DEVELOPMENTS IN AMERICAN POLITICS

Edited by GILLIAN PEELE, CHRISTOPHER J. BAILEY, BRUCE CAIN and B. GUY PETERS

Developments in American Politics 3

Developments in American Politics 3

Gillian Peele
Christopher J. Bailey
Bruce Cain
B. Guy Peters

Editors

CHATHAM HOUSE PUBLISHERS
SEVEN BRIDGES PRESS, LLC
NEW YORK • LONDON

DEVELOPMENTS IN AMERICAN POLITICS 3
SEVEN BRIDGES PRESS, LLC
P.O. BOX 958, CHAPPAQUA, NEW YORK 10514-0958

First American edition, 1998

Library of Congress Cataloging-In-Publication Data

Developments in American politics 3 / Gillian Peele ... [et al.]. —
1st American ed.
p. cm.
Includes bibliographical references (p.) and index.
ISBN 1-56643-048-8
1. United States—Politics and government—1993– I. Peele, Gillian, 1949–
E885.D48 1998
320.973'09'049—dc21 98–23826
CIP

Printed in Great Britain
10 9 8 7 6 5 4 3 2 1

Contents

PART TWO DYNAMICS

PART THREE PUBLIC POLICY

Preface

This is the third *Developments in American Politics* volume. All the chapters are new and, with the exception of the editors there is a totally new group of contributors. We have been fortunate in attracting an outstanding international team of authors and a number of younger scholars of American politics to write for the book.

As in the last volume, individual authors were asked both to analyze recent developments in their area and to balance the theoretical and empirical material. They were also asked to produce chapters which would be accessible and useful to students at an early stage of studying American politics as well as stimulating to more advanced students. All authors were asked to concentrate on the contemporary American scene, but the proximity of the publication of this volume to the turn of the century has prompted us to give the Introduction and the concluding section of the book a slightly broader historical focus than in earlier volumes as a way of encouraging reflection on the significance of recent political development.

In order to make the book user-friendly to its readers around the world and to convey the color and idioms of American politics, we have used American spelling throughout and, where appropriate, the party and state of elected politicians has been included. The references to works cited in the chapters are collected together at the end of the book, and there is also a short Guide to Further Reading for each of the chapters.

The editors would like to thank our publisher Steven Kennedy for the help and encouragement he has given to this volume. We also thank our American publishers Chatham House and record with sadness the death of Ed Artinian, who did so much to improve earlier versions of the book. We also thank our anonymous referees. The editors acknowledge with gratitude the intellectual support given by their respective colleagues at the University of Oxford, the University of Keele, the University of California at Berkeley and the University of Pittsburgh. We are also especially grateful to the secretarial and support staff in our respective institutions. We also gratefully acknowledge the range of fund-raising bodies which have supported our studies and especially the Mellon Trust which has done so much for American research at Oxford. A special vote of thanks goes to Elizabeth McLeish, Samuel Gregg and Teresa Curristine, all in the University of Oxford, who rendered vital and good humoured assistance at various stages in the preparation of this book.

List of Contributors

Christopher J. Bailey is a Senior Lecturer in American Studies at Keele University.

Bruce Cain is Robson Professor of Government and Acting Director of the Institute of Governmental Studies, University of California at Berkeley.

Cornell W. Clayton is Professor of Political Science at Washington State University at Pullman.

Philip John Davies is Professor of American Studies at De Montfort University.

John Dumbrell is a Senior Lecturer in American Studies at Keele University.

Richard L. Engstrom is a Research Professor of Political Science at the University of New Orleans.

James Giordano is a doctoral candidate at Washington State University.

Dilys M. Hill is Professor of Politics at the University of Southampton.

Patricia W. Ingraham is Professor of Political Science at Syracuse University.

Brian D. Jacobs is Reader in the Faculty of Social Studies at Staffordshire University.

Jason F. Kirksey is Hannah D. Atkins Professor of Political Science at Oklahoma State University.

John E. Owens is Director of the Study of Democracy at the University of Westminster.

Jonathan Parker is a Lecturer in American Studies at Keele University.

Gillian Peele is Fellow and Tutor in Politics at Lady Margaret Hall, Oxford.

B. Guy Peters is Maurice Falk Professor of American Government at the University of Pittsburgh.

Steve Reilly is a Lecturer in International Relations at the University of Kent.

Alan Ware is Professor of Politics at Worcester College, Oxford.

Allison Wegner is a doctoral candidate at the University of California at Berkeley.

Graham Wilson is Professor of Political Science at the University of Wisconsin, Madison.

List of Tables, Figures and Maps

Tables

Figures

Maps

List of Abbreviations and Acronyms

AARP	American Association of Retired Persons
ABC	American Broadcasting Corporation
ACIR	Advisory Commission on Intergovernmental Relations
ACLU	American Civil Liberties Union
AFDC	Aid to Families with Dependent Children
AFL–CIO	American Federation of Labor–Congress of Industrial Organization
APEC	Asia Pacific Economic Cooperation
CATS	Conservative Action Team
CBS	Columbia Broadcasting System
CEOs	Chief Executive Officers
CSE	Citizens for a Sound Economy
CETA	Comprehensive Employment Training Act
CIA	Central Intelligence Agency
COS	Conservative Opportunity Society
CPI	Citizens for Public Integrity
CREF	Citizens for the Republic Education Fund
CRS	Congressional Research Service
CSRA	Child Support Recovery Act (1988)
D	Democrat
DAETC	Denver Area Educational Telecommunications Consortium Inc.
DHHS	Department of Health and Human Services
DLC	Democratic Leadership Council
DNC	Democratic National Committee
DOD	Department of Defense
DOE	Department of Energy
DOEd	Department of Education
DOJ	Department of Justice

DOMA	Defense of Marriage Act (1996)
EEOC	Equal Employment Opportunity Commission
EC	Empowerment Community
EMU	European Monetary Union
EPA	Environmental Protection Agency
ESEA	Elementary and Secondary Education Act (1965)
EU	European Union
EZ	Empowerment Zone
FBI	Federal Bureau of Investigation
FCC	Federal Communications Commission
FDA	Food and Drug Administration
FEC	Federal Election Commission
FECA	Federal Election Campaign Act (1971, amended 1974)
FEMA	Federal Emergency Management Agency
FY	Fiscal Year
GAO	General Accounting Office
GATT	General Agreement on Tariffs and Trade
GDP	Gross Domestic Product
GI	General Issue
GOP	Grand Old Party (the Republican Party)
GPRA	Government Performance and Results Act (1993)
GRS	General Revenue Sharing
GSA	General Services Administration
HMOs	Health Maintenance Organizations
HUD	(Department of) Housing and Urban Development
IDEA	Individuals with Disabilities Education Act
IRS	Internal Revenue Service
IT	Information Technology
JOBS	Job Opportunities and Basic Skills (program)
JTPA	Job Training and Partnership Act
JVSVN	Joint Venture Silicon Valley Network
MSA	Metropolitan Statistical Area
NAACP	National Association for the Advancement of Colored People
NAFTA	North American Free Trade Agreement
NAM	National Association of Manufacturers

NAPA	National Academy of Public Administration
NBC	National Broadcasting Corporation
NCES	National Center for Educational Statistics
NES	National Election Study
NFIB	National Federation of Independent Businesses
NGA	National Governors' Association
NOW	National Organization for Women
NJ	New Jersey
NPR	National Peformance Review
NSF	National Science Foundation
OECD	Organization for Economic Cooperation and Development
OMB	Office of Management and Budget
OPM	Office of Personnel Management
PAC	Political Action Committee
PBO	Performance-Based Organization
PPI	Progressive Policy Institute
PR	proportional representation
R	Republican
R&D	research and development
RCCC	Republican Congressional Campaign Committee
RNC	Republican National Committee
SAG	Speaker's Advisory Group
SES	Senior Executive Service
SME	small and medium-sized enterprise
SSI	Social Security Insurance
START	Strategic Arms Reduction Talks
TAFTA	Transatlantic Free Trade Agreement
TANF	Temporary Assistance for Needy Families
UDAG	Urban Development Action Grant
URA	Urban Redevelopment Authority (Pittsburgh)
UN	United Nations
USAID	US Agency for International Development
VA	(Department of) Veterans' Administration
VNS	Voter News Service
WIN	Work Incentives (program)
WLC	White House Legal Counsel's Office
WTO	World Trade Organization

State Abbreviations

Ariz.	Arizona
Ark.	Arkansas
Calif.	California
Colo.	Colorado
Conn.	Connecticut
D.C.	District of Columbia
Del.	Delaware
Fla.	Florida
Ga.	Georgia
Ill.	Illinois
Ind.	Indiana
Kans.	Kansas
Ky.	Kentucky
La.	Louisiana
Maine	Maine
Mass.	Massachusetts
Md.	Maryland
Mich.	Michigan
Minn.	Minnesota
Miss.	Mississippi
Mo.	Missouri
Mont.	Montana
N.C.	North Carolina
N.Dak.	North Dakota
Nebr.	Nebraska
Nev.	Nevada
N.H.	New Hampshire
N.J.	New Jersey
N.Mex.	New Mexico
N.Y.	New York
Okla.	Oklahoma
Oreg. *or* Ore.	Oregon
Pa.	Pennsylvania
R.I.	Rhode Island
S.C.	South Carolina
S.Dak.	South Dakota
Tenn.	Tennessee
Tex.	Texas

Utah	Utah
Va.	Virginia
Vt.	Vermont
Wash.	Washington State
Wis. *or* Wisc.	Wisconsin
W.Va.	West Virginia
Wyo.	Wyoming

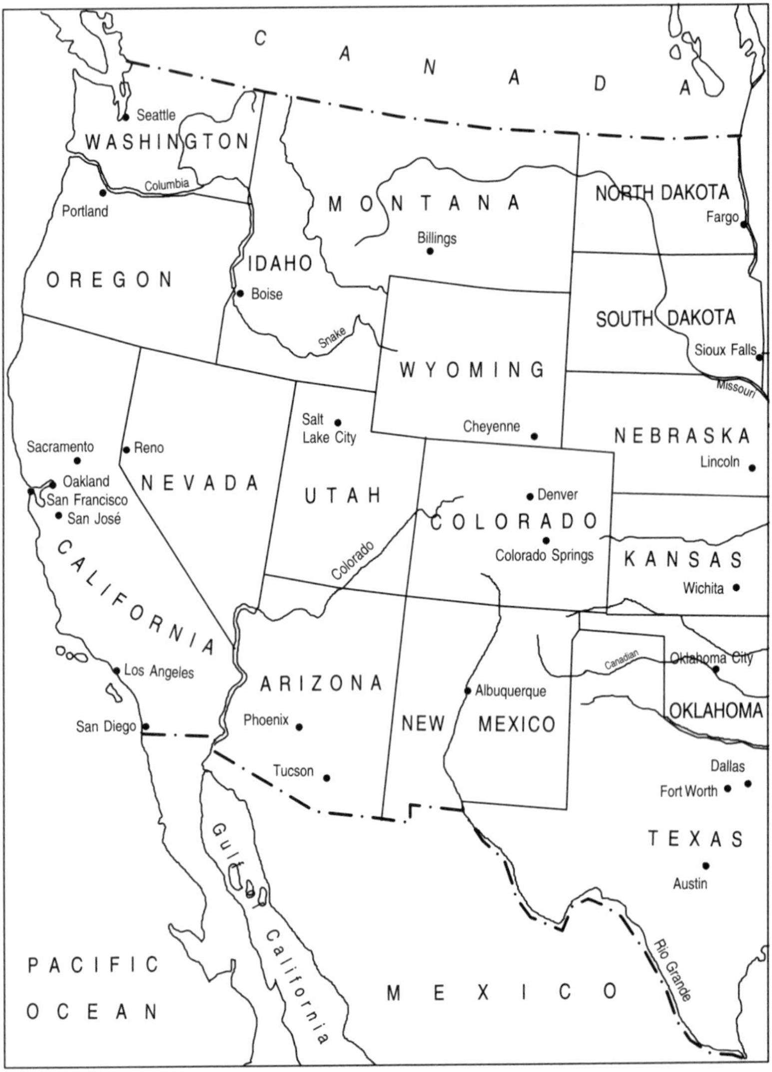

The United States of America: states and main cities

(excluding Alaska and Hawaii)

1

Introduction: The United States in the 1990s

Gillian Peele, Christopher J. Bailey, Bruce Cain and B. Guy Peters

The dawn of a new century encourages introspection in nations as in individuals. In the United States the last years of the twentieth century highlighted the country's uncertainties as well as its tremendous energy, resources and self-confidence. The period of the Clinton Presidency itself encapsulated in its short time-frame many of these competing emotions. As is customary with most new presidencies, Clinton's rhetoric at the beginning of his first term of office in 1993 had been redolent with optimistic calls for a new beginning and held out ambitious promises of large-scale reform. Before long, however, much of the president's initial agenda had been stymied and critics and commentators were focusing on the general discontent of the American public. By the time of Clinton's 1998 State of the Union address, however, the public mood had changed again and there was a much more general confidence in America's future, despite the persistence of strong currents of hostility to government in general and to Washington D.C. in particular. The years leading up to the millennium had also seen the United States veering between self-congratulation at the triumph of democracy in the world under American leadership and a surly nationalism verging on isolationism. And for a country that was usually anxious to embrace the future, there was in many areas of intellectual life a studied retreat to the familiarity of the past.

This tension between self-doubt and self-confidence manifested during the 1990s represents an important element of contemporary

American politics and is apparent in many other aspects of American society and culture. It is not a temporary aberration but a continuing feature of the American scene, pointing up conflicts and dilemmas which will last well into the new century. It generates, and is reflected in, a range of diverse questions about the resilience of the Constitution, about the adequacy of American political arrangements, about the character of the nation's political elite and about the identity of the United States. Such questions are of fundamental importance for the student of American government because they affect American political culture and the policy agenda, and because they may produce significant and enduring changes in the patterns and processes of American government.

The contrasting themes of anxiety and confidence recur throughout the chapters of this book. Across the range of American institutions the observer can see both a range of ostensibly intractable problems thrown up by American society and the political system's seemingly endless capacity for adaptation and adjustment in the face of new agendas. This process of adaptation and adjustment has led to a number of radical changes in the operation and management of institutions and policies, however much they may at first sight appear to display stability and continuity. The dynamics of American politics in the late 1990s have created new institutional patterns and a new politics, notwithstanding the country's historical continuity and traditional adherence to the constitution. The purpose of this introduction is to highlight some of the key elements of the new politics and to explain how the structure of chapters in the book addresses them.

A New (or Old) Public Philosophy?

Running through much of the discussion of the American future was a debate about the values and the principles which should guide the United States as it embarked on a new century. This debate about ideas took place against the background of a thirty-year struggle between liberalism and conservatism in which many critics thought both ideologies had exhausted themselves. In truth both ideologies seem to have been not so much exhausted as modified, although it is probably fair to say that in the clash of philosophical debate liberalism, once so dominant in American thought, had ceded more ground than its opponents. Certainly this would seem to be true if one focuses on the touchstone issue of the role which government should play in American society. Traditionally American liberalism had been associated with a growing role for government in the provision of services to its citizens; and conservatism had placed its faith by contrast in the efficacy and morality of the market. By the time of Clinton's 1998 State of the Union address there was, however, near consensus on the need to reduce the size of government and to eliminate bureaucracy and regulation. Clinton and Gore had pursued "down-sizing" of the government enthusiastically so that by 1998 they could claim to have the smallest government in thirty-five years. But the right had also modified its approach to some extent emphasizing the need for capitalism to exercise civic responsibility.

Clinton's own political synthesis perhaps owed as much to the political realities of divided government as to the emergence of a new ideological consensus. Nevertheless "Clintonism" appeared to tap a set of ideas which fitted uneasily with traditional divisions between the two parties. In addition to the support for a reduced role for the federal government, Clinton's agenda emphasized fiscal restraint and a new approach to welfare which stressed responsibility rather than entitlement and sought to limit both the size and scope of welfare programs. In the international arena, Clintonism was supportive of free trade rather than protectionism and underscored the extent to which a global economy would place new demands on the infra-structure of America's economy, especially its educational and training systems.

Religion, morality and standards in public life

For many critics the growing secularism of American society was also a cause for concern as was the loss of a substantive public philosophy conducive to republican virtue and good citizenship. In fact the United States remained a highly religious country, although there was enormous diversity in its religious beliefs and increasingly profound differences within American society about the extent to which religious practices should be separated from the public arena. For many Americans, however, the country's problem was more the simple deterioration of moral standards among the political elite and the inability of government leaders to set an example to the general public rather than any loss of belief in the population at large.

A series of scandals surrounded both the administration and Congress in the 1980s and 1990s, reinforcing disillusion with ethics inside the Beltway and forcing Congress to put new procedures in place to deal with ethical issues. The lurid allegations of corruption and immorality which whirled around President Clinton himself focused press and public attention on the issue of ethics in government simply because they related to the one figure in the American system who personalizes and symbolizes the nation.

Scandal had dogged the Clinton Administration since its inception and the roots of many of the controversies could be traced back to Clinton's period as Governor of Arkansas. The Clintons' involvement with a failed property venture – the so-called Whitewater affair – was investigated by numerous agencies including independent counsels throughout the Clinton Presidency. These allegations of financial impropriety were paralleled by a well-publicized set of allegations about Clinton's sexual behavior, allegations which generated a damaging harassment suit against the president and serious discussion of the possibility of impeachment.

The public reaction to these scandals, especially the salacious details of the Paula Jones affair, was hard to interpret. On the one hand Clinton's popularity (which had seesawed throughout his presidency but which by early 1998 was at a relatively high level) remained stable as voters apparently drew a distinction between Clinton's private life and his capacity to govern and as some aspects of the investigations took on a highly partisan character. On the other hand, many observers were appalled by the example which Clinton appeared to set, portraying the nation's chief executive as at best a compulsive philanderer who cheated on his wife, and at worst someone who was prepared to lie under oath to cover up his misdeeds.

It is at this juncture difficult to say what long-term damage will be done to the presidency. Assuming that Clinton's personal character flaws are not replicated by his successor, it is possible that no lasting harm will be done. Yet the office has been brought into ridicule and it is clear that, for all his celebrated ability to compartmentalize his life, the need to fend off the welter of accusations at times distracted Clinton's attention from the policy process. Equally it seems certain that these complex scandals have further deepened American disillusion with its national political elite and reinforced other constitutional and political trends serving to weaken the public trust in government.

Political leadership in a divided system

One of the features which made the United States seem hard to govern at the federal level was the persistence of divided government. Although Clinton had been elected in 1992 with a Democratic majority in both the House and the Senate, this was replaced after 1994 by a Republican majority in both chambers of Congress. In fact, in many ways, Clinton fared better in this situation than when Congress was under the control of his own party. Although he came to office with some radical ideas for change (especially in relation to medical provision and welfare) he was not successful in pushing them through. The advent of a Republican congressional majority with its own agenda forced Clinton to retreat to a style of politics which emphasized incremental policy achievements and bargaining around the center of the political spectrum while lowering expectations of presidential achievement. The strategy of "triangulation," governing from a position to the right of the Democrats but to the left of the GOP, turned out to suit Clinton's style of presidential leadership. It played to his particular political strengths, enabling him to exploit opportunities for agreements that crossed party lines.

In some ways the bipartisan thrust of politics after 1995 also suited the public mood. But it had weaknesses of its own. There was a lack of clarity both in programmatic terms but also in terms of legislative leadership. It was hard to articulate a national vision when the implementation of policies was subject to cross-party brokerage and last-minute deals. Inevitably the failure to deliver effective policy reforms through the legislative process cast doubt on the institutional mechanisms of the Constitution both as legislative instruments and as facilitators of political consensus. Not surprisingly, over the 1990s, the failure of political institutions to work smoothly and predictably generated demands for more radical constitutional reforms such as term limits. These radical reform proposals were not intended to undermine the basic design of the founding fathers; rather they were constitutional "quick fixes," intended to meet the needs of an exasperated electorate by transforming the patterns and expectations of routine politics.

Constitutional tensions

One major feature of the Clinton years was a substantial shift of power and responsibility from the federal government to the states. The process of public disillusionment with the balance of federal constitutional power has been long in the making. Partly as a result of the federal government's incapacity to grapple with major policy problems – especially the deficit – but also because of a mounting belief that big government in Washington had become inherently inefficient, the efforts to swing policy-making power and political authority back towards the states gathered momentum in the 1990s. Initiatives which had appeared partisan under Presidents Nixon and Reagan and had foundered not least because of lack of state enthusiasm, under Clinton seemed to reflect a new consensus (Donahue, 1997).

The shift surely represents one of the most significant changes in American government in the late twentieth century, entailing as it did, a transfer of policy-making responsibility in welfare and a reversal of many of the changes associated with the New Deal of the 1930s when the federal government assumed the major responsibility for welfare policy.

The formal continuity of the American Constitution over the 200 years of the country's independent history has, of course, masked a range of substantial shifts in the way the Constitution has worked in practice. The period of Franklin Delano Roosevelt's Presidency (1933–45) itself witnessed a constitutional revolution under the pressure of the depression and world war. In that revolution there was a dramatic growth in the role of the federal government and a concomitant enhancement of the power of the presidency. Looking back at the "Roosevelt revolution" from the vantage point of the turn of the century it is apparent that there was nothing necessary or inevitable about the interlocking changes in American government which occurred at that time. Nor was it inevitable that the dynamic of constitutional change would continue to weaken the states and to strengthen the influence of Washington D.C. Given

American suspicion of centralized government and the country's distaste for the business of its own capital city, it is perhaps surprising that such a marked increase in federal and centralized power was tolerated for so long (Phillips, 1994). By the time of the Clinton Presidency the growth of pressure for devolution, the advent of a Republican congressional majority and the intractable nature of many of the policy problems facing the federal government made a decentralization of power to the states politically expedient for many who did not find the idea theoretically persuasive.

Although the full implications of this major change in the pattern of federal relations cannot yet be assessed, two points can be made here. The first is that such a dramatic shift in the balance of constitutional power is unlikely to be cost-free. While policies may be tailored more closely to the needs of the states, there is also likely to be further fragmentation in the policy process as well as a significant increase in policy variation between the states. Secondly, although the policy debate will doubtless continue (especially about controversial state-imposed conditions for participating in welfare programs) there is unlikely to be a shift back to a greater level of federal control for the foreseeable future.

While the devolutionary thrust of late twentieth-century America was perhaps the most dramatic example of constitutional change, other elements of the constitution remained controversial. There was, for example, much heated debate about the need for, and constitutionality of, formal constitutional limits on the length of time a congressman or senator could serve as an elected representative. This debate went to the heart of American representative theory and reflected a desire to strengthen accountability and revitalize democracy.

Part of the concern which gave rise to the term limits debate stemmed from the high re-election rates of incumbents and the sense that the country's elected representatives, especially at the national level, had become remote from their constituents and immune to their verdict. The reassertion of control and accountability, and indeed of limited government, became important themes on the political agenda and were cleverly exploited by the use of the language of contract by the right, most obviously in Newt Gingrich's Contract with America but also in programs pushed by such pressure groups as the Christian Coalition.

The deficit

Political and constitutional changes do not of course occur in a vacuum. America's late twentieth-century constitutional tensions were a response both to the perceived defects of federal decision-makers and to the issue agenda which was for much of the 1990s dominated by concern about the size of the federal deficit. The deficit had been at the heart both of Ross Perot's third-party crusades and Republican attacks on federal government. It had shaped the character of the new Republican class of 1994 and it had divided Democrats on their own policy priorities (Killian, 1998; Reich, 1997). Although the seriousness of the deficit for American government was almost certainly exaggerated, the issue had acted as a constraint on the ability of federal government to expand its role and had led indirectly to the resurgence of state power in the wider federal relationship. It had also delivered into the president's hands a new tool – the line item veto – which he could use in the annual budgetary battles which had become such defining points in the political calendar.

The federal deficit seemed likely to be eliminated by the time America entered a new century. By comparison with 1993 when the federal deficit stood at $290 billion Clinton in 1998 was able to look with pleasure at a projected federal deficit figure of a mere $22 billion.

The improvement in the federal deficit was not the only area of improvement under Clinton's Administration, and on a number of measures there was a general improvement in the economic outlook of the United States in the last years of the twentieth century. For example, when Clinton entered the White House in 1993 the jobless rate was 7.3 percent; by 1998 it had been reduced to 4.7 percent and welfare recipients had decreased in number from 14.1 million to 10.2 million. Not surprisingly public confidence reflected these figures: consumer confidence between 1993 and 1998 almost doubled, and those satisfied with the nation's direction had risen from 29 percent to 50 percent according to a *National Journal* report in January 1998.

The dilemma of national identity

Perhaps the most basic issue which confronted the United States as it approached the new century was its identity. The United States was self-consciously a country created from immigration and one which expected to grow. Although there had been efforts to stem the tide of immigrants on various criteria throughout the twentieth century, the population of the United States had continued to accept new immigrants. In 1998 the proportion of the population that was foreign born was higher than at any time since the 1930s. And its population was projected to grow massively – from an estimated 261,638,000 on January 1, 1995 to 392,000,000 by the year 2050. But whereas the immigration which had entered the United States in the nineteenth and early twentieth centuries had been overwhelmingly European in origin, the sources of its new settlers at the end of the twentieth century were non-European – predominantly Mexico, Latin America and Asia.

The changes in the character of American immigration together with the dynamics of America's own population raised important questions about the United States' cultural identity. Throughout the nineteenth and for much of the twentieth century it had been assumed that immigrants would sooner or later learn English and be assimilated into a society which was dominated by Anglo-Saxon and Protestant culture. Israel Zangwill's image of the melting-pot assumed the eventual elimination of distinct cultural identities and, although it did not go unchallenged even in its own time, it has structured – subconsciously perhaps but powerfully – the way Americans have addressed the issues of identity (Zangwill, 1914).

It is difficult to pinpoint the moment when traditional assumptions about American identity were challenged but three forces have contributed towards what various scholars have described in terms of "a disuniting" or "fraying" of America or, more dramatically, in terms of "culture wars" (Schlesinger, 1992).

First there was from the 1960s a growing sensitivity towards minorities as America addressed the issue of racial discrimination. Although the issue was most evident in relation to the treatment of America's black minority, the policies and strategies adopted in the process of expanding civil rights had implications for a range of minority groups defined by race, religion and language as well as women and groups defined by sexual orientation. Respect for different identities and subcultures prompted the adoption of a range of policies and strategies ranging from affirmative action to mother-tongue education and ethnic heritage preservation programs. It also prompted a new and often controversial emphasis within the educational system on the role of minorities and women in the history and culture of the United States and equally controversial efforts to reduce the attention given to what had hitherto been seen as the classics of western civilization.

Secondly, minority groups themselves became more assertive of their distinctive cultural identity. This assertiveness had profound public policy implications when it involved the claim that a group's native language should be given parity with English, not simply employed instrumentally to prepare for participation in a culture dominated by the English language and by an intellectual heritage derived primarily from Western Europe.

Finally by the turn of the century, the United States was increasingly forced to confront a demographic future in which Americans of Anglo-Saxon origin would be in a minority. Hispanics in particular seemed likely to grow as a proportion of the population although their cultural presence was already very evident in such states as California, Texas and New Mexico.

Inevitably there was a backlash against these developments and against the threat which they seemed to pose to the dominant understanding of American identity. The status of English as the official language of the United States had never been made clear but from the mid-1980s onwards there were efforts at national and state level to bring forward constitutional amendments to formalize the status of English. Some states – such as California which has radically revised its long-established bilingual education requirements – have held referenda in a drive to eliminate mother-tongue instruction (Bancroft, 1998). This movement towards monolingualism found powerful support in the Republican Party and in Middle America. The important point, however, is that this battle was over much more than the simple issue of language: it was a multifaceted struggle between different elements in American life for control of the country's definition and character.

The problem of equality

In addition to concerns about the identity of the United States there were of course important worries about American society whose divisions were increasingly more salient than its unity. To the familiar and painful divisions of race and ethnicity, American politics had by the turn of the century added important new divisions of gender, age and sexual orientation. Running through the analysis of these divisions was the question of the ability of the United States to treat all its subjects fairly. Poverty had not been eliminated from the United States and problems of social deprivation continued to mark the social fabric and was especially evident in the nation's older cities. Some groups, notably African-Americans, continued to suffer more than others from problems of social disadvantage but other groups such as the elderly and women are also more likely than the population as a whole to find themselves disadvantaged. The uneven incidence of poverty across American society means that few if any issues on the American domestic policy agenda are free of sectional implications and symbolic significance.

Which issues dominate the political agenda at any one period will, of course, reflect a variety of factors including the strength of particular movements and pressure groups, the priorities of the major political actors, especially the president and Congress, as well as the changing concerns of the American public. In the 1990s, although the issue of the budget deficit loomed over the public agenda for much of the time, the familiar distributional issues remained salient as did issues connected to the civil rights of minority groups. Crime remained a major problem and efforts to address the issue were impeded both by the problem of funding and by the extensive and organized opposition to gun control. To the ethical conflicts presented by the abortion issue were added new moral dilemmas relating to the right to die. Yet it is not so much the content of the American issue agenda which strikes the observer as distinctive in the 1990s as its fragmentation and the reluctance or perhaps incapacity of the nation's federal institutions to address directly and comprehensively many of the most pressing issues facing the country.

The chapters in this book address the interlocking themes of US politics and policy-making from a variety of perspectives. In Part One, which examines the framework of American politics, the authors analyze the traditional institutions of American constitutional government. Graham Wilson (Chapter 2) in his discussion of the legacy of the Clinton Presidency argues that Clinton's was necessarily a limited presidency and that the pattern of divided government suggests that public expectations of activist presidential leadership should be modified. The United States, he emphasizes, is not a polity where the executive has sole responsibility for policy-making; Congress has a very important role to play and the policy process is better analyzed as a product of the interaction of executive and legislature. This theme is also emphasized by John Owens (in Chapter 3) which takes as its starting point the political "earthquake" which saw Republicans capture Congress in 1994 in the mid-term elections. Those elections ushered in a new era of congressional policy-making and saw Congress itself transforming its internal structures and instruments of leadership as a result of the pressures from an intensely factional Republican Party. The experience of divided government has also shaped the role of American judicial institutions especially the Supreme Court which in the last decade of the twentieth century has adopted a much more limited and pragmatic role than it had earlier played. Perhaps this more limited role will prove to be cyclical. Justice Jackson for example argued that the Supreme Court went through a tripartite process of assertiveness, followed by criticism from the other two branches and then finally retreat. Much of the argument deployed by Cornell Clayton and James Giordano in Chapter 4 suggests, however, that there are structural factors which make it likely that this cycle will endure well into the next century.

One of the themes which recurs throughout this book is the extent to which our assumptions about the role of government were changed in the late twentieth century. These changing assumptions, which have had an impact beyond the United States have altered both the general evaluation of what responsibilities government should accept and the methods of organizing the public sector. Concern for governmental reorganization and for "reinventing" government has thus been a prominent feature of recent political debate as well as a role in more specialized public administration circles. Patricia Ingraham in Chapter 5 looks at the character of recent efforts to reform the federal bureaucracy and shows how some of these efforts were weakened by conflicting objectives. Nevertheless several important themes emerge from her chapter which suggest that government in the twenty-first century is going to operate in a very different manner from its predecessors.

One obvious development has been the emphasis on devolution both within governmental agencies and organizations and between levels of government. It has already been argued here that the shift away from the federal level of government is one of the most important features of the contemporary American polity. In Chapter 6 on the changing federal system Christopher Bailey analyzes the causes and likely consequences of the trend away from centralized government. Taken together, these five chapters strongly suggest that the institutional framework of the American political system has undergone significant transformation in the last decade, a transformation which must inevitably shape the manner and style in which issues are handled and policy dilemmas addressed.

Part Two of the book analyzes the more obviously dynamic features of American politics: the interacting and overlapping roles of parties, pressure groups and electoral movements which produce the changing issue agenda of American politics and structure electoral politics. Although all three areas of political life display increasing professionalism and sophistication with respect to organization, there is in all three as well a substantial element of uncertainty and questioned legitimacy. Gillian Peele in Chapter 7 examines the role played by the political parties in contemporary American politics. Despite the development of hostility to the existing party system, it is clear that the parties have become ideologically more cohesive entities (though they retain significant internal divisions) and that the competition between Republicans and Democrats has become increasingly intense across the country, giving rise to new styles of leadership and campaigning. Although there have been times when parties have seemed redundant in the United States, the contemporary political scene suggests an enhanced investment at least at the national level in such areas as party organization, and fund-raising as well as new patterns of internal party conflict.

Parties are not the only important forces shaping the political agenda in the United States. Interest groups have always played an important role in American politics; but, as Steve Reilly argues in Chapter 9, it is debatable whether their influence is as benign as some of the traditional pluralist theories of American government liked to suggest. Indeed some commentators have thought that the pluralism of American political culture had by the turn of the twentieth century given way to a hyperpluralism which made it difficult to form a policy consensus at the national level. Reilly details the enormous changes which have taken place in the world of interest groups in the late twentieth century and points up the inefficiencies, inequities and fragmentation that may result from their activity.

Political parties and interest groups both offer opportunities for participation in contemporary politics; both thus attempt to mold public opinion as well as to influence the choices of policy-makers and elected officials. Yet electoral opinion, like so many other features of the US scene, has displayed enormous volatility over the last decade and seems set to continue in this fashion. Bruce Cain and Allison Wegner in Chapter 9 examine the trends in the American electoral behavior and party competitiveness at the various levels of the political system. They analyze both long term factors such as the changing sources of party support across the United States, which are generally strengthening the Republicans, and the shorter term factors which display fewer clear cut trends but which (fortunately for the Democrats) can modify the impact of long-term electoral trends.

The volatility of the electorate is not merely important in its own right for what it reveals about public attitudes to government; parties, pressure groups and legislators also need to take electoral sentiment into account in the policy-making process. Changing electoral constraints add a further dimension of difficulty to an already difficult policy making environment. Part Three of the book addresses the public policy agenda and looks in detail at economic policy (Chapter 10 by B. Guy Peters), social policy (Chapter 11 by Dilys Hill) and foreign and defense policy (Chapter 12 by John Dumbrell). This section has been made somewhat shorter than in earlier volumes of the book in order to be able to include more chapters which focus on important contemporary policy issues and themes which have not been included before. Thus in Part Four Jonathan Parker, in Chapter 13, focuses on education, an issue which President Clinton made central to his New Democratic philosophy, while Richard L. Engstrom in Chapter 14 examines the divisive issue of race and affirmative action. Jason F. Kirksey in Chapter 15 provides an overview of the contentious issue of campaign finance which, although frequently advocated, is rarely implemented. Then in Chapter 16 Brian Jacobs analyzes issues concerned with urban regeneration. This chapter takes one highly successful city – Pittsburgh – as a case study to show how modern city government can address the multifaceted problems of modern cities stemming from economic change. Philip Davies in Chapter 17 then provides an overview of the role of the media in the US focusing not just on its immediate political impact but also on its broader cultural effects.

Part Five consists of a longer chapter (Chapter 18 by Alan Ware) which seeks to place the experience of contemporary America in a broader historical and political context. While it would be unwise to try to draw too precise lessons for the future from history, reflections on the past can, as Ware shows, deepen our understanding of the present. Given that American society often seems to combine a preoccupation with its antecedents and a fetish for novelty, this balanced and nuanced attempt to look both backwards as well as forwards at the turn of the century will, it is hoped, add a richer dimension to the study of American politics.

PART ONE

THE INSTITUTIONAL FRAMEWORK

2

The Presidency

GRAHAM WILSON

A Shrunken Presidency?

President Clinton took office in 1993 after an election in which his predecessor, George Bush, gained a pathetically low share of the vote (35 percent) for an elected president seeking reelection. Within two years, Clinton himself was reduced to arguing that he was "not irrelevant" in Washington as his party lost control of the Senate and, more strikingly, the House of Representatives for the first time in forty-four years. Although President Clinton was able to bounce back in the 1996 elections, no one would have thought that his standing in Washington thereafter was comparable to that of Lyndon Johnson in 1965 or Ronald Reagan in 1985. The president himself remained embroiled in investigations of his past business dealings (Whitewater) and more recent activities in raising campaign contributions. As it is never possible to separate fully the president from the presidency, Clinton's difficulties often prompted suggestions that the presidency itself had declined. It was easy to suggest reasons why the presidency had been diminished. In particular, the end of the Cold War brought to an end the long and unusual era starting in 1939 during which the president had been Commander in Chief of a nation actually or potentially involved in world war. As the most visible politician in the United States, the president could also be particularly vulnerable to the general erosion in confidence in American institutions that had started during the Vietnam War and had never been fully reversed. Though, as we shall see, President Clinton's approval ratings also recovered, he was scarcely a revered figure and the scandals that beset him throughout his term of office raised the issue of whether the institution had entered a new period of decline. Certainly no modern president and probably no president in American history was the subject of so many humiliating inquiries into his sexual and financial conduct.

Perspectives on the Presidency

Attempts to generalize about the American presidency have always encountered the obstacle that the standing of the office has varied so much. Bryce (1891) wrote of a late nineteenth-century American polity in which "great men do not become president." Yet from Roosevelt to Ford, American presidents were substantial figures; at least two of the seven would be regarded as great leaders by the standards of any western democracy. Sometimes the swings have been much more abrupt. In the early 1970s, for example, it was common for commentators to warn of the dangers of the "imperial presidency," a powerful office that had escaped its constitutional bounds and imperiled the standing of Congress and thereby the whole constitutional structure of checks and balances (Schlesinger, 1974). By the end of the 1970s, it was equally common to warn that the presidency was imperiled not imperial, incapable of exercising the leadership role expected by the public.

Several attempts have been made to explain this variation in the standing of the presidency. Some approaches have focused on the personality of the incumbents; Barber (1972), for example, explained the success or failure of administrations in terms of the presidential character. Deep-seated aspects of a president's personality traceable to childhood experiences and treatment determined whether presidents were likely to conduct their office in a manner likely to achieve success or failure. Rockman (1984) suggested that there were several cycles that shaped the standing of a president. The first was one internal to an administration, so that presidents tend to be more powerful and prestigious earlier in their term than later. A second cycle related the standing of a presidency to its predecessors so that powerful or overbearing presidents (Johnson, Nixon) would beget a reaction against the institution itself, enfeebling their successors (Ford and Carter) who in turn would create the climate for stronger presidential leadership. The final element in Rockman's analysis was the impact of very gradual and long-lasting influences such as the increase in the economic and social responsibilities of the federal government and the rise of the United States to being by far the strongest superpower in the world.

In an illuminating book, Skowronek (1993) argues that we should pay attention to two trends that shape the status of a presidency. The first is "political time." Some presidents disrupt a previous political regime, introducing important innovative policies and creating a new political coalition to sustain them. Others preside over the continuation of an existing political order, maintaining the policies and supporting the coalition they inherited. Roosevelt and Truman are the most obvious examples of these two types of presidency. A third and unhappy situation for a president is to preside over the decline of a political order, as established policies are seen to have outlived their usefulness and their supporting political coalition decays. Finally, some presidents are elected against the run of history, "preempting" the dominant coalition by an unexpected victory due to the their popular personality (Eisenhower) or a downturn in the economy coinciding with a presidential election. Skowronek argues that "historical time" may work to reduce the possibilities open to presidents, however. The "thickening" of the political system that occurs over "historical time" involves the creation of more programs, constituencies, and interest groups that can prevent substantial change. It is thus harder for contemporary presidents than their predecessors to be innovative in creating major new programs or political coalitions.

Skowronek's book is open to important criticisms. The first is whether or not he categorizes accurately the place of the presidency in the American political system. Skowronek's book typifies an important tradition in writing on the presidency, placing the president in the center of the American political system, the motor that moves the political system. Yet this approach to the presidency is itself very much in question. The frequency with which "divided government" (one party controlling at least one branch of Congress, the other the presidency) has occurred has reinforced the perspective of political scientists such as Charles O. Jones (1994, 1995), who have emphasized that the presidency is merely part of a "separated system" of institutions, not the focus of leadership. Presidents do not control policy-making, and Congress is as important in shaping policy. Presidents can adopt a variety of approaches in working with Congress, but the reality is of shared power.

How far divided government has reinforced this basic institutional fact is hotly contested. Mayhew (1991) argued that the frequency with which important legislation is adopted under divided government is as great as under unitary government. Yet more recent work has called Mayhew's conclusion into question, suggesting that the rate at which major policy changes fail under divided government (a different but perhaps more accurate test than Mayhew's count of major policy innovation) *is* greater than under unitary government (Edwards, Barrett and Peake, 1997). Mayhew has provided a valuable service in reminding us of factors that promote cooperation under divided government: neither party, for example wants to take the blame for blocking needed legislation or for producing "deadlock." Yet the current state of the debate over divided government seems to be that these important pressures towards cooperation are offset by important pressures towards antagonism. These pressures include both partisan rivalry – elections in the United States particularly for the House are always near – and the fact that the differences between the major parties are unusually clear. Whereas the divisions in the ranks of the Democrats in the 1950s produced a large minority within the party whose conservatism made them congenial to President Eisenhower, both parties in Congress have been unusually disciplined and cohesive in recent times. Even Southern Democrats have been highly likely to vote with their party against the Republicans. Divided government in an era of unusually intense partisan differences has made collaboration between Congress and the presidency hard to achieve.

Skowronek is also open to the standard objections awaiting those who describe anything in terms of cycles. Endless arguments arise about where we are in a cycle, and whether this cycle is really much the same as the last cycle, a question particularly difficult to assess in view of Skowronek's argument that the passing of historical time indeed makes recent political cycles unlike earlier ones. Yet even without necessarily agreeing with Skowronek's cyclical interpretation of American history, we can accept without much difficulty his fundamental point that the relationship between presidents and the broader political situation varies, using his concept of a political order, a relatively enduring set of policies, expectations about the role of government and supporting political forces. Without agreeing that presidents alone create new political orders, we can accept that some are part of the process in which new political orders emerge, others have political programs consistent with the maintenance of a political order, yet others have the misfortune to be part of a crumbling political order and finally some are elected as a result of accident or personality against the balance of prevailing political forces. This unobjectionable simplification of Skowronek's argument continues his valuable perspective on presidents as combining the roles of governing, campaigning and maintaining political coalitions.

The Significance of Clinton

How, in the light of such political science perspectives, may we understand the Clinton Presidency?

The first notable, if obvious, fact about President Clinton is that he was elected to two terms. This is scarcely exceptional among modern presidents: Eisenhower, Nixon, and Reagan achieved the same, as no doubt would Kennedy had he lived. Nonetheless, Clinton's achievement was real, ending a period in which many argued that the Republicans had a "lock" on the Electoral College, winning enough states in successive elections to make it seem unlikely that a Democrat could ever win. The Electoral College "lock" that the Republicans supposedly enjoyed also reflected the divisions within the ranks of the Democratic Party. The problems posed by reconciling the party leaders' enthusiasm for policies such as affirmative action and tolerance of "alternative life styles" with the social conservatism of its white working-class supporters or of obtaining the votes of racial minorities and white southerners had seemed insoluble to three successive Democratic presidential candidates. Yet Clinton did indeed win, defeating not merely an incumbent president but one who had created and presided over a military triumph against Iraq less than two years previously. Clinton's victory in 1996 was perhaps less striking in that he enjoyed all the advantages of an incumbent during a period of high economic growth, price stability, and low unemployment.

Nonetheless these impressive triumphs were not, as many liberals had hoped, the dawn of a new era of policy innovation. A plausible argument can be made that this was due in part to Clinton placing his personal popularity ahead of the causes with which his party had been associated. There is no shortage of people willing to ascribe this to Clinton's own personality, and the need of the stepson of a violent alcoholic to find personal popularity (Drew, 1994; Woodward 1994). There is little doubt that, as his one-time political adviser, Dick Morris, described in his account of his time working for Clinton (Morris, 1997), the president was willing to make almost all his decisions, including where to take his summer vacation, subject to the opinion polls. The more interesting question is why even such a gifted Democrat as Clinton found himself in such a difficult position. A variety of factors support an interpretation of Clinton as a preemptive president, one elected against the balance of political forces and commitments rather than creating or maintaining a new political order.

The first is that the general flow of political argument remained in the direction of conservatives and Republicans, not liberals and Democrats. Expanding the welfare state, strong action in support of racial equality, emphasizing rehabilitation rather than punishment, preferring government spending over private consumption were all policies associated with the Democrats in the past that were now regarded as sure-fire recipes for electoral disaster. This was of course part of a world-wide phenomenon that has been given many names such as "Thatcherism" and "neo-liberalism" which have affected most industrialized democracies including those ruled at the time by social democratic or Labour parties. Newt Gingrich and the Republicans could feel with justice that history was on their side.

Clinton's 1992 campaign was built around a simple set of propositions from his adviser, James Carville ("Change versus more of the same, It's the economy, *stupid*, and Don't forget health care") but it scarcely provided the basis for any claim that he had the support of the people for a shift away from the conservative policies of Reagan and Bush. It can be doubted whether any American president can really claim a "mandate" for policy innovation after an election. The public's reasons for voting for or against a presidential candidate are too rarely linked to policy choices. Under some circumstances, however, presidents do claim successfully to the rest of the Washington community that they have a mandate. Clinton certainly could not make such a claim in 1992 or even in 1996. President Reagan in 1980 is the most recent example of a president whose victory was interpreted – even by his opponents –

as embodying a mandate. Clinton had been helped greatly during the 1992 campaign by Bush's incompetence as a candidate and inability to deal with the fears created by the recession of the early 1990s; the striking feature of the 1992 results was not so much Clinton's victory on a minority of the total vote as Bush's poor showing for an incumbent president. As noted earlier, Clinton's reelection campaign in 1996 took place against the backdrop of almost unbelievably favorable economic circumstances.

Clinton himself made few claims during his campaigns that could be interpreted subsequently as a mandate for a shift in policy priorities towards traditional Democratic concerns. On the contrary, Clinton generally emphasized that he had made a break with "old Democratic" policies. Both Clinton campaigns included very clear messages that this was no liberal Democratic hero. To counteract the politically effective Republican charge in previous elections that Democrats were soft on crime, Clinton flew home to Arkansas, where he was of course still governor during the 1992 campaign, to sign the warrant for the execution of a mentally retarded murderer. Before the 1996 campaign began in earnest, in order to counteract allegations that Democrats were soft on people living on government welfare programs indefinitely, Clinton signed into law a welfare reform measure that removed part of the social safety net dating back to the New Deal (Aid to Families with Dependent Children or AFDC) and thereby placed millions of children in danger of falling into poverty. A combination of action by his administration and Congress and the favorable economic circumstances ended the budget deficit that had been such an effective issue for Ross Perot. In the 1992 campaign, Clinton could always claim that cutting the budget, using the death penalty and reforming welfare were policies that he had favored as Governor and as Chair of the Democratic Leadership Council (DLC), a conservative pressure group within the Democratic Party. Nonetheless, they were all the steps away from traditional Democratic constituencies and were exactly those that most campaign consultants would have prescribed.

The most dramatic refutation of hopes that Clinton's victory in 1992 created the opportunity for a period of liberal activism was the mid-term election of 1994. The Republicans' capture of the House for the first time since 1952 and their recapture of the Senate which they had lost in 1986 was one of the most dramatic developments of recent politics. The significance of the Republicans' victory was increased even further by its apparent ideological significance. The "Contract With America" was remarkable both for the clarity of its conservative ideological commitment and for committing congressional candidates around the nation to a single manifesto. The Republican Speaker, Newt Gingrich, was cast in the mold of a victorious prime minister taking power, and for much of 1995, President Clinton was reduced to arguing that the Republican triumph had not made him "irrelevant."

It is even less plausible to claim a manifesto from congressional elections than from presidential. Turnout is even lower than in presidential elections, the voters in the mid-term elections were not representative of the population in general, and most voters claimed not to have read the Contract With America. As always in congressional elections, local factors played a part. Nonetheless, the drama created by the election of the first Republican Speaker since 1954 and the Contract itself did indeed give the impression of a movement that could claim a mandate. The Republican majorities in the House and Senate were confirmed in the 1996 presidential elections, and the dominant issues on the political agenda during Clinton's second term – balancing the budget, cutting taxes, crime, welfare reform, and increasing the efficiency of government – had a decidedly conservative tinge to them.

Clinton can be seen, therefore, as a prime example of what Skowronek would term a "preemptive president," one elected against the grain of history and limited thereby in what he might achieve. Indeed, whereas a generation of political scientists conditioned by Roosevelt and the dreams of what Kennedy might have been looked to the presidency for heroic leadership, the analytical value of the Clinton Presidency for political scientists is to provide a case study of what a preemptive president might achieve. In the almost inevitable military analogies used about political leadership, Clinton's claim to fame was as a defensive general. Yet probably few generals have experienced such a mixture of defeat and triumph.

Dimensions of Disaster and Triumph

Two of the most obvious and therefore commonly used indicators of presidential standing are the president's success scores in

Congress and his approval ratings in the country. Both indicators are, of course, open to sharp criticism. Congressional success scores do not tell us whether the measures being counted were of considerable or trivial importance, nor do they tell us whether or not the president merely supported measures almost certain to pass Congress whatever he did, or whether he himself created the climate in Congress for their adoption. Proposals that do not even make it to the floor for a vote – such as the Clinton national health insurance proposals – are not counted as failures. Approval ratings measure unstable evaluations of the president by members of the public in the period between elections when electors are unlikely to be paying close attention to politics; and such ratings are also unreliable because they are sensitive to developments such as the state of the economy that the president does not control (McKuen, 1983; West, 1991).

It is nonetheless interesting to note that by these conventional if flawed measures Clinton started out reasonably well compared with his predecessors. In his first year, Clinton had an 86 percent success rate in Congress, and only Eisenhower and Johnson had higher scores during the same period of their presidencies. Only Johnson had a higher success rate in his second year than Clinton, who again scored 86 percent (Duncan and Langdon, 1993; Langdon, 1994). While Clinton was undoubtedly aided by the existence of a Democratic majority in both the House and the Senate during this period, and the unusually high levels of party unity that obtained, his successful adoption of NAFTA (the North American Free Trade Agreement) was carried largely on Republican votes and against the opposition of prominent Democratic leaders in the House. Clinton's approval ratings in his first term averaged 50 percent. Although his highest ratings during that period were less than any of his predecessors since 1945, his lowest ratings were better than Reagan's first-term nadir (see Table 2.1).

Yet even before the 1994 mid-term elections dealt him a stunning setback, Clinton's Presidency seemed to many seasoned commentators to be in trouble. In his classic, *Presidential Power* (1960), Richard Neustadt argued that a high reputation among presidency watchers and fellow politicians – "professional reputation" – was crucial. Clinton's professional reputation during his first two years was not good. The failure of Clinton's major domestic program, national health insurance, was undoubtedly a major blow. Less

TABLE 2.1 *Presidential approval ratings since F.D.R.*

President	Mean	Median	High	Low
Truman	38	35	67	23
Eisenhower I	70	70	77	57
Eisenhower II	61	60	79	52
Kennedy	71	55	83	59
Johnson	57	55	80	36
Nixon	51	56	68	24
Ford	48	47	71	39
Carter	47	43	72	28
Reagan I	50	43	67	35
Reagan II	55	55	68	40
Bush	61	64	87	32
Clinton	50	50	60	38

Note: Eisenhower and Reagan both served two *full* terms and their separate terms have been distinguished in this table. Truman, Johnson and Clinton years in the presidency have been treated as single presidencies.

substantively but politically important setbacks included difficulties in securing Senate confirmation of an Attorney General and Clinton's embarrassed squirming over his attempt to allow overt homosexuals to serve in the military. The latter controversy also confused the president's image as a "New Democrat" who was more in tune with the values of most Democrats. An administration that had sought to conciliate Middle America through emphasizing issues such as health care reform in fact gained most publicity in its first year by promoting homosexual rights in the military, a worthy cause, perhaps, but one that rekindled the fire of alleged Democratic liberal extremism on the "social issues" that the Republicans had fanned for nearly thirty years and that candidate Clinton had worked so hard to extinguish. Even Clinton's ultimately successful fight for NAFTA seemed to many to have been necessary only because Clinton himself had failed to give a clear, unambiguous message of support for the pact. Indeed, it was often thought that the problem was indeed Clinton himself. As we have seen, early interpretations of Clinton's presidency stressed his alleged personal failings. Clinton, it was argued, was a man lacking in self-discipline, a man incapable of saying "no" to whichever group or lobby had talked to him last. Elected as a candidate who could achieve the almost impossible task of pulling the Democrats together, Clinton was criticized during his first two years for being incapable of setting and holding to clear priorities. Faced with the need to choose which policy proposals or components of the Democratic coalition should be given priority, Clinton's instinct was to reply "All!" It was widely thought that Clinton's personality was reflected in the organization, or disorganization, of his administration. Clinton's White House was highly disorganized, with the probable exception of his economic advisers and officials. Only after the debacle of the 1994 mid-term elections was the experienced Washington insider, Leon Panetta, able to impose discipline on a staff that had gloried in its lack of structure and hierarchy. Above all, while claiming early in 1993 to be aware of the need not to overload the Washington agenda, in practice Clinton did precisely that, largely because he was incapable of establishing clear priorities.

As was often the case in late twentieth-century America, the temptation to psychoanalyze was irresistible. Clinton, it was argued, displayed the classic features of a child whose father had died and who had grown up with an alcoholic, sometimes violent stepfather. If the stories of Clinton's sexual adventures are true, they display an ill-disciplined, restless character willing to take risks. Clinton's personality, it was said, displayed a desperate desire to please and to promote harmony, even if it was based on a false consensus. Whether or not such analyses had validity is something best left to those who know Clinton much better personally than most political scientists or journalists who are practitioners of pop psychology. We can, however, point to circumstances that would have made consistency in any Democratic administration hard to achieve. The coalition that had elected Clinton was, as is well known, diverse and composed of antagonistic elements. Prominent African-American politicians, for example, would demand a commitment to affirmative action programs that Clinton's erstwhile colleagues in the DLC would oppose. Twelve years in the wilderness had left nearly all the components of the Democratic coalition with a shopping list of political needs (probably all marked "urgent") that were hard to supply in an era of tight budgets. The complexity of Clinton's ill-fated proposal for national health insurance was due in large part to the need to combine a pledge to achieve this policy goal with the need to avoid increases in public expenditure. Indeed, an effective and successful group within the administration led by the Secretary of the Treasury, Lloyd Bentsen, insisted that reducing the highly publicized (but, in comparative perspective as a percentage of gross national product, modest) budget deficit should be given higher priority than any initiative in domestic policy.

The dramatic defeat of the congressional Democrats in 1994 was a terrible setback to Clinton, among the worst political setbacks short of his own defeat any president has suffered in the modern era. Clinton's ratings and scores plummeted. In 1995, his congressional success score fell to 36 percent, the lowest since the *Congressional Quarterly* began to compile it (Healey, 1996). His popular approval ratings fell to 39 percent in September 1994 and remained thereabouts until early 1995 (*Gallup Poll Monthly*, 1996c). In his second term, Clinton had the satisfaction of seeing his approval rating climb into the highest range for postwar presidents (about 60 percent in the late summer of 1997), and his 1996 congressional success rate climbed back up to 55 percent, the largest year-to-year gain since the statistic was first compiled in 1953 (Doherty, 1996). While Presidents under divided government have sometimes done better (Eisenhower in 1956, Nixon in 1972), Bush fared worse (43 percent) and none had to face a congressional majority as fired up as were the Republicans after their 1994 mid-term victories. Yet the greatest of all the achievements of the "comeback kid" was his reelection in 1996. Even though blessed with a favorable economy and a hapless opponent, Clinton could take satisfaction in a victory that few would have predicted in November 1994.

There are many ways of explaining such a reversal of fortune. Some would emphasize the contribution of key individuals such as Leon Panetta as Chief of Staff or Dick Morris as shadowy promoter inside the White House of whatever policy was popular outside it. Others might suggest that Clinton realized belatedly that his victory in 1992 was more a reflection of the unpopularity of Bush than a mandate for the policies that he and Hillary Clinton favored. The most interesting questions for political scientists, however, are what strategies have worked so well for Clinton since 1994, and what the Clinton Presidency tells us about the position of the presidency more generally at the end of the twentieth century.

Rebuilding a Reputation

The importance of formal powers

It has become something of a cliché that the Republicans' victory in 1994 saved Clinton. Surrounded by dissatisfied Democrats in 1994, Clinton became their sole protector in 1995. Nothing stood between anyone to the left of center and disaster after the mid-term elections except Clinton. The sale of federally owned lands in areas of outstanding natural beauty for development, rescinding or weakening environmental measures, consumer protection, and workplace safety regulations, the abolition of affirmative action and an end to the promotion by the federal government of racial or gender equality, the abolition of abortion rights, and the abolition of federal assistance to the poor were all serious possibilities after the 1994 mid-term elections. The presidential veto and whatever influence the White House still had in Congress were the best guarantees against these changes.

The situation after 1994 gave Clinton many advantages. The Republican Speaker, Newt Gingrich, embodied the Republican agenda from the start and yet was an unattractive figure to most Americans, the epitome of ill-considered and apparently harsh policies. He was also to make numerous tactical errors, most notably forcing the federal government twice temporarily to shut down many agencies as a tactic in budget negotiations with the president: the public blamed Gingrich, not the president. Yet difficulties in coordinating House and Senate Republicans made it impossible for Congress to pass many measures that would confront the president with the agonizing choice of offending Democrats or losing votes. Only in the case of welfare reform was Clinton forced to sign into law a bill that he thought had extensive public support but which was despised by many of his fellow Democrats; in any case, the poor are notoriously weak politically and therefore, from Clinton's point of view, expendable.

A great advantage of this situation for Clinton was that by and large he did not have to do what he had found most difficult in the past for both personal and political reasons, namely prioritize. Rather than being forced to choose between potentially antagonistic elements of the Democratic coalition such as environmentalists and labor unions or African Americans and white ethnics,

Clinton could promise to defend *all* these interests simultaneously. This is not to say that Clinton's strategy was rash or confrontational. As mentioned earlier, Clinton accepted the abolition of AFDC in spite of advice to the contrary from his policy advisers in the field; his political advisers argued strongly for signing and carried the day. Clinton allowed the Republican majority to dominate the political scene for most of 1995, only gradually articulating his opposition to those aspects of their program (such as weakening the National Parks) against which opposition had already emerged. Yet however little Clinton said in defense of any liberal group, they knew that no one else was likely to give them any more effective support. The Clinton revival was based on the belief that he felt the pain of far more groups than he could have helped had there been a Democratic majority in Congress.

A rhetorical Presidency

A related aspect of the presidency that Clinton exploited and was good at was making speeches. Both Tulis (1987) and Kernell (1986) have drawn attention to the growth in the "rhetorical presidency," the frequency with which presidents make speeches or stage appearances to boost support for their programs. There is, in fact, no linear trend in this regard; Clinton was outstanding in this regard even before the Republicans captured Congress.

As opportunities for presidential leadership became fewer after 1994, the importance of appearances and speeches became greater. Clinton called for a wide variety of changes in American practices that were not, for better or for worse, within the power of the president to command. Examples included a call for parents to spend more time reading to their children and the introduction of school uniforms throughout the land, an unlikely reform that would have required action by thousands of local school boards, not the federal government. Not all of Clinton's rhetoric was confined to such relatively mundane issues. In the same year, the president demanded that the nation hold a collective conversation on race relations and followed this within a few weeks with a further demand that there be a national dialogue on the perils of global warming. Whether or not the nation was willing to oblige was doubtful, but Clinton could well argue that faced with a hostile legislative majority, rhetoric was one of the tools available to him.

A similar blurring of the boundaries between speech and action was evident in foreign policy. Warnings to China that it should improve its human rights record became a replacement for making it do so. President Clinton claimed to have brought peace to both Northern Ireland and the Middle East; the continuation of violence after the speech or event marking his peace-making and the contributions of other peace makers were not remarked by the president, or even much by the media. One reason why this opportunity arose was that no matter how great their strength in domestic policy, the congressional Republicans were far less relevant and immediate to the rest of the world than was the president. The conspicuous failure of other actors such as the European Union (EU) in the Balkans emphasized that no matter how weakened domestically, the American president remained at the center of world events.

The Executive Branch Presidency

The rhetorical "action" by the president could be reinforced in a limited number of areas by action he could take without legislation and with minimal interference from Congress. Clinton emphasized his commitment to racial and gender equality, for example, by making appointments to his Cabinet and the Executive Branch more generally at the start of both his first and second term that paid considerable attention to the race, ethnicity and gender of the appointee. (The Senate traditionally interferes little in these nonjudicial appointments, even when its approval is required.) The outgoing Secretary of Transportation, Frederico Pena, whose record in office had been undistinguished, was recalled hastily to be Secretary of Energy for the second Clinton term. Although Pena had no obvious qualifications for the position, it was suddenly realized that otherwise there would be no Hispanics in the Cabinet. Although Clinton deplored "bean-counting" by interest groups representing women and minorities over the share of appointments going to their constituents, there is clear evidence that the president did indeed count legumes (Aberbach, 1996). The Executive Branch has the capacity to make significant policy decisions under powers delegated to it by Congress to make and enforce regulations. In 1997, for example, the president ultimately supported tough new environmental regulations from the Environmental Protection

Agency (EPA), making sure merely that their implementation and costs would be delayed until well after he was out of office.

The primacy Clinton gave to balancing Executive Branch appointments in terms of race, ethnicity, and gender was aided by the modest role that most political appointees out in the departments and agencies – even those at Cabinet level – played in policy-making, as Robert Reich (the first-term Labor Secretary) made painfully clear in his diaries (Reich, 1997). For many department secretaries, their race or gender were more important in signaling the administration's priorities than their views or competence. Power within the Executive Branch resided at the White House to a greater degree than had once been the case; the Secretary of Health and Human Services, Donna Shalala, found that the major policy issue of the first term affecting her department, national health insurance, had been handed over to a special task force led by Hillary Clinton and in which her department played a minimal role. The administration's policy on welfare reform was made in the White House in a contest between Clinton's political advisers and the policy experts from Department of Health and Human Services (DHHS) in which the DHHS lost; several of the Assistant Secretaries in the Department (but not Shalala herself) soon left in protest. While it is true that there has been a long-term tendency for power to be centralized in the White House, in the hands of the White House staff rather than in those of the political appointees in the agencies and departments, the centralization of power in the White House has been aided by current circumstances. Many important policy decisions are made in the context of negotiations with congressional Republican leaders or budget negotiations, or both. As the experienced journalist Nicholas Lehmann (1997) has written:

> Whatever influence the Cabinet once may have had was substantially taken away in the 1970s and 1980s by the advent of the congressional budget committees, the Office of Management and Budget and the big Reagan budget deficit, which have concentrated executive-branch policy-making in the White House by subsuming most decisions under deficit-cutting exercises.

The important exceptions to this rule were the Secretaries of the Treasury (first Lloyd Bentsen, later Robert Rubin), the Secretary of

State and, not because of her popularity with the president but because of her ability to pursue or impede investigations of wrong-doing by officials, the Attorney General, Janet Reno. Both Bentsen and Rubin benefited from the inevitable centrality of their department in discussions about the Budget.

As we have seen, during his first years in office Clinton had found an effective style in running the White House – and the Executive Branch more generally – as elusive as an effective relationship with Congress. In common with many presidents, Clinton struggled to find an effective and congenial approach to running the White House staff. Clinton's first choice was to entrust the management of the White House staff to personal friends, reaching back to his early years in Arkansas to find his first Chief of Staff ("Mack" McClarty). McClarty presided over a White House staff that was regarded by its critics as highly indisciplined and by its members as embodying the virtues of decentralized, team leadership (Solomon, 1993).

An important part of Clinton's recovery involved developing a more effective style of running the White House. It was noticeable that the greatest improvement in Clinton's fortunes coincided with the period during which a Washington insider, Leon Panetta, took over as Chief of Staff. A Washington commentator cruelly referred to the changes Panetta introduced as "the revenge of the grown ups" (Rust, 1996). A former high-ranking Democratic representative from California who had served as chair of the Budget Committee, Panetta struggled to bring order to the decision-making process. Key individuals, such as George Stephanopoulos during the early part of Clinton's presidency, had far more access and input than his formal position as director of communications seemed to warrant. Dick Morris as political adviser had a degree of access after the 1994 mid-term elections that profoundly worried many in the administration, particularly as Morris was quite capable of announcing to other members of the staff that the president had just made a decision that Morris favored; Panetta's deputy, Harold Ickes, developed the habit of checking with Clinton whether such decisions really had been made. Panetta also insisted that no idea of Morris would be implemented without prior approval from himself or Ickes. This problem ended in August 1996 with the departure in disgrace for misconduct of a type more common in British than American politics (a sex scandal involving a prostitute who was allowed to listen in to telephone conversations between Morris and Clinton). In the second term, Clinton made another Southern businessman, Erskine Bowles, Chief of Staff after Panetta returned to California to pursue his own political ambitions. Clinton had not known Bowles until 1992, however, and therefore continued his shift away from Arkansas buddies in his choice. Similarly, the advent of Mike McCurry as Press Secretary helped Clinton achieve a much more helpful relationship with the Washington press corps (Solomon, 1995).

Obtaining sufficient coordination among the White House Staff and between the White House staff and the Executive Branch more generally remained a problem, however, because of Clinton's personal style. Clinton shared with Nixon a fondness for late night, rambling talks with his staff, often on the phone, and his fondness for talking made nonsense of any organization chart of decision-making. Clinton's Labor Secretary in his first term, Robert Reich, describes an hilarious episode in which while in a meeting of aides called to formulate policy options on an issue for Clinton, he was called to the phone in a corner of the room to give Clinton advice directly on the issue under discussion at the meeting. As Reich (1997) put it:

> [Clinton] doesn't give a fig for formal lines of authority. He'll take advice from anyone he wants to hear it from . . . Right now he wants to hear it from me. But how long will this last? And who else is he talking to?

The difficulties of running the White House effectively so evident in the first two years could be contained, but not entirely ended, because of Clinton's own style; they were, however, reduced to manageable proportions. Clinton succeeded, therefore, in creating an effective, minimal presidency. He was not able to promote a radical new agenda, or even to fill in the gaps (such as national health insurance) left by previous Democratic administrations. But he was able to articulate values and concerns that appealed to his core constituency, and to prevent the radical Republican leadership achieving much of its agenda. Deprived of any hope of claiming a mandate by the Republican congressional victory in 1994 (confirmed in the reelection of that majority in 1996), Clinton was forced back on obvious inherent powers of the office – making appointments, making speeches and controlling the actions of Executive Branch officials in making regulations, etc. Like all Presidents during periods of divided government, Clinton relied heavily on explicit or implicit threats of a veto to obtain concessions from the Republican majority in Congress coupled with adroit maneuvering to keep public opinion on his side. His manipulation of Republican calls for a tax cut in 1997 into policy changes increasing medical coverage for poor children and assistance to the working poor will surely be cited as a classic of how under divided government a president can outmaneuver the majority party in Congress. Reconfirming the wisdom of the late Aaron Wildavsky's idea that there are two presidencies – one domestic, one foreign policy – the president was also – and contrary to his wish to devote less attention to foreign policy – to remain at the center of world events.

Yet the over-riding characteristic of the Clinton Administration has been the wide variation in its standing. Some variation is not unusual; as both Rockman and Jones have emphasized, there are important variations in the nature and prestige of the presidency within as well as between administrations. Few administrations, however, have matched the roller-coaster character of the Clinton Administration, starting strongly, plunging to near-disaster in 1994, and recovering for a second term which itself was marred by allegations of sexual impropriety.

"Ours is not a Presidential System" (Charles O. Jones)

The difficulties that confronted President Clinton would encourage many to think that this has been a period of drift in American politics in which little of importance has happened. This is far from the case. Probably at least as many potentially important policy decisions have been made in Washington in the 1990s as in most decades even though these were not the president's top priorities. Not all of these decisions will turn out to be as important as they seemed at the time, and even fewer of them will seem wise in retrospect, for that is the nature of political decision-making. A few of the apparently important decisions will make the point. NAFTA, as Ross Perot complained, had the potential for integrating the

Mexican, Canadian, and American economies. The new World Trade Organization (WTO) created a body that had in theory the right to insist that American laws with discriminatory trade consequences be repealed. The expansion of the North Atlantic Treaty Organization (NATO) to include Poland, Hungary, and the Czech Republic expanded formal American security responsibilities in Europe. The "Welfare Reform" Act of 1996 ended federal guarantees against abject poverty that had been in place for sixty years, with dramatic consequences for both the poor and the nature of the social compact in the United States more generally. The "budget deficit," whose importance as an issue in American politics in the 1980s and 1990s will surely mystify future historians, was effectively ended by a combination of a vigorous economy and budget-cutting. Congress and the president celebrated in 1997 with the first major tax cuts in sixteen years, legislation that, depending on one's choice of economist, would either continue vigorous economic growth or recreate a large deficit later in the twenty-first century.

These policy changes were not the result of decisive presidential leadership, but were more often the consequence of a complicated mixture of partisan rivalry and inter-institutional bargaining. The story of NAFTA, for example, was one in which the agreement was negotiated by President Bush, called into question by Clinton during the 1992 campaign, and finally approved by Congress in an alliance between the Republicans and Clinton against the Democratic leadership in the House. Neither welfare reform nor tax-cutting in 1997 were the president's priorities, but were forced on him by the Republican Congress; Clinton, however, as in negotiations over ending the budget deficit, was adept at redefining issues in a way that was both politically popular and that served his purposes. In the case of the 1997 tax cut, for example, the president was able to insist that the Republican idea of a tax cut be modified to provide assistance to the very poorest who pay no tax at all (Mitchell, 1997). Policy resulted from the interplay of institutions controlled by competing parties fearful of losing their standing with the public, not from decisive presidential leadership. Those who follow Mayhew in believing that divided government does not impede making important policy might note that health care reform died during a period of unified government, and welfare reform passed during divided government.

Implications for Future Presidents

How, then, might we evaluate the state of the presidency as a result of the experience of the Clinton Administration? The question is particularly difficult to answer given its roller-coaster character. The answer one would have given about the state of the presidency in 1993 after Clinton's election, 1995 after the Republican triumph and 1997 after Clinton's recovery would have been very different. Skowronek (1993) might have warned us that this instability was in store for a preemptive president elected against the grain of history. His preemptive presidents often find themselves embroiled in "convulsive" politics including actual or threatened impeachment. President Clinton – the best efforts of the Republicans in probing scandals such as Whitewater or dubious campaign contributions notwithstanding – has escaped that fate. Nonetheless, he has been president through a period of immense partisan instability, even though the stability of the political system itself has rarely been more secure. Most of Clinton's difficulties result not from the stars or even from himself, but from being an accidental Democratic president in an era in which conservatives and Republicans dominated politics.

It is, of course, possible to point to several aspects of the Clinton Presidency with implications for his successors. Like his last politically successful predecessor, Ronald Reagan, Clinton showed that the public's capacity to be impressed by presidential rhetoric and symbolism is immense. President Clinton's favorite form of action often seemed to be talk and, judging from his approval ratings, the public approved. Clinton also showed, as had his predecessors during periods of divided government, the importance of the formal powers of his office. It is an interesting thought experiment to imagine Clinton facing a Republican majority armed with a veto that could have been over-ridden by a simple rather than two-thirds majority; his protestations in 1995 that he was not "irrelevant" in Washington would surely have been in vain. Clinton's experience in running the Executive Branch suggests that, as President Carter also discovered, a White House staff does need a structure, and that a free-wheeling, open-access approach to organizing access to the president does not work.

It is unlikely, however, that Clinton's successor will find very much of value in these observations for the simple reason that so much will depend on the circumstances in which his successor finds himself. Clinton survived scandal in part because he was president while everything – the economy, the crime rate and even the cancer rate – seemed to be going well. But even more normally defined political circumstances might be difficult for his successor. Clinton's adroit use of veto threats, for example, would not work well for a president whose party had a majority in Congress. Speeches about the desirability of school uniforms would not satisfy a public convinced that the president had greater opportunities for action nor, perhaps in less favorable economic times, a public more demanding of policy initiatives. Present indications are that the budget deficits of the 1980s and early 1990s that did so much to shape policy are about to give way to a period of either balanced budgets or surpluses, generating a very different type of politics. The state of the presidency under Clinton's successor will depend to a considerable degree on the way in which that person comes to power, and his relationship to the political order more generally.

Several quite different possibilities suggest themselves, therefore, for Clinton's successor.

The first possibility is that the Republicans retain Congress and recapture the presidency. The second is that the Democrats retain the presidency and recapture control of Congress. The third scenario, and the most probable, is that control of the institutions of government remains shared between the parties. These outcomes would almost certainly yield different presidencies, not because of any simple contrast between unified and divided government, but because they would mark different political orders. Were the Republicans to control all major institutions, the pattern of the Reagan–Bush years of a conservative drift in policy tempered by fears of electoral punishment for ideological excess and the entrenched power of certain interest groups (such as the elderly) would be confirmed. A shift to Democratic, unitary government would be seen as marking the end of the period of Republican dominance and the establishment of a political order to succeed it. The final possibility is that chance circumstances such as the economic boom of the 1990s and shortage of viable Republican candidates result in another "preemptive" outcome in which a Democrat wins the presidency against the balance of political forces.

As election forecasting is in its infancy and has at best a mixed record, it would be folly to predict which of these outcomes will occur. A betting person would probably make unitary Republican government the least likely, unitary Democratic government somewhat more likely (with the Senate being the harder nut to crack), and a continuation of divided government the most likely. We can be more certain that whichever of these circumstances occurs will shape the character of the next presidency. Only one, however, would be likely to create the opportunities for a strong presidency, namely the election of a Democratic president with a Democratic Congress. Freed at last from the constraint of the budget deficit, such a president might indeed be able to provide the strong lead that some have seen as the function of the presidency of the political system but which in reality occurs only intermittently.

3

Congress and Partisan Change

John E. Owens

In 1994, an electoral earthquake hit the American political landscape. For the first time since 1954, the Republican Party won control of the House. A 258–176–1 Democratic majority was suddenly transformed into a 230–204–1 Republican majority as voters turned out the House Speaker – the first holder of the office to be defeated for reelection since 1862 – two committee chairs, and 31 other Democratic incumbents. House Democratic losses were the largest for any party since 1946. In the Senate, a 56–44 Democratic majority became a 54–46 Republican majority, giving Republicans control of the chamber for the first time since 1986.

Uncomplicated by a presidential contest, the 1994 mid-term elections represented a resounding defeat for congressional Democrats, bringing to an end the longest period of single-party rule in congressional history. Democrats had controlled the House of Representatives without interruption for forty years. In sixty of the previous sixty-four years, Democrats had held majorities in the House (Table 3.1), and in fifty-two of the sixty-two previous years in the Senate. No wonder House Republicans were frequently described – and sometimes saw themselves – as Congress' permanent minority (Connelly and Pitney, 1994).

Agenda Change and Partisan Change

Traditionally the party of limited government, Republicans elected to the 104th Congress (1995–96) appeared in many ways to vindicate claims that a new public philosophy was in the offing.

TABLE 3.1 *Party Control of Congress, 1900–98*

Pattern of Control	Years in Control	Total years
Unified Democratic	1913–18, 1933–46, 1949–52, 1955–80, 1987–94	58
Democratic House–Republican Senate	1911–12, 1931–32, 1981–86	10
Republican House–Democratic Senate		0
Unified Republican	1901–10, 1919–30, 1947–48, 1953–54, 1995–98	30
	HOUSE	
Democratic	1911–18, 1931–46, 1949–52, 1955–94	68
Republican	1901–10, 1919–30, 1947–48, 1953–54, 1995–96	30
	SENATE	
Democratic	1913–18, 1933–46, 1949–52, 1955–80, 1987–94	58
Republican	1901–12, 1919–32, 1947–48, 1953–54, 1981–86, 1995–98	40

Source: Bacon, Davidson and Keller (1995).

Gingrich's Contract With America called for "the end of government that is too big, too intrusive, and too easy with the public's money" and for the "beginning of a Congress that respects the values and shares the faith of the American family." Although the legislative achievements of the first unified Republican Congress in forty years were nowhere near as impressive as those of the first New Deal Congress – or indeed some more recent (Democratic) congresses – from an historical perspective they were nevertheless fairly substantial and reflected a significant shift in policy priorities from previous Democratic congresses, which President Clinton was obliged to accept (Owens, 1998). Particularly significant was the overturning of the New Deal's sixty-year-old federal welfare guarantee of cash assistance to all eligible low-income mothers and children; a seven-year "Freedom to Farm" bill which replaced commodity subsidy programs created in the 1930s; a new political commitment to eliminate the budget deficit within seven years; and, after years of languishing, a new federal regulatory framework for telecommunications.

Figure 3.1 shows the extent of change in congressional preferences which was required to effect these shifts in public policy. The figure compares House members' support for four major issue dimensions in the 104th Republican Congress with levels in the previous Democratic congress (1993–4) and two congresses in the late 1970s (Clausen, 1973; Sinclair, 1982, 1985). Congressional support for each dimension fell over this period; the sharpest falls (by twenty points) occurred in support for the social welfare and agricultural support dimensions.

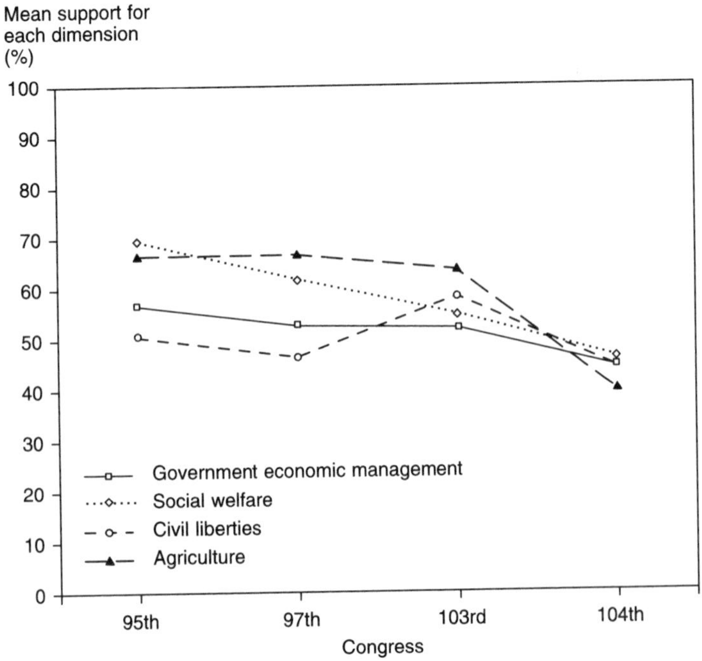

FIGURE 3.1 *House members' changing support for four policy dimensions*
Policy dimensions are those defined by Clausen (1973) and Sinclair (1982). Means for the 95th and 97th Congresses are derived from Sinclair (1982 and 1985) and from Barbara Sinclair.

However, whether these changes in federal law and the associated declines in legislators' support for key issue dimensions signal a long-term policy shift equivalent to that identified by Sinclair for the 1930s (Sinclair, 1982) is too early to state. It became quite clear after the Republicans shut down the government twice in late 1995 that American voters were decidedly leery about scaling back government to the extent demanded by congressional Republicans, particularly when this meant cuts in Medicare spending for the elderly and those with disabilities, Medicaid for welfare recipients, school lunches, and environmental protection. As public support for Gingrich and his party colleagues fell, and Clinton gained in popularity and assumed a lead in the opinion polls over Republican rival Bob Dole, congressional Republicans became much more willing to compromise. In a flurry of legislative activity in the last months of the Congress, a number of important bills were approved with the strong support of Democrats – the Kennedy–Kassebaum Bill providing for portable health insurance, the first increase in the minimum wage since 1989, revised safe drinking water laws, new environmental standards, as well as reform of welfare and immigration policies. This strategic context, constrained by the particular configuration of split-party government, prevailed in the 105th Congress with congressional leaders and the reelected president at once seeking to avoid confrontation and at the same time vying with one another to exploit opportunities for political advantage. However, a new confrontation in June 1997 over the disaster relief bill demonstrated that the president had learned the lessons of governance from 1995 better than congressional Republicans. Despite retaining their majorities in both houses in 1996, it seems doubtful whether a new era of Republican life has been instituted and more likely that we will see a return to what David Mayhew (1996) has called "conventional toss-up politics" in which party control of Congress oscillates and key policy options remain in contention with one another.

Institutional Change

Newly elected congressional majorities have not only been responsible for changing public policy. To further their policy goals and, more generally, to respond to changing external conditions, agendas, and membership turnover, they have also made major adjustments to Congress' formal rules, central leadership structures, divisions of labor, and other organizational features (Dodd, 1986a; 1986b; Foley and Owens, 1996; Fink and Humes, 1996).

Following their election to the 12th House in 1810 the War Hawks elected the dynamic Henry Clay as Speaker. Clay transformed the previously inert speakership into the chamber's political leadership, augmented the office's authority so as to rival the president, and used his new authority to appoint like-minded House members to committees and chairs in order to carry out the War Hawks' wishes. In 1910, insurgent Progressive Republicans stripped their autocratic conservative leader, Speaker "Uncle Joe" Joseph G. Cannon, of his power to appoint committee members and chairs, removed him from the chair of the Rules Committee, and tripled the committee's size. And in 1975 in the wake of Watergate and Vietnam, insurgent Democrats curtailed the powers of committees and their chairs, strengthened the powers of the Speaker, and made their leaders more accountable to the majority caucus.

Put another way then, as the nature of the problems facing American society has changed, the policy positions and agendas that voters have been willing to support have been transformed and so existing political alignments and the nature of the membership in Congress have altered. As successive influxes of new members sharing common perceptions of the dominant issues of the time come to dominate the legislature and seek to promote the newly emerging policy agenda, they have often instituted organizational and procedural change. The fact that the constitution makes no mention of how Congress should be organized – except in respect of how the respective presiding officers should be appointed – allows the House and Senate to make organizational and procedural changes designed to advance designated policy agendas.

Conditional party government

Three competing theoretical perspectives have dominated the literature on institutional change in Congress (Evans and Oleszek, 1997) – clientele rationales (where outside groups push for change), institutional rationales (which emphasize the collective benefits of change), and partisan rationales (where the majority party seeks change). Despite the decline in recent decades in American voters' attachments to the main parties and the rise of candidate-centered politics (Wattenberg, 1996), parties have become the most significant organizational structures on Capitol Hill. This is especially true on the House side where a kind of conditional party government developed in the late 1980s and 1990s (Rohde, 1991; Cox and McCubbins, 1993; Sinclair, 1995; Foley and Owens, 1996; Dodd and Oppenheimer, 1997). From the late 1960s onwards, successive Democratic majorities steadily transferred power from previously deferred-to standing committees and committee chairs to their party caucus and leaders. With strong support from party colleagues, Speakers like Tip O'Neill (D-Mass.) and Jim Wright (D-Tex.) assumed much stronger roles than their predecessors like Sam Rayburn who acted primarily as a power broker mediating between different wings of the Democratic caucus. They began to exercise much greater influence over committee assignments, over which committees would handle legislation considered important to the majority party, over procedures which determined how legislation was handled on the floor, and over the development of party policy and its promotion, particularly in front of the television cameras (Sinclair, 1983, 1992a, 1992b; 1995; Peters, 1990; Rohde, 1991; Cox and McCubbins, 1993; Herrnson and Patterson, 1995).

Even in the more stately Senate, Majority leaders like George Mitchell (D-Maine) and Bob Dole (R-Kans.) became more than managers, enablers, mediators, brokers, and janitors (Davidson, 1985). Increasingly, they sought to exercise much stronger policy leadership and to act as their party colleagues' chief spokesperson (Baumer, 1992; Smith, 1993; Foley and Owens, 1996; Owens, 1998).

So, while the strongly individualistic and entrepreneurial House members and senators of the 1980s and early 1990s (Ehrenhalt, 1982; Sinclair, 1989a; Smith, 1995; Loomis, 1996; Foley and Owens, 1996) still required particularistic benefits to help them cultivate close relations with their constituencies, they also came to depend increasingly on party leaders and coordinated party efforts to tease out from an increasingly complex and conflictual Congress the collective products that the institution was expected to deliver, not least by their own constituents.

These shifts to stronger party influence were necessitated by the more difficult political conditions of the 1980s – split-party control, deficit politics, the decline in inter-committee reciprocity, and the rise in floor amendment activity (Sinclair, 1992a). They were facilitated by significantly increased levels of party voting which resulted from more internally homogeneous parties which became much more distinct from one another (Rohde, 1991).

Republican Party Government in the House

With the election in 1994 of a new Republican majority in the House the continuation of congressional partisanship and party polarization was assured. Frustrated by their long period as the seemingly permanent minority party, House Republicans in the late 1980s had endorsed a more confrontational and partisan style. In 1989, Gingrich – a fiercely partisan conservative with a much deserved reputation as a "bomb thrower" – was elected Republican Whip, the second-ranking position in the House Republican leadership and heir-apparent to Bob Michel (R-Ill.), the party's emollient, Main Street conservative Minority Leader. Gingrich – a strategically minded leader and ardent admirer of Henry Clay – was and is an exponent of party government. House Republicans, he insisted, should become "party activists" rather than "district guys" and "committee guys" (Connelly and Pitney, 1994). To replace "the current welfare state with an opportunity society," he declared, the House and the House Republican Conference needed to strengthen further the instruments of party rule and weaken the labyrinthine, cross-cutting committee system (Owens, 1997).

The Contract With America – a party manifesto

Gingrich's enthusiasm for party government led directly to his and then-Conference chair Richard Armey (R-Tex.) writing the Contract With America – effectively a party manifesto which promised to bring ten specified measures to a vote on the House floor within 100 days if his party won a majority. Before the 1994 election, the strictures of party government led directly to the imposition of the Contract's specific commitments on Republican committee members in the House, sometimes against their wishes;

to a warning by Gingrich in early 1994 that ranking members on House committees should not take their positions for granted; and to the party's nationally coordinated election campaign in which voters were invited to reject the *party* at the next available opportunity if it did not deliver on its promises. "If we break this contract," the document declared, "throw us out. We mean it."

More centralized leadership

Immediately after the elections, House Republicans anointed Gingrich – the architect of their victory – as leader. Enthusiastically supported by the mainly inexperienced, anti-government, anti-Washington, anti-politics-as-usual freshmen and women, Gingrich proceeded swiftly and methodically to implement his party's government vision. With the strong support of other Republican leaders, he quickly restructured the Republican Conference, strengthening his position within it by creating a new and powerful Steering Committee with responsibility for establishing the party's legislative priorities, scheduling items for House and Conference consideration, and for nominating Republican committee members and chairs. Following the practice of previous Democratic speakers (Sinclair, 1998) and eschewing the Conference's decentralized structure, a core leadership directorate was established – the Speaker's Advisory Group (SAG) – chaired by Gingrich's best friend, Bob Walker (R-Pa.).

Party control and committees

Having consolidated his leadership of the party, the new Speaker moved to institute the most important changes to the committee system since the 1970s, significantly strengthening party control over the standing committees and their chairs. In recent Houses, committees and their chairs had been made much more accountable to the majority party, although considerable scope for conflict between party and committee leaders remained (Sinclair, 1995). Speaker Thomas Foley (D-Wash., 1989–94), for example, had frequently deferred to committees and their chairs in the writing of legislation.

Before most of the newly elected Republicans had arrived in Washington, Gingrich claimed the right on behalf of the

Republican Conference to name committee chairs – if necessary, by violating seniority. In nominating Robert Livingston (R-La.) to the chair of the Appropriations Committee, Gingrich passed over four more senior Republicans. Appointments of the chairs of the Commerce and Judiciary committees – Thomas Bliley (R-Va.) and Henry Hyde (R-Ill.) – also infringed seniority. All three hand-picked chairs were judged as more assertive and dynamic (though not necessarily more conservative) and less likely than those they displaced to pursue committee-defined over party-defined priorities. Those thought incapable of exhibiting these characteristics – such as Carlos Moorhead (R-Calif.) who was denied the chairs of both Commerce and Judiciary – were dumped. Gingrich also required Appropriations "cardinals" to pledge their loyalty to the Conference agenda on pain of removal; supported the imposition of six-year term limits on committee chairs; used his position on the Steering Committee to ensure that the new Republican members were heavily involved in committee assignments; and supported the assignment of freshmen and women to some of the most desirable committees (such as Appropriations, Rules, and Ways and Means) over the claims of more senior members and sometimes against the wishes of committee chairs.

Other changes strengthened party influence over committees. Three committees with Democratic-leaning clienteles (District of Columbia, Merchant, Marine, and Fisheries, and Post Office and Civil Service) were abolished while others lost or were threatened with losing some of their jurisdictions. A radical proposal to create an "Empowerment Committee" was abandoned only in the face of strong opposition from senior members – but not before the move had sent a clear signal to committees that should they seek to assert their rights the new Speaker had the power to restructure their jurisdictions (Owens, 1997). Over the objections of some newly appointed chairs, central leaders reduced committee budgets and staff – in order "to restore accountability to the committee process" – and weakened various procedural protections previously accorded committees to help them win floor approval for their bills. Following years of complaints against Democratic majorities, Republicans promised to reduce the number of closed and restricted rules which helped committees protect their legislative products on the floor. Thus, floor debate became more open – and less predictable – with the result that committees and their chairs became more dependent on central party leaders for whipping and other floor assistance. When the Judiciary Committee, for example, reported out a lobby disclosure reform bill in November 1995 the Rules Committee (presumably with central leaders' support) refused to provide for a closed rule but agreed to protect from points of order two floor amendments offered by committee nonmembers. Eleven of the 13 appropriations bills for 1996 were considered under open (or modified open) rules with the central leadership often supporting attempts on the floor to amend the committee's bills. New rules abolishing rolling quorums and requiring members, including committee chairs, to obtain the majority leader's permission to offer so-called "limitation amendments" (which seek to block motions to strike specific items in appropriations bills) had similar effects. Finally, a new rule requiring the Speaker to designate a single committee "of primary jurisdiction" when bills are referred to more than one committee was designed to encourage greater committee responsibility and better accountability to the leadership and the majority party (Owens, 1997).

Centralization within committees

The shift to greater party accountability and more centralized leadership led to greater centralization within committees – thereby reversing the twenty-year trend towards decentralized committees operating primarily through subcommittees (Smith and Deering, 1997). New rules limiting most committees to five subunits were adopted, abolishing thirty-one subcommittees at a stroke. Full committee chairs regained power to appoint subcommittee members and chairs, and to set subcommittee budgets. However, far from signaling a return to the days of powerful committee chairs – to whom central leaders were required to show deference – in the 104th House newly appointed committee chairs effectively became line managers obliged to seek the permission of central leaders before making subcommittee appointments or deciding their agendas. Subcommittees continued to consider major legislation – including welfare reform, telecommunications deregulation, immigration, and Superfund – but fewer meetings and hearings occurred in subcommittees than in full committees than was the case in the 1970s and 1980s (Smith and Lawrence, 1997) and full committee chairs were not accorded the same operational deference as their Democratic predecessors – and, indeed, did not seek it (Owens, 1997).

Enacting the Contract

When House committees began to consider the thirty-two Contract bills, the impact of the shift to party government was only too apparent. Gingrich and Armey agreed on an approved functional division of labor which departed from the practice of previous Democratic leaders (Sinclair, 1998) whereby the new Speaker would concentrate on publicizing and disseminating the Contract message and develop long-term strategy and policies while the new majority leader (and other central leaders) would take responsibility for managing the daily legislative agenda. Once committees were organized, Armey gave committees detailed marching orders: committees were required to give priority to reporting out to the floor legislation enacting the ten items in the Contract in time for a vote within 100 days. So tight was central control that chairmen could not schedule so much as a subcommittee hearing without first asking the permission of the leadership. If they did not meet Armey's deadlines, they risked being replaced. Democratic leaders had used their powers to intervene in committee work after the early 1970s – but nothing on this scale had even been attempted in recent decades. When committees began to consider the thirty-two Contract bills, the impact of party leaders' efforts was evident: over three-quarters of committee bills used initially to write legislation complied with the Contract. Some which did not comply – such as the enhanced rescissions (line-item veto) and unfunded mandates bills – were nevertheless approved by central leaders. Committee leaders who refused initially to use the Contract's provisions were subsequently instructed to do so by central leaders, while others were granted dispensations with the proviso that they did not seek to obstruct committee action. The end result of all this pressure was that less than a quarter of the Contract bills were amended significantly by committees (Owens, 1997).

Having written the Contract and orchestrated the party's election campaign, House leaders then adopted the role of guardians of their party's manifesto. Their guardian strategy involved performing those roles previously assumed by Democratic leaders (Sinclair,

1995), but much more than in recent decades it entailed choosing committee chairs and members; imposing strict deadlines on committee chairs; admonishing committees constantly to keep faith with a manifesto; and in the event that committees failed to deliver legislation which complied with the party program threatening to over-ride committee decisions through the Rules Committee or on the floor. In recent Democratic Houses, central party leaders had increased their involvement in legislation in a major way from 28 percent to 60 percent (Sinclair, 1993). During the Contract period, the comparable figure approached 100 percent – given the leadership's authorship of the Contract.

After the Contract

Experience after the first 100 days reinforced this party government interpretation. Even after all the Contract legislation had been brought to a floor vote, central leaders continued to set committee agendas. More controversially, as in the case of the telecommunications bill which was reported out of the Commerce Committee by a large bipartisan majority, Gingrich insisted that his appointee chair Bliley abandon the committee's bill and support a lengthy leadership amendment which reversed the overall thrust of the legislation. Later in 1995, when the Agriculture Committee rejected the leadership-approved Freedom to Farm bill, central leaders contemplated reprisals against Republican dissidents, and then circumvented the committee by persuading the Budget Committee to include the measure in the budget reconciliation package. In their National Strategic Plan published in early 1996, House Republicans codified the practice of granting the majority leader unilateral power to amend committee bills before they reached the floor.

Throughout the 104th Congress, Gingrich and the Republican leadership made extensive use of task forces which, unlike standing committees, do not have formal organizational rules, a budget or staff, and were even more directly accountable to the speaker. Whereas previous Democratic Speakers had used them to help formulate compromise legislation, manage floor strategy, and to encourage inclusiveness in party affairs, much to the annoyance of some committee leaders and their staff Gingrich used them for less benign purposes to press committees to consider issues and arrive at decisions close to the leadership's positions. Following the Farm

Bill controversy, the entire status of the committee system became a matter of debate when Gingrich was quoted as saying that "eventually, it would be better if committees could be replaced by task forces." Some months later, the party's task force on committee review chaired by David Dreier (R-Calif.) recommended greater use of "ad hoc" committees to handle major legislation, and a number of other measures designed to strengthen party accountability.

And yet, in the last few months of the 104th Congress, as House leaders saw that they had to deliver some legislative products to the voters in the November elections and began to appreciate the virtues of compromise and bipartisan agreement, they allowed the committees and their chairs to write important legislation on health insurance, welfare, the environment, the minimum wage increase and business tax relief. Following the elections, central leaders went further and promised all chairs greater discretion in deciding their committee agendas, although Gingrich insisted on retaining informal veto power over committee decisions. At the beginning of the new (105th) congress, all committee chairs retained their positions – even the chair of the Banking Committee who did not vote for the ethically-challenged Gingrich in the Speakership election. In the new strategic environment comprising Republicans' modest reversals in the 1996 elections, the reelection of Bill Clinton, a narrow majority in the House, and Gingrich's ethics problems, rank-and-file Republicans persuaded Gingrich to replace SAG with a wider 20-member leadership group. In this new context, at least some committees and their chairs were able to win greater autonomy – with predictable results. In one particularly nasty floor encounter over spending priorities, Majority Leader Armey refused to recognize Appropriations Chair Livingston when he tried to offer his committee's bill (Bradley, 1997). Worse still, House leaders who had remained so united in 1995 were fighting among themselves. When Gingrich tried to save his party from the trouncing they received at the president's hands over the disaster relief bill in May 1997, he was opposed by almost all the other Republican central leaders. Not surprisingly, the weakened position of central leaders led to embarrassing lapses in party discipline: central leaders met rank-and-file resistance when they attempted to extract the symbolically important balanced budget constitutional amendment from the Judiciary Committee; 44 mainly moderate

Republicans defected from the leadership over President Clinton's call for the release of foreign funding for family planning groups; party support for congressional term limits declined; conservative Jacobins rebeled over a seemingly noncontroversial committee funding resolution, and openly threatened Gingrich over proposals to postpone tax cuts until an agreement on the budget was reached and over his handling of the disaster relief bill.

However, the threat of leadership intervention is never far away, especially when major issues are under consideration. In March 1998, when Appropriations Republicans (and Democrats) moved to recombine two major emergency spending bills which Republican leaders had split up for political strategic reasons, Gingrich reportedly warned that "if Republicans on Appropriations vote to do this, they'll find themselves on another committee." At the same time, the Speaker also ordered the Appropriations chair against his wishes to find additional cuts to pay for new spending in one of the bills.

Change in the Senate

Notwithstanding its more exalted, more exclusive, position in the perceived hierarchy of governmental institutions in Washington, the Senate was not immune from the effects of the Republican takeover or developments on the House side. While institutional change in the House was immediate and substantial, demands for stronger party government in the traditionally individualistic Senate were more controversial and ultimately not satisfied.

Enacting the Contract

Compared with House Republicans' Contract, Senate Republicans' legislative agenda – modestly titled "Seven More in '94'" – was hardly bold. Yet, immediately after the elections, the new Senate Majority leader Bob Dole (R-Kans.) expanded his party's program to include all the Contract items and within months of the beginning of the 104th Congress, such measures as the balanced budget amendment, the line-item veto, unfunded mandates, term limits, and the Congressional Compliance Bill received Senate consideration. Generally, however, Senate action on the Contract was nowhere near as swift as in the House. Some measures, like the large deregulation package, simply stalled while others reached the floor but were then (like the line-item veto/expedited rescissions and welfare measures) approved in very different form, or (as in the case of the balanced budget constitutional amendment) defeated.

To some extent Senate committees were simply overwhelmed by the sheer volume of additional legislation sent by the House but there was also no mistaking the coolness of Dole and most of his colleagues towards much of the Contract legislation. Dole's strategy for most of 1995 seemed to be to let Gingrich and the House run with the major issues, including many of the Contract items and the budget, and then intervene decisively at the final stage of inter-chamber and inter-branch negotiations. However, when Gingrich and House Republicans were outmaneuvered by Clinton into shutting down the government twice in late 1995, Dole – by then running strongly for the presidency – effectively took charge of the party's overall budget strategy. Ultimately, the Senate leader negotiated a compromise whereby the Clinton Administration would accept the Republicans' seven-year balanced budget goal in return for some adjustments to the underlying economic assumptions.

The individualistic Senate

Senate organization and leadership, of course, are less formalized and weaker than in the House. Rules are fewer, more flexible, and designed primarily to preserve the prerogatives of individual senators – rather than to assure majority party rule, as in the House. Senators' staggered terms usually ensure that membership changes have much less dramatic effects on policy and institutional arrangements than in the House. So, although eleven new Republican senators were elected in the 1994 elections they represented only one-fifth of the Senate Republican Conference. (House Republican freshmen–women represented one-third of their conference.)

Not only is membership change more gradual, influence within this increasingly individualistic chamber (Sinclair, 1989a) is more equally distributed; committees are less crucial in deciding the chambers' final legislative products – because senators have more committee assignments and are better able to offer and amend committee bills on the Senate floor; and the ability of the Senate's central party leaders and party majorities to discipline colleagues and committees is much weaker than in the House. The Senate majority leader lacks the prerogatives and powers of the presiding office and enjoys far less discretion over proceedings than does the House speaker – with the result that Senate floor politics are much less predictable than those of the House. Indeed, the only significant power the Senate's rules provide for the majority leader is the right to be recognized first when other senators are seeking recognition. Almost all other powers rest on the consent and cooperation of other senators and on the majority's leader's ability to manage his party. Former Senate Majority Leader Howard Baker (R-Tenn.) once compared leading the Senate with trying to "push a wet noodle." All these characteristics mean that the capacity of new partisan majorities in the Senate to enact sharp changes of policy and adjust the chamber's internal organizational structure and norms is much weaker than in the House.

Dole and Senate Republicans

Not that Dole's policy preferences or party management style suggested a strong craving for major change. A traditional conservative, Dole would never claim to be a "revolutionary" in the Gingrich mold. His personal legislative style was pragmatic, if somewhat mercurial, and he accepted the need to reach across the aisle to strike compromises. His party management style was far from heavy-handed and allowed for considerable deference towards committee chairs and other senior colleagues.

Increasingly in the 1990s, Dole's ability to manage the widening ideological, stylistic and generational differences among Senate Republicans became increasingly problematic – never more so than after the 1994 elections. Since 1980, the number of Republican conservatives in the Senate – typically from the south and west – had risen sharply. Of the Republican senators elected in 1994, only one – Olympia Snowe (R-Maine) – was a moderate. Not only were nearly all Dole's party colleagues conservatives, many were graduates of Gingrich's House. Most endorsed the hard-line, confrontational approach advocated by the House Republican leader, and embraced his vision of party government. After their

1994 election victory, many Senate Republicans endorsed the Contract agenda. More senior Republicans tended to take a different view, eschewing a confrontational style. When, for example, it was suggested to Senator John Chafee (R-R.I.) that he should support tax cuts because they were included in the Contract, he retorted, "I didn't sign any Contract With America and I don't know who did in the Senate" (Taylor, 1995).

As majority leader, Dole faced increasing difficulties in the 104th Congress trying to straddle these conflicting approaches within his party. In the floor debate on the budget reconciliation bill in October 1995, for example, he conceded ground to a pivotal group of Republican moderates – accepting smaller cuts in health, education, Medicaid, and Medicare spending – and later refused to admonish William Cohen (R-Maine) for providing the only Republican vote against the bill. Hard-line conservatives protested. Echoing the populist party mandate arguments of their House colleagues, they asserted the superiority of their party's electoral mandate. "There are some senators," complained freshman senator Rod Grams (R-Minn.), "who don't think there was a November, but the voters are going to hold us accountable. We should be clear about giving the voters what they asked for" (Cloud, 1995b). They demanded that Dole impose strict party discipline and loyalty to the party program.

Dole's position as Republican leader was made even more difficult by the election of hard-line conservatives to other party leadership positions. In 1993, Trent Lott (R-Miss.) was elected Conference Secretary – the fourth-ranking position in the Republican leadership. Lott was a former House minority whip, and mentor and ally of Gingrich in the Conservative Opportunity Society (COS). In late 1994, immediately after the elections, Lott challenged and defeated Alan Simpson (R-Wyo.), a close ally of Dole's and the incumbent Republican whip. Despite Dole's best efforts, Lott won the second-ranking leadership position by a single vote, and became Dole's heir-apparent. Lott assured his colleagues that "there won't be a separate agenda" but the future direction of Senate Republican leadership seemed unmistakable. Not only had Dole lost a dependable lieutenant, three of the top four Republican leadership positions in the Senate were now held by hard-line conservatives.

Making the Senate (a little bit) more like the House

As the new Republican whip, Lott made it clear that he wanted Senate Republicans to adopt a more disciplined and cohesive approach along the lines he had introduced in the House. The party's whip organization was expanded immediately to ten senators (four more than under the Democrats); and vote-counting became based on member-to-member rather than staff contact. As a result, whip counts became very accurate (Cloud, 1995a).

In contrast with their colleagues in the House, Senate Republicans devoted little attention to the chamber's committee system following the 1994 elections. In obeisance to the Contract, committee budgets and staff were cut and a large Republican task force on internal committee reform was appointed by Dole under the leadership of Senators Pete Dominici (R-N.M.) and Conference Secretary Connie Mack (R-Fla.). In their report, Dominici and Mack recommended reducing the number of Senate subcommittees in the succeeding 105th Congress; abolishing all joint committees; restricting further the number of committee assignments individual senators could hold; disbanding committees whose memberships continued to decline; prohibiting proxy voting; and limiting debate on motions to proceed. Ultimately, the task force's recommendations to reduce committee budgets and the number of subcommittees were approved by the Senate Rules and Administration Committee with Dole's support.

Republican hard-liners who were frustrated by the Senate's slow progress on much of the Contract legislation were clearly dissatisfied with these modest changes and the newly elected Lott's promise to allow committee chairs "a wide berth" in running their committees (Cohen, 1995). They wanted to strengthen the instruments of party rule, rein in the chamber's individualistic tendencies, and streamline its free-wheeling structures. Tension between hard-liners and traditionalists erupted in March 1995. Senator Mark Hatfield (R-Ore.), chair of the Appropriations Committee and the chamber's second most senior Republican, cast the only Republican vote against the balanced budget constitutional amendment, thereby precipitating the new majority's first major legislative defeat. The measure was a core issue in the Contract, and its defeat quickly evoked the ire of Republican hardliners. Immediately after the vote, Alfonse D'Amato (R-N.Y.), chair of the National Republican Senatorial Committee, warned Hatfield publicly that party leaders might withhold funds for his reelection campaign in 1996 and support a primary opponent (the threat was later reversed). Echoing the rationale of Armey and other Republicans in the House, Lott publicly criticised Hatfield, insisting that members of the Republican leadership – which included committee chairs – had a responsibility to support the party's position (Cloud, 1995c). Incensed by Hatfield's action and supported by Lott and other hard-line conservatives, Conference Secretary Mack and freshman Senator Rick Santorum (R-Pa.) insisted that the Conference meet to strip Hatfield of his committee chair. Despite the intense pressure on him, Dole refused to call a Conference vote but agreed to the establishment of a new task force on internal reform chaired by Mack and dominated by hard-line conservatives, including Lott. Had Hatfield been stripped of his position, he would have been the first chair to suffer this fate since 1924 and the only senator ever to lose his post as a result of a single floor vote.

In its report, the Senate task force recommended several organizational changes designed to strengthen party discipline and enhance the influence of the party's hard-liners. Most followed the new House rules:

- the respective party conferences to have sole authority to select and remove committee members and chairs or ranking members (as in the House)
- six-year term limits on committee chairs or ranking memberships (as in the House)
- prohibitions on full committee chairs (except those for Appropriations, Indian Affairs, and Rules and Administration) serving simultaneously as chairs of other full or subcommittees (as in the House)
- all Republican senators to be limited to chairing two subcommittees (House rules restrict members to just one chair)
- the Republican leader to nominate all committee chairs or ranking members with ratification by the full Conference and without necessarily following strict seniority (as in the House)
- the Republican leader to appoint one Republican senator to "A" committees like Appropriations, Finance or Armed Services

when more than one vacancy occurs simultaneously on one of these committees

- the Republican Conference to approve a "Conference Legislative Agenda" by a three-quarters vote before the selection of party leaders and committee chairs thereby enabling Senate Republicans to take into account the positions of committee chairs and leaders on Conference priorities before casting their votes on chairs.

Over the opposition of Republican moderates, all but two of the task force's recommendations were approved by the Conference. New rules providing for term limits on committee chairs were amended to take effect from January 1997. The proposal to allow the leader to nominate committee chairs was rejected in favor of allowing committee members to choose their chairs in secret ballots, subject to approval by the full Conference. A coalition of senior senators and moderates objected to the original proposal on the grounds that it would concentrate too much power in the leader; even so, Republican senators now have greater opportunities to overturn committee chairs than they did. The Conference also refused to endorse the task force's proposal to allow the leader to appoint a Republican to a committee when two or more vacancies occurred.

Taken together these changes represent the strongest movement towards party rule and accountability in the Senate in seventy years. Depending on how the new rule is implemented, the adoption of a "Conference Legislative Agenda" in particular gives Republican hard-liners a powerful mechanism with which to deny committee chairs to moderate colleagues who oppose important items on the party agenda. Possibly with this threat in mind, four committee chairs – including Hatfield and Simpson – announced their retirement in 1996. Besides reinforcing party disciplinary pressures on Republican moderates and traditional conservatives, however, these changes also facilitated a politically useful redistribution of full committee and subcommittee chairs. At the beginning of the 105th Senate, twenty of the thirty Republican senators (58 percent of the total) who had been elected since 1990 became subcommittee chairs at the expense of senior full committee chairs like Dominici, Lugar, Helms, Roth, and Thurmond who could no longer hold their subcommittee posts. After only two years as a senator, freshman Fred Thompson (R-Tenn.) became chair of the full Governmental Affairs Committee with responsibility for leading his party's investigation into the Clinton Administration's campaign finance practices. His predecessor Senator Bill Roth (R-Del.) had to wait ten years before becoming the top Republican on the committee.

A more combative leadership?

Dole's resignation from the Senate in June 1996, to concentrate on running for the presidency, and the election of Trent Lott as majority leader completed the consolidation of hard-line domination of the Republican leadership. Fellow COS graduate Don Nickles (R-Okla.) was elected majority whip while Thad Cochran (R-Miss.) and Mack remained, respectively, Conference Chair and Secretary – producing one of the most politically homogeneous Senate leaderships in recent decades. Lott's election appeared to signal a more combative leadership style and further strengthening of party rule. As Dole's deputy, Lott had continued to promote hard-line conservative causes, sometimes with the aid of the Republican whip organization – as, for example, when he led a move in 1995 to deny federal grants to (generally liberal) groups lobbying Congress. On some occasions, his hard-line approach placed him in opposition to Dole. Dole's efforts to negotiate compromises with President Clinton over US troops to Bosnia and over the FY 1996 omnibus appropriations bill, which would have increased funding for environmental protection programs, were undercut by his deputy. Yet Lott's legislative style was not always confrontational (Barnes, 1996). Even in the heady days of 1995, he did not always support the uncompromising stances of House Republicans whom he sometimes dubbed "the ayatollahs." During crucial budget negotiations with Gingrich and the Senate, it was Lott who advocated an early settlement with the White House; the more cautious Dole feared a backlash among Republican hard-liners. Lott was sometimes willing to cooperate with Senate Democrats – as, for example, in early 1995 over the telecommunications bill – over Dole's objections.

The same mixture of partisanship, principled conservatism, and legislative pragmatism pervaded Lott's leadership of the Senate after June 1996. Like Gingrich in the House, the new majority leader moved early on to strengthen his influence. His penchant for order and discipline led him to increase resources available for leadership offices, particularly the whip office, and to relocate it in more spacious accommodation off the Senate floor. Emulating Gingrich in the House, Lott resorted to using nonlegislative task forces because of his ability to control them. Composed exclusively of Republicans, and dominated by Republican conservatives – Lott used these task-forces to recommend provisions which should be included in legislation. On a number of occasions he demonstrated forceful leadership – for example, engaging the support of the National Right To Life Committee, the Christian Coalition, and other conservative allies to kill campaign finance legislation in 1996. Before the vote to invoke cloture, he warned committee chairs that if they wanted leadership support for their bills they should support him. In the event, only eight Republicans supported cloture; none, except Kassebaum and Simpson who would retire at the end of the Congress, were committee chairs. In 1998, Lott again resorted to tough parliamentary tactics to thwart campaign finance legislation.

Yet, Lott has recognized the limitations imposed by the Senate on strong party leadership, revealing a willingness to compromise in order to produce results beneficial to his party. More than any other Republican leader, it was Lott who understood in the months leading up to the November 1996 elections that both Republicans and Democrats, as well as Bill Clinton, needed some tangible legislative products to take to the voters. Barely a month after becoming Senate majority leader, he shocked hard-line colleagues happy to continue brawling with the president over welfare, health care, immigration, environmental protection, and other measures by summoning colleagues to the Senate floor and chastising them for holding up legislation. Weeks later, over the objections of Republican Whip Nickles and other hard-line conservatives, Lott pushed the Kennedy–Kassebaum health insurance portability bill through the Senate and offered Democrats a new legislative deal which gave them the first increase in the minimum wage since 1989 in exchange for new tax allowances for business. In the 105th Congress, as legislative initiative shifted from the House to the Senate, Lott pushed through ratification of the Chemical Weapons Ban Treaty over the opposition of Jesse Helms (R-N.C.), chair of the Foreign Relations Committee, and other conservative hard-liners; compromised eventually with Democrats over the scope of the proposed investigation of campaign funding abuses, and began negotiations with President Clinton on the FY 1998 budget.

Since his election as majority leader, Lott's party management style has been more inclusive than Dole's and he has developed a highly tuned intra-party communication network based on a much more cohesive Senate Republican Conference. Conscious of the need to assuage moderates' fears of hard-line domination of the leadership, however, Lott recruited moderates like Cohen and Snowe into the leadership organization. At the beginning of the 105th Senate – considerably more conservative than its predecessor – Lott even appointed the pro-choice Snowe to the new position of "counsel" to the majority leader, a post described as "on par" with that of chief deputy whip held by the conservative Judd Gregg (R-N.H.).

The limits of institutional change

The movement towards stronger party rule in the Senate has then been much more tentative than in the House. So, while Gingrich could violate seniority in the appointment of some committee chairs in the House and increase party control over the committee system, in the 104th and 105th Congresses, Republican senators recoiled from such a move. Despite Hatfield's opposition to a key party proposal, the Senate Republican Conference did not press for his removal from the chair of the Appropriations Committee. Following the resignation from the Senate of the disgraced Bob Packwood (R-Ore.) in September 1995, Senate Republicans observed strict seniority in the appointment of his successor Bill Roth (R-Del.) as Finance Committee chair even though Roth's ability to lead the committee effectively was questioned. The appointment of other committee chairs resulting from Packwood's resignation also followed strict seniority; as did chair appointments at the beginning of the 105th Congress. Rumors that the conservative Senator Dan Coats (R-Ind.) would challenge Senator James Jeffords (R-Vt.), the Senate's most liberal Republican and heir-apparent to the chair of the Labor and Human Resources Committee, did not materialize. (Prudently, Jeffords developed a less liberal voting record in 1996, and nominated Lott for majority leader as well as the hard-line conservative Larry Craig of Idaho for the chair of the Policy Committee.) Even hard-line Republicans' attempts to implement the Contract's reductions in committee budgets did not match those in the more tightly structured House. Four senior committee chairs – all like Jesse Helms (R-N.C.) with impeccable conservative credentials – mounted effective opposition to the cuts applied to their committees, while related attempts to abolish the nonlegislative Indian Affairs and Special Aging committees also foundered. Lott's attempts to impose party discipline in the early months of 1997 – over passage of the balanced budget constitutional amendment, over the scope of the campaign finance investigation chaired by Thompson, over the flood disaster relief bill – foundered even though the Republican Conference was larger, ostensibly more conservative, and supposedly more disposed to accepting party discipline. As one Republican colleague after the defeat on the campaign finance investigation observed: "Trent likes to control and manage . . . but the Senate is a collection of 100 independent people who don't always like to be controlled and managed." The Republican debacle over the disaster bill found Lott and other Senate and House leaders insisting on cutting spending while popular feeling and constituency pressure against congressional Republicans grew, aided by President Clinton's veto and public appeals.

Explaining Institutional Change

The strengthening of party rule in the House must be explained by the unusual circumstances of 1994 and 1995, as well as by more familiar factors. Clearly one factor was Gingrich's strategic vision of party government as well as his personal energy and style (which later caused Republicans many problems). Like his Democratic predecessor Jim Wright, Gingrich conceived the role of House Speaker as a sort of prime minister within a parliamentary system. A second unusual factor was that in 1995 House Republicans began with a clean slate, following years as the minority. The newly elected central party leaders did not have to contend with entrenched committee chairs – as Democratic Speakers have had to over recent decades. Nor did they have to contend with a party majority which was either accustomed to being the majority, experienced (61 percent of the Republican Conference had been elected since 1990), or imbued with the House's institutional norms and traditions. A third unusual factor was Gingrich's role and House Republicans' experience in the 1994 elections. There was little doubt in the minds of Republican House members, especially the seventy-three new members, that Gingrich was the main reason for their election and their unchallenged leader. So, when Gingrich called for the speedy enactment of the Contract and greater party accountability within the House's organizational structures, his party colleagues were very willing followers.

Gingrich and other central leaders were, however, also able to push through significant institutional changes in 1994 and 1995 for another more familiar reason. As the previous discussion noted, the essential precondition for more centralized and more powerful leadership is a high level of unity within the majority party. When Speakers Thomas Reed and Joseph Cannon exercised strong centralized leadership in the House in the decades round the turn of the century, they did so under conditions of exceptionally high levels of party cohesion (as well as near-monopolistic control over candidate recruitment) (Brady and Althoff, 1974). Underpinning the consolidation of central leadership power in the 104th House were remarkably high levels of party voting and strong party support among Republicans over and above any levels achieved by majority Democrats over the previous forty years. In 1995, the percentage of House votes which divided House members along party lines reached levels unprecedented since the days of party government in the 1890s and early 1900s. Using *Congressional Quarterly*'s admittedly minimal criterion – at least 50 percent of one party opposing at least 50 percent of the other party – 73 percent of votes divided the parties in 1995 (see Figure 3.2). The more demanding 90 percent versus 90 percent measure yields a level of 31.6 percent – unprecedented since Cannon's heyday in 1905-6. As the percentage of party votes jumped to new high levels, Republican party support increased to 93 percent (Figure 3.3) surpassing any level achieved by majority Democrats either at the height of opposition to President Reagan in the mid-1980s or the period of Wright's speakership.

Table 3.2 shows that partisanship was resurgent in House voting on each of the policy dimensions identified earlier, including social welfare and civil liberties, where as recently as the early 1980s significant internal party divisions had been present in both parties

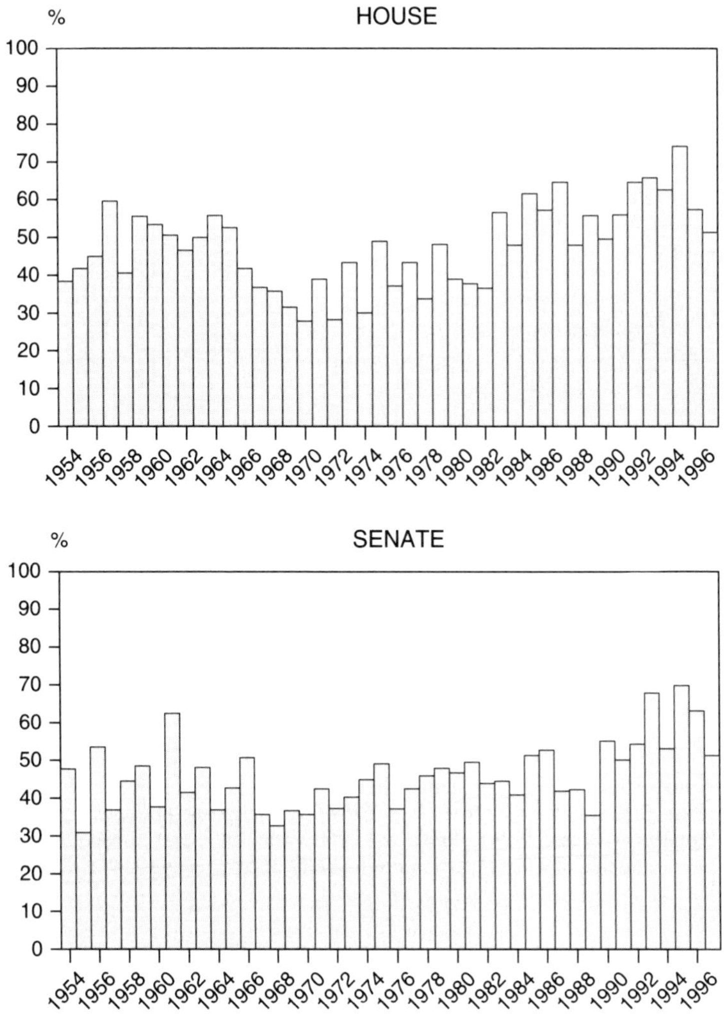

FIGURE 3.2 *Percentage of votes which divided the parties, 1954–97*

A party vote is defined as one in which more than 50 percent of one party opposes more than 50 percent of the other party.

Source: *Congressional Quarterly Weekly Reports.*

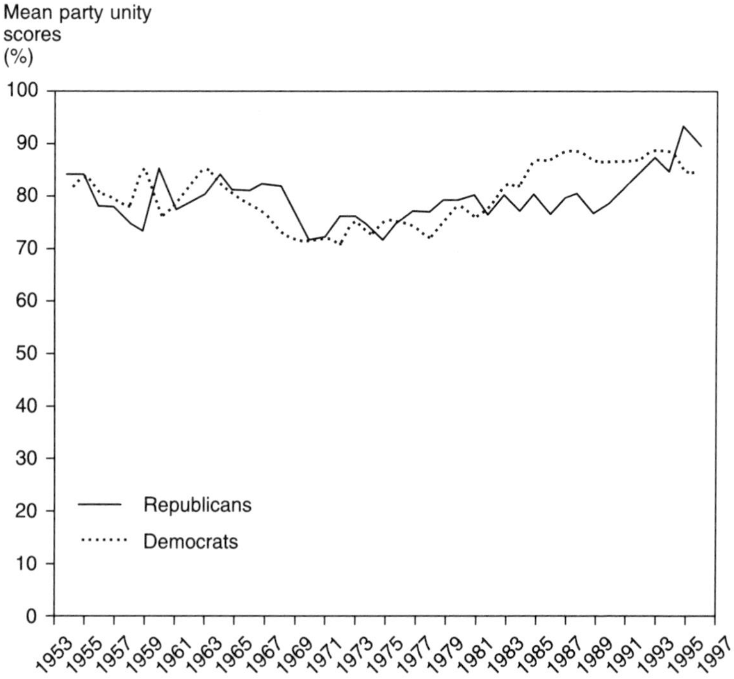

FIGURE 3.3 *Mean House-party support scores, 1954–97*

Note: Data are normalized to eliminate the effects of absences.

Source: Norman J. Ornstein, Thomas E. Mann and Michael J. Malbin, *Vital Statistics on Congress 1995–1996* (Washington, D.C.: Congressional Quarterly Press, 1996), Table 8.4. Data for 1995 and subsequent years recomputed from *Congressional Quarterly Weekly Report*, various dates.

– between northern and Solid South Democrats, and between north eastern and other Republicans. Only when House members voted on military spending–international involvement issues did they display the same (lower) levels of internal party divisions their predecessors exhibited in the late 1970s and early 1980s.

Institutional change in the Senate was more limited, primarily because of the institution's traditions and the political style of the Republican leadership. All these factors combined to constrain central leaders' powers and set real limits to attempts to introduce stronger party discipline and accountability.

TABLE 3.2 *Changing voting alignments in the House across four dimensions, 1981–96*

	Democrats			Republicans			Pearson *r* correlation with party
	All	Northern	Solid South	All	North East	Other	
			Government management				
1981–2	80.5	89.5	60.5	17.0	28.5	13.3	.87
1993–4	85.0	87.8	80.0	3.3	4.4	3.0	.93
1995–6	89.8	92.1	84.5	3.9	6.0	3.5	.96
			Social welfare				
1981–2	85.2	93.1	67.2	32.1	51.9	26.5	.80
1993–4	87.8	91.9	78.9	5.3	8.8	4.8	.93
1995–6	94.7	96.3	91.2	4.3	10.2	3.0	.97
			Civil liberties				
1981–2	65.1	76.9	39.2	22.3	38.2	19.1	.66
1993–4	94.0	95.9	91.0	4.5	7.3	3.8	.96
1995–6	90.3	93.7	82.6	3.9	8.8	2.9	.94
			Military spending scales*				
1981–2	53.7	70.0	21.2	18.6	31.1	14.5	.53
1993–4	57.6	72.3	28.5	16.3	16.0	16.4	.48
1995–6	54.1	66.6	26.6	17.4	23.9	16.0	.51

Notes: Data are means of scores for 1981 and 1982 calculated by Sinclair (1985, Table 13.10). I am grateful to Barbara Sinclar for providing additional unpublished data for 1981–2.

*Contains similar votes to those in Sinclair's international reorientation scale.

Conclusions

It is clear then that congressional debates about organizational change since the mid-1990s have been informed primarily by partisan rationales. In 1995, highly unified Republican majorities in the House shifted power from committees to central party leaders and the party Conference. After 1995, the leadership's tactical mistakes, increasing Republican factionalism and the growing confidence of chairs and committees, introduced more tension into the relationship but the shift in the balance of power to more centralized control remains a reality. In the Senate, reform efforts were driven by the same partisan principles but produced more tentative results in 1996 and 1997. Changes in both chambers were informed by the perceived need for committees and individual members to be more accountable to the majority party. Yet, the congressional world as we know it has not been remade. The House of Representatives is basically a majoritarian institution, even more so now than previously as majority leaders and party caucuses and conferences have become much less willing and able to defer to committees; and the Senate remains basically individualistic albeit much more amenable to limited party government. Nor could the congressional world be remade without subverting a Constitution which upholds institutional competition and power-sharing within as well as among governing institutions.

4

The Supreme Court and the Constitution

Cornell W. Clayton and James Giordano

In recent years, the Supreme Court, like other American governmental institutions, has confronted the destabilizing forces of modernism. These have simultaneously upset established theories of law and unsettled electoral politics. These broad structural forces, more than the personal predilections of the justices, have shaped the contemporary character of Supreme Court decision-making. Indeed, to the disappointment of both the left and right, the 1990s saw a substantial downscaling in American public law. The constitutional activism that marked the Warren and Burger Courts gave way to a Rehnquist Court that was unwilling to expand boldly or abandon established constitutional doctrines. This retrenchment was accompanied by the Court's reluctance to articulate substantive principles to govern constitutional law. Whether speaking in near unanimity while striking down state anti-gay initiatives (*Romer* v. *Evans* [1995]), or in severely divided opinions reaffirming abortion rights (*Planned Parenthood* v. *Casey* [1992]), the Court has become centrist in political outlook and pragmatic in constitutional decision-making. This more constrained judicial role fitted comfortably with the Clinton Administration's legal agenda, which has been modest by comparison with that of his immediate Republican predecessors. Because these broad structural factors are not likely to change quickly, the Court will almost certainly retain its centrist, pragmatic role into the twenty-first century.

The Court's Legal and Political Context

Two historical developments – one legal, one political – profoundly affected the Court's functioning in the late twentieth century. The first is the collapse of a consensual constitutional jurisprudence. During the early part of the twentieth century, legal realists such as Oliver Wendell Holmes and Karl Llewellyn effectively undermined legal formalism by emphasizing law's dependence on political and social forces (Llewellyn, 1931). The way progressives used realist analysis to attack the Court's *Lochner* era jurisprudence and to reconcile the constitution to the political transformations accompanying the New Deal is well known (Gillman, 1993). Roosevelt appointed eight new justices to the Court, each infused with New Deal values. His judicial strategy won judicial acceptance of his legislative program and the Court's shift in jurisprudence ushered in a new constitutional regime in the United States (Ackerman,. 1991).

Realism's impact on the relationship between the Court and the political system, however, was not fully apparent until much later. Following the New Deal, American politics was marked by broad consensus. Both major parties occupied the center of the ideological spectrum and agreed on the values forged during the 1930s. Within the judiciary, that political consensus translated into agreement over constitutional fundamentals and an emphasis instead on the technical aspects of legal process and judicial restraint (Hart, 1959; Levi, 1949; Wechsler, 1961). But as the consensual politics of the 1940s and 1950s gave way to ideological polarization in the 1960s and 1970s, realism's impact on the Supreme Court became more clear. Especially in the wake of the Warren Court's activism, political dissensus in the nation manifested itself in normative debates on and off the Court over constitutional values (Fried, 1988).

Since the 1960s, constitutional theory has become a booming industry in the United States with approaches ranging from critical neo-marxism to a conservative brand of law and economics (Seidman and Tushnet, 1996). On the Court, at least four major approaches to constitutional adjudication have been embraced by the justices: (1) *textualism–originalism*, or the view that the Court should adhere to the literal text or the historical judgments of those who ratified the Constitution; (2) *deference–restraint*, or the view that the Court should defer to the judgments of the elected branches; (3) *independent–interpretivism*, which suggests that the Court must make independent, substantive interpretations on the basis of what best makes sense to the justices; and (4) *democracy–reinforcement*, or the view that the Court should act to improve and protect the democratic process (Sunstein, 1996).

The Supreme Court as an institution has been unable to make an official choice among the various approaches to constitutional adjudication. Even individual justices may be inconsistent, adopting one approach in some cases and a different one in others. Without a consensual constitutional jurisprudence, the Court's decision-making has become increasingly fragmented, affecting both the nature of disputes it can resolve and the clarity of its decisions.

Many have interpreted this dissensus as evidence that the justices simply act on their own policy preferences or attitudes rather than on the basis of "legal" considerations. The justices are thought to decide cases in a result-oriented fashion, using law and jurisprudence as a cloak for their policy preferences (Bork, 1990; Segal and Spaeth, 1993). Within political science especially, analysis of the Supreme Court decision-making has become preoccupied with trends in the justices' voting records or the presence of "liberal" or "conservative" voting blocs rather than with the developments in jurisprudence (Epstein and Knight, 1997; Segal and Spaeth, 1993; but see Smith, 1988; Clayton and Gillman, 1998). The justices themselves have grown sensitive to the perception that they decide cases on the basis of political preferences. In *Mitchell* v. *W. T. Grant* (1974), for instance, Justice Potter warned that:

> A basic change in the law upon a ground no firmer than a change in our membership invites the popular misconception that this institution is little different from the two political branches of the Government. No misconception could do more lasting injury to this Court.

The consequences of the collapse in consensual jurisprudence has been further exacerbated by a second development in American politics. Historically, the US electoral system produced stable governing coalitions that coordinated the work of the various levels and branches of government. Major *realigning elections*, around which governing coalitions emerged, occurred in 1800 (Jeffersonian Republicans), 1828 (Jacksonian Democrats), 1860 (Republicans), and 1932 (New Deal Democrats). The Court's constitutional role coincided with these periods of electoral realignment, as political cleavage issues were constitutionalized and thrust into the courts for resolution. Historically, the Court's most important constitutional decisions corresponded closely to the timing and the issues involved in these electoral realignments. Between realignments, when governing coalitions were stable, the Court tended to play a secondary-branch role, acting to legitimize the policies of the dominant national political coalition (Dahl, 1957; Funston, 1975; Lasser, 1985).

Since the 1950s, however, American electoral politics has been characterized by dealignment rather than realignment. Increasingly, voters disassociated themselves from the major parties, becoming "independents." Split-ticket voting increased and national politics has been characterized not by a dominant governing coalition but by divided government.

Much attention has focused on how electoral dealignment affects Congress and the presidency (Cox and Kernell, 1991; Thurber, 1991). Less well understood, but equally profound, is its impact on the judiciary. Initially, dealignment led the Court to be a more regular and independent source of policy innovation. Without a stable coalition controlling the elected branches, the Court has less fear of institutional retaliation if it makes unpopular decisions. By contrast with the 1930s, recent presidents and Congresses have been unwilling to coordinate an assault on the Court's independence and have even acted to protect it from threats mounted by the other branch. Also, during periods of divided government it is difficult to defer to the elected branches even when the Court is so inclined. For instance, since the 1960s the Court has been deluged with separation of powers and administrative law conflicts where Congress and the executive branch are at odds over the interpretation of federal statutes (Clayton, 1994). Consequently, the Court has become increasingly detached from the political agenda of the elected branches in a way that would have been impossible during previous periods of electoral alignment (Silverstein and Ginsburg, 1987).

The Court's independence was further bolstered by an alliance with interest groups which have turned to courts for reforms that could not be won using ordinary legislative politics in a dealigned electoral system. The Warren Court's relaxation of the rules of standing facilitated this trend (Silverstein and Ginsburg, 1987).

Since the 1960s, older organizations such as the National Association for the Advancement of Colored People (NAACP) and the American Civil Liberties Union (ACLU), were joined by a multitude of new groups such as the Natural Resources Defense Council, the Washington Legal Foundation and the Lambda Legal Defense Fund, all of whom saw the courts as a more effective venue than Congress or the executive for effecting policy change (O'Connor and Epstein, 1989). In addition to litigation, these groups can mobilize campaigns against appointments to the Court that may threaten its independence, allowing the Court to be both a more active policy-maker and less susceptible to traditional methods of control by the elected branches (Silverstein and Ginsburg, 1987).

Judicial Decision-making

The twin developments of electoral dealignment and jurisprudential fragmentation explains much about the contemporary role of the Supreme Court. To begin with, rather than defining moments in the relationship between the Court and the elected branches, judicial appointments during the 1990s have instead become defining moments in the relationship between the president and Congress. As such they have become exercises in conflict avoidance, producing politically centrist and jurisprudentially pragmatic judges. The turning point was President Reagan's unsuccessful 1987 nomination of Robert Bork. The Reagan Administration had a well articulated strategy to remold the federal judiciary (Clayton, 1992; O'Brien, 1988). Reagan made his first two appointments to the Supreme Court – Sandra Day O'Connor in 1982 and Antonin Scalia in 1986 – while the Senate was controlled by his own party, but by 1987 Democrats regained control of the Senate and the Judiciary Committee. Although Bork had impeccable credentials, he was viewed as the leading advocate of original-intent jurisprudence and a sharp critic of the Court's new autonomy from the elected branches and its alliance with interest groups and the politically infused style of law these represented. More than 300 groups took stands on his nomination, which was defeated by the Senate after bitter, nationally televised hearings (Gitenstein, 1992; Bork, 1990).

Following the Bork debacle, Reagan selected Anthony Kennedy. A political moderate, Kennedy distanced himself from the administration's and Bork's controversial legal views and the Senate confirmed him by a unanimous 97–0 vote. Subsequently, when William Brennan retired in 1990, George Bush, in a calculated effort to avoid another confirmation battle, selected David Souter, an unknown, moderate state court judge. Indeed, Souter's political values were so opaque that the *New York Times* labeled him the "Stealth Justice." He, too, won easy confirmation on a 90–9 vote. Bush sparked confirmation controversy, however, when he named Clarence Thomas, a conservative African-American and former head of the EEOC, to fill the seat of the retiring Thurgood Marshall in 1991. Thomas' race split Democratic opposition in the Senate, however, and he narrowly won confirmation by a 52–48 margin, but only after televised hearings in which Democrats savaged his views and aired Anita Hill's explosive charges of sexual harassment against him.

Anxious to avoid confirmation conflicts, President Clinton has also steered clear of controversial nominees. The administration has worked closely with Senator Orrin Hatch (R-Utah), the ranking Republican from 1992 to 1994 and the Chair of the Judiciary Committee after 1994, to assure smooth confirmations. Indeed, Clinton has twice disappointed supporters by passing over prominent liberals such as Interior Secretary Bruce Babbit, etc., after warnings from Hatch that such a nomination would lead to conflict in the Senate. Other prominent liberals, such as former New York governor Mario Cuomo, former Senate Majority Leader George Mitchell (D-Maine), and former Secretary of Education Richard Riley, headed off controversy by withdrawing their names from consideration.

Instead Clinton appointed two moderate, pragmatic jurists to the Court, Ruth Bader Ginsburg in 1993 and Stephen Breyer in 1994. Jewish groups and women's groups strongly supported Ginsburg's appointment. During the 1970s, Ginsburg headed the American Civil Liberties Union's (ACLU's) Women's Rights Project, arguing some of the most important gender discrimination cases, including the landmark *Frontiero* v. *Richardson* (1973). Nevertheless, Ginsburg had developed a reputation, both as a lawyer and later as a judge, for careful and incremental development of legal doctrine. She even infuriated some women's groups by criticizing the Court's decision in *Roe* v. *Wade* (1973) as unnecessarily "extravagant" and "divisive" (Ginsburg, 1992). Her moderate views won her early support on the Judiciary Committee and easy confirmation by the Senate on a 96–3 vote.

Stephen Breyer also had strong support of Jewish groups, as well as early support from Senator Hatch. Prior to his appointment to the federal appeals bench in 1980, Breyer had served as Chief Counsel to the Judiciary Committee, then chaired by Senator Edward Kennedy (D-Mass.). Hatch knew and liked Breyer for his careful work as chief counsel. Moreover, during his thirteen years on the appellate bench, Breyer was known as a legal technician. He authored narrow opinions and his writings had focused on administrative process and regulatory law, rather than constitutional issues. He, too, won the unanimous support of the Judiciary Committee and easy confirmation by an 87–9 vote in the Senate.

With Clinton's appointment of Ginsburg and Breyer, the Court became relatively young in age, center-right in political outlook, and pragmatic in its approach to law. With the exception of Justice Stevens (appointed in 1975) and Rehnquist (appointed in 1972 and elevated to Chief Justice in 1986), the remainder of the Court has been appointed since 1982.

The changing political dynamics of judicial selection during the 1980s and 1990s has created three ideological blocs on the Court: a conservative bloc consisting of Scalia, Rehnquist, and Thomas; a center-right bloc consisting of O'Connor, Kennedy, and Souter; and a center-left bloc consisting of Stevens, Ginsburg, and Breyer. During the Court's 1995–96 term, for example, Justice Scalia voted most often with Rehnquist (82.3 percent) and Thomas (87.2 percent), and least often with Stevens (45.5 percent) and Breyer (54.4 percent). Conversely, Justice Stevens voted most often with Breyer (74 percent) and Ginsburg (72.7 percent), and least often with Thomas (44.7 percent) and Scalia (45.5 percent). Meanwhile, Justice O'Connor and Justice Kennedy often found themselves as swing voters; one or the other voted with the majority in each of the eleven cases where the Court's decision split 5–4, and both voted with the majority in eight of those cases, more than any other justice. The Court's decisions by the late 1990s were the product of shifting coalitions around these three blocs, with O'Connor and Kennedy the deciding votes in most controversial cases and Stevens and Scalia the most vociferous and frequent dissenters. Indeed, during the 1995–6 term, Stevens and Scalia wrote thirty-one dissents, nearly as many as the thirty-six written by the remaining seven justices together (*Harvard Law Review*, 1996).

These ideological blocs were, however, cross-cut by jurisprudential cleavages. Scalia, for instance, was an enthusiastic supporter of a textual–originalist jurisprudence, whereas Chief Justice Rehnquist was a strong advocate of judicial restraint. Thus, in cases such as *Texas* v. *Johnson* (1989), where the Court struck down a statute prohibiting desecration of the American flag, Scalia joined with the majority but Rehnquist wrote a withering dissent. Thus, simply pointing to the political–attitudinal alignments on the Court obscures how the breakdown in consensual jurisprudence affected the Court's decisions.

Even the ability to engage in "behavioral" analysis of the justices individual voting records largely depends on a set of institutional norms that have developed as a result of the breakdown in consensual jurisprudence. Prior to the 1920s, dissenting and concurring opinions were relatively infrequent: the Court tended to produce an institutional opinion which, except in extraordinary cases, the justices would sign even if they disagreed with its specifics. Realism and the conflict between the Court and the elected branches during the 1920s and 1930s led to relaxation of these norms. Justices Holmes and Brandeis earned the title of the "great dissenters," because of their willingness to author dissenting opinions critical of the Court's anachronistic jurisprudence. But Holmes' average of 2.4 dissents per term and Brandeis' 2.9 per term, pale in comparison to contemporary level of dissensus. During the Burger and Rehnquist Courts, the most frequent dissenters included: Justice Douglas (38.5 dissents per term), Stevens (21 per term), Brennan (19 per term), Marshall (15.4 per term), and Rehnquist (12.2 per term) (O'Brien, 1996). Moreover, as an overall percentage of the total number of opinions written by the Court as a whole, the number of individual opinions – dissents and concurrences – went from under 22 percent of the total during the Hughes Court (1933–40) to more than 55 percent of the total during the Rehnquist Court (1986–94) (O'Brien, 1998). During the 1994–5 term alone, in the eighty-six cases the Court decided by full opinion on the merits, fifty concurrences and sixty-four dissents were authored by the justices (*Harvard Law Review*, 1996).

The devaluation of consensual norms on the Court had become clear by the early 1970s. In *New York Times* v. *United States* (1971), the Pentagon Papers case, and *Furman* v. *Georgia* (1972), the Court's first major decision on capital punishment, for example, the Court's nine members authored ten opinions in each case – a *per curiam* opinion, announcing the Court's decision, six concurrences, and three dissents. But what explains these changing norms? The high rate of concurrences in particular indicates that there is more involved than the justices' policy preferences. Because they do not affect a case's policy outcome, concurring opinions can be explained only by a justice's sincere concern that the Court adhere to proper legal criteria in its decision. As ideological polarization during the 1960s led to competing constitutional visions, justices felt compelled to articulate these visions in individual opinions. The dissensus over constitutional jurisprudence thus led to new opinion-writing norms and a more fragmented form of decision making (O'Brien, 1998).

The most obvious consequence of this fragmentation was greater uncertainty and less predictability in law. For instance, in the 1978 *Bakke* case, the Court's first major affirmative action decision, the only part of Justice Powell's opinion for the Court joined by the other justices was a one-paragraph statement of the facts. Even when the Court avoided dissents and reached a unanimous decision, its holding could be unclear. For example in *Church of Lukumi Babula Aye* v. *City of Hialeah* (1992), the Court's decision striking down a city ban on animal sacrifices as violating the free-exercise clause, the opinion alignment for *a unanimous* Court read:

> Justice KENNEDY delivers the opinion for the Court with respect to Parts I, III, and IV, which Chief Justice REHNQUIST and Justices WHITE, STEVENS, SCALIA, SOUTER, and THOMAS join; Part II-B, which Chief Justice REHNQUIST and Justices WHITE, STEVENS, SCALIA, and THOMAS join; Parts II-A-1 and II-A-3, which Chief Justice Rehnquist and Justices STEVENS, SCALIA, and THOMAS join; and Part II-A-2, which Justice STEVENS joins.

The Court even handed down what Rehnquist termed "doubleheaders": judgments in which two opinions announce different and contradictory parts of the Court's ruling for two different majorities in each case (see *Arizona* v. *Fulminante* [1991] and *Gentile* v. *State Bar of Nevada* [1991]). Attorneys and lower courts have had difficulty making sense out of such decisions. Moreover, when the Court avoided fragmentation it often did so only by severely limiting the holding of the decision in order to accommodate the justices' competing jurisprudential views. Thus, jurisprudential dissensus led to a form of decision-making that was not only pragmatic but also minimalist; deciding the case on the most narrow grounds available and avoiding broad principles that would control other cases, future courts, or the ability of the elected branches to correct imperfections in their policies (Sunstein, 1996; Fried, 1995).

With a few notable exceptions, the Court's recent constitutional decisions underline the structural trends towards this more politically moderate, pragmatic and minimalist style of decision-making.

The Right to Privacy and Abortion

Few areas of constitutional law led the Court deeper into the "political thicket" and more clearly demonstrated its retreat to moderate, pragmatic decision making than privacy and abortion. Since 1973, the Court's decision in *Roe* v. *Wade*, establishing a constitutional right to abortion, has been a focus of partisan conflict. As with Reagan and Bush before him, the presidential platform of Bob Dole in 1996 made explicit Republican opposition to abortion. Meanwhile, President Clinton and the Democratic party committed themselves to protecting the abortion right and used the issue as a wedge to open up a "gender gap" over Republicans in both the 1992 and 1996 elections (Graber, 1996).

Five times between 1980 and 1992, Republican administrations unsuccessfully asked the Court to overturn the abortion right. But by 1992, with eight of the nine justices appointed by Republican presidents, the Court seemed poised to reverse *Roe*. In *Planned Parenthood* v. *Casey* (1992), however, the Court stunned many when it instead upheld the right to an abortion and merely altered *Roe*'s trimester framework. The decision was fragmented, with the Court's opinion authored by Justice O'Connor and joined in full only by Souter and Kennedy. While continuing to acknowledge a woman's right to an abortion prior to viability, O'Connor held that states may regulate the abortion procedure so long as they do not impose an "undue burden" on women.

In protecting the abortion right but allowing greater regulation of the procedure, the Court struck a moderate political stance that corresponded to the views of a majority of Americans (Graber, 1996). But O'Connor's opinion included a telling discussion of the problems associated with the Court's style of decision-making and the breakdown in consensual jurisprudence. The perception that the Court acts on the basis of policy preferences, she warned, undermined its ability to carry out the judicial function. Regardless of how individual justices viewed the *Roe* decision itself, she said, the Court should adhere to precedent unless there were compelling reasons to deviate:

> The Court must take care to speak and act in ways that allow people to accept its decision on the terms the Court claims for them . . . (T)he Court's legitimacy depends on making legally principled decisions under circumstances in which their principled character is sufficiently plausible to be accepted by the Nation (at 2814).

By contrast, Chief Justice Rehnquist and Justice Scalia wrote blistering dissents, chiding the Court's moderates for contriving a "novel" theory of *stare decisis* and for clinging to a decision that had

> fanned into life an issue that has inflamed our national politics in general, and has obscured with its smoke the selection of Justices to this Court in particular ever since.

O'Connor's opinion in *Casey*, and the bitterness of the dissents, illustrates well how broad structural forces pushed the Court as an institution toward a more pragmatic constitutional role at the same time as its individual members were becoming more extreme and divided in their views. This trend was apparent in other areas of privacy jurisprudence as well. In *Bowers* v. *Hardwick* (1986), for example, the Court, in a 5–4 decision with five separate opinions, upheld a Georgia statute criminalizing sodomy and refused to expand the right to privacy to cover homosexual conduct. Likewise in *Cruzan* v. *Missouri* (1990), a 5–4 Court concluded that although common law principles protected a patient's right to refuse medical care, that there was no broad, open-ended "right to die" under the Constitution. This limitation on the privacy right was reiterated in *Washington* v. *Glucksberg* (1997), when the Court upheld a state law prohibiting physicians from assisting terminally ill patients to commit suicide.

The Court's pragmatic and minimalist approach to constitutional decision-making, however, rarely ends, and usually only shifts the nature of, judicial involvement in political reform. Following *Bowers*, activists on both sides of the gay rights issue turned their efforts toward the elected branches and state courts. President Clinton found himself locked in a costly political battle early during his first term when he attempted to reverse the military's ban on gays. The resulting "don't ask, don't tell" policy pleased neither side of the dispute and it has produced a stream of litigation in the lower courts (see *Steffan* v. *Aspin* [1993] and *Meinhold* v. *Department of Defense* [1993]). Gay rights groups lobbied local governments to adopt anti-discrimination policies protecting gays. But anti-gay groups fought back with state-wide referenda and initiatives, such as the one approved in 1992 in Colorado, known as Amendment 2 ("No Protected Status Based on Homosexual, Lesbian, or Bisexual Orientation Amendment"). The Colorado amendment was challenged in the Supreme Court in 1996, and a divided 6–3 Court struck down the amendment; not on privacy grounds but under the equal protection clause!

Likewise, in 1996, gay rights groups persuaded the Hawaii Supreme Court to quash under the Hawaii constitution a law forbidding single-sex marriages (*Baehr* v. *Lewin* [Haw. 1993]). In response, the Republican-controlled Congress passed the Defense of Marriage Act of 1996 (DOMA), defining marriage in federal law as a "legal union between a man and a woman," and permitting states to refuse legal recognition of single-sex marriages performed in other states. Not surprisingly this legislation immediately triggered litigation challenging its constitutional validity.

Equal Protection and Affirmative Action

The Court's pragmatism is also evident in its equal protection decisions. Like abortion, affirmative action became an important wedge issue in electoral politics during the 1980s. The Court, for its part, had created two separate inconsistencies in its jurisprudence. First, the Court had treated state affirmative action programs more strictly than federal ones, under the rationale that the Fourteenth Amendment imposed different burdens on states (compare *Fullilove* v. *Klutznick* [1980] and *Richmond* v. *Croson* [1987]). Secondly, the Court had sometimes held that affirmative action could be used only for narrowly tailored efforts aimed at remedying the effects of past discrimination (see *Wygant* v. *Board of Education* [1986]), while other times holding it could be used in a more flexible manner to serve goals such as educational or broadcasting diversity (see *Metro Broadcasting* v. *FCC* [1990]). These inconsistencies led the Court to subject affirmative action programs to strict scrutiny in some cases but to a more relaxed means–ends analysis, or "intermediate level" of scrutiny, in others.

The Rehnquist Court resolved these inconsistencies in *Adarand* v. *Pena* (1995). In a 5–4 decision with six separate opinions, the Court held that all race-based programs would be held to the same strict standard of scrutiny. In other words, race-based affirmative action programs, whether at the federal or state level, would need to be "narrowly tailored to promote compelling governmental interests." The opinion for the Court, authored by Justice O'Connor and joined only by Kennedy, however, made an important concession; it is not true, she said, that "strict scrutiny is strict in theory, but fatal in fact" and government may use affirmative action aggressively to combat the lingering effects of past racial discrimination. In *Shaw* v. *Reno* (1993) and *Miller* v. *Johnson* (1995) the Court brought the same equal protection standards to bear in redistricting cases as well. In 5–4 decisions authored by Justices O'Connor and Kennedy respectively, the Court quashed state reapportionment schemes that used race as the predominant factor in drawing districts. Such districts, O'Connor said, drew upon stereotypical notions about racial groups that were "odious to a free people" and hence would receive strict scrutiny from the Court.

The decisions in *Adarand*, *Shaw*, and *Miller* brought coherence to the Court's equal protection jurisprudence at the cost of restricting governmental use of race-based programs to effect substantive equality. Still, the Rehnquist Court's decisions were relatively moderate, rejecting more conservative positions advanced by the Reagan/Bush Administrations and conservative interest groups.

Thus despite Scalia's and Thomas's opposition, the Court has not prohibited considerations of race altogether in either redistricting decisions or government actions tailored for remedial purposes (see also Chapter 14).

Church and State

The fragmented nature of the Rehnquist Court's jurisprudence is probably most apparent in its decisions on religious freedom, where it has been unable to develop a coherent approach to either the establishment clause or the free-exercise clause. Throughout the 1980s, conservatives advocated greater accommodation of religious belief in public institutions. A focal point of controversy was the establishment test enunciated in *Lemon* v. *Kurtzman* (1971), requiring legislation to have a secular purpose, to neither advance nor inhibit religion, and to avoid unnecessary entanglements with religion. Although most members of the Court have advocated abandoning *Lemon* they were unable to agree on an alternative approach and so the test continues to be invoked.

What kind of religious influences *Lemon* precludes, however, was the subject of constantly shifting coalitions on the Court. For instance, in *Zobrest* v. *Catalina School District* (1993), a 5–4 majority led by Chief Justice Rehnquist upheld public funding for a sign-language interpreter for a deaf student attending a private religious school. In *Lamb's Chapel* v. *Moriches School District* (1993), a unanimous Court held that public schools providing after-hours access to facilities to civic groups must also allow religious groups similar access. But, in *Lee* v. *Weisman* (1992), a 5–4 Court led by Justice Kennedy, rejected the practice of prayer in high-school graduation ceremonies. And in 1994, a 6–3 Court led by Justice Souter struck down New York's creation of a special school district accommodating a community of Hasidic Jews (*Kiryas Joel Village* v. *Grumet*). Justice Scalia's concurrence in *Lamb's Chapel* and his dissents in *Weisman* and *Grumet*, chastised the Court's majority for its pragmatic, case-by-case jurisprudence and its continued reliance on *Lemon*, which he likened to a "ghoul in a late-night horror movie that repeatedly sits up in its grave and shuffles abroad, after being repeatedly killed and buried."

The Court's decisions involving the free-exercise clause were equally fractious. In *Oregon* v. *Smith* (1990), a 6–3 Court led by Justice Scalia upheld a state's denial of unemployment benefits to members of the Native American Church fired from their state jobs for using peyote in religious ceremonies. The central part of Scalia opinion, however, was assailed by Justice O'Connor (concurring) and three dissenters. In that part, Scalia argued that the free-exercise clause requires laws to be "neutral" and "generally applicable," but abandoned the Court's previous insistence that they also be in pursuit of a "compelling state interest" (*Sherbert* v. *Verner* [1963]). The decision drew alarm from those who thought it left unpopular religious practices at the mercy of majority sensibilities. Three years later, the Court seemed to go out of its way to reassure the religious community that government could not regulate religious activity simply because it is unpopular. In *Church of Lukumi Babalu Aye* v. *Hialeah* (1993), Justice Kennedy struck down a city ordinance banning the sacrificial use of animals because the law was not passed for "neutral purposes" but out of animus to the religious practice of Santeria. Although the Court's decision was unanimous, no other justice joined Kennedy's opinion in its entirety. In three separate concurring opinions, Justices Souter, Blackmun and O'Connor vigorously disagreed with the Court's continued reliance on *Smith* and urged a return to the "compelling interest" test.

Not persuaded by *Hialeah*, religious groups successfully lobbied Congress for the Religious Freedoms Restoration Act of 1993. The law essentially reversed the effect of *Smith* by writing the "compelling interest" standards into federal statute. But the law provoked a flood of litigation and in *Boerne* v. *Flores* (1997), a 6–3 Court, again led by Justice Kennedy, struck it down on federalism and separation of powers grounds. While members of the Court continued to debate the propriety of *Smith*, a majority agreed that Congress could not use its powers under the Fourteenth Amendment for the nonremedial purposes of imposing a substantive interpretation of the First Amendment on state governments. Such a power, Kennedy wrote, would not only alter the relationship between states and the federal government but also the "traditional separation of powers between Congress and the Judiciary" which gives the Court "primary authority to interpret" the Bill of Rights.

Free Expression

In contrast to religious freedom, free-expression rights were least affected by the Court's trend toward pragmatic and minimalist decision-making. Here the Court did not hesitate to invalidate statutes or enunciate broad standards of protection. In *Texas* v. *Johnson* (1989) and *United States* v. *Eichman* (1990), for instance, the Court struck down a state and then a federal flag desecration statute as viewpoint-based restrictions on free speech. Dissenting, Rehnquist accused the majority of abandoning a 200-year-old tradition of protecting the flag. But three years later, in *RAV* v. *St. Paul* (1993), Rehnquist joined the Court to invalidate a "hate speech" law that sought to protect minority groups from hurtful and harassing speech. In this case, a group of white teenagers burned a cross on the lawn of a Black family and were charged under a St. Paul city ordinance banning such expression. A unanimous Court, led by Justice Scalia, struck down the ordinance as a viewpoint-based restriction on speech.

In 1996 in *Colorado Republican Committee* v. *FEC* the Court invalidated Federal Election Commission (FEC) regulations restricting independent campaign expenditures as a violation of free-speech rights. Then, in *DAETC* v. *FCC* (1996), it struck down portions of the Cable Regulation Act of 1992, restricting "indecent programming" on public access channels. One year later in *Reno* v. *ACLU* (1997), it invalidated portions of the Communications Decency Act of 1996 that imposed decency standards on internet users. It has also expanded so-called "commercial speech" protections in recent years. In *Ladue* v. *Gilleo* (1994) the Court barred local government from banning the posting of signs on private property, and in *44 Liquormart* v. *Rhode Island* (1996), it limited government's ability to regulate truthful advertisements for harmful products such as alcohol and tobacco.

The Court's expansive protection of free expression continued even in the face of conflicting constitutional values. In *Rosenberger* v. *University of Virginia* (1995), for instance, the Court invalidated a university policy that intended to give force to the establishment clause by denying funds to student religious publications while providing them to nonreligious ones. Writing for the Court, Kennedy said that the policy violated the right to free expression and was not required by the establishment clause. The same year, in

US v. *Treasury Employees Union*, the Court struck down the federal Ethics Reform Act of 1989, which attempted to keep government employees out of partisan politics by prohibiting them from accepting honoraria for speeches and articles. Writing for the Court, Justice Stevens said the law burdened the free market place of ideas established by the First Amendment. Once again, in dissent, Chief Justice Rehnquist argued that the majority had

> understate[d] the weight which should be accorded to the governmental justifications for the . . . ban and overstate[d] the amount of speech which actually will be deterred by such restrictions.

The contrast between the Court's decision-making in free-expression cases and its pragmatic, minimalist approach in other areas of constitutional adjudication, underscores that there was more shaping the Court's role than the justices' political views alone. Few would argue that Scalia favored flag-burning or hate speech. Yet he voted to strike down statutes prohibiting both. The Court's free-expression decisions have been robust precisely because this is an area of significant overlap between competing jurisprudential views. A libertarian conception of free-speech rights can be supported from any of a textual–originalist, democracy–reinforcement, or an independent–interpretivist view. The only approach that would consistently lead to a more narrow conception of the right is a deference–restraint approach, which also explains why Rehnquist, the most enthusiastic supporter of that approach, often found himself dissenting in these cases.

The Separation of Powers and Federalism

Divided government has generated a steady flow of separation of powers disputes over the past three decades. The Burger Court adopted a formalistic approach leading it to invalidate several major congressional acts during the 1970s and early 1980s (e.g. in *Buckley* v. *Valeo* (1976) and in *INS* v. *Chadha* (1983)). By contrast, the Rehnquist Court adopted a pragmatic, flexible approach leading it to be more deferential to Congress and less interested in using rigid principles to create air-tight governmental departments. In *Morrison* v. *Olsen* (1988), for instance, the Court upheld the independent counsel provisions of the Ethics in Government Act against claims that it gave the judiciary an improper role in the executive's prosecutorial function. The following year, in *Mistretta* v. *United States* (1989), the Court upheld the creation of the US Sentencing Commission against claims that it violated the appointments clause and improperly gave the other branches control over the judicial function.

During its 1997 term, the Court continued this more flexible and pragmatic approach. In *Rains* v. *Byrd,* the Court refused to decide a case challenging Congress' decision to give the president a line-item veto over spending bills. The Court said that Senator Robert Byrd (D-W.Va.), who had challenged the veto as an intrusion on the legislative power, lacked standing to bring the suit. Likewise, in *Clinton* v. *Jones* (1997), the Court decided that the presidency was not sealed off from judicial power. Paula Jones had brought a suit asserting that President Clinton sexually harassed her while he was Governor of Arkansas. Rejecting President Clinton's claim that sitting presidents are temporarily immune from civil actions, the Court refused even to consider Clinton's argument that such suits violated the separation of powers by exposing presidents to judicial harassment from frivolous suits. Indicative of its pragmatic approach, the Court said such a problem is hypothetical and ought not to form the premise of a new constitutional rule. Even if such suits became a problem, Congress could in the future legislate to grant the president immunity.

During the 1980s conservatives also championed a revitalization of federalism and the devolution of governmental power. The Rehnquist Court's decisions in *New York* v. *United States* (1992) and *United States* v. *Lopez* (1995) were heralded by some as the judicial embrace of "new federalism." In a series of subsequent cases, however, the Court shied away from any dramatic retrenchment and contented itself with only incremental restrictions on federal power (see Chapter 6).

The Justice Department and Clinton's Legal Policy

The Clinton Administration's centrist policy agenda existed comfortably alongside the Court's pragmatism in the 1990s. Indeed, in contrast to the Reagan and Bush Administrations, Clinton gave the Department of Justice (DOJ) a low priority, making it largely independent of White House control. Partly, this was the consequence of Clinton's leadership philosophy and centrist policy agenda (see Chapter 2). Clinton came to office eschewing judicial strategies of policy-making and believing he could use his considerable negotiating skills to build bipartisan congressional majorities. Moreover, his "New Democrat" agenda focused on such things as health care, education, and parental leave, requiring legislation rather than judicial reform to implement.

But the DOJ's independence from the Clinton White House can also be traced back to early staffing problems. Clinton's Attorney General, Janet Reno, was his third choice for the job since his first two choices had to be withdrawn from consideration. Reno had few partisan ties, no national political experience, and had never even met Bill Clinton prior to discussing her nomination. This stands in marked contrast to other presidents, who have usually appointed close friends or campaign managers to the post. While Reno's background made her less vulnerable to the intense scrutiny turned on Clinton's other Cabinet nominees in the Senate, it also made her more independent of White House influence once in office.

Staffing difficulties hampered other parts of the Justice Department as well. Following the failure to secure Lani Guinier's nomination as head of the important Civil Rights Division it took Clinton another year to fill the post with Deval L. Patrick, a little-known black attorney with moderate views. When Patrick left just two years later, it took another year to nominate Bill Lann Lee, an Asian-American, to fill the post. When Lee's nomination was opposed by conservatives in the Senate, the administration simply left him in the position as an acting head. Delays in appointments and confirmations were further aggravated by a high turnover of personnel during the first term. Indeed, after little more than a year into the administration, two of the top three posts at the DOJ were again vacant. Deputy Attorney General Philip Heymann resigned abruptly in January 1994, citing differences with Reno and the administration over crime policy. Three months later, Associate Attorney General Webster Hubbell resigned when he was investigated and eventually indicted for tax evasion in connection with the Whitewater scandal. Hubbell was a close friend and former law office partner of Hillary Clinton's and his departure further distanced DOJ decision-making from White House influence.

By 1996 many of the most respected officials at the DOJ had left, including Jamie Gorelick, who took over as Deputy Attorney General following Hubbell's departure, Deval Patrick, and Drew Days III, a former official in the Carter Administration, who had served as Solicitor General during the first term. Staffing has thus been a constant problem. Nearly half of the policy-making positions in the Department were still vacant or temporarily filled with acting heads more than a year after Clinton's election in 1992. Six months into the second term, nearly as many top positions at the DOJ were again vacant or had acting heads, including some of the most important policy-making posts, including the Deputy Attorney General's post, the head of the Civil Rights Division, the head of the Criminal Division, and the head of the Office of Legal Counsel.

Further straining White House–DOJ relations were Clinton's problems staffing the White House Legal Counsel's Office (WLC). The post is the key point for coordinating DOJ legal policy and the White House's political agenda. During the Clinton Administration, however, the Counsel's office became mired in scandal (Rabkin, 1994). In 1993, Associate Counsel Vincent Foster committed suicide amidst speculation that he was involved in covering up the Clintons' involvement in Whitewater. A year later, White House Counsel Bernard Nussbaum, a close personal friend of the Clintons, resigned in the face of allegations that he had lied to congressional committees investigating Whitewater. Lloyd Cutler, a former Legal Counsel for Jimmy Carter, accepted the post after Nussbaum, but stayed for only six months. He was replaced by Abner Mikva, a respected judge on the D.C. Court of Appeals. But he too left the position after a little more than a year and was replaced by Jack Quinn. Quinn resigned at the end of the first term and was replaced by Charles Ruff, who became Clinton's fifth Counsel in five years. Ruff has himself come under increasing criticism for his failure to produce documents connected with campaign finance scandals.

Reno's independence, staffing problems, and Clinton's lack of interest in the law as an avenue for policy-making, kept the administration from developing a coherent legal policy agenda. With the exception of criminal justice, where the administration passed the Brady Bill and a major crime bill in 1995, there were few other policy initiatives in this area. In contrast to the years of Republican administration between 1981 and 1992, the DOJ adopted a reactive role and there was little coordination of its activities with the White House. Indeed, Reno quickly demonstrated her independence in the first term by questioning Congress' push for mandatory sentencing and publicly clashed with Clinton over the Crime Bill and over nominations to lower level positions in the DOJ. What most upset the White House, however, was Reno's willingness to launch investigations of the administration. Since 1993 Reno has, on many occasions, asked for the appointment of independent counsels: in 1993 to investigate the Whitewater land deals of the Clintons; in 1994 to investigate allegations that Agriculture Secretary Mike Espy had illegally accepted gifts while in office; in 1995 to investigate whether Henry Cisneros, Secretary of Housing and Urban Development, lied to the FBI about payments he made to a former mistress; again in 1995 to investigate whether Ronald Brown profited from personal business deals as Commerce Secretary; in 1996 to investigate whether Eli Segal personally profited from fund-raising activities for a private group while serving as head of the Americorps national service program; and in 1998 to investigate whether Interior Secretary Bruce Babbitt had lied to a congressional committee looking into campaign fund-raising scandals. Most damaging to the administration (and possibly to the long-term survival of the independent counsel statute), was Reno's decision in 1998 to expand Whitewater independent counsel Kenneth Starr's investigation to include allegations that Clinton may have perjured himself or encouraged Monica Lewinsky, a former White House intern, to perjure herself in connection with the civil suit filed by Paula Jones. Starr, a former official in the Bush DOJ, had already sparked controversy for spending nearly $40 million in what many regarded as an increasingly partisan investigation of Clinton. His entanglement with a private sexual harassment suit and the heavy handed investigatory tactics employed in investigating the Lewinsky affair further fueled criticism of Starr and the independent counsel law which allows federal prosecutors to operate independent of DOJ control (Lewis, 1997). Still, Starr's investigation posed a major threat to the Clinton Administration, causing Clinton to invoke executive privilege (the first time it has been invoked in connection with a criminal investigation since the Nixon Administration) and raised the specter of impeachment. Ironically, Clinton himself had championed the independent counsel mechanism during the 1992 campaign and signed it back into law in 1994 after Bush allowed it to lapse.

Reno, who was praised in the press and on Capitol Hill for her independence during Clinton's first term, became increasingly controversial in the second. After Clinton's 1996 reelection, she was attacked by Clinton loyalists who accused her of mismanagement at the DOJ and disloyalty to the administration. There was pressure from the White House for her resignation but Reno ignored the signals and stayed on.

Reno's independence, however, also proved to hold some advantages for Clinton as well. In 1993, after the government's disastrous siege of the Branch Davidian compound outside Waco, Texas, Janet Reno took full responsibility for the use of force and sending those inside the compound to fiery deaths. Likewise, following the FBI's siege at "Ruby Ridge," resulting in the accidental killing of a boy and his mother, Reno again assumed full responsibility shielding Clinton from any criticism. Reno's fair-minded reputation and independence also allowed her to resist strong pressure from congressional Republicans for the appointment of an independent counsel to investigate questionable White House fund-raising activities during the 1996 campaign. Although Reno launched formal DOJ investigations, her insistence that there was no "credible evidence" of misconduct helped shield Clinton and Gore from mounting criticism over fundraising and the appointment of yet another independent counsel. Ironically, Reno, who was praised by Republicans for her independence during the first term, came under increasing criticism and even calls for her impeachment during the second term as a result of her refusal to ask for the appointment of a counsel to investigate the fund-raising scandal.

The lack of White House control of DOJ policy-making had advantages in other areas as well. During the previous twelve years the work of the Solicitor General, the office responsible for the government's appellate litigation and for arguing cases before the Supreme Court, became highly politicized. Under Charles Fried and Kenneth Starr, in particular, critics accused Republicans of damaging the office's credibility by using it to push the administration's policy agenda and to ask the Court to reverse previously settled areas of law (Caplan, 1987). By contrast, Clinton's Solicitors General, Drew S. Days and Walter Dellinger, have been low key in conducting government litigation and have operated with little interference from the White House. This allowed Clinton to distance himself from unpopular decisions involving government litigation, such as when the Solicitor General angered gay rights groups, first by defending the military's "don't ask, don't tell" policy, and later when it refused to file an *amicus* brief in the *Romer* case.

At other times the lack of coordination resulted in embarrassments and last-minute reversals in government litigations. In 1994, for instance, President Clinton directed the Justice Department to pull a brief just an hour before arguments in an appeals court when he learned the DOJ was supporting a bankruptcy order returning to creditors funds that a Minnesota couple had tithed to a church the year before filing bankruptcy. After meeting with religious groups, Clinton decided the order violated the Religious Freedoms Restoration Act that he had signed into law. The Justice Department also switched sides in *United States* v. *Piscataway* (1998), a case challenging the use of race by a New Jersey school district when making decisions to lay-off teachers. In 1993, the Department won a motion for summary judgment supporting a white teacher dismissed in favor of a black teacher retained to protect diversity. With the arrival of Deval Patrick in 1994 to head the Civil Rights Division, however, the DOJ switched sides, and on appeal the Solicitor General's brief to the Supreme Court supported the school district instead. This case ended abruptly in 1998 when the NAACP, fearing an adverse decision, settled with the school district. The most embarrassing switch, however, came after Drew Days filed a brief in *Knox* v. *United States* (1993), siding with a defendant in a child pornography case. The Solicitor General argued that a pornography statute had been interpreted too broadly by the trial court to convict a man who had pictures of girls who were scantily clad but not nude. Reaction to the administration's position was strong; a unanimous Senate voted for a resolution condemning the brief. In response, the administration switched positions and Janet Reno herself filed a second brief with the Court disavowing the Solicitor General's previous position.

Lower-Court Appointments

Clinton had an unprecedented opportunity to make an impact on the lower federal bench during his first term. There were nearly 115 judicial vacancies when he took office and another 150 judges retired between 1992 and 1996. Again, staffing problems at the DOJ and White House kept Clinton from filling vacancies during his first year in office. But with his judicial selection team finally in place, nominations began to emerge at a record pace by early 1994 (O'Brien, 1996). In November, however, Clinton's momentum was halted by the GOP takeover of Congress. Perceiving vulnerability, Republicans delayed confirming Clinton's nominees in hopes of a presidential victory in 1996. But even after Clinton's reelection, Republicans moved slowly to confirm his nominees, and by mid-1997 there were once again more than 100 vacancies on the federal bench.

Still, by 1997 Clinton had appointed over 200 judges, and by the end of his second term he probably will have appointed more judges than any recent president except Ronald Reagan. Clinton's judicial legacy will be based on the diversity, rather than the politics, of his appointments. Nearly 60 percent of his lower-court judges have been women and minorities. This compares to 34 percent of Carter's nominees, 14 percent of Reagan's, and 28 percent of Bush's (Goldman and Slotnick, 1997). As with his appointments to the Supreme Court, Clinton's fear of confirmation controversy, and his deference to senatorial patronage produced politically moderate and pragmatic lower-court judges. With the exception of the confirmation of Judge H. Lee Sarokin to the Third Circuit Court by a 63–35 vote in the Senate, and the confirmation of Judge Rosemary Barkets to the Eleventh Circuit Court on a 61–37 vote (both of whom were accused of being too soft on crime), there have been few confirmation battles around Clinton's lower-court judges. Moreover, studies of the voting records of Clinton's judges found little difference from those appointed by George Bush (Stidham, Carp and Songer, 1996). Indeed, this has led liberals such as Stephen Reinhardt, a federal appeals court judge, and the liberal judicial watch group the Alliance for Justice to criticize Clinton for failing to redress the rightward drift of the federal courts.

Despite their moderate records, however, Clinton's lower-court judges became an election issue in 1996. In one episode more than

200 members of Congress signed a letter calling for the resignation of Harold Baer, Jr. of the US District Court in Southern New York, after he used a legal technicality to suppress evidence in a drug arrest case. In response, Clinton issued his own statement criticizing the decision and Baer eventually reconsidered his position in the case (Newman, 1997). Following the Baer controversy, Republicans began a campaign to discredit Clinton's judges. Senator Hatch vowed to refuse to confirm the appointment of any more "liberals" to the lower courts, Bob Dole made Clinton's lower-court judges an issue during the presidential debates, and House Majority Whip Tom DeLay, held hearings into the impeachment of liberal judges (Bright, 1997).

In contrast to Roosevelt's, Nixon's or even Reagan's efforts to rein in the judiciary, the Republican assault on the judiciary in 1996 was led by Congress not the president. Moreover it focused on lower courts while conspicuously avoiding any criticism of the Supreme Court. As part of an election year strategy, the attack seemed aimed less at judicial philosophy of judges than at the president in an effort to portray him as part of a liberal elite. The partisan nature of the controversy was underscored when Chief Justice Rehnquist and Justice Scalia, the Court's most conservative members, criticized the Republican offensive and warned against further attacks on lower-court judges (Carelli, 1997).

Conclusion

Between 1932 and 1944, President Roosevelt appointed eight justices to the Supreme Court, transforming its role in American politics and ushering in a new constitutional regime. It is remarkable that Republican presidents Nixon, Ford, Reagan and Bush, with equally clear judicial strategy, together made nine appointments to the Supreme Court over a period lasting twice as long (1968–92) but enjoyed no such success.

Constitutional structures link the role of the Supreme Court to the elected branches of government. But the relationship of the elected branches to each other is equally important in shaping the role of the Court. Mr. Dooley's maxim, that the Court follows the election returns, assumes that the election returns are coherent – an assumption that has been inoperative for much of the past quarter-century. During this time, the Court became increasingly moderate in political outlook as presidents appointed centrists to avoid confirmation battles. In addition, the legacy of legal realism has not proved nearly as simple as many modern social scientists assume. Although realists demonstrated that law was dependent on politics, the politics in courts is not the same as that found in the elected branches. Judges do not simply vote on the basis of policy preferences. The collapse of ideological consensus since the 1960s led to jurisprudential dissensus and changing norms of opinion writing on the Court. This fragmentation has pushed the Court further toward pragmatic and minimalist decision-making.

The pattern of electoral dealignment and divided government that has characterized American politics for the last two decades of the twentieth century seems set to continue. Nor is it likely that constitutional jurisprudence will soon become more consensual. The structural forces generating the politics of moderation and pragmatism on the Supreme Court have also shaped the role of lower courts and other government legal institutions such as the Department of Justice. Thus, in the absence of more systematic transformations in American law and politics, those on the political left hoping for a judicial "counter revolution" as a result of the first two-term Democratic presidency since Franklin Roosevelt will be just as disappointed as those who waited for one on the right during the 1980s.

5

The Federal Bureaucracy

Patricia Ingraham

In 1978 at the passage of the Carter Administration's Civil Service Reform Act, the president and others declared that the reform prepared the bureaucracy to move into the next century and equipped it well for whatever challenges might come its way. That rosy optimism was countered almost immediately by the election of Ronald Reagan in 1980; the succeeding years produced many additional "bumps." Under Presidents Reagan, Bush, and Clinton the federal bureaucracy was downsized, reorganized, reengineered, reinvented and even closed down for a short period of time (Ingraham, 1997). Many federal programs endured substantial budget cuts and some, such as the Energy Department and the Internal Revenue Service (IRS) have had their very existence questioned. Where does the federal bureaucracy, as a set of institutions, stand today?

Assessment of the Role and Effectiveness of Bureaucratic Institutions

It is fair to begin with a variation of Miles' Law: where the bureaucracy stands depends very much on the perspective from which it is analyzed. It also strongly depends on which of the institutions is being examined. For those interested in budget and cost-cutting, or in rapid change, the federal bureaucracy is still perceived to be too big, too slow, and too insular. President Clinton, for example, initially sent a mixed message to the bureaucracy when he announced that it could be a problem-solver, but only if it were first reinvented. The rhetoric surrounding the Clinton "reinvention" initiatives, particularly those related to a "government that works better, but costs less" have emphasized both the need to change and the need to adjust to greatly diminished resources (NPR, 1993, 1994, 1995). Primary attention, however, has been paid to the diminished resources; much less attention has been directed to the myriad internal and external changes that are necessary for the reforms to be successful.

The rhetoric and temper of Congress after its Contract With America efforts and its many attempts to devolve policy and service delivery to state and local governments suggested that there was a strong and continuing interest in reducing the size and scope of federal institutions (Walker, 1997). On the other hand leaders and representatives of the agencies targeted for extensive change – organizations such as the IRS – have argued that those institutions have not merely not resisted reform efforts but have done rather well in very difficult circumstances. From the perspectives of the bureaucracies themselves in the late 1990s, the status and future of bureaucratic institutions appeared troubled, but for reasons which were different from those cited by Congress and by the Executive Branch.

In their assessments of the state of the federal bureaucracy, its leaders have cited the cases of innovation and problem-solving in the Reinvention Laboratories and in the successful downsizing strategies adopted by both civilian and military agencies (Thompson, 1996; Jones, 1995). They have also cited the many examples of the old "brick walls" of rules and hierarchy which have still not been dismantled despite fundamental legislative reform (Ingraham, 1997). Significantly, also, they have cited the lack of political direction and leadership while federal agencies were attempting to navigate the thickets of "doing more with less": at the first major reinvention conference in 1996, laboratory managers took pains to tell Vice President Gore (who had been given charge of the reform efforts) that the Clinton Administration's political appointees were sometimes the most notable source of opposition to the bureaucratic reform initiatives (Proceedings, 1996). Indeed, at the second such conference, one of Gore's chief staffers declared that "the biggest obstacle" to the Clinton Administration's efforts thus far was the "lack of enthusiasm" on the part of its own political appointees (*Government Executive*, 1997, p. 6).

Another perspective on recent bureaucratic change is related to the analysis of the complex impacts of the various reform initiatives of the 1990s. Cutting budgets while creating new partnerships – both with citizens and with other levels of government – eliminating overhead controls where possible, and creating new measures for strategically gauging government performance have created their own management and organizational problems. There have been some obvious successes but there have been many more areas where the effectiveness of change is hard to judge. Tensions in expectations and in the mechanisms created to implement policy have sometimes worked at cross-purposes from each other and have often blurred the results which were achieved. Assessing overall organization health is always difficult in any institutional setting, but it is doubly difficult when the issues extend beyond organizational criteria and are politically charged.

Two concrete examples from the 1990s underline these general points. The IRS is one of the oldest institutions in the federal government and for many years it was numbered amongst its most respected agencies. It is an organization which has necessarily come to rely heavily on technology to achieve its performance objectives, and in the mid-1980s, the IRS began a massive process of acquiring new technology – the so-called "Tax Systems Modernizer" effort. The program was expensive even by federal budgetary standards: nearly $4 billion was spent on a system that essentially failed.

As a result of this episode, there followed a range of varied and not necessarily compatible proposals to reform the IRS. Early in his second term Clinton and his advisers recommended the modification of civil service law to permit greater political authority to be exercised over career leaders of the agency (*Government Executive*, 1997, p. 8). They also nominated a new IRS Commissioner whose expertise was in the field of technology support rather than the traditional fields of taxation and tax law.

Congressional initiatives for reforming the IRS in the 1990s were dramatically different from those of the Executive Branch. Basing its recommendations on a year-long study by a congressional commission, one major congressional proposal was that a major portion of the tax agency's management should be taken over by an independent board of government officials and private sector experts. This reform was necessary, supporters in Congress explained, "to recover the confidence of the public and Congress" (*Washington Post*, June 6, 1997). There was no commonality in the two proposals, and little chance that either reform would commend itself to the other.

The Government Performance and Results Act of 1993 (GPRA) provides a second example of the problems which reform initiatives have encountered. The legislation (which is discussed in detail later) was a congressional initiative designed to link budget and other resources to performance. Once fully operational, GPRA would give members of Congress and their staff unprecedented insight into federal organizations. But, as Rosenbloom (1993) and others have noted, the ever-tenuous balance between the Congress and the president over the direction of the Executive Branch will clearly be affected by this reform and the information it can feed into the decision-making process. While neither the executive–legislative tension nor the need to maintain balance is new to the federal bureaucracy, the budget cuts and dwindling governmental resources of recent years have given them a new dimension. If GPRA works as intended the bureaucracy will have to defend the measures it adopts and the process of implementation more extensively, and bureaucratic choices may be expected to have more directly traceable budgetary and political outcomes.

In order to clarify the complex web of interactions and tensions between the different reform initiatives, it may be useful to examine some of them in more depth. The language and objectives of "reinvention now" have permeated much of the federal bureaucracy that it is important first to analyze the purpose of the reinventing government reforms, thus providing the context for discussion of other changes which occurred.

"Reinventing Government"

Reinventing government was the label attached to a broad set of reforms which have been extensively described elsewhere (Kettl, 1994; Kettl and DiIulio, 1995; Thompson and Ingraham, 1996; Peters and Savoie, 1996; Ingraham, Thompson and Sanders, 1997). For the purposes of this discussion, only a few points about the reforms need to be highlighted. The rhetoric and symbolism of reinvention were transparent and relatively simple, and that simplicity has in fact been a siren song for reformers and members of the federal bureaucracy alike. Reinvention's fundamental ideas were contained in the first report of the National Performance Review (NPR) which President Clinton created immediately following his election in 1992.

The NPR report proceeded directly from the work of Osborne and Gaebler (1992) and contained 384 major recommendations which covered twenty-seven different agencies and one federal system (including procurement, human resources management, and financial management). In line with its objectives of simplifying and streamlining government, the NPR report emphasized the need to cut rules and regulations wherever possible, to decentralize and/or delegate both authority and program delivery, to empower employees and customers and to eliminate any services and programs that were no longer necessary. Improved relations – new partnerships – with labor unions were to be an important part of the new processes. The NPR report also recommended cutting the federal workforce by 12 percent (equivalent to 252,000 positions) over a five-year period and it estimated that $108 billion could be saved by implementing its recommendations (NPR, 1993). Much of the emphasis at this initial stage was on creating new expectations of, and mechanisms for, accountability: the "new" accountability would be to employees, to customers and to performance. "Product" and "performance," rather than process, were to become governmental bywords.

In subsequent annual reports the NPR argued that substantial progress was being made on the reinvention effort (NPR, 1994, 1995, 1996). In 1994, for example, NPR argued that 90 percent of the recommendations were "underway". NPR's assessments of progress were often challenged by other observers such as the General Accounting Office (GAO); there is little question, however, the reinvention initiative did have a significant impact on the size and structure of the American federal bureaucracy.

By 1997 the Clinton Administration was ahead of schedule in reducing the total number of federal employees. The Federal Acquisition Improvement Act of 1994 was a major streamlining of arcane procurement rules and regulations; 200 Reinvention Laboratories had been created in nearly every federal agency and throughout government. The Federal Personnel Manual had been eliminated, although its impact continued to be felt even after its abolition.

The role of the federal central agencies was also altered by the reinvention drive. The Office of Personnel Management (which had been created by the Civil Service Reform Act of 1978) was substantially scaled down leading to a 65 percent reduction in the headquarters staff. OPM semi-privatized its training function and put many of its services on a fee-based system. The General Services Administration (GSA), the central property authority, reduced its staff by approximately one-fifth and also contracted out many of its services.

The Office of Management and Budget (OMB), which was much more closely tied to the White House than the other central agencies, streamlined and reorganized itself based on the recommendations of a report entitled *OMB 2000*. That document argued that the "M" in "OMB" needed to be integrated with analysis functions in each of the agency's units. The restructuring that occurred did not substantially reduce the size of OMB, but it did change its operating style. Furthermore, the coordinating role that the Deputy Director for Management has played in the president's Management Council – a government-wide management and policy group composed of high-ranking political appointees – has given the agency heightened visibility in reinvention efforts. The bulk of the reinvention staff, who were formerly located in the office of the Vice President, were transferred to the OMB in 1997.

Reinvention also had some notable failures, however, and some of them seem likely to shape the long-term impact of the movement. The most important of these failures was the inability or unwillingness of the Clinton Administration to commit itself to fundamental legislative change in the civil service and in other key management areas. Clinton's major legislative initiative in relation to the bureaucracy was the Omnibus Civil Service Reform Act of 1996. Crafted in close consultation with labor leaders, one version of the legislation passed the House but had a quick death in the Senate. It was noticeable, however, that Clinton again emphasized the need for comprehensive legislation in his second term and it seems likely Al Gore will continue to regard such reform as a high legislative priority.

In the absence of any significant change in the legislative foundation of the civil service, the old framework of laws has continued to provide a convenient and well established excuse for adhering to traditional practices. The Clinton Administration tacitly admitted this when it noted in the 1997 *Blair House Papers* that it was "time to urge Congress to remove . . . restrictions so that limited amounts of money [could] be spent effectively" (NPR, 1997).

Overall, then, reinvention has been an essentially informal process which has been firmly anchored in symbolism and rhetoric but less connected to legislative change. (An example of the symbolism was the Hammer Awards, which were lapel pins given to organizations which demonstrated high performance on the reinvention criteria.) Reinvention through its emphasis on empowering employees and on customer satisfaction has created new forces in federal agencies and in many respects made even more complex the accountabilities and expectations for which federal organizations and their employees are responsible. The likely long-term impact on federal agencies is unpredictable, however, and is made more so by the inextricable link between reinvention and downsizing and budget cuts. Doing more (and different things) with less makes for good political rhetoric but its utility as a strategy for governing is less clear.

Downsizing the American Federal Government

How much less do American federal agencies now have, and what difference does it in fact make that they have had budget cuts forced upon them? The answer to those questions inevitably varies from organization to organization and from function to function. To understand downsizing at the federal level of government it is important to stress that the process has been driven by at least three engines: the shift in priorities about the proper size and scope of government; the decline in resources accompanied by increases in fixed costs and mandated program expenses; and the need to balance the budget and reduce the federal deficit. Attitudes towards the proper size and scope of government may change in future years but the other two are likely to continue to play a role in thinking about the organization of American bureaucracy. Downsizing is thus likely to remain a factor in the strategic future of most federal agencies, a consistent reduction of funding in the "cheese slicer powered by the Energizer battery" mode as Allen Schick has put it (Laurent, 1996).

By far the heaviest burden in relation to downsizing has thus far fallen on civilian employees of the Department of Defense, who took 80 percent of the Clinton reductions. Some of these cuts were relatively easy. As the Cold War wound down and military bases and operations were closed or substantially reduced, civilian support needs fell sharply. Because the Defense Department had long enjoyed healthy, if not excessive, budgets, it was also easy to identify surplus and excess.

Cuts have now, however, been spread across government. The Clinton Administration argued that the federal government had become smaller than at any time since 1931 (OMB, 1997) Every major cabinet agency except the Department of Justice (DOJ) reduced its size somewhat over the 1993–7 period and the actual reduction in the Executive Branch workforce during that same period was 12.2 percent (OMB, 1997). Downsizing was facilitated by the Federal Workforce Restructuring Act of 1994 which permitted early retirement buyouts of targeted groups for limited periods of time; most federal agencies have used this authority.

It is important to note, however, that those choosing to exit early from federal service were often employees on the cusp of top management or leadership positions. While this is consistent with reinvention's objective of eliminating overhead controls and reducing middle management, it has had the less salutary impact of removing many high fliers – those with other options but who, had they stayed, would probably have been the next generation of bureaucratic leaders. Furthermore, by 1997 the overall impact of downsizing and buyouts had been to raise the average grade level of federal employees from that in 1992 (Kettl *et al.*, 1996).

As Table 5.1 demonstrates the actual impact of downsizing across government has been uneven. The Departments of Health and Human Services (DHHS) and Veterans' Affairs took substantial cuts (DHHS lost over half of its total 1993 workforce), although in large part these cuts reflected contracting out of health and hospital services by both agencies. Indeed it is difficult to know how many "cut" employees are now contract employees.

The counting of employees and the estimates of actual workforces are made difficult by other complexities of the federal hiring system. The Department of Agriculture, which shows a reduction of

TABLE 5.1 *Budget and workforce reduction in US federal agencies, 1993 and 1996*

Agency	FY 1993 (actual)		FY 1996 (budgeted)		Workforce reduction
	Budget	Staff	Budget	Staff	
Agriculture	$67.857 billion	114,420	$54.064 billion	105,452	8968
Commerce	$3.216 billion	38,343	$3.632 billion	35,842	2501
DOD	$270.300 billion	931,300 (civil.)	$254.500 billion	800,300 (civil.)	131,000
		1,705,100 (mil.)		1,481,700 (mil.)	223,400
DOEd	31.471 billion	4,876	$30.385 billion	4,750	126
DOE	$19.341 billion	20,410	$16.189 billion	19,762	648
EPA	$6.928 billion	17,479	$6.523 billion	17,416	63
FEMA	$3.106 billion	4,476	$4.328 billion	3,930	546
General Service Adm.	$419.2 million	20,249	$242.5 million	14,780	5469
DHHS	591.000 billion	130,366	$325.000 billion	58,924	71,442
HUD	$25.500 billion	13,294	$19.500 billion	11,628	1666
Dept. of the Interior	$7.078 billion	76,880	$6.948 billion	67,150	9730
DOJ	11.209 billion	83,574	$16.392 billion	95,787	+12,213
Dept. of Labor	$46.892 billion	18,003	$33.879 billion	16,655	1348
NASA	$14.305 billion	25,700	$13.821 billion	21,555	4145
OPM	452 million	6,208	$377 million	3,557	2651
NSF	$2.734 billion	1.235	$3.220 billion	1,267	+32
Small Business Adm.	1.10 billion	5,599	$814 million	4,284	1315
Social Security Adm.	$4.905 billion	66,101	$5.890 billion	64,752	1349
Dept. of State	$5.000 billion	26,000	$4.800 billion	23,700	2300
Dept. of Transportation	$36.681 billion	109,242	$37.504 billion	101,232	8010
Dept. of Treasury	$10.131 billion	161,100	$10.402 billion	153,319	7781
Dept. of VA	$36.019b.	234.428	$38.608 billion	223.727	10,301
US Info. Ag.	$1.409 billion	8.470	$1.077 billion	7,311	1159
USAID	$7.942 billion	3.928	$7,443 billion	3,246	682

Source: Compiled from data in NPR documents: Accomplishment/Agency Reports@http://www.npr.gov/accompli.

nearly 9,000 staff in Table 5.1, dramatically increased its part-time and temporary hiring during the period 1992–95. Because these numbers are not reflected in the "full-time equivalent" count by which federal agencies are monitored, the 9,000 reduction figure is quite misleading: part-time and temporary hiring figures at Agriculture were nearly as high as the 9,000 total "reduction."

During the same period, other federal agencies actually increased the total size of their workforce. The DOJ benefitted from congressional and executive attention to law enforcement and drug interdiction. The Patent and Trademark office in the Department of Commerce also hired additional staff in the early to mid-1990s. However, the general trend has been towards reduction, at least in formal full-time employment. The White House argued that 20 percent of the total reduction had occurred in supervisory positions with another 25 percent of the reduction coming in headquarters staff and other control positions (NPR, 1997).

These kinds of reductions, even if accompanied by concomitant hiring of temporary or part-time staff, have inevitable consequences for the structure and method of operation of federal agencies. The Department of Agriculture, for example, accompanied its permanent staff reductions with the elimination of many field offices. The Department of Housing and Urban Development (HUD) eliminated functions and closed its regional offices.

How these downsizing activities will shape the future of federal agencies is not entirely clear. First, as noted earlier, it is difficult to assess the extent to which the downsizing has actually occurred. Secondly, as is generally the case in public organizations, those cuts that have occurred have been aimed at "low-hanging fruit" – the clearly unnecessary, duplicate or obsolete tasks and functions. Even in these cases, initial downsizing decisions have sometimes been reversed by the agency itself or by Congress. Thirdly, in most cases the downsizing activity has been nonstrategic in the sense that it has not been accompanied by significant internal system change or redirection.

Thus in most federal organizations the information technology (IT) system is still not well integrated with other key systems such as budget, financial management, and human resource management. As a result, agencies spend a great deal of time and money collecting information they do not need and continue to operate without information that is critical for effective change.

Finally, in the intensely political environment of the 1990s, downsizing placed many obstacles, some of them unanticipated, in the road to smaller but more effective federal agencies. Although the continuing need to reduce the deficit has created one consistent stimulus, the ability of federal organizations to rethink priorities and to address hard choices about what can be eliminated or streamlined has been attenuated both by conflict between the president and Congress and by the continuing reliance on traditional pork-barrel decisions. For example, actual decisions to close military bases fell to nonpartisan base-closing commissions after it became clear that political considerations would preclude closure choices.

The failure to adopt – or propose – fundamental legislative reform to support basic system changes also constrains both downsizing and predictable outcomes from it. One set of policy decisions, however, is likely to lead to notable changes in how the federal bureaucracy does its business and, in fact, what business it does. Devolution and its implications for the federal bureaucracy is the subject of the next section.

The Administrative Implications of Policy Devolution

John Shannon, of the Urban Institute, has recently argued that a new era in American federalism has arrived (see also especially Chapter 6). Shannon sees the most notable feature of this era as stemming from the fact that for "the first time in American history, neither the states nor the federal government dominate the intergovernmental landscape." The states, Shannon believes, "have lost their privileged constitutional status and the federal government its crisis-bestowed fiscal and public confidence advantage" (Shannon, 1997).

Devolution – not only the movement of funds and programs from one level of government to another but also the search for the appropriate balance – has been cyclical in the US and, as a result, has been a consistent part of the policy dialogue (Walker, 1995). Shannon's point that the foundation of the dialogue has been altered has clear implications for federal bureaucratic institutions. Although many devolution efforts and proposals (such as the 1996 welfare reform legislation) have retained a significant federal role it is likely that this approach will be "refined" over the next few years (NAPA, 1997). Such future changes will probably occur because of improvements in the administrative capacity of many state and local governments and because of the recognition by many state governments that they cannot proceed with their own streamlining and downsizing activities if the current pattern of federal relationships is maintained. The state of Oregon, for example, insisted on new arrangements with the DHHS before it redesigned its social service delivery system at the state level and began benchmarking quality of service and delivery.

Other devolution initiatives were directly related to the reinventing government project. One objective stated in the first NPR report was the creation of new community partnerships. The *Blair House Papers* (NPR, 1997) reaffirmed that commitment in noting that the intergovernmental grant system was "a tangle of good intentions gone awry." There were too many funding categories, suffocating regulations and paperwork – "a misdirected emphasis on solving rather than preventing problems, and no clear focus on measurable results." NPR cited partnerships between states and the EPA, DHHS, HUD and the Department of Labor as successful examples of new inter-governmental relationships and partnerships.

Other observers have not been so sanguine about either the trend or the success in devolving funds and responsibility. Walker (1997) has argued that there was no "consistent strategic design" in the efforts to achieve greater devolution and that it was largely in the "operational federalism field that most of the manifestations of devolution" were found.

Detailing the discretions and new arrangements found in Safe Drinking Water, Clean Air and Food Safety programs, Walker (1997) labelled them "important but not historic." The welfare reform legislation, surely the most controversial of recent policy devolutions, sends decidedly mixed messages. While the legislation does devolve additional administrative responsibilities and some policy functions, it includes very demanding and restrictive mandates: that states spend 80 percent of their current welfare outlays, that case loads be reduced by at least 50 percent in five years, and that legal aliens be barred from receiving benefits (Carroll and Broadnax, 1997).

The redefined administrative capacity that enforcing – or even monitoring – such mandates suggests is quite extensive. This new approach to public policy has many facets, each of which is significant for the future of the federal bureaucracy. First, it suggests both a competence in and a proclivity for information-sharing and monitoring that has little precedent in American government. The IRS case, although not about devolution, is again relevant: creating and sustaining excellent information management capacity continues to elude most federal agencies. How to achieve it is a major challenge for the future and one which is exacerbated by devolution efforts.

Secondly, both devolution and downsizing suggest a fundamental rethinking of what federal organizations do. The push for devolution reflects a common belief that too much time and too many resources have been spent in controlling activities and enforcing arcane rules and regulations. Current federal administrative and management structure is based on this controlling function: field offices and lower level managers and employees control those to whom services are delivered. Central offices and top management control the rest of the organization. The "process is our most important product" guideline has served as the best single definition of what the federal bureaucracy does, and how it does it.

This is where the mixed messages of devolution efforts such as welfare reform are most critical. The "partnering" role that real devolution implies creates one set of performance and management expectations. The mandate and controlling components of the same legislation create another. They are not compatible but both are part of the federal bureaucratic future.

There is another dimension of the administrative capacity part of this equation that is important. Devolution assumes that adequate capacity is in place at lower levels of government for there to be competent agencies to which responsibility may be devolved. There is very little evidence that this is indeed the case. Bowling and Wright (1997) observe that although there have been enormous changes state governments in the past twenty years, there are few concrete assessments of the administrative capacities of each of the individual states. While determining such capacity may constitute a useful research agenda for the next few years, it is of more immediate concern for federal organizations. If adequate capacity does not exist in state and local governments, part of the challenge for those organizations charged with devolution responsibilities is to find and support the transitional arrangements with the states that allow both levels of government to meet their statutory requirements. Given the political pressure of both reinventing and downsizing, this must be done in tandem with internal realignments.

Finding the right balance between discretion and control, however, will not be an easy task because devolution expectations and objectives differ so sharply. If, as welfare reform suggests, the federal bureaucracy is to be less intrusive and more vigilant in monitoring values and behavior, the famous space between a rock and a hard place looks inviting by contrast. What new flexibilities and discretion is the federal government likely to have as it addresses the challenges of the next decade?

The Government Performance and Results Act (1993)

One piece of legislation which is likely to have a major impact on federal bureaucracies and their operations is the Government Performance and Results Act. GPRA, or the "Results Act as Congress wishes it to be known," is a congressional rather than Executive Branch initiative. It is intended (GAO, 1997) to

> improve the efficiency and effectiveness of federal programs by establishing a system to set goals for program performance and to measure results. The Act requires executive agencies to prepare multi-year strategic plans, annual performance plans and annual performance reports and to link these to budget and personnel requests. All federal agencies were required to submit strategic plans to the OMB by the Fall of 1997 and were required to submit government-wide performance plans to Congress in 1999. Full performance reports were required to be submitted to the president, the Congress and the public by the year 2000.

Under the provisions of GPRA, the OMB was directed to establish ten pilot programs in performance planning and reporting to provide experience and lessons in applying the Act's provisions. In fact, OMB created seventy-seven pilot projects, ranging in size from the entire IRS to much smaller programs and agencies. In Phase Two of the pilot effort, the OMB was to designate some of the original set and some additional agencies to explore managerial accountability and flexibility provisions necessary for full GPRA implementation. The OMB did not create any pilots in this area, partly because agencies opted for the more informal Reinvention Laboratory designation to explore potential flexibilities. The final set of pilots, those related to performance budgeting, were delayed because very few agencies had the information management resources and capacity necessary to proceed swiftly (GAO, 1997). Full legislative deadlines were not altered however.

In the first full analysis of GPRA, the GAO concluded that implementation to that point had achieved mixed results which would lead to highly uneven implementation in 1997 (GAO, 1997). The same report also noted that reported examples of substantial performance improvements were relatively few and that many agencies did not appear to be well positioned to provide in 1997 a results-oriented answer to the fundamental Results Act question: What are we accomplishing? (GAO, 1997).

Why is GPRA so important? As the federal bureaucracy moves into the next millennium both declining budgets and new reform expectations will increasingly demand evidence of performance. These demands will come to a system notorious for its difficulties in identifying the bottom line, much less measuring results against it. The results will be accompanied by dramatically differing expectations. They will occur in "reinvented" agencies where the emphasis on discretion and flexibility has often worked at cross-purposes with coordination and strategic effort (Peters and Savoie, 1996). Very importantly, they will occur in federal agencies that do not have in place – or the ability to create – the base systems that are integral to the performance management and measurement activity. One potential solution is to lower expectations for the federal bureaucracy generally and to focus on those agencies that *can* measure bottom lines and have demonstrated commitment to performance and change. That was the intention of the Clinton Administration's Performance-Based Organization (PBO) legislation.

Performance-based Organizations

It is one indication of the federal bureaucracy's current and future state that reforms adopted a decade ago in other major nations are only now on the agenda in the United States. That is the case with the PBO legislation. Clearly modeled on the British Next Steps agencies, the PBO legislation was intended to create organizations with clear missions, measurable services, clear and predictable sources of funding, and clear line SOF accountability (NPR, 1997). The GPRA pilot process provides a natural feeder pool. At the end of 1997 there were proposals for approximately 15 PBOs. Although the initial legislation for the PBOs was introduced and failed in 1996, it was then declared a priority for Clinton's second term. It was, however, a critical part of the strategy that the PBO agencies would be introduced and approved by the Congress one at a time. The first, Patent and Trademark, in the Department of Commerce, has already received a slightly scaled-down PBO status. This approach, while thoroughly "American" and incremental, allows "winners" to proceed full speed ahead. What it does to those agencies troubled by clouded missions, unclear bottom lines, and uncertain funding is not so positive. How, or if, such a performance capacity gap will be addressed does not appear to be on the agenda of either President or Congress (Ingraham, 1997).

Conclusions

Is the American federal bureaucracy well equipped for the new century? The answer is "probably not." Reducing the deficit ensures that budget cuts will continue for many agencies. Reinvention has heightened expectations for management capacity and for performance. It has also argued that federal bureaucracies must be more responsive to customers (which it is hoped translates as citizens), employees, labor unions, Congress, and president. Clearly, there are tensions.

As resources and personnel have been cut, the streamlined processes that the NPR apparently believed would be in place to facilitate change and to allow federal agencies to "do more with less" have not been created. The early GPRA experience is ample evidence that the capacity to manage better, to perform better, to measure better, and to tell everyone about it simply does not exist at the end of the 1990s and is not likely to be created for some time.

This is not to suggest that the future is hopeless. There is some evidence that in some agencies "reinvention," reengineering, GPRA and other reform efforts are having positive impacts and that these lessons can trickle down or over to other agencies (Ingraham, Thompson and Sanders, 1997). As has been the case consistently in the past, however, the future of the bureaucracy will be a political story (Ingraham, 1995). The Clinton Administration's experience is a classic and by no means unusual one.

That the bureaucratic future story will be turbulent is rarely disputed. That it will be one that does not receive high priority attention is also likely. Even with "reinvention" and the GPRA, the focus on the federal bureaucracy has been secondary to other policy concerns. Failure to comply with the GPRA will get congressional attention; but if the past is any indicator, the fundamental need for systematic reform will still not be addressed. The very real changes envisioned by both "reinvention" and the GPRA will require sustained, focused, and consensual political attention: that is not likely to be forthcoming in the foreseeable future.

6

The Changing Federal System

Christopher J. Bailey

Calls for changes in the pattern of American federalism have become a standard chant of politicians in the United States in recent years. President Clinton told the National Governors' Association in January 1995:

> I believe we should ship decision-making responsibility and resources from bureaucracies in Washington to communities, to states, and, where we can, directly to individuals.

Senator Dole claimed in his first speech to the 104th Congress (1995–96): "We will continue in our drive to return power to our states and to our people." Congressional Republicans have repeatedly promised to return "money, power, and responsibility to the states" (Jost, 1996). The platforms adopted by both parties in 1996 called for more responsibilities to be shifted to state and local governments. Republican governors issued what became known as the "Williamsburg Resolves" in November 1994, which called for action to reverse "usurpations by federal legislators and bureaucrats of powers not delegated to them under the Constitution."

Federalism's increased salience as an issue can be traced to four developments. First, public disillusionment with Washington, D.C., reached new heights in the mid-1990s. Fed by news reports and campaign rhetoric that lambasted scandal-ridden, "do-nothing" national politicians, the skepticism that many Americans felt towards Washington, D.C., generated demands for more power to be devolved to state governments. Second, Republican success at the state level led to a greater assertion of state power. Republican electoral success gave a new impetus to demands for both an end to "unfunded mandates" and greater flexibility when addressing societal problems. Third, the Republican takeover of Congress following the 1994 elections established a new majority that was sympathetic to "states' rights." Congressional Republicans saw devolution as a means to reduce the deficit and undermine the position of an alleged liberal establishment in Washington, D.C. Fourth, the "conservative revolution" of the Reagan–Bush years cast doubt on the efficacy of traditional regulatory means. "Big government" became a casualty of a new conventional wisdom that stressed regulatory flexibility and market mechanisms.

Some changes in the pattern of American federalism have flowed from these developments. The Clinton Administration's "reinventing government" initiative (see Chapter 5) has given the states some additional flexibility to manage federal programs. A number of laws passed by the Republican Congress, particularly the Personal Responsibility and Work Opportunity Act of 1996, have devolved responsibility to the states, and the states have provided policy and management leadership on a wide range of issues. Even the federal courts have signaled a willingness to limit the power of the national government. In 1995 for the first time in fifty years the Supreme Court ruled that Congress had exceeded its authority to regulate inter-state commerce.

A number of commentators have suggested that these developments point to a new phase in American federalism. Books have been published with titles such as *The Rebirth of Federalism* (Walker, 1995) and *Reflections on the Fourth Stage of Federalism* (Shannon, 1994). Terms such as "The New Federalism" (Stanfield, 1995), "Middle Class . . . Federalism" (Shannon, 1997), and "The Devolution Revolution" (Nathan, 1996) have been employed as labels for recent developments. The problem with such labels, however, is that they suggest greater certainty about the nature and direction of change than may be justified. A tension can be identified, specifically, between Republican calls for devolution and deregulation. Although laws have been passed which have devolved power to the states, other enactments have preempted existing state power. Nor have the federal courts "always sung only the tune of states' rights" (Weissert and Schramm, 1996). The Supreme Court has continued to use the Fourteenth Amendment to restrict the freedom of the states to act in certain circumstances. President Clinton has also continued to support policies that would expand the role of the national government, despite his declaration in the 1996 State of the Union Address that "the era of big government is over."

Little evidence is available to suggest that recent changes in the pattern of American federalism have been linear. "Kaleidoscopic" is perhaps a better description (Zimmerman, 1992). Economic, social, and political developments have generated pressure for an adjustment of the respective competencies of the various levels of government that has pulled the pattern of American federalism in many different directions.

The Dynamics of Federalism

Martha Derthick (1996) has noted that American federalism is complicated and unstable. The design calls for functions to be divided between the national government and the states, but just how is left open to political and judicial dispute. Although the US Constitution grants the national government specific powers, and reserves all other powers that are not prohibited to the states or to the people, the fact that many of the specific powers are imprecisely defined while the reserved powers are indescribable except in the broadest of terms has engendered endless debate and conflict about which level of government has, or should have, particular powers. Some have argued that the Constitution establishes a system of "dual federalism" in which each level of government is regarded as competent within a particular sphere of activity (Corwin, 1950). The remit of the national government is normally deemed to encompass defense, foreign policy, and the maintenance of economic markets. Others have contended that the Constitution establishes a system of "cooperative federalism" in which the various levels of government in the United States can cooperate in providing goods and services (Grodzins, 1960; Elazar, 1962).

The imprecise demarcation of power between the national and state governments means that the shape of American federalism is largely determined by politicians and judges. An amorphous power structure creates opportunities for state and national politicians to claim power when it suits their purpose and to "pass the buck" when it doesn't. Paul E. Peterson (1995) has suggested that:

> Legislators at all levels of government will seek to distribute governmental benefits for which they can claim credit and, if at all possible, will shift governmental burdens to other levels of the federal system.

Contested claims to power are usually adjudicated in the federal courts, occasionally on the streets, and once on the battlefields of the American South. Judges will employ "literalism, natural law, history, and an eclectic approach" to determine the respective powers of the national and state governments (Fisher, 1995).

The competition for power between national and state politicians is shaped by both the size of the public domain and the matrix of costs and benefits associated with specific issues. Public perceptions that government should address problems that have previously been in the private domain will provide opportunities for national and state politicians to claim power. Such claims to power need not take the form of a zero-sum game. Both national and state governments may become more powerful as they assume responsibilities that had previously been reserved to the people (Hanson, 1996). The willingness of politicians to compete for power will depend upon their calculations of the costs and benefits that will flow from becoming involved in a particular issue. Competition is likely to be fierce when the benefits from action are perceived to be high and the costs low. Inaction or blame-avoidance strategies are likely to occur when the reverse is true.

The importance of the size and nature of the public domain to political competition means that patterns of federalism are sensitive to shifts in socioeconomic variables. This point was noted almost a century ago by Woodrow Wilson (1908), who observed that the relation of the states to the national government

> cannot . . . be settled by the opinion of any one generation because . . . every successive stage of our political and economic development gives it a new aspect, makes it a new question.

Changes in the economy or social conditions will generate new demands upon government as new problems arise and new interest groups emerge. The character, complexity, and cost of these demands will determine the extent of the competition between national and state politicians for control over policy.

In the nineteenth century the pattern of American federalism was determined by the limited nature and size of the public domain. Little was expected of government, and what was expected could be provided by state and local governments. Few national politicians saw much to be gained from seeking to secure responsibility for recording births, deaths, and marriages. Rapid industrialization in the last decades of the century began to change this pattern as new incentives and opportunities were created for national politicians to expand their range of activities. Between 1880 and 1910 the US Congress passed legislation to regulate business monopolies and the railroads, to protect consumers, to conserve natural resources, and to establish some minimum labor standards. The Great Depression of the 1930s provided national politicians with a further set of powerful incentives to intervene in areas that had traditionally been viewed as the preserve of state governments. Laws to combat the consequences of economic collapse were rushed onto the statute books after President Franklin D. Roosevelt told Americans in his First Inaugural Address that only "national" action could "put people to work" (Beer, 1978). The "drift" of power away from state governments towards the national government became a "gallop" from the 1960s onwards as political and economic developments generated new incentives for national politicians to claim even greater power (Zimmerman, 1992). Laws were enacted which partially or totally preempted state authority to act in a wide range of policy areas. These preemption statutes occasionally restrained a state from taking action, but more usually mandated minimum standards which the state had to achieve. Insufficient national funding meant that the states often incurred significant costs as a result of these "unfunded mandates."

The national government's rise to prominence did not go unchallenged in the federal courts. Between 1835 and 1936 the Supreme Court struck down various national laws as violating the "reserved powers" of the states guaranteed in the Tenth Amendment. Belated recognition of the economic and political realities of the New Deal, however, gradually led the Court to abandon its adherence to notions of dual federalism. In *United States* v. *Darby Lumber Company* (1941), the Court effectively eviscerated the Tenth Amendment with a declaration that it was a mere "truism." In *American Power and Light* v. *SEC* (1946), the Court ruled that the national government's power to regulate "inter-state commerce" was "as broad as the economic needs of the nation." Although these decisions in favor of the national government were a blow to advocates of states' rights, they were only a harbinger of things to come as the Court gradually changed its role from "umpire" to "player." From the 1950s onwards the Court moved to uphold individual rights in a way that has severely restricted the flexibility of the states to determine their own policies in areas such as civil rights, criminal proceedings, and abortion. Federal court rulings have effectively preempted state authority in much the same way as national laws.

Economic and social changes have meant that national politicians have won almost every contest for power that has occurred over the last fifty years. The result has been the gradual evolution of a federal system with many of the characteristics of a unitary system (Zimmerman, 1992). Supporters of such changes argue that a number of benefits have flowed from the increased power of the national government. President Johnson argued that "creative federalism" allowed the country to mobilize its resources more effectively to tackle problems such as poverty. Opponents of the growth of national power, however, rail against what they perceive as "coercive federalism." Inefficiency and a loss of freedom are alleged to be the result of national government's rise to prominence.

The Politics of Contemporary Federalism

Calls for changes in the pattern of American federalism are not a new phenomenon. Demands that power be returned to the state governments have been a regular feature of American politics over the last fifty years. Southern Democrats, Goldwater Republicans, President Nixon, supporters of the "Sagebrush Rebellion" of the 1970s, and President Reagan all marched under the banner of "states' rights." But if little is new about the message articulated by President Clinton, Speaker Gingrich and his colleagues, and the new generation of state governors, the same cannot be said of the politics that surround the issue of federalism. A confluence of political forces has not only raised the salience of federalism, but has also generated broad support for change of some sort. Basic assumptions about which level of government should do what, and how such activity should be funded, have been questioned in a way unprecedented since the New Deal.

The debate over basic governmental roles and responsibilities in recent years has revealed both functional and ideological criticisms of the prevailing division of power between the national and state governments. On the one hand, a number of critics have claimed that state and local governments are better positioned than the national government to supply a range of government services. Both conservatives and moderates have argued that the national government has become bureaucratic and unresponsive (Rivlin, 1992; Osborne and Gaebler, 1992; Peterson, 1995). On the other hand, a number of conservative critics associated with the Heritage Foundation, the Cato Institute, and the Progress and Freedom Foundation have championed a reduction in the power of the national government as a means of reducing the size of government at all levels. A candidate's briefing book produced by the Heritage Foundation for the 1996 election stated that "[functional] arguments in favor of federalism are subsidiary to its central purpose: limiting the power of government at all levels" (Seay and Smith, 1996; see also Buchanan, 1995).

Evidence of considerable policy innovation at the state level has bolstered the claims of those who argue that the states can deliver services more efficiently than the national government. Improved institutional capacity, greater professionalization, and stronger revenue bases have allowed many states to play an important role in developing new policy initiatives over the last decade (Henig, 1985). States have promoted radical reform in areas such as economic development, welfare, health care, education, criminal justice, and environmental protection. The range of strategies pursued by the states to promote economic development in recent years, for example, has been particularly noticeable (Clarke and Saiz, 1996). Traditional "smokestack-chasing" approaches like cash gifts, cheap loans, and low taxes have been supplemented by more sophisticated methods of attracting jobs and industry. Some states have sought to foster new enterprises. Pennsylvania's Ben Franklin Partnership program offers businesses inexpensive start-up space, assistance in obtaining federal grants, advice on new technology, and help in securing loans. The Minnesota Partnership Initial Product Assessment Program provides businesses and individuals with grants of up to $9,500 to develop new products. At least seventeen states have established venture capital programs. Other states have tried to find new ways to improve their infrastructure. Public–private partnerships have been used in California and Ohio to provide the infrastructure needed by business. States have also begun to engage in negotiations with foreign countries on trade matters (Dumbrell, 1998).

New York has devised a particularly novel method of promoting economic development that deserves special mention. The Clean Air Act of 1990 sought to control sulfur dioxide emissions by creating a system of tradable pollution permits. Industries and state agencies are given a number of permits which allow them to emit a quantity of sulfur dioxide. Polluters who are able to reduce their emissions are allowed to sell their unused permits to polluters who are unable to reduce their emissions to the required level. What Governor George Pataki (R-N.Y.) has decided to do with the unused permits accrued by state agencies in New York is give them away free to industries that decide to locate in the Empire State. The policy has been denounced by environmentalists who argue that unused permits should be "retired" to reduce the overall level of air pollution, but has been defended by the Empire State Development Corporation as "a unique and innovative idea" (Usborne, 1997).

Some doubt has been expressed about the capacity of all states to deliver services more efficiently than the national government (Lowry, 1993). Not only is considerable variation evident in the institutional capacity, professionalization, and revenue bases of the states, but some states have proved reluctant to engage in policy activism even when able to. Even a cursory glance of rankings of state performance in different policy areas reveals the same states consistently at the foot at the table. The refrain of Nina Simone's song "Mississippi Goddamn" still has a certain resonance when such league tables are scrutinized. Approximately one-third of the adult population of Mississippi, for example, cannot read (Gray, 1996). Others have cast doubt upon the suggestion that the national government has failed to deliver services effectively. National action over the past thirty years has undoubtedly generated improvements in a wide range of areas from civil rights to environmental protection. Even much maligned efforts to eradicate poverty have enjoyed some success (Schwarz, 1988).

Some critics of the states have noted that public discontent about government policy is most pronounced in areas such as criminal justice and education which have traditionally been the responsibility of the states. The charge leveled against advocates of devolution (Chisman, 1995) is that:

> If the states are so good at solving difficult social problems, why have they failed to satisfy the public on issues of far more immediate importance to most people?

Other critics have asserted that devolution may be inappropriate in specific policy areas. Peterson (1995) has argued that devolving responsibility for welfare will cause states "to race to the bottom" to avoid becoming "welfare magnets." "States' rights is about to reign again in America" predicted veteran journalist Carl Rowan in 1995, "and millions of Americans are going to be hurt by it" (Ehrenhalt, 1995).

Constant news stories and campaign rhetoric about the "mess in Washington, D.C." have largely drowned out the voices of supporters of the national government. Polls conducted during the 1990s reveal that Americans have far less confidence in the national government than had been the case in earlier decades (US ACIR, 1994; Conlan and Riggle, 1995; Roper Center, 1995). In 1992 only 42 percent of Americans expressed confidence in the national government compared with 75 percent in 1972. Perceptions of value-for-money have also changed. In 1994, 46 percent of Americans identified the national government as the level of government that delivered the fewest services for their taxes compared with 36 percent in 1989. Confidence in state and local governments, in contrast, has remained relatively high. In 1992, 51 percent of Americans expressed confidence in their state government and 60 percent expressed confidence in their local government. States and local governments were also perceived as providing better value-for-money than the national government. In 1994, 21 percent of Americans identified their state government as the level of government that delivered the fewest services for their taxes and only 19 percent fingered their local government. A mammoth 75 percent of those polled believed that the states should take over more responsibilities from the national government.

State governors took advantage of the strength of public opinion to campaign for greater power to be devolved from Washington, D.C. Republican success in the gubernatorial elections of 1994, which gave the GOP a majority of state governorships for the first time since 1970, reinvigorated efforts to change the pattern of American federalism. At a meeting in Williamsburg just three weeks after the election, Republican governors issued a manifesto which called for action to enforce the Tenth Amendment. The "Williamsburg Resolves" also urged Congress to enact legislation to end the practice of unfunded mandates. Some governors even campaigned for a Conference of the States in the United States to be held in 1995 to discuss ways of reducing the power of the national government. Governor Mike Leavitt (R-Utah), co-chair of the National Governors' Association (NGA) at the time, argued that such a Conference would provide a forum in which the states could demonstrate their determination to assert their authority.

Opposition from extremist groups and individuals who "fanned fears that the Conference would undo basic American rights" meant that a Conference of the States of the sort envisaged by Governor Leavitt did not take place (Pagano and Bowman, 1995). Representatives of the Council of State Governments, the National Conference of State Legislatures, the American Legislative Exchange Council, the State Legislative Leaders' Foundation, and the NGA did hold a conference in October 1995, however, to discuss ways to coordinate their activities. The five groups agreed to explore ways in which the states could propose constitutional amendments, force the national government to reconsider laws that were not wanted by a supermajority of states, end the practice of conditional grants, and require Congress to specify the constitutional sources of its power to legislate on specific matters. At a second meeting of the five groups in November 1997 an eleven point plan was adopted which sought to alter the balance of national–state relations. Although nothing concrete followed from these initiatives, the concern expressed by the state organizations about their appropriate governmental role sent a message to national politicians.

Several states have taken initiatives to assert their authority in recent years. Arizona, California, Colorado, Hawaii, Illinois, Missouri, Oklahoma, Pennsylvania, and Utah have passed resolutions which demand that the national government honor the spirit and letter of the Tenth Amendment. Arizona and Utah have established so-called Constitutional Defense Councils to defend state interests against encroachment by the national government. Arizona, California, Florida, and Texas have launched suits against the national government to secure reimbursement of hundreds of millions of dollars incurred by mandatory expenditures on health care, education, and incarceration of illegal aliens. Other states have sought to force national politicians to think about the implications of their actions on the pattern of American federalism. Initiatives in Alabama, Arizona, California, Delaware, Michigan, Pennsylvania, and South Dakota have sought to force their congressional delegations to account for their votes on unfunded mandates.

President Clinton had displayed some willingness to give the states more discretion in managing federal programs as part of his "reinventing government" initiative, but the Republican-controlled Congress that assembled after the 1994 elections was a far more sympathetic audience. Congressional Republicans had already signalled a commitment to restrict unfunded mandates in the "Contract With America," and were more than willing to listen to the arguments of Republican governors. Both individual governors and the NGA gained new access to Capitol Hill (Weissert and Shram, 1996; Norquist, 1996). Governors Tommy Thompson (R-Wisc.) and John Engler (R-Mich.) were active participants in the process of drafting a welfare reform package in 1995 that devolved some power to the states, and the NGA played a key role in breaking the impasse on the issue:

> Never before in American history has there been as close a working relationship between any set of governors and members of Congress as this one on a project as large stated one Republican congressional staffer (Vobejda and Havemann, 1995).

Although Speaker Gingrich told the governors in November 1995 that he regarded them as "full partners in the process of creating a better 21st century America for our children" and claimed that "state and local government does a better job of understanding local communities than does some Washington bureaucrat," the willingness of the Republican Congress to devolve power to the states was mitigated by two factors (*Rockefeller*

Institute Bulletin). First, the Republican credo that the size of government needed to be reduced generated a deregulation impulse that was at odds with the desire to devolve power to the states: deregulation involved enactment of statutes that preempted state authority to regulate various industries. Second, the state of public opinion was not as unambiguous as a casual reading of the polls might suggest. Despite protestations that the states should be given more authority to tackle problems in their own way, the public continued to support national leadership in important policy areas such as economic policy, civil rights, and environmental protection. High levels of public concern about crime and education also prompted national intervention in policy areas that had traditionally been the reserve of the states.

The commitment of the Republican Congress to devolution has been unimpeachable in terms of rhetoric and symbolic politics. The pages of the *Congressional Record* since 1994 have been filled both with speeches praising state governments and reports of bills introduced to enforce the Tenth Amendment. Less convincing have been the products of all this huffing and puffing. Not only have elements of coercive federalism been retained in legislation which purports to devolve responsibility to the states, but the Republican Congress has actually taken action to limit state authority in a number of areas.

The "Devolution Revolution"

Public demands and academic arguments for power to be devolved to the states have prompted both the Clinton Administration and the Republican Congress to take action to alter the balance of American federalism. Executive Orders and administrative waivers have been used to give the states greater flexibility in implementing federal programs. Laws have been enacted which devolve some responsibilities to the states. The federal courts have also proved willing to reconsider the limits of national power. In a decision that brought a halt to sixty years of constitutional jurisprudence, the Supreme Court ruled in 1995 that Congress had exceeded its power to regulate inter-state commerce when it passed the Gun-Free School Zones Act of 1990 (Weissert and Schram, 1996). The flow of power, however, has not been all one way. President Clinton campaigned in 1996 for changes to 911 emergency systems, the introduction of school uniforms, and restrictions on gun ownership near schools (see Chapter 2). The Republican Congress has enacted laws which have increased national power both as a response to public demands for action and as a means of deregulating the economy. The federal courts have also acted to uphold national power and restrict the autonomy of the states.

President Clinton launched an effort to establish a better "partnership" between the national government and the states in the first year of his administration (Walker, 1996). Executive Order 12866 (issued in September 1993) required federal bureaucracies to draw up plans for regulatory relief and banned new unfunded executive agency mandates. Executive Order 12875 (issued in October 1993) required states and local governments to be consulted when new regulations with an intergovernmental impact were being considered. Far more important as far as federalism was concerned, however, was the National Performance Review (NPR) report published by Vice-President Al Gore in September 1993 (see Chapter 5). Among the reforms deemed necessary to "reinvent government" were a number of proposals to "empower state and local governments." The report called for the creation of a Cabinet-level board to oversee community empowerment initiatives, a reduction in the number of unfunded mandates, the consolidation of fifty-five categorical grants into a "flexible grant," increased state and local flexibility to use other grants, deregulation of the public housing program, and greater leeway for federal bureaucracies to waive rules and regulations.

The effects of this willingness to grant waivers to state governments have been most noticeable in the area of welfare. The US Department of Health and Human Services (DHHS) has given 40 states the opportunity to test new approaches to welfare. Considerable innovation has been apparent in the reforms tested by the states. Wisconsin's "Wisconsin Works" (W-2) abolished Aid to Families with Dependent Children (AFDC) and introduced workfare. Michigan's "Project Zero" provided subsidized child care and transportation to those seeking work in the Detroit area. Arizona's "Empower" program limited able-bodied recipients to no more than twenty-four months of welfare benefits in a five-year period, ended additional payments for welfare recipients who have further children, and required minors to live at home to receive benefits.

California's "Work Pays" project established a "learnfare" program which provided a range of incentives to encourage welfare recipients to graduate from high school.

Other aspects of the "reinventing government" initiative have had a less tangible impact on the pattern of American federalism. To a certain extent this has been a consequence of the limitations of executive fiat. President Clinton did create a Cabinet-level board to oversee community empowerment initiatives, but most of the other recommendations required congressional action. The devolution aspect of the NPR report has also been subsumed by the politics of the deficit. "Reinventing government" has come to be seen more as a means of saving money rather than devolving power. President Clinton spoke entirely in terms of "cuts" and "reductions," for example, in a revealing speech to the NGA on July 31, 1995. Devolution was not mentioned in a speech which cataloged reductions in federal personnel and the burden of regulations. "[Government] is smaller than it used to be," Clinton informed the assembled governors.

The administration's commitment to devolution has been further compromised by President Clinton's need to respond to public concerns about problems such as crime and education. Political competition has forced Clinton to support measures that increase the power of the national government despite consistent protestations that he wishes to devolve responsibility to the states. The administration has vigorously supported the Brady Bill, for example, even though the law establishes new national requirements for purchases of handguns. President Clinton also intimated in his 1997 State of the Union Address that the national government should take a closer look at education provision (see Chapter 13).

Similar contradictions can be seen in the commitment of the Republican Congress to devolution. The Republicans seized control of Congress following the 1994 elections and promised to transfer power from the national government to the states. "We should not be here to dictate to the states," declared Senator Dirk Kempthorne (R-Idaho), "Return the responsibility for local decisions back to local people and to the leaders they elect" (Hosansky, 1996). Promises to devolve power are one thing, but giving up newly won reins of control are quite another. Republicans have shied away from devolution when confronted with the prospect of losing the ability to respond to public concerns. Not only have some laws that purport to devolve power contained "coercive" provisions, but efforts to promote deregulation have led the Republicans to enact laws which have preempted existing state authority.

Republican intentions to change the pattern of American federalism have been signalled in the introduction of a number of symbolic bills to limit the authority of the national government. The Tenth Amendment Enforcement Act introduced by Senator Ted Stevens (R-Alaska) would require a clear statement of intent to preempt and a factual finding of the need for preemption for every bill that proposed to preempt state authority. It would also limit the power of the federal courts and agencies to preempt state law. Legislation introduced by Senator Spencer Abraham (R-Mich.) and Rep. John Shadegg (R-Ariz.) would similarly require all bills to contain a statement that described the specific constitutional authority under which Congress was acting. Rep. J. D. Hayworth (R-Ariz.) introduced a Sense of Congress Resolution that the US Constitution is a document establishing delegated and limited powers, and that Congress must act within such parameters. Senator William Roth (R-Del.) proposed that a commission to restructure the national government be established. The focus of this commission would be on whether the national government should be involved in a particular activity.

Provisions to devolve power to the states have been included in a number of laws passed by the Republican Congress. The national 55–65 m.p.h. speed limit has been abolished, states have been given greater flexibility to take account of local health needs when setting drinking water standards, and state officials have been granted an enhanced role in determining how rural development funds are to be distributed.

Action has also been taken to restrain the future use of unfunded mandates. The Unfunded Mandates Reform Act of 1995 requires a report to be prepared by the Congressional Budget Office (CBO) on the costs that states will have to bear if proposed legislation is enacted, and allows any representative or senator to raise a point of order against a bill that contains an unfunded mandate. Although critics have questioned the effectiveness of the legislation, the NGA has argued that fewer unfunded mandates have been imposed on the states as a result of its enactment (Zimmerman, 1997). Points of order have been used to block mandates in bills on immigration, gambling on Indian reservations, Medicaid, minimum wage, and occupational health and safety. The NGA has reported that only two unfunded mandates have been created since enactment of the Unfunded Mandates Reform Act (*Governors' Bulletin*, 1996).

The most important devolution measure to pass Congress has been the Personal Responsibility and Work Opportunity Act of 1996 (see Chapter 11). This law devolved some responsibility for welfare to the states by converting a categorical grant-in-aid program called Aid to Families with Dependent Children (AFDC) into a bloc grant called Temporary Assistance for Needy Families (TANF). Increased state control over the award and level of benefits has replaced a national entitlement to welfare assistance which was established during the New Deal. National control over welfare policy, however, has not been completely abrogated. The Personal Responsibility and Work Opportunity Act specifies that individuals may receive welfare assistance for a total of only five years, and requires states to have at least 25 percent of welfare recipients working a minimum of twenty hours a week by FY 1997, and 50 percent working at least thirty hours a week by FY 2002. Failure to achieve these goals will result in a reduction in federal funding.

The Personal Responsibility and Work Opportunity Act has set the states a number of difficult challenges (Tweedie, 1997). First, increases in welfare payments will have to be funded almost entirely from state funds. This means that states will have to anticipate economic cycles that increase or decrease welfare rolls. Second, the states will have to find more than one million jobs for welfare recipients by the end of FY 1997 if they are to avoid cuts in their federal funding. More than 2 million jobs will need to have been created by FY 2002. Third, work mandates mean that the states will have to double the number of child-care slots that are available. Although TANF provides increased federal funding for child-care needs, the CBO has estimated that the start of the two-year work requirement will rapidly deplete these increased funds. Fourth, the states will have to establish some form of safety net for the children of those welfare recipients who have spent over five years on welfare. Demand for child welfare services and foster care will undoubtedly rise as the number of families passing the five-year barrier begins to increase.

Congressional Republicans have essentially "used" the states to offload an unpopular program. State politicians rather than their counterparts in Washington, D.C., have been given the responsibility of making difficult choices about welfare spending and eligibility. The unwillingness of national politicians fully to cede power, however, means that these choices will have to be made within a "prescribed framework of unusual specificity and severity" (Derthick, 1986). Traditional methods of "coercive federalism" have been employed to deny state politicians particular policy options: "Unfunded liabilities have replaced a funded mandate" (Goldberg, 1995).

The Republican Congress has proved willing, in fact, to abandon all pretense of devolution when faced with public concern about issues such as violent crime. Laws enacted during the 104th Congress have not only made arson or bombing of a place of worship, inter-state stalking, and rape committed during a carjacking federal crimes, but have also required states both to arrest a larger number of violent criminals and to ensure that convicted felons serve at least 85 percent of their sentences. Public concern about illegal immigration has even led Congress to establish national standards for birth certificates and driving licenses. Devolution has also been abandoned in pursuit of deregulation. Laws have been passed which partially or totally preempt state authority to regulate telecommunications, pesticides, and mutual funds. President Clinton even vetoed a tort reform measure passed by Congress that restricted the amount of punitive damages that could be awarded by juries on the grounds that it constituted an intrusion on state power.

Arguments about the respective powers of the national and state governments have obliged the federal courts to consider the nature of American federalism in some detail. Although no clear constitutional position has emerged from the federalism cases heard by the courts, the Supreme Court under the leadership of Chief Justice Rehnquist has proved willing to restrict the power of the national government. The Supreme Court has become "more willing to play the umpire role and to call more strikes against the federal government," as Weissert and Shram have noted (1996). Tentative limits, in particular, have been placed on the "elasticity" of the inter-state commerce clause.

The most important federalism case of recent years has been *United States* v. *Lopez* (1995), in which the Supreme Court ruled that Congress had exceeded its constitutional power to regulate inter-state commerce when it enacted the Gun-Free School Zones Act of 1993 which made it illegal to possess a gun within 1,000 yards of a school. The Court ruled that there was no "empirical connection" between gun possession near schools and inter-state commerce. Some lower federal courts have used the precedent established in *Lopez* to strike down other assertions of national power based on the inter-state commerce clause. Federal district courts in Arizona, Pennsylvania, and Texas have ruled that the Child Support Recovery Act of 1988 (CSRA), which forces absent fathers to pay increased child-support payments, is unconstitutional. No "empirical connection" between child support and inter-state commerce was deemed to exist. Similarly, a federal judge in Virginia has ruled in *Brzonkala* v. *Virginia Polytechnic Institute and State University* (1996) that the Violence Against Women Act of 1994 is also unconstitutional. Judge Jackson Kiser opined that the law went beyond Congress' power to regulate inter-state commerce and "had the practical result of excessively extending Congress' power and of inappropriately tipping the balance away from the states."

In another case with important implications for federalism the Supreme Court injected new life into the Eleventh Amendment which protects states from being sued in federal courts by citizens. The Court ruled in *Seminole Tribe* v. *Florida* (1996) that a provision in the Indian Gaming Act of 1988, which allowed tribes to sue states in federal court to force negotiations over gambling on reservations, was deemed to violate the Eleventh Amendment. Lower federal courts have even tried to reinvigorate the Tenth Amendment. A federal appeals court in Texas ruled in *Koog* v. *Texas* (1996) that provisions in the Brady Handgun Violence Protection Act of 1993, which require local law-enforcement officers to conduct background checks on handgun buyers, was a violation of the Tenth Amendment. The Supreme Court upheld this view in *Prinz, Sheriff/Coroner, Ravalli County, Montana* v. *United States* (1997). Writing for the majority, Justice Scalia declared that "Congress cannot compel the states to enact or enforce a federal regulatory program."

Not all recent decisions of the federal courts have been in favor of the states. The Supreme Court has used the Fourteenth Amendment, for example, to limit the power of the states. In *Romer* v. *Evans* (1996), the Court ruled that a constitutional amendment in Colorado which discriminated against homosexuals was an infringement of the equal protection clause of the Fourteenth Amendment (see Chapter 4). In *US* v. *Virginia et al.* (1996), the Court similarly ruled that Virginia's efforts to restrict entry to the Virginia Military Institute to men also violated the Fourteenth Amendment. Nor have all federal district courts viewed the CSRA as unconstitutional. District courts in Connecticut, Florida, and Indiana have upheld the right of the national government to regulate child-support payments. A federal appeals court in New York has also upheld the CSRA. In *US* v. *Sage* (1996), the 2nd US Circuit Court of Appeals ruled that

> Nothing about the act threatens the existence of the states or interferes with the exercise of their powers. On the contrary, the act aims to help the states in their efforts, often unsuccessful, to enforce their child support decrees.

Conclusions

The patent failure of both politicians and judges to act upon a consistent philosophy of federalism is a consequence of the kaleidoscopic nature of American federalism. As Lenny Goldberg (1995) has observed:

> Every public policy area has an involved and evolved set of federal, state, and local relationships that have far more to do with institutional histories, the predilections of long-powerful congressional chairs, and lobbying groups with particular preferences than with any coherent federalist principles.

With each government program raising a different set of intergovernmental issues the pattern of American federalism has been pulled in contradictory directions. The states have gained power in some areas, but have ceded authority in others.

Continued uncertainty about the purpose and funding of government means that federalism will remain a salient political issue in the near future. Debate will continue to rage about which level of government is best suited to deliver particular services, and how such provision should be funded. No systemic solutions to such concerns, however, will be acted upon. The pattern of American federalism will continue to be shaped by the competition between national and state politicians over the fate of individual programs.

PART TWO

DYNAMICS

7

Political Parties

Gillian Peele

American political parties are complex and sometimes perplexing institutions. While their long-term decline has been forecast frequently by academic analysts and journalists, they continue to function in most respects like parties in other advanced democracies. They play a key role in the promotion of policy ideas, in the recruitment and servicing of candidates for office at various levels of the political system, in the mobilizing of the electorate, and in the structuring of electoral competition. Unlike parties in many other systems, however, they frequently have to compete with other actors (such as pressure groups and independent consultants) in the performance of these functions. Many of these themes are addressed elsewhere in this book (see especially Chapters 8 and 9). This chapter will concentrate on the factors which shape the character of American parties today, and especially their values, strategies, and internal factions. Understanding the changing interplay of ideology, organization and personality within and between the two major parties remains a crucial prerequisite for understanding the dynamics of American politics more generally.

A large part of the explanation of the character of American parties can be traced to the constitutional environment in which those parties have been forced to operate. Although the United States is a two-party system, traditionally neither the Democrats nor the Republicans have been monolithic organizations. The separation of powers has created many different, and substantially autonomous, arenas for the conduct of party politics. Not surprisingly, the presidential and congressional wings of the parties have developed different perspectives on political issues. Federalism has also created a range of intra-party divisions and factions. State parties have frequently displayed great variation reflecting the diversity of the United States itself and the unique character of individual state political systems (Mayhew, 1986).

One of the most marked features of postwar American politics is that American parties are now nationally competitive. Yet regional concerns remain important and have created distinct approaches to politics and policy inside the parties. While some divisions (such as the conflict between Southern Democrats and the rest of the Democratic Party) may have eroded, differing regional perspectives can still be found in both parties. The Republican Party, for example, is now heavily dependent on the South and the Rocky Mountain states, regions with their own distinct interests and an anti-governmental ideology.

It is sometimes difficult to distinguish the role of ideology and interest in American party politics. Certainly there has been an enhancement of ideological issues in American political debate in recent years, giving political debate and rhetoric a more hard-edged style than previously. One element in this sharpening of ideological debate has been the emergence of a self-conscious and politically successful conservative movement which has challenged the dominance of liberalism in the United States. Intellectual conflict has not eliminated more long-standing conflicts over interests and constituencies; rather, the advent of a more ideological style of political controversy has interlocked with sectional concerns and complicated the internal management of both major parties. Thus, although the United States is clearly a two-party system in form, it is also a highly fragmented one.

An Anti-party Environment?

Despite the dominance of the two major parties in American politics, there have been frequent challenges to their hegemony even in the twentieth century. The last decade has seen extensive criticism of the two-party system and substantial efforts to change it. Such criticism was hardly novel. At the beginning of the twentieth century the Progressive Movement's critique of the party system focused on both the need to use governmental power to deal with problems of social deprivation and the urgency of cleansing

American democracy of corruption. Yet the dilemma of those who have self-consciously set out to reform the American political process has always been that parties, not individuals or social movements, have been the most durable instruments for achieving political goals and the most successful party organizations have frequently operated in ways which were authoritarian or corrupt. Thus the now defunct big city machines which for long played such an important role in the politics of the Democratic Party combined ruthless use of patronage with extensive provision of social services.

In the 1990s revulsion against a series of scandals involving national politicians contributed to a series of distinct political phenomena which seemed to challenge the existing political order: the Perot presidential candidacies of 1992 and 1996 and the growth of support for a third party, speculation about a bid for the presidency by Colin Powell, the growth in female representation in Congress, the hostility to incumbency and the growth of demands for such devices as term limits as well as calls for campaign finance reform. This reaction against the existing political elites, however, also affected the framework of party competition and the nature of the parties themselves in other ways. The Republican Congressional triumph of 1994 (which was narrowly sustained in 1996) profoundly altered the character of political debate in Washington and transformed assumptions about the way the two-party system operated. For the first time in forty-four years Republicans gained control of Congress, depriving Democrats of the resources of incumbency (see Chapter 3). This re-emergence of divided government (after a brief period of unified Democratic control) produced an initial increase in partisan behavior but then calls for bipartisanship in the conduct of government policy and some softening of partisan rhetoric. Faced with evidence of public distaste for Washington politics, both the Democrats and the Republicans after 1996 emphasized policies and themes based on decentralization and populism, even though in the case of the Democrats this strategy meant accepting a rolling back of federal welfare policies and their transfer to the uncertain care of the state governments (see Chapters 6 and 11).

Party leaders were thus faced with a series of dilemmas in the period after 1995. How should the parties operate in this new environment? Should they give priority to their electorate's agenda, insofar as it could be determined? Or should they interpret the outcome of divided government as a signal that the public wanted less rather than more politicking?

Perot and the Third-party Phenomenon

One of the most tangible signs of public alienation from the existing party system was the support generated by Ross Perot and his third-party movement. Minor parties and third-party movements have played an important part in American history, as is evident from the sagas of the Progressive Party, the Prohibition Party, the Socialist Party and the Communist Party.

Third parties also remain a vital force in contemporary American politics. Although only four parties (Democratic, Republican, Reform and Libertarian) had candidates on every state ballot in 1996, there were nineteen candidates running under a third party or independent banner in the presidential race (*World Almanac of US Politics*, 1997).

It was perhaps Ross Perot's Reform Party which had the most dramatic impact on the party scene of the 1990s. Perot's third-party candidacy in 1992 proved a magnet for angry voters. At 19 percent of the popular vote, Perot secured the best third-party showing since 1912, crystallizing the dissatisfaction with both the Republicans and Democrats, and underlining the volatility inherent in the political system.

Supporters of the call for a third party in the 1990s were, however, faced with a seemingly intractable problem. Although there was no doubt of the existence of the army of activists anxious to take the message to the electorate, the party lacked collective leadership at the top and was always liable to be dubbed a "one-man band" tied to the eccentricities of its founder. Equally, although the opposition to the existing parties was tangible, there was no coherent policy strategy which could unite the voters. Perot's 1996 presidential bid (which gained 8 percent of the vote) was nowhere near as successful as his 1992 run and further effort by Perot himself seemed unlikely. Moreover by 1998 the Reform Party was itself deeply divided, despite the pledge to field legislative candidates.

The Perot candidacies, while highlighting dissatisfaction with the existing party system, also underlined how difficult it is to challenge it. The United We Stand Movement and its successor the Reform Party, like other third parties, have faced a range of structural barriers including limited access to the ballot, money, and media credibility. Access to the ballot is determined by state electoral law and, in a system which assumes a two-party structure, the simple task of getting a third-party candidate onto the ballot absorbs energy and resources. Money, of course, remains crucial both for launching and sustaining a campaign. The Perot candidacy of 1992 was only possible because of the candidate's enormous personal wealth; but even a wealthy candidate will make a rational analysis of the benefits of bankrolling a campaign that seems likely to fail. In 1996 Perot's second presidential bid was financed in part from public matching funds and any further bid would get limited funding on the basis of 1996; but it remains to be seen how much future political activity will be funded by Perot himself. Media credibility is also problematic; while Perot was able to participate in the 1992 presidential debates, he was excluded in 1996 on the basis that his standing in the polls did not suggest he was in fact a realistic candidate.

The Perot movement, though it failed in its primary objectives, had an effect on the major parties. The Perot vote in 1992 lost Bush the White House and secured Bill Clinton the presidency. It focused attention on government failures in Washington, D.C. – notably the failure to eliminate the budget deficit – and initially made it harder for Clinton to govern, especially given the limited mandate which the three-way contest gave the winner in 1992. Perot thus had long-term effects on the policy process as well as jolting the major parties' complacency. Certainly for much of the 1990s Perot's presence remained a symbol of public dissatisfaction with the status quo and reminded Republicans about the gains to be made from populist-style attacks on Washington. Perot's crusade also stands as a colourful reminder that the two-party system in the United States has to coexist with a rich and multifaceted tradition of protest politics which still retains its potential to disrupt "politics as usual."

Ideology, Issues, and the Party Response

The public mood which sustained the Perot movement also reflected and itself prompted more extensive speculation about the character of American society and its public philosophy. Different critics brought their own perspectives to bear on the problem; but what was surprising was the convergence of opinion that a nation normally self-confident and optimistic had become more negative and doubtful about its future (Shafer, 1997; Alexander and Finn, 1995).

This is not the place to examine the detailed arguments about the changed nature of American democracy (but see Lowi, 1995). It is perhaps sufficient to note the recurrence of two broad themes in the debate about what had caused the American malaise and what would constitute a solution. The first theme was the perception that the United States had lost its sense of purpose, the moral quality which made it a distinctive political entity. This theme can be found in the writings of academics, journalists and practical politicians. Academic analysts, such as Michael Sandel (1996), couched their arguments in terms of the contradictions of contemporary liberalism and its deficiencies as a public philosophy. Sandel stressed the extent to which the political system had substituted a process-based political system for one committed to shared substantive values.

Some of the same themes emerged in more polemical writings. William Bennett (who had served under Reagan and Bush), whose views achieved wide popular appeal (see for example Bennett, 1992), emphasized the importance of rebuilding a sense of shared morality in the political system. As Bennett put it in a speech before the Christian Coalition (quoted in Dionne, 1996):

> Our problem is not economic. Our problems are moral, spiritual, philosophical, behavior . . . crime, murder, divorce, drug use, births to unwed mothers, child abuse, casual cruelty, casual sex and just plain trashy behavior. The decay of older values, it was suggested, explained the decay of family structure, personal alienation, and national decline.

A second theme which recurred in the debates was the loss of civic virtue and political autonomy. Independent citizens, on this argument, had been transformed into dependent clients of government, their capacity to govern themselves reduced by an emphasis on rights rather than obligations.

At the heart of both themes was an implicit linkage between the growth of federal government and the decline of civic virtue in the 1990s. Critics alleged that as the federal role had grown, the responsibility of the individual and the family for their own well-being had been undermined. And, as the federal government had come to dominate state and local government, the process of democracy had become more remote. Yet at the same time federal government and the federal courts had neglected, and indeed made more difficult, the inculcation of ethics by adopting an allegedly neutral and secular approach to values.

The starting assumptions of many of these arguments was that a return to tradition was needed. These themes, therefore, played out differently in the Democratic and Republican parties, reasserting a conservative outlook and denying the efficacy of large government. Republicans found the emphasis on "values," although not completely unproblematic because of the individualism inherent in much market-oriented thinking, chimed well with their broad political strategy. Republicans were generally unhappy with much of the so-called "rights revolution," and opposed cultural and moral relativism and alternative life-styles. They also attacked the style of distributional politics traditionally practiced by the Democrats.

The Democratic Party, by contrast, was placed in an awkward situation by the theme that "values mattered most." It had been the party most associated with large government and with a style of politics which emphasized brokerage not principle. Moreover the Democratic Party by the late 1990s was seen as the natural home of groups (such as the gay movement and the women's movement) who were skeptical about traditional cultural values centered on a conservative view of the family.

What is important about these debates is that they enhanced the ideological dimensions of factional divisions in the parties and in the wider politics of the United States, altering both the style of political debate and the issue agenda.

The Democratic Party

The process of political change in the 1990s continued to undermine the Democratic Party's majority party status, a transition which inevitably has had a demoralizing effect on the party as a whole even if some analysts thought that the process could be reversed (Starr, 1997). The 1990s also continued the process of changing the demographics of support for each party and the balance of factions within each party. At the end of the twentieth century, as it had been in the 1930s, the Democratic Party remained a diverse coalition of constituencies and factions. There have, however, been some marked changes in the character of those constituencies and factions, making them less clear cut and arguably more difficult to manage.

Franklin Roosevelt's achievement had been to use federal government initiatives to create a broad national coalition of diverse social groups behind the Democratic Party. Essentially in the New Deal era it welded the "outsiders" and "have nots" of American society – labor unions, blacks, inner cities, ethnic minorities, Jews, Roman Catholics, and the poor – with intellectuals, anxious to use the power of government creatively. The Southern Democrats were a distinct faction in the Democratic Party determined to preserve segregation in the states of the Old Confederacy and skillful at using their congressional power (based on seniority) to preserve their position (Rae, 1994).

The conflict inherent in the Democratic coalition was obvious; but even without the peculiar tensions which came from combining southern white supremacists and inner-city minorities in one party, by the end of the Second World War the coalition was increasingly fragile. The unravelling of the New Deal coalition was a product of many different factors. Structural change in the economy, as well as political intervention, weakened the power of the unions. Demographic change produced new living patterns and changed the character of the cities. Suburban Democrats developed new agendas quite different from those of urban activists. The solidarity of some ethnic minorities dissolved as white ethnic minorities experienced upwards mobility and blacks (and to a lesser extent Hispanics) mobilized behind more radical programs. The civil rights issue and the political transformation of the South altered the character of the Democratic party in that region.

Foreign policy issues of the 1960s further fractured the Democratic Party. Until the 1960s the majority of the Democratic Party had adhered to a strong anti-communist line which went hand in hand with a commitment to internationalism. Vietnam created new divisions in the party, separating "hawks" (consisting of anti-communist intellectuals, regular political leaders and middle American patriots) from "doves" (consisting of new left activists, students and liberal politicians). New cultural and social issues also began to divide the Democrats, although they also added new sources of support. As Democrats became the natural recipients of support from newly mobilized social movements – environmentalists, women, and gays – they found it harder to appeal to their older core constituencies, some of whom became receptive to Republican appeals.

Increasing internal division weakened the Democrats' ability to command a national majority. When Lyndon Johnson left the White House in 1969, his legacy was a demoralized and riven Democratic Party. Between 1969 and 1993, there was only one brief period of Democratic control of the White House when Carter won the presidency in 1976.

The effort to find a successful Democratic presidential candidate in the 1969–93 period saw the party oscillating between traditional Democrats such as Walter Mondale and more technocratic politicians such as Gary Hart and Michael Dukakis. The dilemma for Democrats, however, always seemed to be that traditional "tax and spend"-style liberalism had lost credibility in the 1960s while new-look Democrats lacked depth and substance. At the same time there were demands from minority groups within the Democratic Party, especially blacks, for a greater say in its processes, a demand which stimulated successive rule changes and reviews of their impact (Shafer, 1983). These procedural changes in many ways highlighted the internal tensions of the party since they strengthened the representative and internally democratic nature of the Democratic Party at the expense of its ability to operate efficiently or to appeal to the wider national constituency. Substantive policy disagreements within Democratic ranks were further exposed in the presidential primaries which often weakened the party prior to the general election.

After the loss of the 1984 presidential election, a new faction (the Democratic Leadership Council or DLC) was founded with the aim of making the Democratic Party more responsive to new ideas by breaking the grip of established interests, especially labor, over party policy. It also had the aim of making the party more electable, by relocating it in the mainstream of public opinion and ending its role as a vehicle of minority causes. The key thinkers in the DLC (such as William Galston) argued that the separation of the Democratic Party from its association with minority agendas was a prerequisite for the success of the most important items of the Democratic case, especially its progressive economic message (Dionne, 1996).

The DLC had strong southern support, and Bill Clinton (who served as its president in 1990), Chuck Robb, and Sam Nunn were prominently associated with it. Although Clinton's 1992 campaign and his presidential record could not be completely attributed to the new thinking promoted by the DLC and its associated think-tank (the Progressive Policy Institute or PPI), new ideological divisions were created in the Democratic ranks. On the key issues of the economic and trade policy, the role of government, and social issues the DLC's analysis and policy prescriptions conflicted with those of traditional democratic constituencies, especially organized labor and blacks.

A number of themes illustrate the new thinking espoused by the DLC. On the related issues of economic and trade policy, the DLC had been from the beginning pro-business and anti-organized labor (Dionne, 1996). The DLC also fully accepted the implications of a global economy. While unions and their allies in the Democratic Party were protectionist, the DLC embraced free trade, recognizing that the main priority for the United States was to maintain its international competitiveness, especially in new areas of high technology. The internal party divisions surfaced in the debate over the North American Free Trade Agreement (NAFTA) which many unions opposed because of the fear that cheap labor from Mexico would undercut their bargaining position. These divisions continued to manifest themselves during the Clinton presidency as Clinton battled in 1997 to secure renewal of fast-track trade negotiating authority from Congress against the opposition of House minority leader Richard Gephardt (D-Mo.) and Senate minority leader Tom Daschle (D-S.D.).

The DLC also distanced itself from the traditional high-spending approach to the role of government which had marked the Democrats until the end of the Johnson Presidency. Although the DLC recognized the intellectual and political factors which had prompted opposition to the continuing growth of the federal government's role, the DLC wanted to promote activist government engagements in selected spheres, especially education and training. What it was less enthusiastic about was any federal commitment to across-the-board intervention by government to solve problems which might be more effectively dealt with either by the private sector or the states.

The most visible point of division between the DLC and the traditional Democratic Party related to social and cultural issues. Here the DLC wished to identify the party with the mainstream of American opinion, even if this meant antagonizing such historically important constituencies such as blacks, a group which remained solidly within the Democratic camp. (It also meant antagonizing new and potentially crucial groups for the Democrats such as Hispanics.) The issue of affirmative action was an obvious cause of conflict, as the DLC advocated a retreat from policies which had alienated whites (see Chapter 14).

Inevitably the intellectual clarity of the DLC message became blurred as Clinton himself attempted to deal with the problems of governing. (Indeed, there were relatively few DLC appointments to senior levels in Clinton's Administration and the DLC was critical of Clinton's first term.) But the combination of the DLC's efforts to address the problems of the party's philosophy and the substantive experience of the Clinton Presidency have combined to produce a new broad division within the Democratic ranks between self-styled progressives and traditionalists.

In the 105th Congress elected in 1996 (in which there was a good deal of scope for organization around the center ground of politics) Clinton-style Democrats were organized into a New Democrat Coalition, a successor to the Mainstream Coalition, a DLC-affiliated caucus. This New Democrat Coalition had three co-chairs, Tim Roemer of Indiana, Jim Moran of Virginia and Calvin Dooley of California. In addition, a new group of centrist Democrats – the Blue Dogs – emerged, with an agenda of furthering progressive Democratic policies and building centrist coalitions.

However, two important points should be noted about contemporary Democratic divisions. First, they are by no means clear-cut since the Clinton Presidency self-consciously adopted at different stages a populist style and used symbolic politics to appeal to different minority groups in the party. Secondly, while these divisions now seem to have a strong ideological core, they have to interact with other factions in the Democratic ranks which have a more interest-based content. Thus Democratic factions in Congress revolve as much around around constituency and electoral base as ideology. Groups such as the black caucus are as much interest-based as ideological, while urban members clearly have different ideological and constituency agendas from their rural or suburban counterparts. Finally, there are a large number of Democrats who describe themselves as "centrists" or "moderates" and whose policy preferences will change depending on the issue. Unpacking the factions of the Democratic Party is a more complex process than it once was, not least because of the large number of cross-cutting divisions and issues within the party. The internal fissures of the Democratic Party at the very least make the process of governing more difficult and risk exposing party disunity on a fairly constant basis.

The Republican Party

The Republican Party in the late 1990s had expanded its electoral base and, at least temporarily, gained the advantage in congressional and gubernatorial elections. As a party it had a very different culture and organizational pattern from that of the Democratic Party since it was generally more hierarchical and less conflict-ridden. The Republicans had been traditionally the party of small towns and farms and of Protestantism in America as well as of wealth and big business. Regionally its strength had been in the Midwest as well as in the North East. By the late 1990s this profile had changed markedly. Particularly noteworthy was the growing strength of the party in the South. In 1994, for the first time since Reconstruction, the GOP gained the majority of southern House seats, southern Senate seats, and governorships, reflecting the growing Republican partisanship of the region. The Republican Party had also become very much stronger in the western states, where opposition to federal government intervention was an important ideological force and fitted well with the increasingly devolutionist sentiments of the GOP. Perhaps most significantly of all, the Republicans had become the party of the suburbs and the party of those who supported conservative life-styles.

Divisions had existed in Republican ranks in the past. On foreign policy issues, there was historically a strong regional split, with mid-westerners (such as Robert Taft) tending towards isolationism and easterners tending towards an acceptance of international commitments. For much of the twentieth century the leadership of the Republican Party had been in the hands of moderates and pragmatists within the party and had been powerfully influenced also by some self-consciously liberal Republicans such as Nelson Rockefeller. From the unsuccessful presidential bid of Barry Goldwater in 1964, however, the party had seen a steady rise of the right and the eclipse of the party's liberal wing at the federal level (Rae, 1989). By the late 1990s the Republican Party's center of gravity had shifted firmly to the right, although there were several different strands in its ideology and marked differences of emphasis between different intra-party groupings.

Economic doctrine was an increasingly important element of Republican Party thinking. The GOP had always been the party of business and the better-off groups of American society but the dominance of New-Deal liberalism had caused a split between the minority who remained wedded to free market doctrines and the majority who had accepted much of the New Deal's public philosophy. From the mid-1970s, however, there was a resurgence of free market thinking providing new intellectual impetus for the right. The exploration of supply-side economics and libertarian ideas in universities and think-tanks helped fuel the Reagan revolution of the 1980s and the Republican Party transformation (Peele, 1984). Although the Bush presidency (1989–93) was seen by many conservative intellectuals as a period in which much of the right's intellectual momentum was lost, there was a resurgence of such activity after Bush lost the presidency in 1992. However economic conservatives were not themselves united. The increasing significance of the deficit in American politics in the late 1980s and 1990s divided those politicians (such as Jack Kemp) who were supply-siders from those who were "deficit-hawks" and whose top concern was the elimination of the budget deficit.

Divisions over social issues created a different pool of support for the Republican Party in the late 1990s. From the point at which the Democratic Party in the 1960s had become identified with the "counter-culture," the Republicans had reinforced their commitment to traditional morality, frequently striking a distinctly populist line on cultural issues such as funding for the arts as well as on such themes as the women's movement and gay liberation (Mellich, 1996). This strand in Republican politics was reinforced by the mobilization of conservative religious groups, especially conservative evangelicals and fundamentalists. This mobilization created a new constituency for the Republican Party and a new cadre of activists while at the same time consolidating the party's emphasis on moral and social issues. It also, however, created new fault lines in the Republican Party and alienated some important sources of support, notably women.

The mobilization of religious groups had attracted attention in the late 1970s and early 1980s but was then associated with organizations such as the Moral Majority which had limited success (Peele, 1984). By the late 1990s the relationship between conservative religious groups and the political universe had been transformed in a number of ways which had important consequences for the Republican Party. Essentially, the religious right had become more party-oriented in its activities. Instead of the independent activities of groups such as the Moral Majority, the mobilized religious conservatives of the 1990s became involved in state and local party politics, becoming in states such as Virginia significant elements in party expansion as well as a source of internal tension (Wilcox and Rozell, 1996).

The term "religious right" is an umbrella term which can be used to denote groups like the "Christian Coalition," the largest organization in this area, as well as some related groups primarily concerned with traditional social values such as Beverley La Haye's "Concerned Women of America." This group had been founded in 1979 to counter the activism of liberal women's groups such as the National Organization for Women (NOW). Also important in the religious right network was Gary Bauer's group, "Focus on the Family" which was especially concerned with social and moral issues.

By the late 1990s the religious right had acquired considerable political sophistication. It had dropped some of its earlier "absolutism" and had, especially under the guidance of Ralph Reed, executive director of the Christian Coalition for eight years until 1997, learned skills of negotiation and compromise as well as the importance of providing candidates with the services and resources which they needed. In 1994 the Christian Coalition claimed a large responsibility for Republican electoral successes because of the strategy of distributing voter guides. The local and state level were especially fertile territory for groups such as the Christian Coalition because they could capitalize on local knowledge and sentiment and organize around preexisting networks provided by congregations and religious activists.

The domestic agenda of the religious right centered on such issues as abortion, school prayer, textbook selection, and opposition to homosexuality, but the Christian Coalition also had a foreign policy agenda, opposing extension of trading advantages to countries which impeded the free exercise of religion. In addition to claiming a seat at the GOP's political table by the late 1990s, the Christian right had developed important links with a number of sympathetic think-tanks and pressure groups, especially those concerned with social issues.

Republican Presidential Politics

Ronald Reagan's two-term Presidency constituted a defining moment for the modern Republican Party and legitimized the ascendancy of conservatism within it. The period of George Bush's Presidency, by contrast, saw much internal dissent in the party, not least because Bush was never seen by the right as a true believer and because of the manner in which he reneged on his promise not to increase taxes. In 1992 Bush was strongly challenged by Pat Buchanan who ran a highly populist primary campaign which brought out a range of new ideological, social, and personal divisions in the Republican ranks. The rise in support for Buchanan-type populism and the enhanced clout of the religious right at the GOP's 1992 national convention forced Bush to move right, although it is doubtful whether this helped his standing with the GOP activists or enhanced his appeal to the electorate. As a result the legacy of the Bush Presidency for the Republican Party after 1992 was limited by comparison to that of Reagan.

Although very different from Bush, the 1996 presidential nominee Robert Dole, the former Republican Senate leader, also left a limited impact on the Republican Party. Dole had captured the nomination by exploiting superior organizational resources but he had proved an inappropriate candidate against the much younger Clinton. By 1996, also, Dole was clearly out of harmony with the more ideological leadership style offered by Gingrich in the House and even his selection of a Republican crowd-puller, Jack Kemp, as his running-mate, could not galvanize his campaign. Dole inevitably encountered major difficulties with a party that was radically changing at the grass-roots. Thus the process of delegate selection in 1996 saw some Dole loyalists forced off state delegations in favor of Christian right and anti-abortion activists (Edsall, 1996).

The Bush Presidency and the Dole candidacy highlight a recurrent dilemma for the Republicans at the national level. The selection of a candidate with the ability to appeal strongly to party activists tends to result in the choice of someone too ideologically extreme for the electorate as a whole. The selection of a politician with nation-wide appeal risks isolating the presidential nominee from his party. As the Republicans look towards future contests, it remains to be seen whether their choice will be a candidate shaped by the right and the Gingrich revolution or a more moderate Republican perhaps from the ranks of Republic governors.

The Republican Party in Congress

Like their Democratic counterparts, Republicans in Congress have long been divided on ideological, interest, and constituency grounds. Ideologically, the right had made much of the running in Republican ranks since the 1970s, but there were by the 1990s divisions within the right, especially between Republicans primarily motivated by economic policy and Republicans primarily motivated by cultural conservatism. In addition, there remained some moderates and pragmatists in Republican ranks.

An entirely novel situation in Republican ranks was created when Republicans swept the House and Senate in the mid-term elections of 1994. The triumph of Newt Gingrich as the symbol of a new style of Republicanism was important both for the dynamics of the Republican Party in Congress and for the character of the GOP as a whole, as a new generation of freshmen in the House stamped their own zealotry on the party (Killian, 1998).

Gingrich became Speaker of the House in 1995, inheriting an office which had become increasingly powerful under Democratic Speakers Tip O'Neill and Jim Wright. The fact that Gingrich could claim much of the credit for the Republican victory of 1994 enabled him to exercise his leadership powers in a highly personal fashion, concentrating powers to select committee chairs and committee assignments in his own hands and by-passing seniority norms (see Chapter 3). (Gingrich also threatened to remove committee chairmen for not following leadership strategy.) His approach to party leadership went beyond the immediate legislative agenda, as he was keen to identify key congressional races which Republicans could win and to link party donations to candidates to party responsiveness. This manipulation of the Speaker's powers enhanced the ability of the Republicans in Congress to enact their party program; but it also created a system of leadership in the Republican Party which was only as stable as the Speaker's own political authority and popularity.

Although Gingrich had strong support from the freshmen Republicans elected in 1994, the Republican Party in Congress exhibited increasing factionalism from 1995 onwards. In 1995 the right had regrouped around two organizations, both with paid organizers: the Conservative Action Team (which had grown to about sixty members) and the Family Caucus, headed in Congress by Tom Coburn (R-Okla.) a Southern Baptist deacon, which had started as a prayer breakfast. The Family Caucus concentrates on the issues dear to the Christian right, including abortion and such symbolic issues as funding for the arts and legal services, and had by 1999 grown to some seventy-five members. In addition to these groups there were others with varying defenses of organizational muscle, including the New Federalists and the Freshman Breakfast Group.

In the 105th Congress self-conscious moderate Republicans mobilized to resist the highly visible onwards-march of the right. The Mainstreet Coalition was formed, with a paid organizer, and this new voice of moderate Republicans complemented a series of informal groupings which had been active in the 104th Congress, including the House Wednesday Group, the Mainstream Republican Alliance, and the Tuesday Lunch Bunch.

Some of the cutting edge of Newt Gingrich's leadership seemed to have been blunted by the time of the 105th Congress. Gingrich's own ethical problems (which had earned him a fine and a reprimand) and more general concerns about his leadership style meant that his re-election as speaker in 1997 was by no means a forgone conclusion. There was widespread criticism of his lack of responsiveness to members, his management of the House, and his failure to build on the Contract With America with a planned legislative strategy. In July 1997 there was an abortive but significant attempt to remove Gingrich from the leadership involving several senior Republican figures including Tom DeLay (R-Tex.), the Republican whip, and Bill Paxon (R-N.Y.), the former chairman of the House Republican Congressional Committee, and until then a close ally of Gingrich's.

The attempted ousting of Gingrich had several effects on the Republican leadership in the House. Inevitably it created an atmosphere of suspicion and enhanced some of the factionalism which had already been manifest inside the congressional party. Gingrich's handling of the Speakership became an issue in other Republican congressional leadership battles. Most significantly, the Special Advisory Group (SAG), the small group which Gingrich had used to support his leadership, was disbanded and a broader group of Republicans was coopted to help set party strategy. Thus from an inner core of leaders (majority leader Dick Armey of Texas, House Republican Whip Tom DeLay and Republican Conference Chairman John Boehner (R-Ohio)) the group around the Speaker has been extended to include Jennifer Dunn (R-Wash.) Deborah Pryce (R-Ohio) and Dennis Hastert (R-Ill.) (Koszczuk, 1997).

The change should not, however, be interpreted to signal much dilution of Gingrich's emphasis on personal loyalty. Most of the people included in the broadened leadership group were allies of Gingrich, and his move to rely more on committee chairs entailed a move towards a group which owed its position to him (Koszczuk, 1997). Gingrich's authority had been weakened, however, and he was forced to run party affairs in a more inclusive fashion and to spend more time on the internal affairs of the House rather than acting as a national party spokesman.

The Republican Party in the Senate was initially less marked by the ideological shift which characterized the House in the 104th Congress. Indeed, it became a constant complaint of conservative activists that the Senate was stalling on the conservative agenda and there was frequent criticism of Dole's leadership. When Trent Lott replaced Dole as Senate leader in 1996, the Senate leadership seemed likely to shift in a direction more acceptable to conservative Republicans. Also by the 105th Congress Phil Gramm (R-Tex.) had provided additional strength for the right as the chair of the Republican Steering Committee.

Lott's leadership was not regarded with general enthusiasm even on the right, however. He incurred criticism for supporting Clinton's chemical weapons treaty and failed to deliver supporting votes for either the balanced budget amendment or a ban on partial birth abortions. Lott's leadership style in any case had to be tailored to the Senate's norms, which are much less conducive to aggressive partisanship than those of the House. Also the individual Senate committee chairmen still wield substantial power, as witnessed by the ability of the conservative Jesse Helms (R-N.C.) after 1995 to use his chairmanship of the Foreign Relations Committee to pursue an aggressive right-wing and populist agenda against the United Nations and the State Department. Helms' venom was not reserved for Democrats; in 1997 he blocked Clinton's nomination of former Republican governor William Weld as ambassador to Mexico because Weld was too liberal for Helms' taste on such issues as drugs. And on the liberal wing of the Republican Party, Senators John Chafee (R-R.I.) and James Jeffords (R-Vt.) retain powerful committee chairmanships.

Republican Governors

Any analysis of the internal factions of the Republican Party also needs to take into account the increasingly important role of Republican governors. Republicans in 1998 had the majority of governors, and this section of the party has proved consistently more pragmatic than the congressional wing of the party. The 1990s' emphasis on state welfare reform and the retrenchment of federal government gave the states, and hence governors, a new national prominence. In 1994, Republican governors issued their own manifesto (the Williamsburg Resolves) and spearheaded new approaches to social policy. Individual governors such as Tommy Thompson (Wisc.), John Engler (Mich.), Christine Whitman (N.J.), and Pete Wilson (Calif.) acquired national prominence, although Whitman's liberal stand on abortion rights made her a controversial figure in the party. Ironically, however, as a group within the Republican Party the governors were almost too policy-oriented and pragmatic to exercise extensive influence in a climate so strongly affected by ideology.

In addition, there are a range of issue-oriented pressure groups within the GOP which represent liberal rather than conservative views – for example, the well organized Log Cabin group which represents gays in the Republican Party.

The 1990s thus present a mixed picture for the Republican Party. It has experienced and continues to experience growth at the grass-roots and has, of course, expanded its electoral base. Yet much of the success of the Republican Party in recruiting new members has produced internal conflicts and risks alienating important sections of the electorate, including women and minorities.

Party Organization

The 1990s has continued the trends at the national level of party organization evident since the 1970s. First, the increasing integration of the different levels and activities of the parties has continued. A new model of national party innovation had been set by Bill Brock, chairman of the Republican National Committee from 1977 to 1981. Increasingly thereafter the national party committees took the lead in developing national strategies for the parties, moving further away from the older model of party organization in which national parties were essentially shells and any real activity which occurred took place at the level of the state party. Secondly, the national party committees became increasingly concerned with the delivery of services to candidates. Thirdly, the national committees devoted ever more time to raising funds to support increasingly costly election campaigns (see Chapters 9 and 15).

These broad trends marked both parties in the 1990s, although the Republican Party was frequently the innovator of new developments while the Democratic Party emulated them. There were, however, some differences between the parties, and both experienced periods of growth and decay.

Democratic Organization

The political party which holds the presidency tends to experience a certain loss of momentum. The fact that Clinton did not come from the Democratic mainstream may have reinforced the natural tendency of presidents to neglect the party organization; certainly by the time of the second Clinton term there was a strong feeling that the White House had neglected the Democratic National Committee (DNC) as well as a sense of low morale following poor congressional showings in 1994 and 1996, a $4 million debt and the fund-raising scandals associated with Clinton's 1996 re-election campaign.

The organizational core of the Democratic party is the DNC. The DNC has however been less supportive of its state parties than the RNC and Democratic Party organization has generally proved more unwieldy than its GOP counterpart. For much of the first Clinton term there had been a dual arrangement at the head of the DNC with Christopher Dodd of Connecticut acting as the public face of the party and Donald Fowler exercising more organizational responsibilities in relation to the state parties. Certainly Fowler's role was one which was much appreciated by the state parties, not least since he had been committed to party-building activities including the promotion of training academies for activists. In 1997, the Democrats appointed Colorado Governor Roy Romer as general chair and Steve Grossman of Massachusetts as national chairman. Both found they faced formidable difficulties stemming primarily from the Democratic Party's financial problems which threatened to impede the DNC's organizational support to candidates and to state parties.

State parties have on the whole become more organized and active in recent years, not least because of the Federal Election Campaign Act (FECA) amendments of 1979 which encouraged giving for party-building activities through "soft money." Indeed it is part of the argument for keeping "soft money" that without it state parties would be starved of cash since political donations tend otherwise to be targeted at the national level of party organization (see Chapter 9). Nevertheless the picture at the state level is patchy with some strong state Democratic parties such as Massachusetts and Minnesota balancing organizationally weaker ones.

Republican Organization

The late 1990s saw a significant transfer of power at the key Republican National Committee (RNC) when Haley Barbour, who had been chairman from 1993 to 1997, was replaced by Jim Nicholson. Barbour, a southerner, had enjoyed enormous prestige and was credited with being the organizational inspiration of the 1994 Republican legislative majority, not least because he had helped create the Contract With America. His influence extended beyond organizational matters to policy, both because his views on strategy were valued by the legislative leadership and because he had the capacity to unite the different factions of the Republican Party (Barnes, 1995).

The RNC itself had been galvanized under Barbour's chairmanship. His fund-raising drive had been a major factor in reestablishing the financial heath of the GOP, but it had also been crucial in the financial strategy of directing funds to candidates who needed it most. Following the trend towards greater integration of the party at all levels, Barbour played a key role in securing Republican governors' agreements to national initiatives such as the balanced budget amendment. Part of Barbour's strategy had been to demoralize the Democrats, by publicizing the many switches from Democratic to Republican ranks at all levels of the system. His successor, by contrast, has tried to complement this emphasis on converts by an effort to refine the Republican message and to develop strategies for groups who had been neglected in the 1994–97 period. Thus growing Democrat advantage among female voters was countered in 1997 by a new Republican initiative to mobilize women under the direction of Senator Kay Bailey Hutchison (R-Tex.) and Congresswoman Sue Kelley (R-N.Y.) (Greenblatt, 1997).

Candidates, Campaigning, and Money

The decision to run in an election is a rational one based on an assessment of the chance of winning and the ability to raise resources to fund the race. Parties have an interest in encouraging good candidates to come forward and they also have an interest in directing their funding (once the primary is over) to the races where the party as a whole is likely to benefit. Generally the Republicans were thought to have secured better House candidates than Democrats in the 1990s, a product in part of the revitalization of the Republican Congressional Campaign Committee (RCCC) under Paxon's chairmanship and his ability to encourage able new candidates to run (Killian, 1998). Paxon also improved the RCCC organization and reduced its debts.

The raising and spending of money absorbs a vast amount of time in both parties, especially given the legal requirements imposed by the FECA. The late 1990s were an especially difficult period for money-raising because of the general hostility to the parties, growing demands for further regulation of campaign finance and the persistent calls on parties and candidates to fund expensive campaigns.

The legacy of the 1996 presidential campaign was initially most keenly felt by the Democrats who were severely criticized for the alleged solicitations for cash from the White House – breaches of the spirit and letter of the law which led to a quartet of inquiries and subsequent allegations of attempts to stymie them. The sensationalism of the charges against the Democrats tended to obscure other developments in political funding. The 1996 Supreme Court decision in *Colorado Republican Federal Campaign Committee* v. *Federal Election Commission* effectively allowed the expenditure of money on the promotion of issues, provided that such promotion was not expressly linked with a candidate. This ruling stimulated the Republican Party to rethink its campaigning strategy. It established the I-division at the RCCC as an independent legal and organizational entity, a strategy which was later copied by the DNC (Corrado, 1997).

Other changes in the way in which money operated in American politics shaped party strategy in the late 1990s. First, the 1994 elections and the immediate post-election period saw Gingrich and Barbour targeting funds in a highly strategic manner. In 1994 party funds had been used to support forty of the seventy-three Republican freshmen elected and the RNC more than doubled its spending over previous mid-term elections, investing more than $20.2 million on the campaigns themselves for both House and Senate, national advertising and transfers of funds between the RNC and state and local parties (Barnes, 1995). After the 1994 mid-term successes Gingrich encouraged early fund-raising by incumbents to prepare for the 1996 elections. For its part, the RNC under Barbour's direction funded a $200,000 television advertising campaign promoting its congressional reform initiatives and the balanced budget amendment as well as a campaign against Democratic Senators.

Much of the money raised had come from successful direct mail campaigns, which both parties used. The Republicans, however, were especially successful using this technique and Barbour was able to fund an almost bankrupt RCCC and to commit the RNC to greater involvement in district campaigns. Republicans had always enjoyed the edge in direct mail fund-raising and the capture of the House and Senate in 1994 brought further dividends as Republican incumbents began to receive additional Political Action Committee (PAC) money. However, the Republicans were good at spending as well as at raising money and by the end of 1997 it was alleged that the RNC was between $4 million and $9 million dollars in debt and would be unable in 1998 to fund anywhere near the number of candidates it had supported in the previous cycle. The Democrats for their part experienced organizational turf-wars between the DNC and state parties as state parties (through the Association of State Democratic Chairs) sought to negotiate a deal which would allow them to benefit from DNC fund-raising in the individual states by ensuring that a 7.5 percent share of funds would go to state parties.

As far as campaigning is concerned, the parties have continued the trends of the early 1990s. Negative campaigning remained a prime weapon in the parties' armor. Thus Joseph Gaylord, a Republican strategist in 1994, emphasized the need to "go negative" early on in a campaign and never back off (Dionne, 1996). The technology of communication remained vital for campaigning as well as fund-raising and more general party activities. The role of television continued to expand but there were also a series of new initiatives with cable, satellite and the internet (see also Chapter 17).

Conclusions

American parties approached the end of the twentieth century with enhanced vigor in some areas yet somewhat weakened in others. The trend towards stronger and more professional party organizations had been institutionalized at the national level and the national committees had become significant players on the national political stage. Parties continued to show resilience and innovative capacity in a changing fund-raising and campaigning environment. In Congress party not merely retained its salience but in many respects increased it. On the other hand, state parties, especially in the Democratic Party, had to fight to maintain a role. And the American public's apparent disenchantment with the existing party system and the exigencies of divided government operated as barriers to extensive strengthening of the role of party in the governing system. If this balance is not the strong party system advocated by some critics of American government, neither is it one which implies the death of party. Quite the contrary, it is a balance which provides substantial space in which parties can operate flexibly and one which is consonant not just with the dynamics of the American system but also with more general political patterns in modern democracies.

8

Organized Interests in National Politics

STEVE REILLY

Debate about the character and impact of interest groups in the contemporary United States is as vivid as ever. An extraordinary number of groups jostle for position in every policy area, using a wide and sophisticated variety of lobbying techniques. Although the increased diversity and number of organized interests may lessen the likelihood of any single group dominating a major policy area, there are undoubtedly patterns of both exclusion and bias. If interests cannot buy the tools of organization, they are seriously under-represented. If the rich matrix of business interests, right-wing think-tanks and discreetly funded "citizen groups" lacks the cohesion to control the parameters of policy-making, it is neither for lack of resources nor for want of effort.

Interest Groups and Organized Interests

There have been three major phases, the third of which is far from complete, in the development of the politics of organized interests since the watersheds of the New Deal and the Second World War enlarged the reach of the state. The first was that of the long generation from 1945 to 1960, when a broad and sometimes artificial consensus was underwritten by growth, the erosion of radicalism and the neglect of racial issues. Politics was largely articulated through a relatively stable matrix of interest groups operating in a rough harmony with the party system. The second phase (1960–80) has been amply documented elsewhere (Schlozman and Tierney, 1986). Suffice to say that in the 1960s and 1970s, as the party system lost much of its limited coherence, the number, variety and impact of interest groups grew explosively, and the two channels of representation became arhythmic and detached. Observers needed a new vocabulary to describe a more populous, unpredictable form of interest politics. Although this period did not conform to the model of "iron triangles," geometric metaphors remained in vogue: the evocative but imprecise concept of issue networks was supplemented by "policy spheres," "sloppy hexagons," and the even less elegant "doughnut" (Salisbury *et al.*, 1992).

A new metaphor is needed, however, to capture the essence of the third phase of interest politics which has endured since 1980. There are three features which distinguish this phase from its predecessors. First, it is no longer adequate to use the term "interest groups" to describe the wide variety of different institutions which attempt to influence national policy.

Secondly, the true purpose of groups is often different from their apparent mission. Institutes bearing the most neutral and innocent of names to advertise their public-interest virtue turn out on close inspection to be the partisan mouthpieces of corporate interests. "Grass-roots" organizations are often far more attuned to their foundation donors than to a mass membership, or are hard to distinguish from the "astroturf" lobbies constructed by the illusionists of K Street. Thirdly, the formal institutional character of organized interests are, increasingly, a poor guide to their activities. Many groups roam freely across boundaries of policy areas or mix functions which used to belong to different classes of institution. The Christian Coalition is no respecter of "policy domains," as shown by its vigorous opposition to President Clinton's 1993–94 health care reform proposals and its broad engagement with issues of crime, taxation, education and trade policy. The Heritage Foundation is at once a think-tank, a key axis in the conservative movement, a base for numerous policy entrepreneurs, and a sponsor of smaller institutions and one-off advocacy projects.

The system is, then, not one of interest-group politics, but of the politics of organized interests. If any geometric metaphor is apt, perhaps that of a kaleidoscope of interests is useful. It is merely a metaphor, not a model: but it reminds us that within the whole system of interest representation there are an almost uncountable number of pieces – as one sees when finding widely different estimates of the total in various guides and directories to Washington's plethora of organizations. The pieces are certainly of different shapes and sizes: the Christian Coalition dwarfs the liberal Interfaith Alliance; the business lobby on China outweighs the human rights advocates. Some parts of the spectrum are more vividly present than others: the deeper hue of more radical environmental groups such as Greenpeace is more than offset by the moderate tones of the Wilderness Society and the National Wildlife Federation. Fragments cohere as issues change: pieces form transitory blocs to resist disruption. There may be discernible patterns, but they are likely to be intricate and shifting.

Organized Interests in the 1990s

Business groups

Business groups are often assumed to dominate American politics. They spend millions of dollars attempting to influence election campaigns, lobbying officials, and often move with ease into senior government posts. It is easy, however, to exaggerate the power of business groups. While corporations and their peak associations are clearly more influential than any other individual sector of interests, the business community is neither monolithic nor united. American business seldom has a single mind; it certainly has no single voice, not least as both major political parties compete, albeit with differing balances of purpose, for the chance to articulate the interests of capital.

The fragmentation of legislative authority and executive structures in a federal system induce interests to compete for influence. The US Chamber of Commerce (itself a national federation of local units), the National Association of Manufacturers, the Business Roundtable and the National Federation of Independent Businesses (NFIB) represent substantial fractions of business: but so also do hundreds of associations in every industry. There are at least eighteen major trade associations within the energy and natural resources industry, including such groups as the American Petroleum Institute, the American Gas Association, and the Edison Electric Institute, each of which has an annual income of over $60 million. The degree of specialization of the world's most sophisticated consumer market encourages the existence of such arcane bodies as the National Pasta Association and the Outdoor Advertising Association of America. This fragmentation has been furthered by the fact that business groups have not had to unify to fight challenges to the capitalist system, particularly since the late 1940s.

The most politically striking change in business representation in the last few years concerns the NFIB In the early 1990s the NFIB was a significant but generally low-profile organization. It had a full-time director in each state, a cadre of activists who were often mobilized to lobby state legislators, and a quiet presence in national politics. It had only a small PAC, and the state groups played no part in federal campaigns. Within five years the NFIB became a powerful political force, "with the far-flung organization, resources and binding ideology of a national political party" (Johnson and Broder, 1996), close ties to, and influence upon the Republican Party, and a reputation founded on its ability to combine traditional and newer lobbying tactics. The NFIB's constituency has grown as corporations have hived off many specialist functions, as service and leisure industries created yet more niches for entrepreneurs, and as deregulation freed capital and lowered start-up costs for small businesses. In 42 percent of US households at least one member is employed by a small business. The NFIB has over 600,000 member companies, of which about 60 percent employ fewer than ten people, and an annual budget of some $22 million. It also has a strong sense of mission. Many large corporations have not only adapted to an environment of dense government regulation, but prospered by influencing and exploiting the web of subsidies, direct grants, and tax breaks that constitute the "corporate welfare state." In contrast, many smaller businesses object to such federal largesse as the $1.4 billion sugar price support program, of which over 40 percent goes to the largest 1 percent of growers. The NFIB combines a pragmatic aversion to the costs of environmental, consumer, employment and other "burdensome" laws with a zealous faith in a slimmer state more detached from a lively market.

The Republican takeover of Congress following the 1994 mid-term elections provided the NFIB with new opportunities to exercise power. The organization became an established partner, for example, in the House Republican leadership's weekly "Thursday Group" legislative strategy meetings. The NFIB has grown to become a potent organization connected to the conservative wing of the GOP, able to combine any useful mixture of electoral strategies, direct lobbying, media-based tactics and grass-roots mobilization. Many large corporations, however, have had to adjust to the unfamiliar ideological zealotry of some congressional Republicans, who have proved reluctant either to deal with companies which pragmatically defend their interests by making large campaign contributions to incumbent Democrats and Democrat campaign committees, or to defend the secure regulatory and corporate welfare environments which gave large companies the advantage. Party leaders have made clear their view that the Business Roundtable, a discreet but potent group of some 200 chief executives of large corporations, is too bipartisan in its donations and connections. Some have suggested the need either for the Roundtable to revise its approach, or for a new, more reliable big-business group. The tensions are a vivid reminder that it is often misleading to talk of a single "business community" in the kaleidoscopic world of interest politics.

Labor unions

Conventional wisdom suggests that the labor movement has become a shadow of its formerly powerful self. Not only have most of the nation's heavy industries declined, and manufacturing firms relocated abroad or in the anti-union Sunbelt, but the influence of the movement in the Democratic Party declined as other minority groups mobilized from the late 1960s. The Reagan Administration's attacks on the rights and status of unions further diminished their size and effectiveness. Consequently, many observers were surprised by the strength of union activity in the 1996 elections, and by other signs of reinvigoration in the movement. In 1996 the AFL–CIO supplemented its PAC expenditure with a $35 million effort at unseating targeted Republicans in Congress. Some $20 million was largely devoted to aggressive television and radio advertisements; the remainder supported a field organization of thirteen paid campaign coordinators engaged with 102 House districts and fourteen Senate seats.

The labor movement set new standards for the use of campaign expenditures which are notionally nonpartisan. In the final two months of the campaign, the AFL–CIO spent an estimated $10 million on advertising against twenty-one first-term Republicans, and about $1.1 million in open House districts.

The effects of these efforts are, however, hard to judge. While the AFL–CIO claims a large role in defeating eighteen Republican incumbents in the House, critics suggest that these were vulnerable members who would probably have lost anyway, and that the movement made unnecessary enemies by attacking moderate Republicans who, having survived, are now more hostile. Nevertheless, the Republican response implies some real sense of a threat from labor, in the 1996 elections and in the future. They were disturbed not only by the AFL–CIO effort, but by the early and large expenditure of other unions, which between January 1995 and June 1996 gave Democratic challengers $4.4 million, compared to $4 million in the whole 1993–94 cycle. From April 1996 the Republican Party ran a series of advertisements to counter the union effort, including an $8 million advocacy campaign in July and a series of explicitly anti-union ads in October, and orchestrated the creation of "The Coalition" of business and other conservative groups under the umbrella of the US Chamber of Commerce. It raised less than was hoped for, in an election year in which business groups were already giving unprecedented amounts to parties and candidates. Nevertheless, it financed two television advertising campaigns in thirty-three House districts at a cost of $7 million. The Heritage Foundation initiated a "Union Watch" program to seek out funding irregularities and attempted to link a dozen conservative groups and think-tanks. The party itself funded anti-union advertisements, pressed broadcasters not to air AFL–CIO messages, filed complaints with the Federal Election Commission alleging misuse of union funds, and used its congressional committee dominance to initiate hearings designed to expose unions as corrupt and anachronistic. The party's unease continued in 1997, when Speaker Gingrich stressed to corporate donors the need for increased spending to combat union advertising, and called for an extended "debate" on the role of unions.

Some evidence of a revival may also be seen in efforts at grass-roots organizing and political education. The recently-created

AFL–CIO Organizing Department had a $20 million budget for 1997–98, and a Working Women's Department was set up in 1996, showing a somewhat belated recognition of the potential implied by the relative success of unions in some heavily female occupations – such as in health care, garments and textiles, and clerical work – in maintaining or increasing membership in recent years. Strategists also see increased female membership as helpful to unions' general public image and to the mobilization of popular support for union positions, and therefore for unionism, on "nonworkplace" issues such as education, welfare reform and health care. They have already begun, through Project 96 and its successors, to revive or create alliances with environmental, consumer and senior citizens' groups – recognizing that there are few issues in which a solely union position will prevail.

These limited but striking signs of revival tend to be attributed to just two factors: the shock effect of the Republican takeover of Congress in 1994, and the election in 1995 to the AFL–CIO presidency of John Sweeney, seen as a reformist committed to the modernization and aggressive promotion of a declining movement. In fact, the story is not so simple, not least because Sweeney's earlier record raises doubts about his wish or capacity to overcome the insularity, oligarchism and corruption which still bedevil many private sector unions. The "revival," if it qualifies as such, has earlier origins. Labor's weakened position during the Reagan Presidency was eased first by the Democratic recapture of the Senate in 1986, then by Speaker Jim Wright's determination to repair the party's alliance with labor. During the same period, the growing influence in the movement of public sector unions (which represented 38 percent of the sector's workforce) and their often younger leaders diffused some of the tensions between labor and other liberal groups, suggesting a possible return of labor to the politics of coalitions and alliances – a form of politics severely damaged in the years of Vietnam, black radicalism and the women's movement.

It could therefore be argued that some preconditions existed for a labor revival before the catalyst of the Republicans' unexpected and threatening victory in 1994. The picture has, however, been mixed. Union leaders remained uneasy with the Clinton Presidency, and did not forget Clinton's successful creation of a congressional coalition to overcome their resistance to the North American Free

Trade Agreement (NAFTA). The Democratic Party has remained tentative about union associations because most of its contemporary leaders (with a few exceptions such as Richard Gephardt) are fearful of jeopardizing middle-class support and corporate acceptance especially given that unions represent only some 15 percent of all workers. The general climate for unionism is thus still discouraging. Organized labor needs to recruit some 300,000 workers a year merely to sustain its current share of the workforce. Small businesses are both hard and expensive to organize, legal constraints inhibit not only recruitment but most forms of union action, and the US media tend to pay little attention to union conflicts or successes. Few newspapers now have a "labor beat," union perspectives are rarely seen on TV, and the media tend to under-report corporate excesses or view them as threats to consumers, the environment, or minorities rather than to workers *per se*. Despite the wealth of union PACs, it will not be easy for labor to improve rather than at best defend its public image, its membership and its influence within the Democratic Party.

Other membership groups

It is hard to classify the multitude of interest groups of other kinds which have expanded so dramatically in number and variety in the last thirty years. To call them "noneconomic" (Wilson, 1992), to distinguish them from business associations and labor unions, is for some purposes misleading. If the American Association of Retired Persons (AARP) protects its 33 million members from higher health care costs, it is certainly serving their economic interests. Groups representing women, racial minorities or welfare claimants may be as concerned with their constituencies' economic well-being as with their legal rights. A commonplace alternative term – "public interest group" – which is applied to numerous groups devoted to consumer, environmental, "good government," and many other issues which ostensibly should concern any virtuous citizen, is also inadequate. It usually refers to groups which exist principally to seek benefits to be shared by the broader population rather than solely or disproportionately by the group's members – as with such groups as Public Citizen or the Sierra Club. However, the corporate chief executives who constitute the Business Roundtable, an elite group which addresses issues related to economic growth, are surely as likely as are the members of a consumer group to believe that their aim is the common good and that they would benefit the adoption of their recommendations no more than would the CEOs of large companies which choose not to join the Roundtable. Terms such as these and "advocacy," "single-issue" or "cause" group should be seen as little more than shorthand for a range of groups with widely differing aims, united if anything by the existence of a substantial membership of private citizens, who provide a considerable part of the group's funding and a significant voice in setting the organization's goals and priorities.

It is also notoriously difficult to enumerate this rich matrix of groups. Although many have a durable existence and a real membership base, others may be very transient, or exist as no more than a facade for a corporate interest. At a cautious estimate, excluding business and professional associations and labor unions, there were slightly over 300 membership groups with offices in Washington in the mid-1990s. That figure (*Capital Source*, 1997) excludes the numerous groups which do not maintain offices in Washington, but retain professional lobbyists to act on their behalf.

The growth of such groups in the second and third phases of post-1945 interest politics at first encouraged high hopes of a new form of politics, more pluralistic in content and more democratic in structure. The first hope has been at best only very imperfectly realized. Ironically, the early success of public-interest groups raised the cost of politics and stimulated counter-mobilization by wealthy corporate groups. Costs were first increased by political reforms which opened up congressional committee meetings, required more public hearings and open files, and forced executive agencies into the sunlight. Many groups are unable to match business' capacity to conduct research, offer and analyze data, or attend hearings. It became even harder than before for constituencies of the poor to buy their way to effective representation, or for radical groups unsupported by wealthy foundations to compete for legitimacy in the information-rich, specialized policy arenas of a more open but complex system. Organizations which rely on voluntary efforts to support the work of a small professional staff are at a severe disadvantage. Time and money are not similar political resources; politics frequently involves conflicts between the more and the less wealthy, but seldom between the harried and the leisured (Verba *et al.*, 1995). Consequently, a rough hierarchy of interests has evolved in recent years: business remains most resourceful, if not necessarily always best able to translate its wealth and general legitimacy into wide popular support for particular policy measures. So-called public-interest groups have some chance of success through carefully focussed efforts, particularly if they can draw on the financial backing of foundations and philanthropists to supplement membership revenues. Poorer citizens, lacking the resources to organize or the active voters to reward or punish politicians, are woefully under-represented. Although Americans have been credited since Tocqueville with an unusually strong habit of "voluntary association," the habit is unevenly distributed by class and education, and its high level compared to most other nations has depended substantially on the catalyst of church membership, which itself has remained unusually high in the United States. In an era of union decline, churches are the only substantial and relatively egalitarian social institutions which act as sites for learning political skills or for sharing the growth of a political sensibility. Despite the existence of significant politically progressive–liberal wings in each of the main denominations, their prevailing bias is toward social conservatism and market economics. As Verba *et al.* observe, "churches can pinch-hit for unions" in providing skills, but not in bringing the interests of the poor to the forefront of politics.

Hopes for a more participatory politics have no more been realized than have aspirations for a more inclusive pluralism. Most citizen-based groups "are not very participatory or popularly rooted at all" (Skocpol, 1996). Instead, they tend to be professionalized and hierarchical organizations, run by their full-time staff and by boards of directors who often represent the perspectives of staff or of large institutional donors. In most "public-interest" or advocacy groups, most members' involvement is limited to the payment of dues, or at best to dutifully redirecting to congressional offices the letters and faxes drafted for them by the national staff. Such groups tend not to reflect the radicalism or diversity of an active membership, but the moderation favored by large donors and the "inside the Beltway" habits of caution likely to infect professional staff. There is also the risk that such groups' partial dependence on foundation or corporate finance may compromise their activities.

The contemporary group environment is also marked by fragmentation and by competition for resources, access and influence. In most issue areas there is no monopoly of representation by a single group speaking for an entire constituency. Even the massive and influential AARP has faced competition from the National Council of Senior Citizens, which has ties to organized labor and the Democratic Party, and from the National Council to Preserve Social Security. More recently, a trio of conservative groups, the Seniors' Coalition, the 60 Plus Association and the United Seniors' Alliance, has been partly sponsored and certainly encouraged by the Republican Party leadership, which regards the AARP as dangerously liberal.

It is not clear whether the fragmentation of groups generally adds to or detracts from the effective representation of an interest. It may, for example, be argued that the anti-abortion movement, which includes at least half a dozen sizable single-issue groups and numerous concerned allies, gains from creating the impression of a busy matrix of groups united by a common goal but divided by tactics, membership, and structures, or if it loses by having no single "legitimated" voice with a unified message and a clear strategy. Similarly, Mexican-American groups such as the League of United Latin American Citizens, the Southwest Voter Registration and Education Fund, the Mexican-American Legal Defense Fund, and the National Council of la Raza have differing histories, funding sources, primary concerns, and points of access. It is hard, if not impossible, to gauge if Chicanos would be better served by a single association with a sharper focus and more leverage on politicians inclined to respond attentively if they hear the approaching footsteps of a bloc vote.

In recent years membership groups have had to adapt to several changes in the political environment. Levels of discretionary spending in the federal budget have reduced their chances of winning policy changes which require increased government spending (Peterson, 1992). The shifting center of gravity in the Democratic Party, and the Clinton Administration's determination to reduce the federal deficit and also shake off the party's image as an aggregation of "tax and spend" interests, made life tougher for liberal groups. So too did the advent of a congressional Republican majority in 1994 with an agenda hostile to regulation, redistribution, higher taxation, cultural liberalism, and the use of the state as an instrument for racial equality. Liberal groups were largely forced onto the defensive, while conservative groups enjoyed a broad harmony with the Republicans and with a bipartisan resistance to extending state authority.

Think-tanks

The American political system is often criticized for elevating the urgent over the important, and sound bites over policy. There is more than a little truth in this, as the last days of any congressional session show. However, US politics is not only a matter of expediency and compromise: it is also a contest of ideas. Until recently their quality was generally enhanced by "think-tanks': nonprofit institutions distinct from the academic world and unattached to party or government. Their role was to conduct independent research into policy issues and to disseminate the findings to politicians, administrators, and the media. Ideally, their work was disinterested, available to anyone: and if they promoted individuals as spokesmen, it was as experts not as "combat intellectuals" (Maynes, 1997). Think-tanks such as the Hoover Institution or the Brookings Institute had discernible leanings, to the right and the liberal left respectively, but their work was essentially serious and scholarly, and disseminated with more care for accuracy and utility than for headlines. A generation ago they would not have been regarded as organized interests.

In recent years that model has been all but destroyed. Think-tanks have become more ideological and partisan, tied by one hand to the corporations and foundations which fund them and by the other to the political parties for which they provide intellectual weight and a veneer of disinterested legitimacy. There are several reasons for the change. These include, simply, the continuing specialization of policy, the surplus of foundation wealth, and the vast range of information resources and research technologies available in contemporary America. But the main reasons are more specific. First, since the late 1970s, the counter-mobilization of business interests and the growing political voice of a market-oriented, anti-statist conservative movement created a demand and supplied the funding for an ideological channel of policy proposals and analysis running from think-tanks into the political arena. Second, the major parties, historically seldom noted for intellectual rigor, have in recent years been preoccupied with organization and campaigning, and have also tried to dilute ideological conflict by subcontracting the responsibility for ideas. In the 1990s neither the demand nor the supply diminished. Across the conservative spectrum, institutions from the moderate and respected American Enterprise Institute (AEI) and the libertarian Cato Institute to the aggressively partisan and entrepreneurial Heritage Foundation and the urban-oriented Manhattan Institute have been the main pillars of an increasingly dense structure of think-tanks which combine research, advocacy, and partisan campaigning. Some, such as the Project for the Republican Future (later transformed into a magazine, *The Weekly Standard*), were virtually adjuncts of the Republican Party. Others have been essentially parts of the personal network of senior Republicans: Empower America, The Progress and Freedom Foundation, the Better America Foundation, and the Institute for Policy Innovation associated, respectively, with Jack Kemp, Newt Gingrich, Bob Dole, and Dick Armey. Not all these survived the ambiguities of their role, but all have accelerated the transformation of the world of think-tanks, as did the Democratic Leadership Council's (DLC's) creation of the partisan and factional Progressive Policy Institute (PPI).

Many of these organizations bear impressively neutral names which disguise their main purpose: few emphasize the sources of their budgets. The Foundation for Economic Progress was mainly funded by the American Petroleum Institute, itself the peak association of the oil industry. It has conducted expensive "public education" campaigns via radio and television to oppose higher environmental protection standards. The Civil Justice Reform Group, an alliance of forty or more large corporations, has attempted to weaken regulations governing product liability. There were in the mid-1990s about 105 think-tanks of very different sizes and wealth in Washington. They have had to adapt to a changed media environment as news values have been corrupted by "infotainment." Think-tanks have therefore ceased to expect coverage of their research findings and policy proposals unless they were presented with an eye to color and controversy (see also Chapter 17). Think-tanks have also had to adapt to the changing ideological balance and to the demands of corporate and foundation funders. Some are little more than bespoke policy shops, providing interest groups with studies whose conclusions are ensured before a project is started. John Motley, head of the NFIB, has observed that

> Anytime you get into a lobbying effort you'd like to have some unimpeachable source out there ... [A] study done by somebody you can turn to and say, see, they agree with us. Usually these things are thought up for a specific purpose, they are funded for a specific purpose, and they are used exclusively inside the Beltway. (Center for Public Integrity, 1995)

Modern think-tanks have to compete for funds in a buyers' market: most are essentially right-wing, and most have diminishing independence. Major funding sources include the John M. Olin Foundation, the Lynde and Harry Bradley Foundation, the three foundations created by the Koch family, and the Sarah Scaife Foundation, the flagship of Richard Mellon Scaife's network of funding for conservative causes which has given $200 million to right-wing projects over two decades. The supply of policy proposals comes from groups such as the Institute for Justice, the Heartland Institute, the Individual Rights Project, and many other small institutes. Foundations are also increasingly likely to design and administer their own programs, to enter joint projects with think-tanks, and to impose strict constraints on the latter's authority. As with "membership groups" which depend more on corporate and foundation funding than on their mass membership, the think-tank element in the Washington kaleidoscope is not what it first seems and not what it was a generation ago. Nor is it a net contributor to any real increase in the pluralism of political voices – except, perhaps, to evoke Schattschneider's famous phrase, that they sing with a greater variety of upper-class accents, because the upper classes are seldom of one mind (Schattschneider, 1960).

Trends in Strategy and Tactics

Many of the means by which organized interests operate are familiar enough, and need only brief mention here. They may be broadly categorized as "insider" and "outsider" strategies. The former are the long-established means by which interests seek to gain direct, often personal and discreet, access to policy-makers and their senior staff. In the traditional world of the lobby, personal networks, the capacity to supply policy-makers with reliable information, and a keen knowledge of congressional procedure and the labyrinth of executive agencies remain important. "Outsider" methods developed with the second phase of modern interest politics, as groups such as environmentalists sought to compensate for a lack of established access by mobilizing public support. In the current phase, groups exploit the opportunities offered by technologies which allow, for example, for rapid polling of closely-targeted groups, computerized contact lists for members, donors, or sympathetic allies to be reached by phone, fax, E-mail, or letter, whether in a search for funds or to promote a flood of calls and letters to government offices. Groups make increasing use of television and radio ads in specific campaigns (as with the Health Insurance Association of America's "Harry and Louise" spots, which were then given much free media attention in the early stages of opposition to President Clinton's health care reforms), and in elections as "independent" actors. Not surprisingly, business interests have adapted and extended techniques first developed by public-interest groups, and can devote far more money than their opponents in either traditional or "outsider" lobbying.

Coalitions

There is nothing new about organized interests forming alliances and coalitions. However, the frequency with which substantial coalitions are now constructed, and their ability to manipulate the various possibilities of traditional lobbying, media advertising, election campaign funding by "hard" and "soft" money, and more or less "natural" grass-roots activism, adds up to a significant trend. The reasons lie not only in such tactical opportunities. The growth of coalitions or "superlobbies" partly reflects the greater difficulty of achieving costly policy changes in an era of budgetary limits, and of strong partisan divisions in Congress. It is also a consequence of the sheer weight of numbers of individual actors, particularly in the business sector, in interest politics. According to the *National Journal*'s "Washington Directory," in 1991 there were 288 professional and trade associations in Washington: in 1997 there were 858, while the number of nonbusiness groups has remained nearly constant. Finally, of course, organization begets counter-organization: the creation of a large coalition to fight on one side of an issue is likely to stimulate an opposing coalition.

One example of a large coalition in the 1990s was "Keep America Moving," an alliance of highway users, the auto industry, labor unions, and roadbuilders and contractors. It was constructed to fight for more "road-friendly" allocation of revenues from the federal tax on gasoline under the terms of the Intermodal Surface Transportation Efficiency Act (1991) and was the largest coalition yet assembled on a transport policy issue. It was opposed by the Surface Policy Transportation Project, an alliance of environmental, community, and conservation groups, with links to the mass-transit lobby, the National Conference of Mayors, and the National League of Cities. Other examples exist in most policy areas, and sometimes bring together odd bedfellows – as in the "Stop Corporate Welfare" coalition, constructed in 1997 and consisting of nine groups, including Citizens for a Sound Economy and Friends of the Earth.

Even foreign policy is far from immune. Since the end of the Cold War, policy has been less determined by any single axis of conflict or by giving constant priority to national security issues. The 1980s' trend towards a growing number of "intermestic issues" (combining international and domestic political elements) has continued, with a consequent increase in the number of organized interests seeking to influence policy, often through the formation of ad hoc coalitions. For example, US policy towards China underlined the kaleidoscopic interplay between alliances of economic interests, advocacy organizations, think-tank professionals, ideological activists and the state itself. In 1997 the annual conflict over the renewal of China's status as a "Most Favored Nation" (MFN) in US trade policy was yet more intense than previously, largely because of the involvement of interest coalitions on either side. Opposition to renewal was articulated by alliances of religious conservatives led by the Christian Coalition, the Family Research Council, and other "traditional-values" groups such as the Eagle Forum, in concert with anti-communist ideologies and defenders of Taiwan's sovereignty, combined with human rights groups, labor unions, environmental groups, and foreign policy specialists who distrust China's nuclear policies and strategic intentions. On the other side of the battle was an array of business interests: China is potentially both a vast market, particularly for the aviation, engineering, automobile, tobacco, and agricultural chemicals industries, and a source of cheap labor for American companies. Business efforts were coordinated through the Business Coalition for US–China Trade, which represented more than 1,000 companies and trade associations, and whose steering committee included representatives of about thirty of the largest, including the National Association of Manufacturers, the Business Roundtable, the US Chamber of Commerce, the National Retail Council, Boeing, Motorola, and Rockwell. Given the level of organization and the combination of resources brought to bear, through a mixture of techniques, ranging from conventional lobbying to the creation of local grass-roots networks via local and state Chamber of Commerce chapters, industries, and firms with much to gain from greater access to Chinese markets, it is no surprise that business interests overwhelmed the substantial, but less unified, opposition.

Organized Interests and Campaign Finance

No treatment of trends in the politics of organized interests can avoid mention of changes in the nature of their involvement in election campaign finance. It is, of course, generally true that money buys organization, staff, and technical resources, from phonebanks and databases to computerized mailing lists and opinion polls. It also buys the services of K Street lobbyists, PR firms and "astroturf" specialists. But, most strikingly, organized interests have poured vastly increased funds into election campaigns. It is not easy to prove that money buys votes. The usual claim is that it "merely" buys access – a claim which sounds particularly hollow if one remembers that what is bought must be sold, and that even "selling access" hardly fits the nation's own loudly proclaimed democratic standards.

The general pattern of spending by interest group, labor and corporate PACs in the 1995–96 election cycle was largely familiar, with minor exceptions which may be seeds of future changes. First, even if one discounts the tendency of lobbyists to protest too much, it appears that the traditional picture of interest groups throwing money at candidates needs to be supplemented by that of the major parties pursuing group and corporate donations with more zeal than ever (see Chapter 15). Secondly, the Republican Party in particular was reported as being intolerant of business groups and companies which, in line with modern practice, also gave money to Democratic candidates. Thirdly, there have been signs that the GOP has been tending to use conservative tax-exempt groups as agents for campaign expenditures which undermine their legal status. The Republican National Committee (RNC) gave, for instance, $4.6 million in 1996 to Americans for Tax Reform, to underwrite the group's distribution of a reported 20 million pieces of mail and for numerous phone-canvass calls in 150 House districts.

However, there were also two major changes in the role of organized interests in the 1996 elections. First, they were able to take advantage of the increasingly porous state of FEC regulations, following the 1996 Supreme Court ruling in *Colorado Republican Federal Campaign Committee* v. *Federal Election Commission*, which allowed almost unlimited spending by the political parties on behalf of candidates. This change, combined with the existing capacity for parties to spend on "issue advocacy ads," which carefully avoid explicit demands for the election or defeat of a candidate, transformed the possibilities for "soft" money. Organized interest groups, often under strong pressure from the recipients, donated huge sums to the national House and Senate campaign committees of the two major parties.

The other substantial change in 1996 was the sharp increase in the amounts of money spent by interest groups and corporations running their own issue advocacy adverts. The pattern was in part set by the AFL–CIO's expenditure of $20 million on ads attacking Republican party or incumbent records and positions. If interest groups cannot be shown to have colluded with a party or candidate, and avoid a clear voting recommendation, there are few restrictions on their potential spending. The consumer watchdog group Citizen Action spent some $7 million on ads attacking Republican positions on Medicare, the environment and educational spending. The Sierra Club's PAC contributed $750,000 to candidates, but the organization itself spent approximately $6.5 million on issue ads and voter guides. For example, in the 21st District of Pennsylvania (Gugliotta, 1997) about a dozen groups were running numerous ads:

> the firefight among the interlopers frequently left candidates feeling like bystanders at their own elections . . . if it wasn't the American Hospital Association, it was the AFL–CIO; if it wasn't the liberal Citizen Action it was the conservative Citizens for the Republic Education Fund (CREF). During one 20-hour stretch in early November, more than 500 campaign ads aired on Erie's television stations and on election eve the CREF placed more ads than either candidate.

The Internet

New technologies have transformed the operations of organized interests. Virtually every tactic other than the most traditional insider methods has been affected by the availability of multiple means of telecommunications and fast, cheap computers. The political uses of the Internet in particular are growing at a furious pace, and are seen by some observers as barely the beginning of a transformation in forms of political information, communication and mobilization (Swett, 1995).

The causes of the Internet's growth as a political medium are several, and include the Clinton Administration's enthusiasm (Vice-President Gore's "Information Superhighway"), which stimulated media attention, the rapid creation of sites in federal departments and agencies, and a rapid imitative response from Congress.

The major parties and organized interests were also quick to see the Internet's potential. Numerous conventional membership groups, think-tanks, labor unions, corporate associations, and the numerous national and local fragments of social movements and of the radical press of left and right have all established their presence on the net. The phenomenon is developing too quickly to allow any precise measure of the number of political sites, politically inclined users, represented groups or networks of discussion and attempts at mobilization. However, one recent estimate suggests there are at least 2,000 political sites. Few major groups lack a website, and there already exists a startling range of sites offering links and connections within particular issue areas. Some reflect the efforts of individuals and small groups to collate information and help build networks of interested citizens. Others are highly institutionalized and lavish: the Heritage Foundation, through its Town Hall site, sits at the center of a network of thirty-five conservative groups, publications and policy entrepreneurs. Its neo-liberal counterpoint, the Electronic Policy Network, is maintained by the journal *The American Prospect*. It has thirteen other member organizations and thus not only links visitors to such bodies as the Brookings Institute and the Twentieth Century Fund, but uses the air of legitimacy given by their presence implicitly to assure the visitor of the probity of lesser-known organizations such as the Citizens' Budget Commission and the Center for the Future of Children. Many other groups, particularly in the environmental, consumer, and "good government" areas, maintain sites which combine access to substantial bodies of material with links to related sites, allowing a user quickly to be drawn into a widening network of connections.

It is far from clear if the Internet represents a gain for the democratic process: it has been described variously as an electronic town hall, a junkyard, and the 1990s equivalent of the hula-hoop. Optimists emphasize its innately democratic character and rapidly widening use: pessimists point to the mass of conspiracy-theory nonsense which clogs it up. Certainly there are already many examples of its potential. In 1994 a net-based group contributed to the defeat of House Speaker Thomas Foley: the publication on the Net of leaked tobacco company documents, and the activities of the Smoking Control Advocacy Resource Center Network, have both been important to the growing success of the anti-smoking lobby; the formation of LatinoNet, linking local and national Latino organizations, is seen as a model for other dispersed ethnic groups. The net is said to have several features which suit it well as a democratizing and mobilizing medium. It allows the dissemination of research materials, data, documents, and opinions, and facilitates the formation of communities of values and attitude independently of the commercial mass media. It can connect any permutation of citizens, groups and governing institutions (not least at local level), prompting the claim that "the 'many to many' model is going to eat the 'few to many' model alive" (Swett, 1995). It is a relatively cheap medium for less affluent groups, and gives them the means to raise funds, distribute action alerts, launch E-mail lobbies on government institutions, and strengthen membership participation in group policy-making.

Not everyone is convinced by these sanguine views. It is as yet unclear if use of the net will remain so biased towards the educated, male middle-classes. Even if it does not, critics suggest that technology alone will not induce higher levels of genuine activism; that an already balkanized electorate will become yet more fragmented by the insular character of "Net communities"; that the existing problems of astroturf lobbying and figleaf organizations will be more widespread and harder to detect; and that elected officials will be even more inundated by E-mail stimulated by unreliable and emotive appeals. Ultimately, the debate may be between those who favor a more Jacksonian model of American democracy and those whose distrust of either pure or corrupted populism extends to the fear of an "electronic republic."

Conclusions

The kaleidoscopic interplay of organized interests inevitably affects the functioning of American democracy. It is true that, at least in principle, groups and associations perform useful roles. They represent the values and attitudes of citizens and of constituencies which cut across the geographical boundaries of a diverse society. They provide governments with expert information, with early warning signals of policy conflicts and with personnel for the array of task forces, commissions, and advisory committees. But they do not necessarily do these things well. It is often hard to reconcile democracy and efficiency, advocacy and neutral expertise.

More importantly, perhaps, the system of organized interests has two major damaging effects. Although no single interest exercises monopolistic power in American politics, the system as a whole has a bias towards business while certain groups such as the poor remain under-represented. The system is also highly inefficient. Organized interests often clog the arteries of the body politic. The consequences of this sclerosis are various: stasis, log-rolling, and public disillusion with a political system that is perceived not to deliver.

9

Electoral Politics

Bruce E. Cain and Allison Wegner

American elections in the 1990s have been unkind to conventional wisdom, familiar patterns, and incipient trends. Accustomed to Democratic Congresses and Republican presidents throughout the 1980s, many observers were surprised by the dramatic 1994 congressional election results and the ease with which Clinton was able to recover from his administration's rocky first years to become the first reelected incumbent Democratic president since FDR. Conventional wisdom dictated that the Democrats had a "lock" on Congress (see Chapter 2), because the incumbency advantage and personal vote worked against Republican challengers, but in 1994 the Republicans took control of both congressional houses for the first time since 1952. Supposedly, Republicans had a "lock" on the presidency, because voters preferred fiscally conservative executives to balance off programmatically responsive legislatures, but Bill Clinton not only defeated George Bush for the presidency in 1992, but became only the fourth Democrat in history to win re-election in 1996. So far in the 1990s, the characteristic trends of one election have not carried forward into the next. The "year of the woman" in 1992 became the "year of the angry white male" in 1994, and then the "year of moderation" in 1996. In short, the defining pattern of recent American elections has been abrupt reversals and unexpected shifts.

Yet ironically, the heightened unpredictability of American electoral politics comes at a time when more time, effort, and expertise than ever before have been poured into understanding, monitoring and catering to the perceived interests and whims of American voters. The professionalism of American elections advances with each election cycle. Political campaigns study voters with the latest in poll and focus group technology. They target swing voters with more precision and develop efficient campaign plans that aim to place resources where they will matter the most. Consultants know more about the dynamics of political advertising and the strategy of media buys than they did before. And yet ironically, the more they know, the less predictable and stable the political system as a whole. Despite the formidable amount of science and craft that has been thrown into recent political campaigns, the electoral landscape has become less rather than more predictable. The simple question this essay addresses is "Why?"

Volatility Examined

One theory to explain this electoral volatility is that the process of partisan dealignment in effect since the end of the New Deal era has recently accelerated, creating more voters in the 1990s without stable ties to a party or ideology. These unattached voters would, theoretically, be more easily swayed in their vote choice from election to election, and they thus could be a reason for the inconsistency in recent American elections. This theory of accelerated dealignment is quite attractive for its simplicity; unfortunately the evidence does not support it.

First, partisan identification shows no major shift away from voter–party allegiance during the 1990s. The number of voters who identify as pure political independents – independents who do not lean toward one party or the other – has remained stable at approximately 11 percent of the population since the early 1980s. Adding those people who identify as independents but who lean towards one party or another, the percentage hovers around 35 percent for the same time period (Keith *et al.*, 1992) (see Table 9.1). Within the last ten years, despite the unstable voting pattern, there seems to be no further movement away from the two-party system toward independent or third-party identification.

Second, the level of split-ticket voting – another indicator of dealignment – also appears to have declined. The correlation between a district's vote for its member in the House of Representatives and for president has increased from approximately 72 percent in 1980 to 85 percent in 1996, a level not seen

TABLE 9.1 *Independent party identification, 1952–94*

Date	Pure independent identifiers (%)	Pure independent identifiers *plus* independents who lean towards either party (%)
1952	6	23
1956	9	23
1958	7	19
1960	10	23
1962	8	21
1964	8	23
1966	12	28
1968	11	30
1970	13	31
1972	13	35
1974	15	37
1976	15	37
1978	14	38
1980	13	34
1982	11	30
1984	11	34
1986	12	33
1988	11	36
1990	11	36
1992	12	39
1994	10	35

Note: Cross-section samples only; pre-election surveys in presidential election years.

Source: Keith *et al.*, (1992). Data for 1992 and 1994 provided by Raymond E. Wolfinger, University of California at Berkeley.

since the 1950s. The correlations began rising in 1992 after a twelve-year low in 1990, rising again in 1994 and 1996 (Jacobson, 1997b) (see Figure 9.1). One normally associates unpredictability with the weakening of party ties, but clearly something is different in the 1990s. Voters are adhering to party lines more closely than in the 1980s, but even so, outcomes have shifted and reversed from election to election.

Having failed to find the reasons for electoral volatility in a theory of dealignment, we turn to other long-term political factors for an explanation. Here we are again confounded, however, for

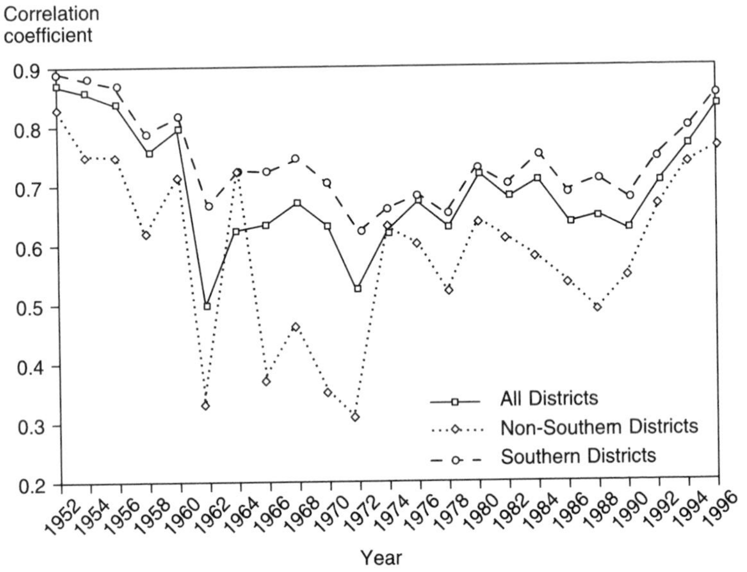

FIGURE 9.1 *Correlations between District Presidential vote and House vote, 1952–96*

Source: Jacobson (1997a), p. 8.

other such factors would actually seem to encourage electoral stability. For instance, one interesting development in the long-term factors shaping American politics is the new geographic balance between the parties. The post-New Deal realignment favoring the Democrats was a national movement, but the Democrats were particularly strong in the South and the cities. Republican power was centralized in New England and the Midwest. During the past forty years, however, this pattern has reversed. Democrats maintain their hold over the cities, but also now include New England and the far West in their stronger areas. Republicans have become much stronger in the South, the mountain West and the plains states. In the 1950s, less than a fifth of House Republican seats came from these regions whereas approximately half of the Democratic seats were won there; in 1996, approximately five-sixths of Republican seats came from those regions while only one third of the Democratic seats did (Jacobson, 1997b) (see Figures 9.2 and 9.3.).

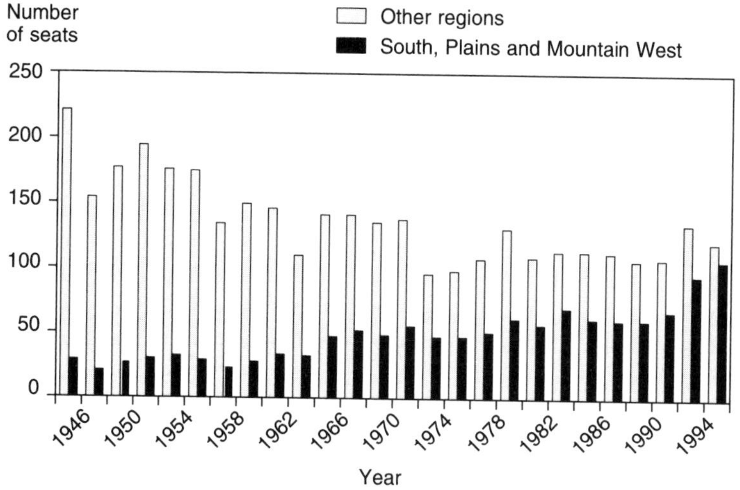

FIGURE 9.2 *Republican strength in the House, by region, 1946–96*
Source: Jacobson (1997a), p. 7.

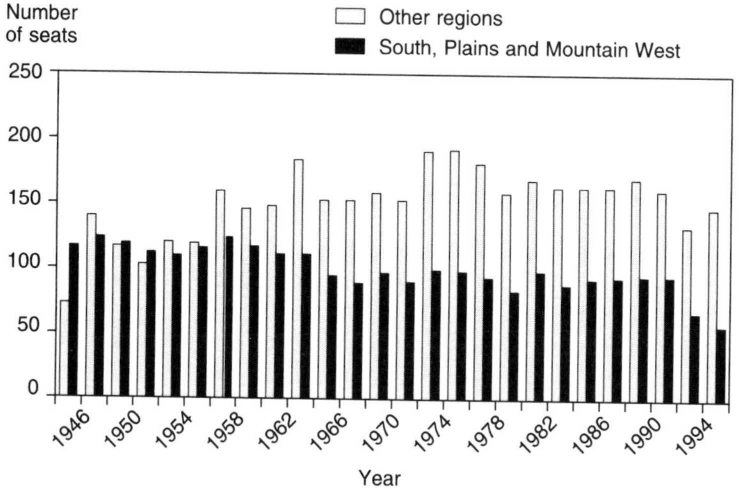

FIGURE 9.3 *Democratic strength in the House, by region, 1946–96*
Source: Jacobson (1997a), p. 7.

The growing Republican strength in these areas is particularly important when one realizes that the South and mountain West are the fastest-growing regions in the country. Between 1990 and 1995, the US national population grew by 5.6 percent. During this same time period, population in the South grew by 7.5 percent and the mountain West grew by 14.5 percent (US Bureau of the Census, 1996; *Congressional Quarterly*, 1993). In 1980, seats from these regions made up 145 of the 435 total House seats. In 1996, there were 164 and the 2000 census is expected to increase these numbers again. In short, we are seeing a significant geographic shift in party support, a shift which, because of regional growth trends, favors the Republicans.

The rise of the Republican Party in the South (the eleven states of the former Confederacy) has been particularly noteworthy and problematic for the Democrats. Beginning with the civil rights reforms of the 1960s, white southern voters began to switch party affiliations, away from their traditional post-Civil-War alliance with the Democrats toward the more conservative, pro-states' rights and anti-government intervention program of the Republicans. Between 1952 and 1982, Republican Party identification among nonblack southerners rose from 14 percent to 32 percent while support for the Democratic Party declined from 81 percent of the nonblack population to 55 percent. The Reagan revolution increased the flight of white southerners from the Democratic Party. Between 1982 and 1984, the percentage of white southerners identifying with the Republican Party jumped five points, to 37 percent; by 1994, fully 50 percent of this population allied themselves with the Republican Party and, for the first time since the Civil War, affiliation with the Democratic Party dropped below a majority to 41 percent of southern nonblacks (Keith *et al.*, 1992; Miller and Shanks, 1996).

For a while, white southerners split their votes – voting Republican for president but protecting conservative Democratic members of Congress who had built up seniority, and thus could protect the interests of the home district. In the 1990s this changed. First, the congressional scandals of the early 1990s – the House Bank check-bouncing scandal and the House Post Office drug and money laundering charges – led many members to retire, causing many seats to open up. In 1992, the Republicans made slight gains in southern seats, but the Democrats held their own in many areas and maintained a majority in Congress by electing sixty-three freshmen members to the House (*Congressional Quarterly Almanac*, 1992). Being first-term members of Congress, these Democrats were still vulnerable two years later when the Republicans launched their Contract With America, a campaign strategy that included not only the party platform, but more importantly a well organized and targeted money and campaign assistance strategy and, even more importantly, top-level candidates recruited in many cases by Newt Gingrich's organization. Although a success nationally, these Republican efforts worked particularly well in the South, where voters had particularly strong responses to the perceived ultra-liberal bungling of Clinton's first two years. Gays-in-the-military, the Lani Guinier and Joycelyn Elders appointment fiascoes, Whitewater, and the health care reform disaster – all these events resonated strongly in the South. By the end of 1994, the Republicans were moving toward solid control of the South, taking a majority of the southern House seats for the first time in US history as well as 59 percent of the southern Senate seats (Ladd, 1995). After the 1996 elections, the Republicans had tightened their grip on the South, with the former Party of Reconstruction holding 71 out of 125 House and 15 out of 22 Senate seats from the South (Leadership Directories, 1997).

As dramatic as the shifts in the South are, the Republican renaissance was actually felt around the country. While sixty-four of the seats won by the Republicans in 1994 were in the South and thirty out of thirty-nine were in the mountain West and plains (Arizona, Colorado, Idaho, Kansas, Montana, Nebraska, Nevada, New Mexico, North Dakota, Oklahoma, South Dakota, Utah and Wyoming), 136 were from other areas in the country. Thus, although the most significant Republican gains have been in the South, the 1994 Republican takeover of the House was in many ways a national revolution.

The foundation for this revolution was really laid during the Reagan years. In 1980, the Democrats were still holding on to their post-New Deal advantage in party identification; when asked, 41 percent of Americans in 1980 said they identified as Democrats while only 23 percent claimed Republican affiliation. If one adds in the voters who claim to be independents but who lean towards one party or another (and who, in their voting behavior, are indistinguishable from partisans), early-1980s' Democrats were still

TABLE 9.2 *Partisan party identification, 1952–94*

Date	Democrat identifiers (%)	Democrat identifiers *plus* independent Democratic leaners (%)	Republican identifiers (%)	Republican identifiers *plus* independent Republican leaners (%)
1952	47	57	28	35
1956	44	60	29	37
1954	49	56	28	33
1960	45	51	30	37
1962	46	53	28	34
1964	52	61	25	31
1966	46	55	25	32
1968	45	55	25	34
1970	44	54	24	32
1972	41	52	23	34
1974	39	52	22	31
1976	40	52	23	33
1978	39	53	21	31
1980	41	52	23	33
1982	44	55	24	32
1984	37	48	27	39
1986	40	50	26	37
1988	36	48	28	41
1990	36	48	28	41
1992	35	49	26	39
1994	33	46	31	43

Note: Cross-section samples only; pre-election surveys in presidential election years.

Source: Keith *et al.* (1992). Data from 1992 and 1994 provided by Raymond E. Wolfinger, University of California at Berkeley.

strong, holding the affiliation of 52 percent of the voters; Republicans lagged with 33 percent. Reagan's leadership changed all this. By 1988, Democrat affiliation (including independent leaners) had dropped to 48 percent of the population; the number of Republicans had increased to 41 percent (Keith *et al.*, 1992) (see Table 9.2). Not only was the geographic balance tilting in the Republicans' favor during the 1980s, but party identification moved towards the GOP as well.

The significance of this shift is greater than the numbers indicate, however, because the groups that make up the Republican voting

TABLE 9.3 *1996 vote compared to population statistics, 1995*

Population Stats/ Characteristics	% v. population in 1995[a] (%)	% 1996 vote[b]	% Dole[b]	% Clinton[b]
White	73	83	46	43
Black	12	10	12	84
Asian	3	1	48	43
Hispanic	10	5	21	72
Married	61*	66	46	44
Family income < $15,000	23**	11	28	59
Family income < $50,000	70**	61	36	52
Family income > $50,000	30**	39	48	44
H.S. graduate or less	52**	30	53	34

Notes:
* 18 or over; all others out of total population.
** 1994 data; all others from 1995 data.
[a] Source: US Bureau of the Census (1996), pp. 19, 25, 54, 160, 461.
[b] Source: *New York Times* (1996), p. 28.

base – white voters, married people, the wealthy and Protestants – are also the groups most likely to vote in a US election (see Table 9.3). The most loyal Democratic voters – minorities, the poor, the uneducated – also have the lowest turn-out scores. In other words, winning should be easier for Republicans who only have to do better among the large voting groups who favor them. Democrats, on the other hand, have to put together a coalition of many small groups (in addition to those groups noted above, Jews, union workers, the very well educated) and must ensure turnout of their loyal voters as well. The slight disadvantage in party identification suffered by the Republicans is more than made up for by the high voter turnout of their most loyal groups (Polsby and Wildawsky, 1996).

Much has been made of the gender gap providing a big advantage to the Democrats electorally because of their purported issue strength among women voters. At first glance, the data supports this reading. In 1996, women supported Clinton over Dole 54 percent to 38 percent. In 1992, women favored Clinton over Bush by seventeen points. But at closer examination, what first

TABLE 9.4 *Gender and the vote, 1992 and 1996*

	1992		1996	
	Bush (%)	Clinton (%)	Dole (%)	Clinton (%)
Men	38	41	44	43
Women	37	45	38	54
White men	40	37	49	38
White women	41	41	43	48

Source: *New York Times* (1996), p. 28.

appears to be a Democratic advantage among women turns out to be a Republican advantage among men. The gender gap is not the result of women moving toward the Democratic Party over the past twenty years, but of men – specifically white men – moving away from the Democrats to the Republicans. The gap now, particularly among whites, is wider when it comes to men. In 1996, the gap between white women who voted for Clinton over white women who voted for Dole was 5 percent; the gap between white men who voted for Dole over Clinton, however, was 11 percent (*New York Times*, 1996) (see Table 9.4).

The evolution of this shift was traced by Warren Miller and Merrill Shanks, who showed that the partisan balance among the genders was defined by a marked shift by men toward the Republicans during the Reagan era. Among nonsouthern men, the partisan balance shifted from two points in favor of the Democrats in 1980 to nine points in favor of the Republicans in 1992. In the South, the switch was even more pronounced, dropping from a twenty-three-point advantage for the Democrats to a one-point advantage for Republicans (Miller and Shanks, 1996).

In addition to the shift in party identification towards the Republicans, there has also been a shift in the ideological leanings of the American public towards the conservative perspective. In 1996, the Gallup Poll organization asked Americans whether they supported or opposed certain policies. The respondents supported the conservative position on fifteen out of twenty issues, and on eleven of those issues – such as supporting the balanced budget amendment, designating English as the official language, term limits and school prayers and opposing racial preference programs, legalization of marijuana and gay marriages – more than two-thirds of the respondents supported the conservative position. The liberal, Democratic position did better on three issues – supporting a ban on assault rifles, raising the minimum wage and opposing social spending cuts; only on the minimum wage, however, was the support overwhelming in the Democrats' favor – 83 percent supported the minimum wage increase (Dougherty *et al.*, 1997).

During the 1996 election, *Washington Post* conducted a similar survey. They compared the policy views of delegates to the Republican and Democratic national conventions with the views of voters, and their results were very similar to those of the Gallup organization. Out of eleven issues tested, Republicans were closer on eight issues, Democrats on three. But perhaps more significantly, the Republicans "won their issues by a landslide, while Democratic wins were far more modest" (Morin, 1996).

In summary, what this tells us is that in the past twenty years there has been no increase in voter dealignment with the two-party system (no increase in independent identification and a slight decrease in split-ticket voting), but there has been a significant shift in the electorate – geographically, psychologically and ideologically – toward the Republican Party. The advantage these factors give the Republicans is not overwhelming – it is not even near the scale of Democratic dominance after Roosevelt's election in 1932 – but it is significant and we should expect it to have effects in American politics. Specifically, we should expect greater Republican dominance in elections. Nationally, we have not seen this dominance emerge but much of American political activity takes place in the states, to which we now turn.

Trends in State Government

The ability of political parties to take advantage of realignments and forge a powerful electoral mandate has always been greatly compromised by certain key features of the US political system. In particular, the length and openness of the general election ballot affords American voters ample opportunities to split their votes across party lines. When enough voters split their tickets (i.e. vote across party lines), it results in divided government. The most common forms of divided government are those in which the legislative and executive branches at the state or federal level are controlled by opposing parties. Throughout most of the 1980s, for instance, the Democrats controlled both houses of Congress while the Republicans won the presidency. However, since 1994, the positions have been reversed, with a Democrat in the presidency and the Republicans holding onto both the Senate and House of Representatives. Periods of unified government at the federal level have been short-lived and not obviously more successful (Mayhew, 1991). The two years that Clinton had to work with a Democratic Congress, for example, resulted in a failed attempt at health care reform, ongoing investigations of his Whitewater investments, a series of unsuccessful confirmations, and ultimately, a voter backlash that resulted in the electoral triumph of Newt Gingrich's Contract With America.

Unified government has also been a less frequent occurrence than divided government at the state level. As Table 9.5 shows, the total number of unified state governments remained constant in the period between 1988 and 1996, but that statistic actually masks some important changes. During the same period, the number of unified Democratic state governments dropped from fourteen to six (in southern and border states such as Arkansas, Mississippi, Louisiana, Tennessee, Virginia and West Virginia) and the number of unified Republican governments increased from four to twelve (especially in the mountain West and plains states such as Arizona, Idaho, Montana, North Dakota and Wyoming). This is consistent with what we said earlier about Republican gains in the 1990s.

As to the pattern of divided governments, the most common alignment is the pre-1992 federal model with a Republican executive and a Democratic legislature. However, as Fiorina (1996) discovered earlier, there are a handful of states where the positions are reversed as happened nationally in 1994. In Alaska, Colorado, Florida, New Hampshire, Oregon and Washington, the Democrats control the governorship and the Republicans the state legislatures.

This blows rather large holes into theories that explain split-ticket voting based on the varying functions of the different offices or on the inertial forces of the incumbency advantage. The former argued

TABLE 9.5 *Divided government at the state level, 1988–96*

	State races			Federal races		
	1988	1992	1996	1988	1992	1996
Total unified	18	21	18	7	12	16
Total split branch[a]	31	26	29	43	38	34
Total split leg[b]	14	13	10	33	36	30
Unified Democrat	14	16	6	2	10	6
Unified Republican	4	5	12	5	2	10
Dem exec.–Rep. leg.	4	5	6	0	0	3
Rep exec.–Dem. leg.	13	8	13	10	2	1
Dem exec.–split leg.	10	8	4	7	22	21
Rep exec.–split leg.	1	3	3	0	0	0
Other	1	3	3	0	0	0
House and Senate delegations controlled by different parties				7	8	8
Equally divided Senate delegation				17	16	17
Equally divided House delegation				5	7	3
Equally divided House and Senate delegation				4	5	2

Notes:
[a] Excludes nonpartisan legislature and independent governors.
[b] Combines Dem. exec.–split leg. and Rep. exec.–split leg.

that voters split their tickets in order to put more conservative officials in executive positions and more liberal representatives in law-making roles. But, if so, how do we explain the reasoning of voters who put liberals in as governors and conservatives in the legislature (e.g. Washington State)? The incumbency and redistricting theory maintained that the seats that Democrats won in the 1970s would be hard to retake because the ability of incumbent Democrats to raise money, draw favorable district lines and cultivate a personal vote with diligent constituency service put Republican challengers at a severe disadvantage. However, aided in some cases by term-limits-induced turnover, the Republicans have tripled the number of state legislatures they control (i.e. from six to eighteen) in the last eight years. This is more evidence of a general shift towards the Republicans.

When parties control different branches of government, it alters the costs of negotiations and the calculus of coalition-building.

Governors need to find support from members of the opposite party in the legislature and legislative leaders must be wary of the gubernatorial veto. But often overlooked in the discussion of divided government is the situation of divided legislatures – i.e. when the houses in a bicameral system are controlled by different parties. At the federal level and in most states, the two legislative houses have different terms of office and district boundaries, and hence it is possible for one party to capture one legislative house and another party the other. The overall frequency of divided legislatures has dropped slightly in the 1990s from fourteen to ten states. Also it appears that whereas there were more Democratic governors dealing with split legislatures in 1988, it became a more common situation for Republican governors in 1996. Like divided-branch situations, dealing with a divided legislature complicates the policy-making process and tempers the electoral mandate.

One last way of looking at the effects of split-ticket voting in the 1990s is to look at the consistency of party voting for federal offices within a state. Looking at which presidential candidate carried the state, which party controls the two US Senate seats and the party split in the state delegation to the House of Representatives, it is interesting to observe the complex and diverse patterns of party voting in federal elections. As we saw with state governments, less than a third of the states exhibit consistent party line results across the three types of federal races. By 1996, only sixteen states were unified in their voting pattern (i.e. the winner of the presidential vote, both US senators and the congressional delegation all belonged to the same party), and this is up from a mere seven in 1988. The gains by the Republicans in this period were largely attributable to an increase of sixteen in the number of House delegations they controlled during this period. Situations in which the presidential vote goes one way and control of the House and Senate delegations goes the other are infrequent, especially in the 1990s. Only four states (Arizona, New Hampshire, North Dakota, and Tennessee) fell into that pattern in 1996. The most typical cases are those in which either or both of the federal legislative delegations are split between the parties in one of various ways. There are states where the House delegation is controlled by one party and the US Senate seats are held by the other; states where either the House or the Senate delegation is split down the middle; and states where both delegations are evenly divided.

The complexity of these patterns reveals the problem of translating electoral advantage into party control at either the state or federal level. Despite fundamental changes in long-term factors which favor the Republicans, American voters continue to pick and choose across party lines, and the cumulative result of this ballot freedom is electoral volatility and a mishmash of party influence at various levels. Republicans saw some gains at the state level in 1994, but it was not enough to fundamentally alter the balance of power in the states.

Republican Gains and Frustrations

But if the evidence is correct and active realigning forces have favored the Republicans in congressional and state legislative races, why did they fail to win the big prize, the presidency, in 1996? Although the economy was strong and Clinton's favorability ratings were high, in 1995 most commentators thought the Democrats would have a tough fight hanging on to the top office. First, there were the geographic, psychological and ideological shifts towards the Republican Party. Second, although Clinton's approval ratings were moderately high, his unfavorable rating was also high – a sign of vulnerability. In January 1995, 56 percent of a Gallup Poll sample held a favorable opinion of Bill Clinton while 42 percent had an unfavorable view. The ratings remained essentially unchanged in January, 1996: 54 percent favorable, 44 percent unfavorable (*Gallup Poll Monthly*, 1996a). Just before the election, 59 percent of the sample had a favorable view while the unfavorable population had dropped to 35 percent (*Gallup Poll Monthly*, 1996c).

Third, the recent geographic shifts had given the Republicans a significant advantage in the Electoral College. In the past five presidential elections (1976–92) there were only ten states which had favored the Democrats a plurality of times, for a solid 100 electoral votes. The remaining states had all favored the Republicans by various margins. An examination of the Electoral College map shows that the critical swing states are in the South. As William G. Mayer wrote in 1994, speculating about the Democratic prospects in 1996: "it is not impossible for a Democratic presidential candidate to concede the South and win the White House – but it is extraordinarily difficult" (Mayer, 1994). And with Republican fortunes riding higher in the South than ever before, it seemed early on that the Democrats were heading for a tough fight.

Which, of course, is not at all what happened. Bob Dole's presidential aspirations were dashed again, for several reasons. First was the quality of the candidate himself. After three Republican primary contests, Dole had proven himself to be an inept national campaigner, unable to cover up his cynical personality with charm and lightness *à la Reagan*. Also unlike Reagan, Dole was never able to overcome the perception that his age was a factor; scenes of Dole stumbling verbally or physically, even falling off stages, did little to help his image.

Second, although the Republicans did much to repair the damaged image of their party following the mean-spirited 1992 convention, ideological disunity in the party still came through. First Dole had to endure a difficult primary season, where Pat Buchanan continued to stir up fears in the American public that the Republican Party had become the party of hatred and extremism, and Steve Forbes, with his flat-tax proposal exempting all trusts and capital gains from taxation, became the symbol for the press wanting to label Republicans as the party of the rich. At the convention in San Diego in July, Dole's team did a nice job keeping most of the battles off the air, putting charismatic Elizabeth Dole on prime time and spotlighting Republican Congresswoman Susan Molinari and her infant as a way of appealing to female voters.

The Republicans could not avoid the abortion issue however. A few weeks before the convention, Dole began publicly toying with the idea of removing the anti-abortion plank from the Republican platform and adopting a more moderate party position on the issue. Almost immediately, he was forced to retreat on the issue by organized opposition in the form of conservative party leaders and Christian coalition and anti-abortion delegates. Having raised the issue however, his retreat was then met by a backlash from moderate Republicans, led by California Governor Pete Wilson, who threatened to bring the abortion issue to the floor for a debate. This protest, too, was shut down, but not after once again highlighting party divisions over the abortion issue.

Finally, what may have hurt Dole just as much as his own errors of judgment was the decision by his fellow party members in Congress to concentrate on holding the House and abandon Dole to his loss (Drew, 1997a). Congressional Republicans had lost certain key battles with Clinton over the preceding two years which threatened to hurt them at the polls. Most significantly, the Republicans had lost the battle of public opinion when they refused to compromise with Clinton on the budget, forcing two separate shut-downs of the federal government. The effect of this strategy was immediately apparent in public opinion polls. In January 1996, 47 percent of a Gallup Poll sample preferred that the Republicans in Congress "have more influence over the direction the nation takes this year" than Clinton, who was preferred by 41 percent. By April, however, 50 percent of the respondents now preferred Clinton and the Republican percentage had dropped to 42. More significantly, the percentage of respondents calling the Republican Congress a "success" dropped from 52 percent in August 1995 to 43 percent in May 1996 while 49 percent called it a failure. Finally, the public was clear about whom they blamed for the stand-off of the previous year; in April 1996, only 46 percent of the respondents felt that Clinton had not cooperated enough with the Republican Congress; fully 66 percent felt that the Republicans had not done enough compromising (*Gallup Poll Monthly*, 1996b).

Thus, in the Spring of 1996, many congressional Republicans were feeling insecure about their own positions. According to Drew, a calculation was made by the congressional leadership that holding the majority in Congress was a more important (and perhaps a more attainable) goal given Dole's performance. So, in order to protect their own jobs, congressional Republicans agreed to give Clinton two big victories in 1996 rather than stall on the legislation and allow Dole to use the issues in the campaign. First, the welfare reform bill, which Clinton was desperate to sign to prove that his claims of moderation were legitimate. Second, a minimum wage increase which, although disliked by conservatives, was so widely popular in the voting public that Republicans felt they had to give in.

Clinton's expert campaign team moved quickly to capitalize on these electoral victories, using them to reinforce their chosen image of Clinton as a moderate (welfare reform) who cares about the working class (minimum wage). More significantly, however, they went on the offensive and initiated warfare over the Republicans' proposed budget cuts which included a cut in the planned increase in Medicare spending. Claiming the Republicans wanted to "cut

Medicare spending," Clinton's campaign aides highlighted the one issue (besides the minimum wage) where they had a majority of the public backing them – defending social spending. Republicans tried to respond that they were not *cutting* Medicare spending, but merely cutting the *increase* in Medicare spending, but this was a distinction without a difference for the majority of voters. Clinton's team was successful at convincing the voters that this election was about whether or not to cut social spending, and that Clinton was necessary to protect the public from the extreme Republicans who would drop the budget axe if left in sole control of Washington.

In sum, the 1996 election can be explained by several factors. First, the economy was healthy, eliminating the most significant risk factor for Clinton's reelection. Second, the Republicans were disorganized, without a message and hindered by a poor-quality candidate. Third, the Clinton team excelled at taking advantage of political factors moving in their favor and defining the campaign on terms advantageous to their candidate. Compare this election to what happened in 1994. That year, the Republicans benefitted from both the long-term forces acting in their favor (shift in party identification, ideological appeal, and their edge in voter turnout) and their ability to expertly exploit the political environment at the time to frame the election in their favor. A favorite campaign tactic of Republican congressional candidates in 1994 was to show a picture of their Democratic opponent morphing into Bill Clinton as a voice-over slowly recounted the ultra-liberal political misjudgments of the past two years: "Gays in the military, government run health care . . . is this the government you want?" The ads read: "Vote Republican."

In 1997, again, the Republicans had both the long-term and short-term forces in their favor. Three major seats were contested that year: the New Jersey governor's race, where Republican incumbent Christine Todd Whitman faced challenger Jim McGreevey, a Democratic state senator; the Virginia governor's race, an open seat contest between Republican former state Attorney General James Gilmore and Democratic Lieutenant Governor Donald S. Bever; and the Staten Island, New York, congressional district where the retirement of moderate Republican Susan Molinari instigated a contest between Republican New York City Councilman Vito J. Fossella and Democratic state representative Eric Vitaliano. Republicans won all three seats, a sweep explained in part by low turnout (which favors Republicans), an ideological advantage in all three races and the strong economy, which favors incumbents and works against change (the previous office holders in both Virginia and Staten Island had been Republicans.) More importantly, however, the Republicans had a huge financial advantage which allowed the party to pour significant resources into all three races; the Republican national party spent $5 million on the three races, the Democrats could only put together $1 million (Greenblatt, 1997). The Republicans used this money to pay for television ads depicting the Democratic candidates as extreme liberals; without money to pay for a similar campaign, the Democrats had no way to respond.

In 1996 and in 1992, however, the Republicans failed to capitalize on their electoral advantages. The Democrats, on the other hand, who were at a disadvantage with the long-term forces, had all the short-term forces in their favor. Economic conditions favored the Democrats both years, and the Clinton campaign teams did an excellent job of manipulating the short-term political forces in their favor as well. In 1992, it was the poor economy and Bush's apparent lack of interest in the anxiety of the voters (as the Clinton team themselves put it: "it's the economy, *stupid.*"). In 1996, the issue was the extreme actions of the Republican Congress and Clinton's crucial role in protecting social spending.

To conclude, the electoral volatility in the 1990s is about the inability of the Republicans to capitalize consistently on their advantage in long-term forces shaping elections. What is clear about the elections of the 1990s is that the victories went to the team who best took advantage of the short-term forces at work in the election. So the next question is: How did this state of affairs come about?

The Quest to Control Short-term Forces

The unpredictability of American electoral politics in the 1990s is deeply ironic in the sense that it coincides with an explosion of campaign professionalism and expertise at all levels. Paid consultants of various sorts – pollsters, fund-raisers, media advisers, etc. – have established permanent roles for themselves in presidential, House and US Senate races. For these races, it is almost inconceivable to think about running for office without polling and targeting first (i.e. identifying voters who should receive particular information, messages or attention). In some states, grass-roots organizing is so professionalized that it is has been nicknamed "artificial turf work." There are consultants for every campaign task, including specialists who work exclusively on making TV and radio buys, opposition researchers who carefully examine a candidate's prior statements and personal life for items that can be used in negative attack ads, and computer experts who identify and make mailing labels based upon voter characteristics such as race, age, gender, and previous voting record. On the margin, campaigns at all levels with better campaign advisers are more successful than those without them. But, marginal advantages in individual races do not seem to add up to a higher level of overall predictability in the system. The more candidates know about and do for voters, the less control they seem to have over the general mood and swing of the electorate. Why?

One possibility is that campaign professionalization is itself the product rather than the cause of greater electoral volatility. To some degree, the unpredictability of the electoral environment leads candidates to grasp for any advantage, however small and expensive, they can get. But campaign professionalism has been on the rise since the 1960s, certainly predating the peculiar patterns of the 1990s. If there is an internal dynamic that causes increasing professionalism, it is usually a sense that one has to keep up with or best the opposition rather than a feeling that voters are harder to understand *per se*.

Perhaps a more important explanation for the ironic correlation between electoral volatility and campaign expertise lies in what campaign management tries to do and what it chooses not to. The consultant's primary goal is to control what we call "short-term forces." There are two main types of short-term forces that vary in the degree to which they can be controlled by campaign management. The first are short term, circumstantial factors such as events or conditions at the time of the election. For instance, there is a great deal of political science evidence that presidential election outcomes are heavily determined by economic conditions at the time of the election. A high growth rate, and low levels of inflation and unemployment favor the incumbent over the challenger (Lewis-

Beck, 1988; Lewis-Beck and Rice, 1992; Markus, 1992). Thus, Dole had very much an uphill battle against Clinton, because economic conditions were generally favorable, whereas Bush in 1992 and Carter in 1980 were not favored by the timing of the economic cycles. Events (e.g. military operations) and scandals near an election can also affect the outcome. For the most part, the short-term circumstances of an election are outside the control of the candidates and their consultants. The consultants can try to "spin" media coverage towards or away from prevailing conditions depending upon whether they work for or against their candidate, but they cannot control the circumstances *per se*. Despite Tufte's suggestion that presidents manipulate business cycles in order to maximize their chances of reelection, the evidence suggests that instruments of economic control are far too coarse and unpredictable to allow for that sort of manipulation (Tufte, 1978).

Hence, the focus of political consulting is not on short-term circumstances, but rather on short-term political factors such as issue positioning and character presentation. Consultants typically distinguish between strategies and tactics. Strategies determine what the messages of campaign will be and to whom the messages are targeted. Tactics are the logistics of a campaign, or how the message is delivered. An example of strategic decision would be the Dole camp's deliberation in the Fall 1996 campaign about whether to make anti-affirmative action a major campaign theme, and their calculations about which voters would be most persuaded by that issue. The Dole campaign decided not to pursue the issue as it was unlikely to bring added value to the campaign. The voters likely to be invigorated by an anti-affirmative action message (e.g. white males) were likely to vote for Dole *anyway*, while other potential voters – women, for example – might be driven away by the message.

Most strategic decisions deal with how to establish a "favorable contrast" between your candidate and the opponent. Sometimes this involves positioning the candidate advantageously on particular issues, and at other times it means making a favorable contrast more salient so that voters not only know about it, but think that it is important. In 1996, Dole was blocked from making a strategic contrast by Clinton's move to the right on most issues. Dole could not highlight many traditionally conservative issues such as welfare reform, the balanced budget amendment, and so on, because Clinton's position on these issues so closely resembled Dole's own. Trying frantically to find a contrast, the Dole campaign came up with a huge tax-cut proposal – a 15 percent reduction in taxes across the board. The effort failed dramatically. Dole himself never seemed fully committed to the plan and he never satisfactorily explained how he would pay for it. The Clinton team, for their part, were overjoyed. Dole's huge tax cut proposal ended up reinforcing the Democrats' message that the Republicans would slash social spending if in control. There was no way Dole could implement his plan, the Democrats argued, without cutting Medicare and Social Security. With his tax-cut plan, Dole succeeded in defining a contrast between the candidates, but it was a contrast that in the voters' minds ended up favoring Clinton, not Dole.

Once campaigns agree upon a strategy and message, they plan the tactical decisions or the "how" of campaigns – i.e. how to get the message to voters most effectively. For instance, an example of a tactical decision would be designing a TV ad that vividly contrasts the positions of two candidates on crime, or figuring out how often and in which media markets to show a TV spot in order to maximize effective exposure.

The goals of political consultants can be characterized as intentionally marginal, efficient, and candidate-specific. They are marginal in the sense that the consultant knows that typically three-quarters of the voters are going to vote in predictable ways and have made up their minds early in the campaign. The focus of the campaign is on the "persuadables," that minority of voters who have not yet made up their minds how to vote. Consultants can make a difference if the number of potential persuadables is greater than the initial margin between the candidates, but their marginal efforts cannot succeed if the underlying support for one candidate is overwhelming.

Their goals are efficient in the sense that their resources are usually limited and hence have to be devoted to the activities that yield the greatest return. In recent years, for instance, many campaigns have concentrated their efforts on frequent voters only (i.e. those who regularly vote in local, state, and national elections), ignoring the occasional and infrequent voters, because the effort at persuasion seems wasted (i.e. inefficient) if the voter does not go to the polls in the end. This is called "diminished universe targeting."

Lastly, their efforts are typically candidate-specific in the sense that most campaigns are run autonomously and have little coordination with other campaigns of their own party. Sometimes, the state party will undertake to register voters state-wide, or clusters of candidates will combine to put out a "slate mailer" (i.e. a piece of mail endorsing a slate of candidates), but for the most part, key strategic and tactical decisions are made independently by the candidate and his or her consultants. Moreover, each candidate is primarily responsible for raising the money and organizing the team that will run the campaign. Any assistance that comes from the party in the form of transfers of funds from other candidates in the same party or "soft" money transfers from the national to the state parties comes after the candidate has demonstrated his or her viability by finding the resources and personnel to start a campaign.

Some commentators describe the 1994 election as an exception to the above rule as the Republican congressional campaign was nationalized to an extent unseen in the modern era. The vast majority of Republican congressional candidates joined in signing Newt Gingrich's "Contract With America," promising to deliver on ten issues-oriented promises if elected. In addition, the candidates were, to a large degree, recruited and coached in their campaigns by Gingrich's organization and the candidates themselves appeared to feel indebted to Gingrich. It is not entirely clear how these efforts to nationalize the election actually played out. Shortly after the election a Gallup poll showed that fully 65 percent of the individuals polled had never heard of the "Contract With America," undercutting Republican claims that the election was an issue mandate (Moore *et al.*, 1994). In any case, by 1996 Republican unity had been undercut as Republican members of Congress sought to distance themselves from Gingrich and from the popular perception that they took extreme positions on the issues (Jacobson, 1997b).

The candidate-specificity of modern elections is particularly important in understanding the ironic correlation between volatility and campaign professionalism. The goal of the consultant, and more generally the campaign effort, is not to build a stable base, but to exploit the instability of the swing voter for a candidate's electoral benefit. The intentionally marginal focus concentrates efforts away from loyal base votes toward independents and weak partisans. The norm of efficiency dictates against investing in voters at the periphery of political participation in order to avoid wasteful efforts. And the candidate-specific focus creates a collective action problem in which individual candidates do not find it worthwhile to undertake long-term investments to build up the party base, and candidates satisfice with divvying up the diminished universe of frequent voters.

The other pieces of the puzzle are the structural factors that contribute in the US system to chronic under-investment in long-term political and base-building activities. Just as there are two forms of short-term forces, there are long-term circumstantial and political forces as well. Political scientists have long recognized the importance of events and structural features that determine long-standing political interests and cleavages. These include realigning events (e.g. civil wars, economic depression, etc.), structural changes in the economic (e.g. declines in blue-collar employment and the rise of the service sector) or social systems (e.g. the propensity to join groups), and technological innovations affecting communication and the dissemination of information (e.g. new forms of media, the web, etc). Long-term forces of this sort can alter the overall nature of political alignments in the United States. For instance, the migration of northerners into the South in pursuit of jobs has played an important role in ending the domination of the Democratic Party in southern states (Rohde, 1991; Polsby, 1983; Polsby and Wildavsky, 1996). To an even greater degree than short-term circumstantial forces, long-term factors of this nature are not manageable by candidates or their consultants.

But the last category in our fourfold distinction, long-range political activities, is the distinctively neglected part of American politics. These are the strategies and activities that build party ties and memberships, that disseminate ideological perspectives tying together positions on a variety of particular issues, and that foster organizational links between extra-political groups and elected officials. None of these things is likely to win over swing voters needed to win a close election, nor are they actions that any one candidate would have the resources or incentive to undertake on his or her own. But if they are successful, they create the basis for stable coalition-building among groups in the electorate which, in turn, diminishes the volatility of electoral results.

To a certain extent, the under-investment in such activities in American politics is a chronic feature, relating to the oft-discussed weakness of American political parties. Stronger parties tend to make greater efforts at recruitment and to take programmatic and educative responsibilities more seriously. Currently, efforts of these sort are ad hoc and subsumed by short-run electoral demands. A good example of this is party registration efforts. In the US system, voter registration requirements are set by the states, and most states require registration well in advance of the actual election date. A pure party-building strategy would register potential voters wherever they might be found, or in areas of greatest concentration and potential loyalty. When registration is subsumed in the short-run consideration of winning a given race, more effort will be put in areas that are electorally marginal than in safe areas, since registering additional voters in safe areas has little likelihood of affecting the end result. Again, the norms of efficiency and effectiveness dictate that even potentially long-term activities like voter recruitment be subordinated to the need to marshal scarce resources in the most electorally influential manner.

US political parties have undergone something of a revival in recent years, but in a curious way, as instruments of short-run electoral management, rather than forces that build and maintain a base. The proliferation of "soft" money transfers in the 1996 election from the national to the state parties was made possible by a ruling of the FEC that these funds could be exempted from the limitations of the campaign finance law (FECA) that governs presidential elections, because they would be used for party-building as opposed to campaigning. In fact, Clinton and Dole used the "soft" money transfers as the primary means for getting around the inadequate expenditure limits that federal law placed upon them. What were called "party-building activities" were in fact merely extensions of the presidential campaigns.

The tendency to under-invest systematically in building the base of stable coalitions can be traced to a number of factors. A more precise way to talk about the weakness of American political parties is to say that, compared to other political systems, they are more dominated by the elected officials than by activists and constituency parties. Perhaps uniquely in the US system, there is a wide gulf between the party as elected officials and the party as constituency, leaving the party as elected officials virtually unchecked by the party as constituency and free to do what it has to to be electorally competitive. Since elected officials tend to have more invested in being electorally responsive than activists, this gives the system a more short-run, politically opportunistic cast.

But in addition, other features of the US system weaken the incentive to invest in stable coalition-building. For instance, the complex overlay of American federalism – with independently elected offices at the state, local and federal levels – raises the coordination costs and makes it harder for groups to forge a common agenda. The fact that states have a great deal of power with respect to electoral organization gives state parties enormous leverage to resist the centralizing efforts of the national party organizations. US demography also makes long-term coalition-building harder. The high mobility of the population, both within and across states, makes it hard to keep people registered and to form the strong neighborhood organizations that characterize other political systems.

In sum, the proliferation of campaign professionalism not only does not dampen but quite possibly exacerbates the underlying instability of political coalitions in the United States. The ever-increasing amounts of money and professional expertise are devoted to the short-term force management, not long-term base-building. Stability, to the degree it is achieved, is incumbent and race-specific. A particular elected official might build a personal base to survive better transient trends, but the collective and long-term activity of developing stable coalitions is largely neglected. If and when it occurs, it is the unintended byproduct of trying to win one or a number of individual races. Of course, it is always possible that as yet unforeseen long-term circumstantial forces – a realigning event, the ultimate effects of dramatic demographic change – might over-ride the effects and short-term focus of modern campaign management. Until then, the irony of greater professionalism and greater electoral uncertainty is likely to persist.

PART THREE

PUBLIC POLICY

10

Economic Policy

B. Guy Peters

By early 1998, the economy of the United States was performing at a level that surpassed the expectations of even the most optimistic analysts. High levels of economic growth, the lowest level of unemployment for over two decades, a dollar stable or even increasing in value compared to other major currencies, the stock market reaching numerous record highs, and an inflation rate near zero combined for one of the best economic pictures in years (see Table 10.1). The only dark spot in this otherwise agreeable economic picture was the continuing problem of a huge balance of payments deficit. President Clinton ran for office in 1992 using the phrase "Its the economy, *stupid*" to guide the campaign, and in 1998 he was presiding over one of the best periods of economic performance in recent memory. This successful position was solidified by the negotiation of a balanced budget and tax reform

TABLE 10.1 *Economic growth*[a] *of the United States and other industrialized democracies, 1970–79 to 1996*

	1970–79	1980–89	1990	1991	1992	1993	1994	1995	1996
United States	1.7	1.6	0.2	−1.5	1.4	2.3	3.1	1.8	2.1
Japan	2.6	3.4	4.5	3.9	0.8	−0.5	0.3	0.8	2.8
Germany	2.7	1.9	2.3	2.0	1.4	−1.9	2.6	1.7	1.0
France	2.1	1.4	1.6	0.0	0.5	−2.2	1.9	2.6	0.4
United Kingdom	1.7	2.2	0.2	−2.6	−0.9	1.9	3.5	2.2	1.8
European Union countries	1.6	1.2	2.2	0.2	0.6	−0.2	1.0	2.4	1.5
Total OECD	2.0	1.8	1.5	0.0	0.8	0.5	2.1	1.7	2.0

Note:
[a] Annual rate of growth of *per capita* GDP

agreement between the president and the Republicans in Congress, an agreement that may help institutionalize this positive economic performance.

The Challenges of Economic Policy

The government of the United States, like that of other countries, now bears a major political responsibility for the economic performance of the country. Ever since the Full Employment Act of 1946 the federal government has declared that it is responsible for managing the economy in a way that will produce "full employment." At that time faith in Keynesian economics provided a technology that would permit government to intervene effectively and efficiently to manage the economy. Even when faith in Keynesian economics waned, monetarism and supply-side economics were believed to be methods that could make the economy behave in ways that would benefit the public (as well as the politicians responsible for economic policies).

The contemporary treatment of economic policy in the United States is somewhat paradoxical and asymmetrical. On the one hand, political leaders reflect an increasingly dominant ideology that influences both parties. This view is that government cannot effectively manage the economy, and when it tries too hard to do so it generally reduces real economic performance. On the other hand, there has been a pervasive belief that the federal deficit that had been used (often successfully) to influence the economy through Keynesian demand management has more recently become the central economic and political problem in the country. The current climate of ideas is that government actions are capable of undermining the economy but there is little or nothing that government can do that will assist the economy.

The public assessment of American economic performance is in some ways even more paradoxical. As will be demonstrated later, the economy of the United States has been performing well. That statement is true when recent achievements are compared with the performance of the American economy during the 1970s and 1980s. It is also true when American economic performance in the 1990s is compared with that of most other major industrialized nations.

Despite that relatively strong performance, the American public continues to be somewhat negative and uncertain about the economy. There are some obvious reasons for their concerns, but apparently little justification for the extreme skepticism that many Americans have been expressing about their economic future.

There is yet another paradoxical element of the economic behavior of American citizens. Although public opinion polls show that the public remains skeptical and anxious about the future of the economy, their behavior appears quite the opposite. Millions of small investors have been clamoring to put their money into the stock market; over 60 million Americans now own stocks privately and over 125 million own stock through investment funds. In some ways this increased level of personal investment may represent popular anxiety about the future of employer-provided retirement programs, as well as of the Social Security program; but it also represents some real faith in the future of the economy. On the one hand, this spate of investment helps to address the long-term problem of inadequate savings in the American economy; on the other, it places the economic future of a very large number of citizens at risk if there is a significant downturn in what has been a booming Wall Street. This is all the more true if these citizens have little or no other savings if they lose some or all of their investments in the equities market.

The Goals of Economic Policy

The basic goals and instruments of economic policy in the United States are little different from those of other countries. There are five basic goals, although it may well be difficult for a country to achieve all five simultaneously. The most fundamental goal is economic growth. Almost everyone in the society is happier if there is an increasing total aggregation of goods and services available to them; and international league tables, as well as increased foreign travel, permit citizens to know how their economic fortunes compare to those of citizens in other countries. The goal of economic growth is closely associated with a second goal of increasing real wages for citizens, especially for the average worker in the economy.

Economic growth also helps to achieve a third economic policy goal – low rates of unemployment. Governments at all levels are now assessed by how many jobs they "create" – President Clinton argued in his 1996 campaign that some 20+ million jobs had been created during his time in office. Senator Dole had to concede that the jobs were there but argued that many of these jobs were minimum wage, "hamburger-flipping" jobs that were not capable of supporting the individual worker, much less a family. Total unemployment is important, but the rates of joblessness for certain key groups in society – minorities and youth – may be equally important politically. Even historically low unemployment rates are now in rapid decline.

Low rates of unemployment are often perceived to threaten another important economic goal – stable prices or, phrased differently, low rates of inflation. The connection between these two economic variables is now less direct than it once was and emphasis has shifted from the "Phillips Curve" to the "Wage Curve" (Roberts, 1995; Blanchflower and Oswald, 1994). Nevertheless, policy-makers still hesitate to direct too much attention to reducing unemployment for fear of "overheating" the economy and raising inflation. In the United States, the Federal Reserve Board, and especially its chairman, Alan Greenspan, has been especially concerned about the potential for inflation when the economy is performing as well as it is in the late 1990s. Inflation creates economic uncertainty and it especially hurts people such as retirees who must live on fixed incomes. On the other hand, inflation can benefit debtors since their debts decline in real terms year after year. As the biggest debtor in the United States, the federal government can benefit from inflation more than any other institution or individual.

Finally, governments also seek to have a positive balance of payments from international trade. In other words, governments would like their economies to earn as much or more overseas than is spent. Continuing negative balance of payments tend to erode the value of the currency and put a country in debt to foreign interests. These international factors are in some ways especially important for the United States given that the dollar is a major international reserve currency. For this reason, preserving the value of the dollar is important for maintaining international confidence in American economic management. On the other hand, the domestic American economy is so large that it is less influenced by international trade than most other industrialized countries.

We should also point out that these economic policy goals must be assessed in conjunction with social policy goals and programs. The growth of the economy has been purchased with increasing income inequality and the loss of benefits from both public and private programs. On the other hand, the expanding economy makes changes in social policy like "workfare" more feasible than they might have been at the opening of the decade; there now appear to be jobs for former welfare recipients. Further, economic growth is now more linked with education and training than in the past, so these policy areas must be brought together. Finally, the linkage between the budget deficit, basic entitlement programs like Social Security, and the success of the American economy continues to be a central issue in American politics.

The Instruments of Economic Policy

Governments have a number of instruments at their disposal to help attain their multiple economic policy goals. The consensus that once characterized the use of policy instruments has now been shattered and governments now utilize a variety of "tools." None of these instruments is new, but the mixture of approaches and the uncertainty about how to approach economic policy have made economic management something more of an adventure than it was when there was the certainty associated with Keynesianism. Indeed, some critics attributed the success of Clinton's economic policy to the lack of interference in the functioning of a domestic economy that appears well suited to the increasingly globalized economy surrounding it (Weatherford and McDonnell, 1997).

One central element of economic policy is fiscal policy – the central element of Keynesian economic management (Hall, 1988). The fundamental idea is that effective demand in the economy can be managed by using the public budget to put more or less money in the hands of the public. If there is a deficit people have more money, spend more and stimulate the economy (reducing unemployment but possibly fueling inflation), while government surpluses would reduce demand and deflate the economy. One major problem is that public spending is more popular than taxes, so that "one-eyed Keynesianism" (Rose and Peters, 1978) and high deficits have been the norm for almost all governments, including those of the United States. During the Reagan Administration, "supply-side economics" (Roberts, 1984) was the alternative version of fiscal policy to Keynesianism. Rather than manipulate demand, supply-side economics argued that the better approach was to create a greater supply of goods and services by lowering taxes, especially on the upper-income earners, so that there would be higher levels of investment. Although ideologically popular at the time, the major consequence appears to have been a massive increase in the public deficit.

The major alternative to fiscal policy is monetary policy. The argument supporting this approach to economic policy is that rather than manipulating the public deficit, a more effective approach is to vary the supply of money in the economy through manipulating interest rates and other details of the banking system. Again, if there is more money around the public finds it easier to spend, interest rates may go down, borrowing for investments goes up and there should be more economic growth, albeit with possible inflation. Likewise, if the money supply is constrained, the economy will grow more slowly but inflation should be controlled. Also, monetary policy in the United States has the additional virtue of being controlled by a largely autonomous Federal Reserve Bank that is more resistant to political pressures than are the budgetary policy-makers responsible for fiscal policy (Woolley, 1986).

Governments also use regulatory policy extensively to control their economies. Rather than influencing the overall performance of the economy directly this instrument tends to target particular industries (public utilities), to control certain types of behavior (anti-trust laws, exploitation of labor), protect consumers from fraud and/or unsafe products (Peters, 1997b). These policies may direct economic activities in certain directions, or protect citizens from monopolies, or simply provide a climate that is conducive to economic expansion. In some cases, however, regulation may go too far in pursuing those goals. Indeed, for the past several decades governments have been more concerned with deregulation than with regulation, and some of the relative success of the American economy has been attributed to the absence of controls over the labor market (but see Reich, 1991). The one exception to that trend has been the slight increase in the minimum wage (from $4.25 in

1995 to $4.75 in 1996 and then $5.15 in 1997), the effects of which are rapidly being superseded by the increasing demand for labor since many "hamburger-flipping" jobs now earn well over the minimum wage.

Governments also use a number of other powers to promote economic growth and development. As the international economy has become more important for the American economy, government can, and must, utilize its power to intervene in that economy in a variety of ways. These powers include acting as an advocate in a number of international fora such as the World Trade Organization (WTO) and the General Agreement on Tariffs and Trade (GATT) and supporting international trade directly through the Export–Import Bank. At the national level there are a variety of programs to support business through loans, subsidies, insurance, and a variety of other policy instruments. Even the power to "jawbone," or persuade, can often be a powerful economic policy weapon, given that so much in economic policy depends upon the confidence of consumers and trading partners.

Finally, we should remember that in the United States the federal government is not the only public actor of importance for economic policy. The states have a great deal of autonomy to make their own budgetary decisions, so that even if the federal government attempts to manage the economy through its budget those efforts may be thwarted by subnational governments. State governments also play a major role in promoting economic growth within their own borders and in regulating industries that have an impact on their citizens. Even local governments have substantial autonomy in budgeting, regulation and economic promotion, including having trade representatives in foreign countries. The tax incentives offered by subnational governments often help businesses, but the multiple and often competing regulations can be harmful to those same industries.

In summary, governments have a number of instruments through which to affect the economy. There is not a consensus about the relative importance of these instruments or how each of these instruments should be used. Despite this lack of consensus, the American government continues to be involved in the economy and even to be successful in doing so. The economy and the public household also continue to be central issues in the politics of the United States.

The Public Household

The nature of the public household continues to be a central concern in American politics. There is a long tradition of concern about taxing and spending (Hughes, 1991). This tradition is to some degree reflected in America's relatively low levels of both taxation and public spending when compared with most other industrialized democracies. There is also a long tradition of concern about the public deficit and commitment to balanced budgets is almost theological among the American public and many politicians (Savage, 1988). State and local governments perform much better on this criterion than does the federal government, partly because of provisions in almost all state constitutions that outlaw deficits.

Allegedly, the size of the deficit (a maximum of $290 billion in 1992) presents a number of problems for the American economy and society. Conservatives argue that the debt slows economic growth by public borrowing "crowding out" private investment opportunities. It is also argued that it places the American economy at risk of excessive influence by foreign interests who may hold the debt. Liberals also argue that the debt and the interest on the debt (over 14 percent of federal spending in 1996) prevent government from undertaking needed social and economic development programs. For almost all sides in the economic debate, the debt represents the failure of government to make difficult choices and serves as a tax on generations to come.

Tax policy is another major political issue about the public household. American politicians at all levels have been falling over each other attempting to be more anti-tax than their opponents. This opposition to taxation is phrased in terms of letting the individual retain as much as possible of his or her earnings to support a family, in terms of promoting greater economic growth, and in terms of an ideological opposition to "big government." This anti-tax sentiment appears to be shared by most citizens so that it remains good politics (if not necessarily good government).

As well as the general opposition to taxation, there are several specific issues about tax policy that have been on the political agenda in the mid-1990s. One of the most persistent is the repeal of the capital gains tax. Citizens are taxed (at a maximum level of 28 percent) on the profits they may receive from the sale of a capital asset, whether real property, stocks and bonds, or whatever.

Although the rate of taxation is lower than for ordinary income, many conservatives believe that this is still a disincentive to saving and investing. More liberal politicians, on the other hand, argue that there is already a tax break for this form of income, and that the benefits for repealing the tax would accrue almost entirely to the wealthiest 5 percent of the population.

The one type of tax that does appear acceptable to the American population in the late 1990s is excise taxation of products such as alcohol and tobacco – so-called "sin taxes." Especially after the major tobacco companies have virtually admitted the harm produced by smoking there has been a flood of legislation at the state level attempting to impose much higher taxes on cigarettes and other tobacco products. The only problem for the states is that these taxes have produced significant amounts of revenue in the past so that if they attempt to tax tobacco off the market they will have to find other, less popular ways to raise revenue.

Emerging Issues in the Economy

In large part because of the increased impact of the international economy on the American domestic economy, a number of new economic policy issues are arising. In reality these issues have been around for decades, but they are now being conceptualized more as being "economic" or as having important economic elements. One of the most important of these is training and education. Since the 1950s Americans have wondered "Why Johnnie Can't Read," but the nature of the emerging economy makes educational issues more than just questions about personal growth and capacity. If the emerging international economy is to be a knowledge-based economy, especially for wealthy, high-wage countries such as the United States, then education and job training become central to national prosperity. For this reason, among others, the Clinton Administration launched a number of major education initiatives shortly after being reelected (see Chapter 13).

The other old, but new, issue is income inequality. Incomes are unequal in all capitalist (and noncapitalist) systems but the level of inequality has been increasing in the American economy. The rich have been getting richer rapidly, while the poor and even the lower middle classes have been losing ground (see Lawrence, 1997). Part of the cause of this change is the influence of the international economy and the loss of many manufacturing jobs to lower-wage countries. Moreover, the manufacturing jobs that have remained in the United States have been faced with increased competition and pressures for lowering wages and especially nonwage costs such as health insurance. Families have been maintaining their incomes by working longer hours and both partners working, a pattern which has created greater pressures on the structure of families. The public sector in the United States is not expected to play the role in creating equality that is expected in Europe, but the rapid increase in inequality is beginning to raise questions about the management of the economy.

Associated with the above issue of equality is the more general question of the structure of employment in the United States. The idea that an individual would work at one full-time job and receive an adequate income for a family is becoming a thing of the past except in some managerial and professional occupations. Even in those jobs there is a greater chance of being laid off than in the past, often during what would be the peak earning years, because a firm has wanted to reduce costs to make itself more competitive in the international market. Americans never had the job security that has been characteristic of the Japanese economy but there was some sense of commitment by firms to their employees that most analysts now argue has been lost. There is also an increasing reliance on part-time employment, one of the major issues in the 1997 strike by the Teamsters Union against United Parcel that has to some extent redefined labor management issues in the United States. In short, the average American employee is now more threatened and more exposed to competition than at any time in memory.

The Basic Paradox: Doing Better and Feeling Worse

The American economy is performing far from perfectly at the turn of the twentieth century. There is a large and persistent balance of payments problem, and there is still a large (by historical standards) public debt. There is also growing inequality. Despite those problems there is a strong record of achievement to note as well. There have been twenty-one quarters of uninterrupted economic growth – the best record for the past several decades. There is also a relatively low, and decreasing, rate of unemployment and yet inflation has remained low. Despite that strong performance, the economy is still a great concern for most Americans and many do not believe that the economy is performing well. Why are Americans, in economic terms, "Doing Better and Feeling Worse"?

Macro-Performance

We should substantiate our argument that the economy of the United States has been performing reasonably well during the years of the Clinton Administration, and to some extent even before that time. The slogan "It's the economy, *stupid*" played a significant role in the 1992 Democratic campaign, but even during much of the Bush Administration the economy was not performing badly by international or historical standards.

The American economy has been growing regularly, and it has been growing without significant inflation. Tables 10.2–10.4 clearly demonstrate the positive performance of the economy. Growth rates in the 1990s compare favorably with all but a few periods of the postwar years, including those of the so-called "Reagan boom" to which campaigning Republicans tend to hark back. When compared with the recent performance of other industrialized democracies that performance appears equally positive (see Table 10.1). The American economy has grown somewhat faster than major economic competitors such as Germany and France, and almost as rapidly as Japan. That growth rate can be seen reflected in unemployment figures which, in April 1997, were better than at any time since December 1973. The performance on inflation is also very good, by historical as well as comparative standards. When their incomes are compared using purchasing power, Americans are almost the richest people in the world.

They may be rich, but many Americans do not *feel* rich, and anxiety about the economy persists. At an individual level there is a great deal of uncertainty about employment and the levels of wages that employees can expect. For example, in a poll in September 1997, 70 percent of Americans responded that they felt less secure in their jobs than in the past, and almost 60 percent said they had to work harder to earn a decent income.

TABLE 10.2 *Unemployment rates, 1980–96*

	1980	1985	1990	1991	1992	1993	1994	1995	1996
United States	7.2	7.2	5.6	6.8	7.5	6.9	6.1	5.6	5.4
Japan	2.0	2.6	2.1	2.1	2.2	2.5	2.9	3.2	3.3
Germany	3.2	8.0	6.2	6.7	7.7	8.9	9.6	9.4	10.3
France	6.2	10.2	8.9	9.4	10.4	11.7	12.3	11.7	12.4
United Kingdom	5.3	7.2	5.8	8.2	9.9	10.2	9.2	8.2	7.6
European Union	5.6	10.2	7.9	8.5	9.6	11.1	11.6	11.2	11.4
Total OECD	5.6	7.7	6.0	6.8	7.5	8.2	8.1	7.8	7.8

Source: *OECD Economic Outlook* (monthly).

TABLE 10.3 *Inflation rates*[a]*, 1980–96*

	1980	1985	1990	1991	1992	1993	1994	1995	1996
United States	10.9	3.7	5.1	4.2	3.3	2.6	2.4	2.4	2.1
Japan	7.5	2.3	2.6	2.5	1.9	0.7	−0.5	0.0	
Germany	5.8	1.8	2.7	3.7	4.7	4.0	2.9	1.9	1.7
France	13.3	5.8	2.8	3.2	2.4	2.2	2.1	1.6	1.8
United Kingdom	16.2	5.3	5.5	7.5	5.0	3.4	2.5	2.6	2.6
European Union[b]	11.0	4.2	4.4	4.3	3.4	2.8	2.3	2.1	1.9
Total OECD									

Source: *OECD Economic Outlook* (monthly).

Note:
[a] Annual percentage changes in consumer prices.
[b] Excluding countries with chronically high inflation, mostly recent entrants into the OECD.

TABLE 10.4 *The public deficit as a percentage of GDP, 1985–95*

	1985	1990	1991	1992	1993	1994	1995
United States	4.1	3.6	4.5	5.4	4.4	3.5	3.1
Japan	0.8	−2.9	−3.0	−1.5	1.9	2.1	1.9
Germany	1.2	2.1	3.4	2.3	3.1	2.0	3.2
France	2.9	1.6	2.2	4.0	6.1	6.0	6.3
United Kingdom	2.8	1.5	2.6	6.3	7.8	6.8	5.1
European Union	4.7	3.6	4.3	5.1	6.4	5.6	5.7
Total OECD	3.9	2.5	3.2	4.2	4.8	5.5	6.1

The early 1990s were a period of immense downsizing of companies in the United States with large employers laying off thousands of people. Unlike the layoffs when steel and other large manufacturing industries were downsizing, many of the job reductions in the 1990s have been white-collar workers, including a large number of middle-management positions. Moreover, although there have been a large number of jobs created, many of these have been low-paying jobs in service industry. The image of "hamburger flipping" as the only jobs being created has been greatly over-stated for political reasons; many Americans nevertheless do believe that they are under-employed if not unemployed. Many people who lost jobs in the 1990s have been forced to accept jobs that pay only a fraction of what they had been earning previously. The downsizing also feeds into social policy issues, since many people losing jobs also lose benefits – most importantly health insurance.

The changing nature of employment in the American economy contributes to the insecurity Americans feel about the economy. As well as trading manufacturing jobs for service industry jobs, there is a shift toward part-time employment. As previously noted, the flexibility that this pattern of employment creates in the labor market is considered to be one component of the success of the economy in the 1990s. Although it may be beneficial for the economy as a whole, this mode of employment is not so beneficial for the part-time employees. Not only are there less security and generally lower wages in part-time jobs, but there are usually few if any benefits so that part-time employees must pay for their own health care and look after other needs that employers might otherwise provide for them.

The fears of personal insecurity are heightened somewhat by changes in social policy and the pressure to get welfare recipients into paying jobs. Many employees at the lower end of the job market believe that they will potentially lose out to these new workers almost desperate to find work. This insecurity is compounded by resentments over some of the benefits that people on "workfare" will receive, at least in the short run. Those benefits include, perhaps most importantly, subsidies for child care and for transportation. Many of the working poor feel that they are once again being treated shabbily while those who have been, or who still are, on social assistance receive undeserved benefits.

As well as personal unease, there is also anxiety about the national economy. The most important element is the competitiveness of the American economy in an increasingly global economy. As already noted, the United States continues to run a large balance of payments deficit. This deficit is largely with the countries of Asia, and is in both low-level manufactured and semi-finished goods (textiles, shoes, etc.) and in high value added products such as automobiles and consumer electronics. The dominant question is whether the American economy can continue to be competitive in the international market-place or whether there will be a slow but perceptible decline in the economic place of the United States.

Associated with the above fear is whether the United States is becoming just a nation of service industries with high levels of unemployment in "dead-end" jobs or whether there is a more viable future in actually producing goods. In the first place some of that fear may be misplaced, given that although the number of jobs in manufacturing has been declining the value added by manufacturing actually has been increasing. Further, although service employment has been increasing not all service jobs are in fast-food restaurants as is sometimes assumed. Services like insurance, computers, and banking are actually important competitive industries for the United States.

If there is confusion about the relative success or failure of economic performance and economic policy in the United States, the discussion of the state of the public household appears beset with overt myth-making and/or conscious deception. The average American has come to believe that he or she is paying abnormally high taxes and that the American public deficit in the 1990s is of monumental proportions. These issues have been central in contemporary political discussion; they were a major part of the 1996 presidential campaign. The consequent crusade to lower taxes and the deficit is placing severe restraints on the capacity of government to meet its obligations to the public in a number of policy areas.

The first point to be made about the mythologies abounding in this area is that Americans do not pay very high taxes, either in historical or cross-national perspective. To the extent that there is still big government in the United States, it is at the state and local level rather than in Washington. Indeed, among all the developed democracies only two – Japan and Australia – have lower rates of total taxation as a percentage of GDP The developed democracies in Europe average almost 41 percent of GDP taken as tax, while for the United States taxation takes only 27.6 percent. It is difficult to justify the common perception that Americans are burdened by excessive taxation. Yet that perception is an important political reality.

Similarly, the public deficit, while seemingly immense when described in absolute figures (it was about $100 billion in 1997), is actually not particularly large when seen as a percentage of GDP The current deficit is not close to the size of that of the Reagan and Bush years when compared to available economic resources, and the level of total federal debt also has begun to decline as a percentage of GDP. Also, compared to many other developed countries the public sector deficit has not been particularly large (Table 10.4). Most European countries have been reducing their deficits in order to meet the Maastricht criteria for joining the European Monetary Union (EMU), but even without that spur the American deficit has been coming down consistently and is lower than that of many other countries.

Despite the reality of deficit, deficit reduction has played a major part in politics. In late 1996 Congress passed a piece of legislation permitting the president to veto parts of spending bills coming to him from Congress, rather than having to veto the entire bill. Governors of the majority of the American states have this "line-item veto," and are meant to use it to eliminate wasteful spending proposals – especially "pork-barrel" proposals benefitting one or another constituency. The president has never had this power before, and the fact that Congress was willing to give up some of its fiscal powers is a strong indication of the general concern about the deficit. President Clinton vetoed several items contained in the 1998 budget agreement with Congress and the line-item veto looks set to become an important weapon available to the executive.

It is not, however clear that the line-item veto will have all the positive effects assumed by its sponsors. The principal problem is that the veto provision may encourage congressmen to place pieces of "pork" into spending bills, or put special exemptions into tax bills. The legislators can introduce those provisions knowing that even if they are removed by the president they can still claim political credit for having proposed them. Even if the president has the fortitude to remove all the provisions – Bill Clinton did remove a number of both taxing and spending items from the 1998 agreement and then thirty-nine projects in a Defense Appropriations Act – the fiscal culture of employing the budget for political gain will be reinforced rather than weakened.

With or without the line-item veto, a vigorous debate was waged between President Clinton and Congress over the fiscal 1998 budget. Both sides had pledged their strong intention to reduce the deficit significantly, although they tended to disagree about what the policy priorities were for the federal government. In addition, the congressional Republicans were having difficulty reaching agreement among themselves on whether the more important goal was reducing the budget or reducing taxes. The conflicts were resolved in a package that seemed to provide all sides with something. The president was able to have some of his policy priorities funded, while the Republicans extracted some tax concessions and some budget cuts. All sides proclaimed they would produce a balanced budget by 2002. The strength of the economy in 1997 meant that the budget was close to being balanced already, and there was already a discussion of what to do with the possible budget surplus – reduce taxes, pay off some part of the federal debt or, less likely, expand programs (*New York Times*, October 27, 1997).

Any budget deal is, however, only between the president and the congressional leadership and therefore may not survive once the Appropriations Committees and their subcommittees begin to work out the details. Further, even if the budget is balanced by the year 2002, there remain crucial underlying problems which are driving public expenditure, especially the continuing aging of the American population and the massive expenditures for entitlements such as Social Security and Medicare. Until those issues are addressed, or higher taxes are accepted by the public, there is little hope for a continued balancing of federal accounts.

Concern about balancing the budget and proposals for reforming the process go well beyond the line-item veto and any one year's political negotiations. A balanced budget amendment was one element of the Republicans' 1994 Contract With America, and that provision came close to passing during the past several Congresses. Should the proposal ever pass Congress, the states are virtually standing in line to ratify the amendment. A majority of Americans also appear to support the balanced budget amendment, most using the analogy of the need to balance an individual's budget to justify the need to balance the national budget. The assumption that most citizens make is that the national debt is a drag on the economy and on their economic future, and that it must be eliminated.

If passed, the balanced budget amendment would prohibit Congress and the president passing a budget with a deficit. The only way to overcome that constraint would be for an extraordinary majority of Congress to declare that a financial emergency existed. The advocates of the amendment argue that enshrining the measure in the Constitution is the only effective means of preventing politics as usual from leading to budget deficit after deficit. The political advantages of spending money, and the political costs of taxation, are sufficiently high that ordinary legislation, e.g. Gramm–Rudman–Hollings and the Balanced Budget Act of 1991 have been ineffective in eliminating the deficit (see Kettl, 1992). Thus, the advocates of the amendment argue that only by passing a strong "formula" for the budget is there any hope of adopting a more responsible fiscal policy (Hanuschek, 1987).

The critics of the balanced budget amendment view the issues quite differently. They argue that this amendment is unnecessary and once in operation it would only tend to increase the (already immense) cynicism of the American public about politics and politicians. In the first place, they assert that a balanced budget could be passed any time there is the political will to do so. The same conflicts over spending priorities, and the political difficulties in raising adequate revenue, will remain after the passage of the amendment and there is no reason to expect any greater ease in resolving the conflicts. The amendment might help force some decision-making, but it could not resolve the inherent political conflicts.

If there is the formal need to pass a balanced budget, it is argued by the critics, the budget that is adopted is likely to be balanced on paper, but not balanced in practice. This deception is often the case for budgets in the states that have balanced budget provisions in their constitutions. The budget figures could be based on faulty assumptions and erroneous data but so long as they balance on paper the document meets the formal criterion. If the public sees "balanced" budgets being passed year after year but each of them actually producing more deficits, then the conventional belief that government is incompetent and/or corrupt will only be reinforced.

In addition to the political problems associated with a firm legal restriction of the capacity to run deficits, a balanced budget might also present fiscal and economic problems. We have already maintained that faith in Keynesian management of the economy through the public deficit has waned, but it has not died totally. Hence, eschewing the instrument of the unbalanced budget could weaken the capacity of government to control the economy, and perhaps also its capacity to respond to future needs of the population (e.g. natural disasters, or economic recession). Critics of the balanced budget amendment further argue that the analogy with state governments' budget restrictions is fundamentally flawed, given that state governments do not have the responsibility for macroeconomic management of the federal government.

Finally, critics of the balanced budget amendment suggest that it should be considered only if the federal government modernizes its budget system and separates capital and current expenditures. The figures commonly used to represent the budget deficit do not provide an adequate picture of what portion of the deficit is appropriate investment in capital projects, and what portion represents spending on current programs that might well be restrained within an operational budget constraint, especially during good economic times. Even if the popular analogy of the private household is used, it is reasonable for the average citizen to differentiate borrowing to buy a house, or even an automobile, from credit card debt for expensive meals in restaurants. One is a reasonable use of borrowing while the other is more questionable. Indeed, with the declining budget deficit in 1997 the operating budget was apparently in surplus.

Conclusions

The American economy performed extremely well during most of the Clinton Administration. Whether this was because of, or in spite of, Clinton's economic policies is difficult to determine. The good performance might be thought to represent good economic management, given that the increasing globalization of the economy should have had a negative impact on the US economy. It appears that the combination of a flexible labor market, the growth of small high-tech firms, and continued deregulation have all produced positive economic outcomes.

Despite the good economic news there are also continuing concerns, some of which are directly economic whilst others reflect the impact of the economy on society. The American economy is supporting a heavy debt burden, both public and private. The savings rate of the economy is also extremely low compared to other developed economies, despite growth of personal investments. Real wages had been declining for almost a decade until the end of 1996 when they registered a slight increase; workers thus had their buying power eroded. American earnings in the international market do not equal US spending overseas so that there is a continuing drain of resources overseas. Finally, there has been increasing economic and social inequality. It is clear that any American president has little time to rest on any laurels he may receive but must get on with the fundamental task of making the economy perform for the benefit of all Americans.

11

Social Policy

Dilys M. Hill

Clinton, though elected on a minority 43 percent of the popular vote, promised major domestic policy legislation on gaining office. The twin goals of health and welfare reform were to fulfil campaign promises but also to distance the Democrats from the "tax and spend" label. In the event, the promotion of health care reform, and its failure, had important consequences for the strategy for welfare reform. In campaigning for office, Clinton had made health care an important plank of his Democratic heritage, a new "New Deal" whereby a national health insurance program completed what was essentially the agenda of the Roosevelt and Johnson years – a liberal inheritance. But Clinton was the New Democrat, seeking the votes of Middle America after twelve years of Republicans in the White House. Promising to "end welfare as we know it," candidate Clinton had stressed education and job training, support for low-income families through the Earned Income Tax Credit, stricter enforcement of parental obligations for child support, and changes to the Aid to Families with Dependent Children (AFDC), which would promote entry into the workforce and child care for recipients.

However, health and welfare reform both failed in 1994. And, in August 1996, Clinton signed, with reluctance, a Republican welfare bill, the Personal Responsibility and Work Opportunity Reconciliation Act. Critics attacked this move on the grounds that it ended the sixty-years entitlement program of the New Deal, reneged on federal responsibility for the needy, turned power over to states with widely varying records on welfare aid, and threatened a harsh future for the poor. The focus of this chapter, then, is on the health and welfare reform projects which were the dominant themes of the incoming Clinton Administration's social policy. The early 1990s, however, offered a severely constrained arena for dramatic changes in social policy, particularly if additional expenditures were sought.

The Policy Climate

America is a "reluctant welfare state" (Janssen, 1993). Poverty levels are high, income disparities are wide, and wages for the working poor have stagnated since the early 1970s. There is no universal health insurance, but a complex of industry, private, state, and federal programs that cover the employed, the elderly, and the poor. Similarly, benefits to the needy and indigent include entitlement (Medicare, the health program for the elderly) and means-tested (Medicaid, for the poor) benefits, federal and state programs, and wide variations in benefits. The United States differs from other countries, particularly European ones, in that it does not provide direct income transfers (family benefits or child allowances) to all or almost all families with children. The main welfare program, AFDC, is means-tested, eligibility is restricted and assistance levels are low. Childless adults who have exhausted unemployment benefits receive no aid beyond General Assistance which is a state-level program providing very meager income support. The welfare system came under further strain during the Reagan Administration, which reduced domestic spending across a wide range of social programs (AFDC, child care, nutrition programs, food stamps, housing, energy assistance, family planning, public and mental health services, alcohol and drug abuse counseling, and legal aid).

The constraints on social policy arise from the inter-related ideological and economic factors of the Reagan and Bush years. The attacks on Keynesianism and New Right arguments to reduce state power questioned the role and effectiveness of federal social programs. In the 1980s, "supply-side economics", with its emphasis on tax cuts and deregulation, at a time when defense expenditures were expanding, produced escalating budget deficits. Any proposals for new or greatly expanded domestic programs fared badly in this economic environment. These trends continued after Reagan left office. In 1990 President Bush agreed to tax increases in return for preserving a high defense budget, but the agreement laid down that any reductions in defense spending could not be used to increase social spending. The legacy of the 1980s has been, however, not only financial constraints but an important emphasis on federal devolution to state and local governments. Though President Reagan's "New Federalism" was not fully realized, the use of block grants, combined with deregulation, has effectively cut and controlled expenditures on federal programs. These constraints and the use of block grants were pressed forcibly as a means of dealing with social issues following the Republican victory in the congressional elections of November 1994.

Of equal importance in the development of social policy has been the discourse on values. The New Right thinking of the 1980s stressed the need to reduce the role of government and increase individual responsibility. In the 1990s, the emphasis on family and community – and on communitarianism by scholars of both right and left – has reinforced the moral context of policy. The view of welfare dependency as evidence of moral turpitude has grown over the past two decades, moving from a New Right stance to one which dominates the mainstream agenda. Debate on social policy is essentially one on how to deal with the problems of the inner cities and the supposedly defective work ethic of poor people, favoring behavioral and culture-of-poverty explanations (Mead, 1986, 1992). Speaker Newt Gingrich's publication *To Renew America* (1995), for its part, called for the abandonment of the welfare state and its replacement with the opportunity society and volunteerism.

There is also a less palatable strand to these value arguments. Dealing with the supposedly defective work ethic of the indigent, and reasserting the American values of family and individual responsibility has, it is asserted, been permeated with racial connotations. Though the majority of poor people are white, problems of inner-city poverty are problems of black, Hispanic and other ethnic minorities. The "feminization" of poverty has similarly highlighted the numbers of black families headed by lone parents, usually women, who are in receipt of welfare benefits, and has singled out for attention the numbers of teenage, never-married mothers. All too easily, ethnic minorities become the target of the strictures on dependency, taking on the mantle of the "undeserving poor" of nineteenth-century values.

The academic and political debate on big government, supply-side economics, budget deficits, individual responsibility, and "dependency" have shaped the agenda of social policy. An incoming Democratic president in the early 1990s faced uneasy maneuvering within these limitations. In welfare, the "New Democrat" president, campaigning for radical reform, finally accepted a Republican plan. At the same time, he claimed that the bill reflected his own objective of limiting welfare aid while promising to mitigate its worst features in his second term. But the factors which limited welfare reform, and drove it down the path favored by the Republicans, appeared far less burdensome in the case of health policy. The reasons for the awesome failure of Clinton's health reforms lie not in value arguments or congressional Republican triumphalism, but in organizational and leadership weaknesses.

Health Care Insurance for All

The demands for change

In the early 1990s, the prospects for a new health care policy to give universal coverage looked favorable. A Democratic president, with a Democratic Congress, was riding a tide of demand for reform. Rising costs meant that health care spending accounted for 14 percent of GDP and would reach 19 percent by the year 2000. At the same time, 38 million people, 17 percent of the population, were without health coverage and an estimated further 50 million people had major gaps in their benefits. Health outcomes vary widely by socioeconomic status and ethnicity: white Americans have infant mortality rates comparable to those elsewhere in the developed world, but rates for black Americans are similar to third world levels.

Opinion polls showed that 90 percent of the population thought that the system was in crisis, while the American Medical Association, the trade unions, and the American Chamber of Commerce initially favored the Clinton reform proposals. A majority of the public backed change which included a significant government role, support which extended to those who already had adequate medical coverage. This momentum was dissipated by

President Clinton's failure to mobilize support in his early days in office – in Congress, among powerful interest groups and from the wider public. Organizational problems exacerbated, but did not cause, these difficulties. Political commitments, however, did set limitations. To disavow the "tax and spend" label of old-style Democrats, Clinton rejected both the financing of health care through new payroll or income taxes, and the delivery of health services through new or expanded government programs. This effectively ruled out single-payer proposals on the Canadian model whereby one health insurer (which could be state or federal governments) collects contributions and pays providers. Additionally, Hillary Clinton's fears of the health insurance industry's bitter opposition to the single-payer model eliminated it from the agenda (Marmor, 1994).

The groundwork of the plan

The President moved quickly on the health reform project, appointing his wife to lead a task force to produce the plan. Chaired by the First Lady, the task force was made up of six Cabinet secretaries and a number of White House advisors, including Ira Magaziner as its Executive Director. But the detailed work was carried out by a separate, unwieldy structure of working groups with over 500 members drawn from congressional staffs, federal agencies, and experts from around the country. A core of close advisors worked out the key elements of the plan which were then tested-out on the working groups and wider audiences. The document as presented by Clinton to Congress ran to 1,364 pages. The charge that an air of secrecy surrounded the work of the task force is questioned by Fallows (1995), who reports favorably on Magaziner's statements that it met with members of Congress and their staffs and was "the biggest outreach effort ever in laying the groundwork for a bill." It remains the case, however, that the task force did not contain any representatives of organized outside medical, pharmaceutical, or insurance interests, and neither President Clinton nor his close aides worked with congressional leaders in establishing the prior parameters of legislation.

The final plan was an amalgamation of related objectives: government regulation with employer-based insurance to finance it; universal coverage and standardized benefits but through the "managed competition" of market forces; and state-level administration and regulation. The details of coverage were complex. Essentially, individuals would be enrolled into new health care alliances, made up of regional groupings of doctors, hospitals, and other providers. These alliances would offer enrollees a variety of health plans to choose from, and would bargain with health insurers to obtain the best deal for their members. This process was termed "managed competition" and would, it was argued, drive down costs as insurers competed to offer the best health insurance plans. At the same time a new National Health Board would be established to set quality standards and supervise costs.

States would have new powers and responsibilities, including the power to choose between a single-payer or managed-competition system. The states would set up the health alliances, which would be quasi-governmental bodies coordinating the health care system for consumers in a region. A regional health alliance could be set up as a private nonprofit corporation or as a state agency. Most doctors would have to join health care networks with hospitals and other providers to be part of a health plan and have access to patients. Consumers would primarily be full-time and part-time employees of businesses of fewer than 5,000 workers, the self-employed, and the working and non-working poor whose health care would be subsidized by the government. Large businesses with over 5,000 employees would have the option to buy their health insurance outside the plan, but would pay an additional 1 percent tax for opting out.

The implications for the federal health programs, Medicare and Medicaid, varied. The entitlement program, Medicare, would remain largely unchanged, but the price would rise steeply for wealthier beneficiaries and the rate of growth of the system would be sharply reduced with most of the cuts to be borne by doctors and hospitals. Medicaid, the means-tested program for the poor, faced greater uncertainties, given its links with the main welfare benefit AFDC As well as AFDC beneficiaries, Medicaid includes the aged, blind, and disabled on Supplemental Security Income, low-income pregnant women and children. States may also choose to provide Medicaid coverage for the "medically needy," and some thirty-one states and the District of Columbia do so. Unlike Medicare, all the Medicaid provisions would be subsumed in the new health alliance system.

Challenges to change

Health care for the poor is a difficult area. Medicaid is a state-administered program that operates under federal guidelines. It is jointly financed by federal and state governments, with the federal government paying from 50 to 80 percent of the funding. States have considerable discretion over eligibility and the amount of services. Expenditure has been growing rapidly in recent years and both the federal and state governments have been trying to curtail costs. Recent legislation has required states to increase Medicaid coverage; the 1988 Family Support Act, for example, laid down that people who lost their AFDC eligibility on moving into employment should be guaranteed six months of Medicaid coverage for themselves and their families, with no premium requirements. More limited coverage would be provided for a further six months.

In spite of the rapid growth of Medicaid expenditures for adults and children in low-income families, the program in fact spends far more on care for the elderly and disabled. In 1990 although almost 70 percent of Medicaid users were low-income families, they received only slightly more than a quarter of Medicaid payments. This is because the average payment per user for the former was less than one-sixth of that for the elderly and disabled (primarily for long-term care). Thus this is an area where two value judgments clash: the elderly and disabled are far more likely to be viewed as the "deserving" poor, in contrast to those assumptions that Medicaid goes to the (less deserving) households headed by lone (and minority group) parents.

Cost savings in Medicare and Medicaid were crucial to the main plan. The Clinton proposal envisaged that the new health care system would be funded primarily through a 75 cent increase in the federal cigarette tax (bringing the tax to 99 cents in total), intended to raise $65 billion; the 1 percent levy on large corporations that set up their own health plans, worth $24 billion; and savings in Medicaid and Medicare of some $189 billion. As debate progressed these funding figures looked increasingly uncertain, with potential federal costs rising steeply.

In September 1993 President Clinton announced his plan to a joint session of Congress, saying that reforming the "costliest and most wasteful system on the face of the earth" was the most urgent task facing the country. In the following week, Hillary Clinton testified to five congressional committees, gaining wide admiration for her analytical and presentational skills. But opposition to the task force process, and criticism of her policy role in the White House, made the First Lady a focus of attack. The bill was introduced in Congress in October 1993 as the Health Security Bill. Clinton faced difficulties in that there were only fifty-seven Democrats in the Senate, not all of whom were firm supporters. Thus to avoid a successful filibuster against the bill, the support of some 10–15 Republican senators was needed. Fears were aroused when, in January 1994, Clinton returned to the health care theme in his State of the Union Address. To his original pledge of guaranteeing health insurance for all, the President added that he was not prepared to compromise, threatening to veto any legislation passed by Congress that did not fulfill that pledge. These ominous words reflected the difficulties that the plan had already encountered. These included the mobilization of opposition, particularly among the small business community and sections of the health insurance industry, and the number of alternative bills being launched in Congress.

From opposition to defeat

The long-drawn-out process of producing a health plan, far from mobilizing public opinion around a consensus, resulted in an intense politicization of the issue. Health insurers, large and small business, trade unions, health providers and user groups were caught up in extensive debate, including the use of sustained television advertising. The most contentious television attacks came in the famous "Harry and Louise" advertisements which played on middle-class fears that existing coverage was insecure, supported by segments of the health insurance industry (though the five largest companies and the Blue Cross/Blue Shield not-for-profit organizations disassociated themselves from it). These were important factors, given that 80 percent of Americans who did have health care coverage, held as a prime value the choice of a personal physician, and feared the apparent prospect of increasing bureaucracy and the implied rationing of cost control. The Clinton reforms would have affected nearly one-fifth of the economy and resulted in a major expansion of federal intervention – a "big government" solution which the public rejected.

In Congress, a variety of bills were circulating. Some were variants on Clinton's bill (HR 3600, S 1757), while others included a single-payer plan, based on the Canadian system by which government collected premiums and paid the health care providers. Others expanded Medicare to include the poor and uninsured or promised universal access to health insurance rather than universal health coverage. Yet another version avoided an employer mandate but required those employers who purchased insurance to do so through regional health insurance cooperatives, and gave subsidies to poor families. There were four main types of arguments in Congress on health care changes. The first surrounded the so-called "employer mandates" – by which employers would pay 80 percent of the health insurance for their employees, while workers themselves would pay the other 20 percent of the premiums. The second set of arguments centered on the federal government's regulation through a National Health Board. The third concerned the compulsion on individuals to enroll in the regional health alliances, while the final argument arose from the opposition to the increased cigarette tax.

The proliferation of bills reflected not just differing party, ideological or interest positions, though the divisions between the right and left of the Democratic Party produced major difficulties for the White House. It was the working of the congressional committee system, where some eight panels had jurisdiction over health care matters, which significantly increased friction. Among the major committees involved in the House were: Ways and Means and its Health Subcommittee, the Labor Management Relations Subcommittee of the Education and Labor Committee, and the Energy and Commerce Committee. In the Senate, while Labor and Human Resources favored a regulatory approach, Finance supported more market-led solutions. Daniel Patrick Moynihan, (D-N.Y.) chair of the Senate Finance Committee, was cautious on health care reform (saying that although there were problems, there was no "crisis"), while Edward Kennedy (D-Mass.) sponsored a bill close to Clinton's own.

Health legislation revealed the ultimate workings of the long-remarked fragmentation of the federal policy process. Divided government – even when, as for the first two years of Clinton's presidency the Democrats controlled the White House and both houses of Congress – was a factor. But that it was not the dominant issue was highlighted by the ability of Clinton to secure passage of his crime control legislation which banned certain types of guns, together with social legislation which aimed to tackle the root causes of crime. It was the internal divisions within Congress which were the formidable obstacles. These conflicts were fuelled, both inside and outside Congress, by the power of the health care lobby. In March 1994, Clinton denounced the $30 million lobbying campaign mounted by the health insurance industry and other interest groups, but by then control had passed from his hands.

The turmoil inside Congress was increased by several difficulties. The first and perhaps most important was the failure of political leadership from the White House, allied to the unwieldy and secretive nature of the task force process. Commentators are agreed that the fatal error was to present Congress with a finished plan of great complexity. A simpler approach, based on well-prepared working between president, task force and leading congressional committee chairs, might have had greater chance of success. A second difficulty surrounding White House–congressional relations arose from the way the health care reform process was allowed to drag out into the summer of 1994 – a year of congressional elections when individual legislators were concerned with reelection problems. In addition, the Spring and Summer of 1994 saw rumors and announced retirements from Congress, with key House members considering bids for Senate seats and governorships in the November elections. Acknowledgement that the process was failing came with Senator Majority Leader George Mitchell's willingness to stand down from consideration for a Supreme Court nomination in order to remain in Congress to steer the health reform process. Moynihan (1995a) has suggested that the legislation was doomed from February 7, 1994, the day that a White House meeting decided not to attempt a bipartisan approach. But the Democratic votes were not there either: failure was complete in the summer of 1994 when the White House abandoned health care reform, with no bill being considered or voted upon in Congress.

Though the loss of health care reform was a personal and institutional failure for the presidency in 1994, the debate has not ended. In 1996 Congress passed the Kennedy–Kassebaum bill, the Health Insurance Reform Act, which provided portability of health insurance protection for workers losing or changing jobs (see also Chapter 3). Individual states are experimenting with reform schemes, including Hawaii with its comprehensive medical care for all citizens, and Pennsylvania where health care is available for all children in the state. Waivers of federal requirements have also enabled states to develop managed care programs for Medicaid recipients. The health care industry is also stressing change. The industry favors "managed" care which restricts choice of physician and doctors lose some controls over treatment, an extension of the Health Maintenance Organizations (HMOs) systems in which the five largest insurers, and Blue Cross/Blue Shield, already have a major involvement.

The failure of the policy process in health care reform in 1993–4 did not augur well for the other major Clinton campaign commitment, the radical restructuring of welfare.

Welfare, Work and Dependency

The American approach to welfare

American responses to the problem of poverty have been fragmented, ad hoc and targeted programs rather than comprehensive policy. The New Deal established protection for the "deserving poor" through universal social security based on entitlement principles. But the most vulnerable received means-tested programs. Images of the poor, especially the black poor, were those of a class apart, a position reinforced rather than eliminated by the "War on Poverty" programs of the Johnson years.

Targeted welfare programs have reinforced those divisions in social policy between programs for the broad middle class and those for the poor. These divisions have been manifested in a welfare backlash over the past two decades and ultimately in those "tough love" policies from both the Republican and Democratic parties in the 1992 presidential campaign. Such reactions appear exaggerated given the tiny proportion of the federal budget represented by welfare aid: some 7 percent of the federal budget is spent on income security programs for the poor, with the combined cost of all welfare programs totalling $107 billion in federal funding and $17.5 billion from the states. Overall, this amounts to some 10 percent of the combined federal, state and local expenditures (United States GAO, 1995).

The "retreat from caring" reflects a pessimism about the intractability of poverty and the failure of welfare programs (Lawson and Wilson, 1995). The backlash was also reinforced by the issue of "welfare cheats." Welfare mothers lack education and skills and thus have low participation rates in the workforce. Some 47 percent of people on welfare have less than a high school education, and nearly 40 percent lack work experience. Welfare benefits, even in the more generous states, are at subsistence level or worse. In constant dollars the average AFDC monthly payment per family has dropped from almost $600 in 1975 to $374 in 1994. As a result, many women are resorting to unreported work or dangerous sources of income such as prostitution or drugs, further undermining the political acceptability of welfare aid. At the same time, in spite of research evidence to the contrary, policy-makers as well as the public assume that the poor lack a work ethic, and that welfare promotes family breakdown and fosters irresponsible child-bearing among young unmarried women.

Undoubtedly, in the United States as in other advanced societies, family structures have changed markedly over the past three decades. One-parent families have increased in number from some 6 percent to around 30 percent, with similar increases in births to unmarried mothers. In 1993, more than one-quarter of all children under the age of eighteen lived with a single parent; for Hispanic children the rate rose to one-third and for black children to more than one-half, trends which are still rising (Peskin, 1995). Attributing these situations to the availability of state support is simplistic (Ellwood, 1993). Nevertheless, the welfare stigma remains; thus welfare must be reformed, however intractable the problem of poverty appears. Moreover, it must stress the obligations not the rights of citizenship and thus require work in return for welfare benefits.

"Workfare" has a number of meanings, but generally incorporates requirements to enroll on education, training, job-search schemes, and community work to quality for benefits. Its stress on citizen obligations as opposed to rights is now widely accepted on both sides of the Atlantic. But the requirement that women with children should work is a long way from the original objectives of the Aid to Dependent Children, as the program was originally called, instituted by Title IV of the Social Security Act 1935. That aid provided cash benefits for needy widows to care for their children at home. In the early 1960s the emphasis was still on services rather than on work, a position which eroded under the rising costs of welfare. By 1967, with the introduction of the Work Incentives (WIN) program, AFDC recipients with no preschool children were required to register for training and employment services, but the results were disappointing. This argument is well documented by Bane and Ellwood, Harvard scholars who served in the first Clinton Administration (Bane and Ellwood, 1994); both resigned following Clinton's signing of the 1996 bill, disappointed at its harsh provisions.

By the mid-1980s workfare had become widely accepted, as working mothers were now part of the normal family and employment structure, and hostility grew to what were seen – often erroneously – as irresponsible lone mothers opting to stay on welfare over long periods. The result was a change in political perspectives that culminated in the 1988 Family Support Act. Even at this stage, the legislation combined some of the social service approaches of the 1960s with more stringent work requirements. These requirements were also paralleled by the extension of child care and medical benefits, for up to a year, to families leaving the welfare rolls for jobs. The outcome was disappointing as work targets in the legislation were hit by the onset of recession and by the costs of the Job Opportunities and Basic Skills (JOBS). program. Critics have also argued that some forms of workfare are designed to force poor minorities into entry-level, poorly paid and casual jobs in the service industries.

Wider structural forces are also evident. The United States is subject, like other western states, to the impact of global economic restructuring. This has undermined the ability of nation states to withstand international capital and labor market forces and maintain welfare economies. Nation states are moving to decentralize and devolve responsibilities to local levels, private agencies, and voluntary sectors. Collective action for citizens with rights gives way to individual responsibilities of citizens with obligations. This is reinforced in the United States where attacking poverty has never been the same as attacking dependency: America has always favored the latter over the former as the prime social policy goal.

Attacking poverty or attacking the poor?

These assumptions underpinned not just the Democratic and Republican 1992 presidential campaigns but the 1988 welfare reform legislation, the Family Support Act. Since 1988, with the passage of the Act, welfare to work has become the main objective of the welfare program. The Act required states to run a JOBS program. But it has had only limited success, with only about 9 percent of some 5 million adults now receiving AFDC being in work. It has been the black poor who have been disproportionately affected by these developments: while the economic restructuring of the 1980s had had widespread effects, it was the inner-city black poor, increasingly concentrated in segregated ghettos with severe housing, education and employment problems, and beset by crime and drug street-cultures, who were most vulnerable.

In the legislative attempts of the 1994–96 period to reform welfare, the congressional Republicans reversed the assumptions of the debate on the role of welfare in helping families out of poverty: instead of helping children, AFDC was said to harm them. In August 1995 both the Republican majority and the Democratic minority in Congress introduced bills which threatened to abolish AFDC. The Democrats' attempt to add more child care, child nutrition and foster care were, in Senator Moynihan's words, "Literally arranging flowers on the coffin of the provision for children in the [1935] Social Security Act" (Moynihan, 1995b). But the problem has been compounded by the fact that, in deference to the priority given to health care reform, the Clinton Administration had not presented a plan until June 1994, far too late for the 103rd Congress to consider, and thereafter prone to defeat in the Republican-dominated 104th Congress.

Clinton's welfare plan, in the spirit of the times, proposed changing the one federal income support program for the nonelderly, AFDC, into a work-based system. This approach exemplifies the general feeling of despair in American society at the seemingly intractable problem of black poverty: by the end of the 1980s 48 percent of the black poor had incomes below half the official poverty level. By the early 1990s the value of AFDC support was only about half its value a generation earlier, but neither the White House nor Congress showed much willingness to increase it. Candidate Clinton had already promised to limit the receipt of welfare to a two-year period. In office, the Democratic Administration took the view that, in spite of the 1988 reforms, welfare was still a prime policy issue. Following the increase in earned-income tax credit for poor working families in 1993, Clinton emphasized his determination that this was the key to change: "rewarding work over welfare, making it possible for people to be successful workers and successful parents. Now that's real welfare reform" (State of the Union Address, 1994).

The Clinton plan

In his State of the Union Address of January 25, 1994, Clinton offered a compact with welfare dependents:

> We'll provide the support, the job training, the child care you need for up to two years. But after that, anyone who can work must – in the private sector, wherever possible; in community services, if necessary. That's the only way we'll ever make welfare what it ought to be – a second chance, not a way of life.

In spite of the time constraints, Clinton in the 1994 State of the Union Address had been adamant that tackling both health and welfare was inevitable and imperative. One million people, he argued, were on welfare because that was the only way they could obtain health coverage for their children (leaving the AFDC rolls meant loss of Medicaid eligibility). Welfare reform proposals were announced in June 1994, and emphasized individual (parental) responsibility, the work ethic, "families," and a "second chance" (not a needs-based right). The Clinton plan targeted education and training benefits for those recipients born after 1971 (i.e. young mothers) but which meant that in effect two-thirds of AFDC beneficiaries would remain virtually unaffected. For the targeted families, AFDC would be limited to a single two-year lifetime benefit. Following training, recipients would have to find jobs (in the private, public or community service sectors) or face termination of their benefits. Additionally, there would be more aggressive child-support enforcement and some limits on welfare benefits for legal immigrants. The plan also gave individual states the latitude to cut welfare altogether for mothers who had more children while on welfare. The polls showed that the public endorsed the two-year limit coupled to job requirement.

The White House decision to delay welfare reform until after health care had been considered sidetracked the plan, delaying it to the 104th Congress and thus coinciding with the Republican victory. The Republican-controlled Congress after 1994 sought to eliminate welfare dependency through three strategies: limiting federal spending by consolidating funds into a block grant and capping federal outlays; handing welfare programs to the states; putting welfare recipients to work. Speaker Newt Gingrich announced that welfare reform would be a priority, in line with the much more stringent proposals already outlined in the Republicans' Contract With America. The prime target was teenage mothers, who would be denied benefits and urged to place their children for adoption. However, the proposed building program for new orphanages, greeted with outrage by Hillary Clinton who called it "unbelievable and absurd," was dropped.

The Clinton welfare plan attempted to distance itself from the Republican proposals by stressing the opportunities it offered and the support, particularly child care, that it provided for those passing from welfare to work. But the flaw was that eligibility for education, job training, and transitional benefits was available only to those on welfare, not the working poor, fuelling opposition to welfare. At the same time, however, Clinton promised to defend Social Security and Medicare, the entitlement programs for the elderly, against Republican depredations, and in 1994 he signed a bill making Social Security a separate Cabinet department.

Though workfare provisions and time limits were common to both sides, Clinton's signing of the Republican bill was widely seen as ending the New Deal's main entitlement program for the poor. Governing as a centrist Democrat in a period when congressional elections were producing a polarized legislature between liberal Democrats and conservative Republicans demanded time and attention if the approach to welfare reform was to have any chance of success. Clinton, however, was not able to devote the necessary attention to reform until the agenda had slipped firmly into Republican hands. The welfare bill which passed the Senate in July 1996 did so by a margin of 74–24 with the Democrats split down the middle: 23 for and 23 against. Though Clinton had previously vetoed the Republican Welfare Reform Bill in January 1996 – once as part of the seven-year balanced budget plan, and once as a free-standing bill – he finally signed the congressional version in August

1996. Clinton, however, claimed that it fulfilled his original reform commitments to replace welfare with opportunity.

The Personal Responsibility and Work Opportunity Reconciliation Act (1996)

The Personal Responsibility and Work Opportunity Reconciliation Act of 1996 was based, as the constrictions of the policy climate outlined above predicts, on cuts in expenditure, not its expansion. The new law was expected to save the federal government $54.2 billion between 1996 and 2002, largely through cuts in the Food Stamps program ($23 billion, which would hit hardest at those very poorest families on half the official poverty level) and making legal immigrants ineligible for most welfare benefits including food stamps, Medicaid and SSI ($23.8 billion). Other savings were expected from the SSI budget, including restrictions on children qualifying for SSI on grounds of disability. One of the harshest provisions was that unemployed adults between eighteen and fifty without children would only be eligible for food stamps for three months in every three years.

The Act integrates a number of previously separate programs, including cash assistance, JOBS funding, child-support enforcement, food stamps and SSI. It terminated the main welfare program, AFDC, established in the 1935 Social Security Act, thus ending sixty years of federal assistance to poor families. The legislation also laid down work-participation rates that increase over time, so that by 2002 at least half of each state's adult welfare recipients must be in work. Failure to meet targets leads to a penalty of 5 percent of the state's block grant, increasing by 2 percent each year the failures continue, up to a maximum of 21 percent. Unlike earlier Republican versions, the new law does not require – but does permit – states to deny benefits to unmarried teenage mothers and to impose caps on monthly payments to families where additional children are born while the mother is receiving welfare.

The Act marked a fundamental change in the relations between federal and state governments, with federal funding moving from open-ended aid to block grants to states. Individual (means-tested) entitlement to benefits was ended, and AFDC was replaced with a federal block grant called Temporary Assistance for Needy

Families (TANF). The requirement for state matching funds was also dropped, though states have to spend at least 80 percent of existing outlays, reduced to 75 percent for those states meeting work participation targets. The block grants would remain largely unchanged over the six-year period to 2002. This faced states with a potentially onerous burden, given that the capping of the grants would not allow for any growth in welfare rolls or costs.

The Act's requirements that more welfare claimants would have to seek and hold jobs was not matched by additional federal support for job training. In fact, job-training programs have been declining steadily over the past few years. The main federal training program is the Job Training and Partnership Act (JTPA). In 1994 this provided some $5 billion for training, and another $1.1 billion for the basic welfare-to-work provision of the 1988 Family Support Act's JOBS program. In fiscal year 1997 (beginning on October 1, 1996), the funding was reduced to $4.7 billion for JTPA, with the JOBS program being eliminated entirely under the new welfare reform legislation. The outcome of these factors was that states themselves would have to fund much of the additional training that welfare recipients would need in order to enter the labor market, and this has meant additional outlays in the short term (as in Wisconsin, for example).

Some commentators argued that the result of the legislation would be to add a further 1 million to the 9.7 million children already in poverty. In the longer term, the reality would be that many adults would not achieve self-sufficiency, given their lack of skills and the instability of the low-wage labor market. There was also concern that, given the change of federal funding from entitlement aid to a block grant to states, together with the capping of federal funds, there would be a financial shortfall which states could not fill. It was estimated that the 1996 Personal Responsibility and Work Opportunity Act would cut federal welfare outlays by some $54 billion. This sum includes the cuts in the Food Stamps program and the rules making legal immigrants ineligible for funds.

Even allowing for these elements of the cuts, however, it was believed that between 1996 and 2002 the states would have to spend $13 billion more than Congress had authorized, if the employment targets in the new legislation were to be met. Child care difficulties increased the uncertainty. Even though federal spending was set to increase by $3.5 billion to a total of $14 billion, that still fell short of what would be needed if states were to meet the work targets. Indeed, Wendell Primus, Deputy Assistant Secretary of the Department of Health and Human Services, resigned when President Clinton decided to sign the 1996 law. He argued that its funding predictions were unrealistic, given that the workfare provisions requiring claimants without jobs to undertake community service already cost about $6,000 a year more per recipient than reliance on benefits alone.

Outputs and outcomes

It is clear that the pressure is now on states to reduce their welfare caseloads and, over the longer term, cut rather than contain costs. This outcome is reinforced by the fact that the new legislation will allow states to reduce their own welfare spending by $40 billion between 1996 and 2002 without penalty. There is, however, an irony here. If the 1988 Family Support Act was hampered in execution by the onset of recession, the strong economy of the late-1990s aids the position of the states, at least initially. The number of families on welfare fell between 1994 and 1996 by some 18 percent. Because the new welfare block grants are based on state expenditures in the early 1990s, most states will be cushioned in their budgets and will also find it easier to move welfare recipients into jobs if the economy continues to grow. This in turn will reduce the targets set by the new legislation for the percentage of caseloads that must be in work. In effect, states had a federal windfall.

This felicity is unlikely to persist, given the investment needed in training and other costs, and the continued disparities between standards in differing states – disparities reinforced by the historically based criteria of TANF funding. There are concerns that such disparities will force down standards, as states strive to deter in-migration from those seeking better welfare aid (the so-called "welfare magnets" problem). Moreover, once the most employable of welfare enrollees have been placed in jobs, reducing caseloads becomes much more difficult.

Requiring movement from welfare into work depends on available training, child care provision, and jobs. The financial restrictions on training and child care are evident; difficulties over jobs are equally clear. The United States has had an impressive record on job creation since 1992. Now, at around 5 percent, unemployment is regarded by economists at near full employment level. But the figures conceal two problems. One is the nature of the jobs themselves, which are in service industries and are of two kinds: low-wage entry-level jobs in retailing (including catering) and skilled work in high-tech business and industry. Low-paid jobs do not necessarily remove families from poverty, and there is evidence that wages for workers with less than a high school education have fallen dramatically in the last decade and a half. The other problem follows from this trend. Those without skills and with other difficulties – trapped in inner cities where manufacturing jobs have declined dramatically and without family support – are increasingly disadvantaged. Such problems affect urban blacks disproportionately and adversely (Wilson, 1996). Fulfilling state obligations to move claimants from welfare to work in such situations becomes problematic.

As well as the devolving of responsibility to states under the 1996 Act, greater freedom from federal regulation has been in progress since the late 1980s. Forty-three states have conducted their own reforms of welfare by obtaining waivers from federal laws, an approach begun in 1988 when the Reagan Administration granted Wisconsin a waiver from federal AFDC rules which allowed the state to reduce welfare benefits to parents who failed to prevent truancy among their teenage children. Such waivers, including many imposing time limits on welfare benefits, accelerated under Bush and gained further momentum in 1993 under the Clinton Administration. Notably, in May 1996, Clinton commended the reforms of Republican Governor Tommy Thompson in Wisconsin which eliminated the existing system entirely and required every recipient to take a job, subsidized or otherwise, placing a five-year limit on the time anyone could receive welfare. Now, the widespread use of waivers reflects the fact that it has been the states who have seized the initiative in setting welfare policy.

Ending the New Deal assumptions

It would be wrong to assume that the change in federal–state relations brought about by the 1996 Act was solely the result of radical Republican ideology attacking federal big government. States, too, played their part in ending the New Deal assumptions. In addition, Clinton's inability to resolve the tensions inside his administration between helping those on welfare and imposing more stringent obligations upon them, added to the ambivalence about federal and state roles. These tensions, and the decision to give health reform top priority, fatally delayed the agenda to the summer of 1994. By then support in Congress was slipping away, with liberals concerned about the two-year limit on welfare aid, and conservatives believing they had the administration's resolve on the run.

Conclusions

Clinton came into office as a "New Democrat," advocating a "New Covenant" with the American people in domestic policy. But his first term was marked by contradictions in social policy. On the one hand there were successful policy outcomes (improvements in Earned Income Tax Credit, Family and Medical Leave Act, Goals 2000) and increased funding (for Head Start, nutrition programs, Food Stamps, the homeless, and low-income housing). But these and other successful measures were, in David Stoesz's words, to be judged as merely the "small change" of a Democratic domestic agenda (Stoesz, 1996). It is as yet too early to tell how these achievements will be weighed against the Clinton Administration's capitulation to the Republican determination to end federal involvement in welfare.

Leadership flaws, poor timing and fiscal constraints are not the whole explanation for these problems. Institutionally, as Desmond King has stressed, the universal basis of contributory programs such as Social Security, unemployment assistance, and Medicare makes them resistant to political attack. By contrast, the noncontributory nature of AFDC limits its political support (King, 1992). The result is a popular distinction between the "deserving" and "undeserving" poor, and the aid due to each. A prime difficulty is what commentators have pointed to as the increasing "plebiscitary" nature of American policy-making in which policy is exposed to close public observation and dependent on immediate mass approval (Quirk and Hinchliffe, 1996). At the same time, the separation of powers between the three branches of government at federal level, and among the federal, state and local governments, means that the United States lacks a single point of policy initiation and makes focused leadership very difficult. Health and welfare reform illustrate these tensions all too well. In health care, president and Congress produced different and multiple plans, interests and lobbies took up entrenched positions, and consensus over the need for change eroded. In welfare, the states' use of waiver dispensations gave them a leading voice in reform, public support underpinned the extension of the workfare obligations from the 1988 legislation, and Republican congressional victory triumphed over Clinton's weakening momentum.

Ironically, as the 104th Congress drew to a close, its opposition to the Clinton Administration appeared much more muted. Bills were passed on Clinton's terms: for an increased minimum wage, for the portability of health care when workers changed jobs, for extra money for education. But in defense and welfare policy, the Republican goals triumphed. Moreover, those on the right believed that the next feasible target would be Social Security; to those on the left the very idea of universality appeared to be under threat. In the spring of 1997, however, Clinton appeared to regain some ground. In May, the budget accord between Clinton and Congress promised to soften (but not eliminate) the cuts in the Medicare and Medicaid programs, and restore to legal immigrants benefits imposed by the 1996 Personal Responsibility and Work Opportunity Act. These gains came at a high price: large parts of the tax cuts that the Republicans had demanded, and reductions in agencies.

12

Foreign Policy

JOHN DUMBRELL

James Baker, Secretary of State under President Bush, reflected accepted wisdom when he wrote that during his tenure in office (1989–92) "the very nature of the international system as we knew it was transformed" (Baker, 1995). Since 1989, it has been almost universally accepted that the ending of the Cold War shattered America's foreign policy compass. Foreign policy elites have felt impelled to develop new doctrines to replace anti-communism, and to assemble new justifications for US global activism.

Almost inevitably, by the mid-1990s, some shades of academic opinion had begun to question these orthodoxies. Had the demise of Soviet communism really changed *everything*? After all, from one viewpoint, the communist collapse merely removed the ideological icing from East–West conflict, leaving the underlying geopolitical cake intact (Gray, 1996). Were global *North–South* relations radically transformed by the post-1989 upheavals? "World system" theorists would deny that they were, maintaining that structural relationships between "core" (Northern, exploiting) capitalism and "peripheral" (Southern, exploited) capitalism remain in place, pending a more general transformation (Wallerstein, 1995). From a liberal vantage point, G. John Ikenberry (1996) has argued that America's post-Cold War task "is not to imagine and build a new world order but to reclaim and renew an old one" – the liberal order created by the United States in the late 1940s. In some underlying sense, it may also be upheld that essential American aims persist: "to create an environment in which democratic capitalism can flourish in a world in which the US still remains the dominant actor" (Cox, 1995).

Despite elements of continuity, it is nevertheless clear that policy-makers can no longer make sense of the world in terms of anti-communist containment. They are faced by a bewildering array of paradigms, predictions, and prescriptions for the new order. By turns, various commentators assert that the world is becoming a single, globalized, even homogenized, liberal order; that we are on the brink of a "clash of civilizations" (Western *versus* Islamic); that the post-Cold War order is collapsing into fractionated anarchy; that democracy is on the march, and with it an international "democratic peace"; or that the future is one of a borderless world, radical interdependence and a transcendence of the traditional nation state (Russett, 1993; Huntington, 1993; Wittkopf, 1994; Dumbrell, 1997b). As for America's role in the world, a range of options has been put forward – among them: promoter of democracy, leader of a security-imposing multilateral alliance, reinvented Pacific power, and solo superpower (Hames, 1993). In the early 1990s, isolationism even emerged as a serious course for the United States. Eric Nordlinger (1995) was one of the few commentators actually to embrace the "I-word," which still survives primarily as a term of abuse. Nevertheless, since the end of the Cold War various forms of (usually unacknowledged) isolationism have conspicuously re-entered American discourse. In some quarters, the United States has been enjoined to look after its own interests and resist the "imperial temptation" (Tucker and Hendrickson, 1992). By far the most visible species of neo-isolationism is the "new populism" of the Republican right: a cluster of ideas organized around "America First" nationalism, and the perception that global leadership tends to involve neglect of America's own interests. Less well known versions of neo-isolationism also exist on the left: critiques of continuing American imperialism, militarism, and arms production (Klare, 1992; Nordlinger, 1995; Bacevich, 1996; Gottlieb, 1997).

The Clinton Administration and Post-Cold War Internationalism

At one level, the removal of the Cold War template for understanding international issues promised to liberate US foreign policy. No longer need America's understanding of regional conflicts be distorted by excessive preoccupation with Soviet behavior. The domestic agenda need no longer to be sacrificed to the global. The end of the Cold War held out the prospect of innovation, of presidents being able to choose new issues, to elevate new international agendas. It also opened the possibility that American administrations might not feel obliged to even *have* a policy for every world region and for every potential crisis.

Unquestionably, the Cold War simultaneously constrained and overloaded America's foreign policy resources. Yet it also provided guidance and purpose. With the template removed, there was always the danger of US foreign policy slipping into mere reactivism – into a series of ad hoc responses to international stimuli and perceived crises. To some extent, of course, reactivism was a feature of Cold War foreign policy, too, albeit within the constraints of the overarching doctrine of anti-communist containment. It is also the case that reactivism, defined as the ability *to* respond to unexpected challenges, is at least to some degree a positive asset within foreign policy repertoires. No administration can ever hope to run successfully an entirely proactive foreign policy; to pretend otherwise would be both arrogant and absurd. To paraphrase a comment once made by journalist James Reston: that is the problem with foreign affairs – they are foreign and will not always conform to America's whims and expectations. It became a common criticism of the first Clinton Administration that its foreign policy was rudderless and reactive. If President Bush had neglected the "vision thing," then Clinton's foreign policy was – to quote one commentator, writing in the wake of the 1996 elections – "distracted by crises that were made vivid by constant television coverage but did not involve America's central security interests." The second term Clinton team (Secretary of State Madeleine Albright, Defense Secretary William Cohen and National Security Advisor Samuel Berger) were "all better known for their political sensitivities and skills than for grand strategic theorizing" (Zakaria, 1996).

In fact, the first Clinton Administration was continually preoccupied with the search for a doctrine to underpin post-Cold War internationalism. It was utterly unable to fulfill the expectations of some commentators on the 1992 elections by ignoring foreign issues. In military terms alone, this was a highly activist administration. Clinton inherited an extensive US Marine Corps deployment in Somalia, a quarantine around Haiti and Air

Force actions in Iraq. Between his inauguration and December 1995, Clinton presided over foreign use of US armed forces on some twenty-five occasions; this compared with seventeen during the two terms of President Reagan and fourteen during Bush's one term (Sicherman, 1997). The guiding words in Clinton's search for doctrine were "engagement" and "enlargement." Clinton's 1996 National Security Strategy report (submitted in accordance with the Goldwater–Nichols Defense Department Reorganization Act of 1986) outlined the key themes: "Never has American leadership been more essential – to navigate the shoals of the world's new dangers and to capitalize on its opportunities." American troops would be sent abroad "only when our interests and our values are sufficiently at stake." However, in an interdependent world, "the boundaries between threats that start outside our borders and the challenges from within are diminishing," so that "the problems others face today can quickly become ours, tomorrow." International "engagement" must be "selective," with the US being committed to the "enlargement of the community of market democracies" (The White House, 1996).

Clear prioritization of US trade and economic interests, the doctrine of "selective engagement," the commitment to "enlarge" the global sway of market democracies: these themes essentially represented the administration's response to charges of simple reactivism. As developed especially in the early Clinton years, "selective engagement" seemed to embody a hierarchy of conditions which would tend to impel the United States towards diplomatic and/or military activism in particular arenas. Early formulations of "selective engagement" clustered around differing understandings within the administration of its commitment to "multilateralism": the view that American power should be exercised within coalition or alliance structures. For example, when Madeleine Albright, as US ambassador to the United Nations (UN), lobbied in 1993 for a UN resolution to transform the Somalian commitment into a nation-building one, she used the term "assertive multilateralism." A more constrained form of the doctrine was advanced by Under Secretary of State Peter Tarnoff, who appeared to argue that US (especially military) power was unlikely ever to be used except in a multilateral context. (Tarnoff was taken to task by his boss, Warren Christopher, Clinton's first Secretary of State: "our need to lead, our determination to lead," insisted Christopher, "is not constrained by our resources") (Christopher, 1995; Dumbrell, 1997a). Clinton himself in a 1993 speech to the UN returned to the theme of "constrained multilateralism," setting very demanding standards for UN military interventions (serious threats to international security, anticipatable costs and a clearly defined exit-point).

Despite these early differences over the concept of multilateralism, the administration did seem to have settled by 1994–95 on a reasonably clear understanding of "selective engagement." Activism in regional crises would be most likely where there were particular security concerns, especially regarding nuclear proliferation and crises relating to the Caribbean; where particular domestic constituencies were closely involved; where high-priority domestic issues, like drugs, immigration or terrorism, were implicated; and where the United States had special trading or resource-access interests. National Security Advisor Anthony Lake also developed the doctrine of "backlash states": international "bad boys" like Cuba, North Korea and Libya, who were always likely to provoke US-led policing action. The policy of containing Saddam Hussein's regime in Iraq was to come close to war in early 1998. US policy in North Korea, Haiti and the former Yugoslavia – where the United States failed to provide activist leadership prior to the summer of 1995 – seemed to fit this general picture of "selective engagement." Bosnia lacked the regional proximity or implications for immigration of Haiti, where US troops landed in September 1994 in an attempt to restore the position of the legally elected leader Jean-Bertrand Aristide. Unlike North Korea, Bosnia raised no immediate issues relating to nuclear proliferation. (Former President Jimmy Carter secured a complex agreement in 1994 whereby North Korea would dismantle its nuclear weapons fuel complex.) In contrast to Northern Ireland, where the United States embarked on a vigorous and unprecedented program of involvement, there was little public support for Bosnian activism: the administration appeared to have learned the lesson of the Somalian overstretch. During 1995, however, the caution over Bosnia collapsed: partly in response to action taken by the Republican Congress, partly due to acceptance of the view that only the United States could resolve a conflict which threatened to disrupt security across the Balkans, much of Eastern Europe and even the Near

East. Despite the early and apparent success of the 1995 Dayton accords, and subsequent US troop commitments to Bosnia, the new Balkan activism essentially represented a retreat from earlier ideas of "selective engagement" and constrained multilateralism.

Anthony Lake's commitment to "enlargement" and to the promotion of market democracy were at the heart of the Clinton team's efforts to solve the venerable problem of balancing American ideals and interests. The policy had some links with the Carter administration's 1970s human rights policy and it linked up also with notions of the post-Cold War "democratic peace," with contemporary theories of economic globalization and the emerging international free market order (Russett, 1993; Layne, 1994). Any hopes or fears that "enlargement" would involve a humanitarian crusade for democracy and human rights were dispelled following the Somalia debacle, where US intervention rapidly lost public and congressional support as casualties were taken. Rather, "enlargement" and democracy-promotion came to be defended in the following terms (by Strobe Talbott, architect of the first Clinton Administration's Russian policy and Deputy Secretary of State at the start of the second):

> The larger and more close-knit the community of nations that choose democratic forms of government, the safer and more prosperous Americans will be, since democracies are demonstrably more likely to maintain their international commitments, less likely to engage in terrorism or wreak environmental damage, and less likely to make war on each other.

According to Talbott, Americans "want their country's foreign policy rooted in idealpolitik as well as realpolitik" (Talbott, 1996).

The most common charge against Clinton's foreign policy in the 1992–94 period was simply that the president allegedly lacked both commitment and interest. James Baker tried to develop this critique during the 1996 presidential election campaign: "When they say that Bill Clinton knows his way around, and knows the ways of the world, they sure ain't talking about his foreign policy" (Walker, 1996). More substantially, Clinton's attempt to balance "idealpolitik" and "realpolitik" came under intense attack not only from Republicans in Congress, but also from a wide spectrum of academic opinion. For Michael Mandelbaum (1996), for example, the main Clinton interventions (Somalia, Haiti, Bosnia) signified a "foreign policy as social work" – a denial of true US security interests in the name of a half-baked "neo-Wilsonianism" (Rubinstein, 1996). Clinton was also taken to task for *downgrading* "idealpolitik" in the name of economic pragmatism, notably in his finessing of concern over China's human rights record and his administration's policy on arms sales. The whole "enlargement" doctrine clearly did rely on some rather uncritical assumptions about the interpenetration between political democracy and free markets. Some internationalist commentators also saw the administration's preoccupation with "economic security" as encouraging isolationism (Muravchik, 1996). Supporters of Clinton, on the other hand, tended to present a "best possible in the circumstances" defense. Their interpretations credited Clinton with developing a manageable internationalist agenda, which while centered on "economic security" was also sensitive to the case for American leadership (Cox, 1995).

As Clinton embarked upon his second term in 1997, the outlook for his foreign policy was far from unpromising. During the 1996 presidential campaign, Clinton successfully preempted some important Republican stances (for example, by opposing the renomination of Boutros Boutros-Ghali as United Nations Secretary General, and by supporting sanctions on firms trading with Cuba). Familiar problems, such as the uncertain status of the Middle Eastern peace process, remained. However, Somalia apart, Clinton's critics were unable to point to any major US battlefield casualties. The biggest first-term gamble, the commitment of 20,000 troops to Bosnia, had not developed into "another Vietnam." The power of Saddam Hussein's regime in Iraq appeared to have been contained, albeit untidily. Against all the odds, President Yeltsin held on to power in Russia. From the renewal of the nuclear proliferation treaty, to the rescue of the Mexican currency, the administration could point to foreign policy successes. In addition, the second-term priorities appeared fairly well defined. Immediate concerns included likely destabilization on the Korean peninsula and the developing relationship with China. Transition to a unified, noncommunist Korean peninsula presented itself as a long-term objective, as did the integration of China into US-led security and economic networks. The administration also needed to develop credible policies for post-Cold War Africa and for a post-Castro Cuba.

At an even deeper level, the Clinton Administration – as it contemplated its second-term options – looked to a new balance between Pacific and European engagement. If coherently achieved, this new balance would be likely to shape US foreign policy well into the new century. Significant shifts had become apparent well before 1997. Certainly, investment patterns still closely connected the United States to Europe (by the mid-1990s, over 40 percent of US direct investment was in Europe). Increased Pacificization of US foreign policy is likely rather than inevitable; it could easily be deflected by developments in Russia. Despite demographic changes in the United States, important Atlanticist lobbies are still in place. However, by 1996, the United States had 50 percent more of its trade with Asia than with Europe. American troop levels in Europe declined by over two-thirds between 1993 and 1995, by which time America's Asian and European troop deployments were on a par. Regarding Europe, the most pressing issue for the new Clinton Administration involved enlargement of the North Atlantic Treaty Organization (NATO). More precisely, a way had to be found of admitting former Warsaw Pact countries into NATO – and thus achieving a new security consensus in Europe – without inciting and reviving anti-Western Russian nationalism. At the NATO summit in Madrid in July 1997, the United States prevailed in its wish to restrict invitations for new NATO membership to Poland, Hungary and the Czech Republic. The 1997 Founding Act had tried to quell Russian anxieties, by setting up a joint NATO–Russia council. Yet ambiguities in the Founding Act, and the vagueness of NATO's undertaking not to station nuclear weapons or large troop numbers in the new member territories, made future Russian reactions uncertain. Also problematic was the US Senate debate over ratification of the NATO enlargement. Worries about costs and about US over-extension seemed likely to reignite disagreements over the preferred scope of post-Cold War American internationalism. Articulation of a "strategic partnership" with the cause of Russian reform was a major first-term priority. Redefinition of NATO's purpose, along with the drawing of Russia into new security and economic relationships, seemed certain to preoccupy US policy-makers into the future (Papacosma and Heiss, 1995; Kaplan, 1996).

Republicans and Foreign Policy

Commitment to NATO expansion, along with hostility to "foreign policy as social work" (especially in the context of UN operations) represented important aspects of the Republican program as presented during and after the 1994 congressional elections. The national security section of the Contract With America sought to prohibit the use of US troops in UN operations under foreign command; to prevent savings from defense being used to fund social programs; to develop anti-missile defense; and to cut US financial contributions to UN peacekeeping.

Though a modified version of the national security portion of the Contract passed the House of Representatives in 1995, no action was forthcoming in the Senate during the 104th Congress (1995–96). Certainly, the post-1994 Republican Congress was an important influence on foreign policy – adding to the defense budget, cutting foreign aid, causing the executive to switch policies. However, the story of the 104th Congress was one of containment and channeling by the executive of the GOP's foreign policy "revolution." Some reasons for the counter-revolution are familiar to observers of the domestic aspects of the Contract: the greater caution of Republican Senators as compared with Representatives, for example, or the potency (potential and actual) of the presidential veto. The GOP's eagerness to increase defense outlays could be offset by its desire to cut deficits. Other reasons for the blunting of the Republican challenge, however, go to the heart of the difficulties faced by the GOP in developing coherent post-Cold War foreign policy.

However much Republican leaders accused Clinton, in Senator Gramm's phrase, of "channel surfing" on foreign policy, they could not disguise disorder in their own ranks. Insularity, isolationism and even nativism had been apparent on one wing of the Republican Party since the termination of the Cold War. On October 24, 1995, the UN's 50th anniversary, Republican Congressman Joe Scarborough of Florida introduced legislation calling on the United States to quit the UN Upon assuming leadership of the Senate Foreign Relations Committee in 1995, Senator Jesse Helms (R-N.C.) began a sustained assault on the UN, on the foreign aid budget, and on State Department spending and organization. According to Helms, the United States should leave the UN by the century's end if the 33,000 strong UN bureaucracy was not "reformed," and if America's share of the peacekeeping budget (currently 30 percent) was not made "voluntary." Helms could point to strong cases for both UN and State Department reorganization. The accumulation of around $1.5 billion in American back-dues to the UN by 1997 reflected a dissatisfaction with the UN which was not confined merely to the right wing of the GOP. Helms' swingeing assaults on State Department bureaucracy (notably the proposal to eliminate the Agency for International Development) deliberately echoed earlier downsizing plans advocated by Secretary Christopher and Vice President Al Gore. (In April 1997, Clinton signed a plan which would combine the formerly independent Arms Control and Disarmament Agency and the US Information Agency with the State Department by 1999.) However, Helms' post-1994 attacks on the State Department, and on the "rat hole" of foreign aid, failed to acknowledge that the US foreign affairs budget had declined by half in real dollars since 1984. By the mid-1990s, the entire US international affairs budget (excluding defense, but including foreign aid and State Department funding) amounted to around 1 percent of federal spending. Yet defenders of Republican internationalism, such as Senator Richard Lugar, were forced on to the defensive. Clinton was thus able to condemn the entire Republican Congress as "isolationist."

Though an exaggeration, Clinton's depiction did capture the failure of the GOP not only to develop its own version of "constrained internationalism," but also to articulate what might be called a "Reaganite" response to the Cold War's end. Robert Kagan (1995) gave his opinion that

> once it found itself in opposition to the Clinton presidency, the Republican party might have been expected to be the first to insist on the need for maintaining America's preponderance of power and influence, and to attack the Democrats' foreign policy from a Reaganite direction.

Instead, Clinton was criticized "not for doing too little, but for doing too much; not for being afraid to use American power but for using it too indiscriminately." The Pentagon's leaked "No Rivals" plan of 1992 had outlined a new American "preponderant power" strategy for the post-Cold War order. Its effective abandonment by the Republicans was the result of the provincialist wing of the party, so long overshadowed by GOP internationalism, reasserting itself in the new era.

The congressional Republican dynamics were reflected in the 1996 presidential race. Candidate Bob Dole sought both to resist, and to adjust to, the insularist upsurge represented by Republican primary contender and victor in New Hampshire, Pat Buchanan. (During the campaign, Buchanan called for a complete end to foreign aid; for a five-year moratorium on legal immigration; and for a consumer tax on imported goods.) Between isolationism and Dole's hesitant internationalism lay the "unilateralism" of House Speaker Newt Gingrich, and a large swathe of Republican opinion. Gingrich's self-defined status as a "cheap hawk" aligned him with aid-cutters and set him against the "preponderant power" strategy. However, Gingrich generally supported free trade and declared in 1995 that "the US must lead, period," because the alternative for the twenty-first century is "a dark and bloody planet." The United States should neither practise multilateralism nor act through the UN. Rather, America should hold to the military's post-Vietnam War doctrine: "We don't come in unless we're really pushed, and if we're really pushed, we're unstoppable" (*Time*, April 7, 1995). The attachment of congressional Democrats to multilateralism – not "assertive multilateralism" necessarily, but certainly a commitment to positive US stances on international cooperation – underlined the degree to which bipartisan approaches to foreign policy had collapsed in the new era.

Beyond its failure to develop a coherent and deep-rooted internationalism, the post-Cold War GOP was beset by some very specific difficulties in challenging Clinton. The legacy of anti-communism tended to push Republicans towards opposing policies such as the normalization of relations with Vietnam. Many Republicans feel, with justification, that administration policies towards China tend unduly to disregard not only Chinese human rights violations but also US promises towards Taiwan. Yet such stances could also be held to contravene the GOP's earnest embrace of hard-headed national interest, along with Republican antipathy to "foreign policy as social work." The legacy of Republican Party support for presidential discretion in foreign affairs – the famous attacks of the Reagan and Bush eras on the 535 Secretaries of State on Capitol Hill – also caused problems for a Republican legislature facing a Democratic president. (After 1994, both Gingrich and Dole – Senate majority leader until 1996 – were publicly committed to scrapping the 1973 War Powers Resolution, with its attempts to limit the executive's authority to commit troops) (Cooper and McGinniss, 1995; Clarke, 1996; Rodman, 1996). The worries expressed by some Republican senators over the wisdom of expanding NATO in 1997 – despite the commitments of the 1994 Contract – indicated the continuation of GOP rifts.

Defense, Intelligence, and Trade

US post-Cold War defense conversion has been unsurprisingly slow. The Clinton Administration had to pick its way between demands for a "peace dividend," invocations of new international insecurity, and vested interests. As Edward Luttwak (1995) put it: "The Cold War lasted so long that no-one remembers any prewar normality to which the military should return." Clinton's 1993 defense reassessment concluded that US interests still demanded spending of over $1.3 trillion over the following five years.

Significant defense cuts have occurred nonetheless, with impacts on domestic defense industry employment. The Pentagon's Quadrennial Defense Review, published in May 1997, reported that "since 1985 America has responded to the vast global changes by reducing its defense budget by some 38 percent, its force structure by 33 percent, and its procurement budget by 63 percent" (Department of Defense, 1997). What has not fundamentally altered is the US military and strategic commitment. The "bottom-up review" conducted by Les Aspin, Clinton's first defense secretary, essentially produced a scaled-down version of the Cold War military structure. The review's main assumption – that the United States should be capable of fighting and winning two near-simultaneous regional conflicts – continued to dominate strategic thinking into the late 1990s. Yet both Aspin, and his successor William Perry, admitted that a significant mismatch existed between spending and America's "prevent–deter–defeat" global strategy. Early in Clinton's first term, Republican critics like Senator John McCain were speaking of a "new hollow force," and criticizing the administration's inability to hold a balance between defense readiness and modernization. The Clinton team was attacked for reneging on a promise to reverse Pentagon procurement budget cuts by FY 1996. However, the use of the presidential veto in the 104th Congress, along with divisions between Republican "defense hawks" and "deficit hawks," secured important victories for executive priorities. When William Cohen, former Republican member of the Senate Armed Services Committee, became defense secretary, he warned against defense spending increases. The American people, declared Cohen, simply "do not see [any] identifiable threat on the horizon" (*Congressional Quarterly Weekly Report*, February 15, 1997). The administration's defense budget requests for FY 1998 followed the precepts set by Aspin in 1993. Following the 1997 defense review, Cohen argued that the military should retain its current missions and strategies. It would continue to plan for peacekeeping and humanitarian operations, as well as "asymmetric threats" (such as terrorism, chemical, biological, and information warfare). Modernization would be achieved through cuts in the support "tail," through base closures and transfer of jobs to the private sector (*Congressional Quarterly Weekly Report*, May 24, 1997; Department of Defense, 1997; Betts, 1995; Perry, 1996; Brown and Dunn, 1996; Ciambala, 1996).

Future spending battles – over issues such as the B-2 stealth bomber, digital communications for the Army, anti-missile defenses, base closures, and manpower cuts – seem inevitable, and will be played out in the context of executive–legislative agreements on deficit reduction. In the short run, however, the White House has just about managed to keep pace with realistic congressional and military expectations. Clinton was prepared to back some highly expensive and controversial items (like the C-17 wide-body cargo jet and the Marines' V-22 Osprey airplane/helicopter). In the absence of a reawakened public perception of external threat, major long-term defense disputes will center on any proposals significantly to cut US global military commitments. The defense outlook, of course, especially in regard to nuclear weapons, could be radically altered with a nationalist, anti-Western takeover in Moscow. In late 1994, Clinton accepted military arguments by opposing nuclear cutbacks to a "core strategic force" of 500 each for Russia and the United States. At the beginning of Clinton's second term, the 1993 START II treaty (dealing with long-range nuclear missile control) remained nonoperational, pending action by the Russian Duma. In March 1995, however, Clinton and Yeltsin agreed to guidelines for START III: a reduction in long-range missiles to between 2,000 and 2,500 warheads each by the year 2007 (an 80 percent cut from the highest Cold War levels). Regarding nuclear weapons development, the Clinton Administration moved to a laboratory testing strategy – "science-based stockpile stewardship and management" – designed to halt underground tests and to restrain the qualitative arms race.

If US defense policy after the Cold War has struggled to achieve a balance between spending and commitments, American intelligence strategy for the new era has entirely lost its way. The termination of the Cold War left the US intelligence community bereft of purpose and prestige. Far from being credited with winning the Cold War, the Central Intelligence Agency (CIA) in particular was widely assailed for failing to keep America abreast of Soviet economic weakness. The Aldrich Ames and Harold Nicholson spy scandals further weakened the CIA's bureaucratic standing, as did blundering attempts by the agency to develop economic espionage. The "scrubbing" of over 1,000 overseas informants by CIA Director John Deutch merely added to the public fund of horror stories about US intelligence. A major dispute arose concerning massive, and apparently wasteful, spending associated with the National Reconnaissance Office (overseer of US spy satellites). Persistent reports of botched attempts by the CIA to unseat Saddam Hussein in Iraq continued to harm the agency's reputation. Clinton's appointment of Anthony Lake to head the CIA (and hence the entire intelligence community) was designed to bring order and purpose to a byzantine, sprawling bureaucracy. (Besides the CIA, the United States has thirteen other intelligence agencies, most with overlapping jurisdictions; their annual budget by the late 1990s amounted to around $30 billion.) The CIA has tried to redefine its purpose, setting up counter-narcotics and counter-terrorist units. Yet Lake's withdrawal from the nomination in early 1997, amid partisan attacks in Congress, boded poorly for coherent future direction and consolidation (Johnson, 1994; McCurdy, 1995). The CIA is unlikely to be abolished, despite some voices, like that of Senator Daniel Moynihan, being raised in favor of abolition. Yet its purpose needs to be defined, and standards of accountability established.

The old Cold War question – how far should the CIA be involved in operations rather than in intelligence-gathering – must also be settled.

The major foreign policy successes of the first Clinton Administration were in the area of trade policy; notably, in securing 1993 congressional passage of the North American Free Trade Agreement (NAFTA) (setting up a regional free trade area, comprising the United States, Mexico, and Canada) and the 1994 legislative ratification of the General Agreement on Tariffs and Trade (GATT). In fact, a good case can be made to the effect that any Clinton claim to post-Cold War vision lies, not so much in doctrines of "engagement" or "enlargement" *per se*, but in free trade strategy. According to this strategy, itself of course largely inherited from the Bush Administration, the United States should become the capstone in a series of interlocking regional free trade pacts. The vision is not only of a world saved from protectionist fragmentation, but also – in true Wilsonian fashion – of a reaffirmed identity between US and global interests. Enlargement of NAFTA, to include populous South American nations, emerged as a major second-term priority. Enthusiasm for regional free trade was maintained by US activism in APEC (Asia Pacific Economic Cooperation) and, to a significantly lesser degree, for TAFTA (the nascent Transatlantic Free Trade Agreement). Inter-branch conflict over NAFTA, however, cast something of a shadow over Clinton's second-term free trade agenda. The 1993 campaign for NAFTA ratification involved the abandonment of some traditional Democratic Party constituencies. Organized labor, in particular, argued that NAFTA was designed to augment corporate profits, rather than protect American jobs. By 1997, it was widely perceived that NAFTA's "side deals" (designed to safeguard labor conditions and to ameliorate environmental damage) had proved ineffectual. Conflict centered on the admission of Chile to NAFTA, and on congressional withholding of "fast-track" negotiating authority – Clinton's ability to ask Congress to vote trade deals up or down, without continually unraveling the whole process through amendments. Protectionist Republicans found themselves allied with pro-labor Democrats against "fast-track" reauthorization. Aside from NAFTA, the World Trade Organization (WTO), the body set up by GATT to adjudicate trade disputes, looked set to figure in future trade policy disagreements. China aspires to full membership of the

WTO, while the WTO is also implicated in debates surrounding US economic sanctions on Cuba, as well as in wider disputes involving American sovereignty.

Underpinning Clinton's trade policy were a number of commitments and recognitions: acknowledgement of increasing US trade dependency; acceptance that the post-Cold War order is structured around geo-economics rather than geo-politics; a desire to lead public and congressional opinion away from protectionism – all within the framework of an almost neo-mercantilist commitment to "competitiveness." According to Clinton, the United States is "like a big corporation competing in the global marketplace" (quoted in Krugman, 1994). Promotion of US economic interests must, in this view, be rescued from its Cold War status as "low policy" and accorded high bureaucratic and operational status. Such a policy has its hazards, despite Clinton's undoubted successes in furthering it. For one thing, as Krugman (1994) has argued, the conceptualization of the United States as "like a big corporation" is misleading. Big corporations, for example, do not sell the majority of their products to their own workers. An "economics-first" foreign policy also raises severe problems of how to finesse and integrate competing objectives. Burgeoning American arms sales (almost half of global sales) sit uneasily with White House statements on the dangers of unrestricted arms proliferation. In Asia, in particular, the United States will continue to juggle economic, security and human rights goals. The first Clinton Administration did achieve some degree of exchange rate cooperation with Japan, but America still needs to tackle the huge trade deficits with China and Japan. Regional security arrangements, designed to spread burdens and to resist Chinese expansionism, need to be developed. And all this must be done within the scope of American "idealpolitik"!

Post-Cold War Foreign Policy-making

Clinton's "economics-first" foreign policy has involved both adjustment to, and a desire to resist, the logic of liberal economic globalization. Unquestionably, globalization has impinged on state sovereignty as traditionally conceived, and will continue to do so. "Competing for world market shares, whether oil or semiconductors or air travel, means accepting the established structures and customs of those markets" (Strange, 1995). Yet the logic of globalization, and the consequent enervation of state authority, can be over-stated. For one thing, as Clinton's preoccupation with state-led economic competitiveness exemplifies, globalized processes do not automatically necessitate atrophy of the state (Cerny, 1997). By many measures, the global economy was as integrated before 1914 as in the 1990s (Hirst and Thompson, 1996). The extreme integration of global financial markets has not been replicated in all other areas. As the only remaining multidimensional superpower, the United States retains a unique ability to set the terms of international economic competition (Nye, 1990). The regionalist strategies adopted by the Clinton Administration themselves indicate the extent to which the absolutist imperatives of globalization may be resisted (Gamble and Payne, 1996).

As a general rule, the more that traditional security yields to economic agendas, the more control over US foreign policy tends to shift away from the White House. Recent years have witnessed new actors entering the foreign policy arena, especially as divisions between domestic and international policy agendas have blurred. Particular attention has been paid to foreign governmental lobbying (Hrebenar and Thomas, 1995). Pat Choate, the nationalist economist who ran alongside Ross Perot in the 1996 presidential race, has publicized the extent and intensity of Japanese lobbying in the United States (Choate, 1990). Alleged Chinese governmental involvement in campaign fund-raising for the 1996 federal elections rapidly became the subject of Justice Department and congressional investigations. The new economic foreign policy has also activated domestic interest groups, notably the environmental and labor lobbies which opposed NAFTA State and local governments have become involved in trade promotion, and also to some extent in immigration issues, in ways which may be held to conflict with constitutional and statutory prohibitions on subfederal foreign policy-making (Shuman, 1992; Hatcher, 1996). Even within the Executive Branch itself, unlikely bureaucratic forces, such as the Commerce Department, emerged to play important roles. The circumstances of post-Cold War international politics have also called forth new domestic ethnic group formations – such as the Central and East European Coalition, founded in 1993 to represent the foreign policy interest of ethnic minority or "hyphenated"

Americans from the old Soviet empire (Kirschten, 1995). Foreign policy "think-tanks" have also become more heterogeneous than in the Cold War era, less likely to replicate the world view of liberal internationalism (Clough, 1994; Newsom, 1996). There is little sign of this decentralized complexity receding.

Yet it would be extremely rash to proclaim the end of presidential foreign policy dominance. The trajectory of the first Clinton Administration's foreign policy-making style followed a familiar Cold War pattern. Early State Department prominence, both in strategic conceptualization and in operationalization of foreign policy, gave way to firm White House direction. National Security Adviser Anthony Lake, as had so many of his Cold War predecessors, benefitted from his proximity to the president and from his sensitivity to Clinton's electoral needs.

Regarding Congress, Clinton was sometimes able (for example, in votes on policy in Bosnia) to exploit alliances between Democrats and senior, internationalist Republicans. Nevertheless, several important presidential victories were clearly achieved only after complex horse-trading and the granting of expensive concessions to powerful legislative factions (examples include the 1993 NAFTA ratification and 1997 Senate approval of a treaty banning chemical weapons). This is likely to be a continuing feature of post-Cold War inter-branch bargaining. The end of the Cold War has made it less easy, though by no means impossible, for presidents to invoke "national security" as a way of mobilizing legislative support. In the early Clinton years, "national security" was effectively invoked in relation to aid to the Soviet successor states, and policy towards North Korea. As Jeremy Rosner (1995) noted:

> When the national security stakes on an issue appear to be low . . as on peacekeeping or development aid, Congress increasingly flexes its muscles. This . . . pattern was clear *before* the Republicans took control . . . and it is likely to continue.

Patterns are difficult to discern. The removal of the Soviet threat undoubtedly made Congress more confident in its ability to tackle policy areas traditionally left to executive discretion. For example, Paul Stockton (1995) concluded that, in regard to the defense budget, "Congress has moved beyond micromanagement into strategy." Yet the president, perhaps to a surprising degree, managed to keep a tight grip on the foreign policy reins. Clinton's

1996 record on congressional defense and foreign policy votes (seven wins out of twelve in the Senate; eight out of seventeen in the House, including the sustaining of his veto on the defense authorization) was respectable, given the partisan context. His neglect of the legislature's war powers prerogative – from Iraq to Haiti and Bosnia – has been in line with precedents set during the Cold War. When war with Iraq appeared imminent in early 1998, Congress was unable to pass clear resolutions either backing or opposing Clinton's strategy. Academic attempts to enthrone a putatively "imperial" Congress – relentlessly micromanaging foreign and defense policy, setting agendas and strategies – are premature and unrealistic (Ripley and Lindsay, 1993; Lindsay, 1994; Hinckley, 1994; Weissman, 1995).

The president's ability to lead foreign policy continues to derive in large measure from his special relationship to public opinion. Post-Cold War public opinion in the United States has frequently been characterized as "homeward bound." Certainly, there is little indication of public enthusiasm for high-spending liberal internationalism. Alvin Richman (1996) notes that all poll measures of "global altruism" (democracy promotion, human rights, aid to developing nations) have experienced significant reductions since the Cold War ended. Against this background, Democrats and internationalist Republicans in Congress have found it difficult publicly to defend foreign aid. However, despite academic and journalistic preoccupation with an apparently rising insular populism, public opinion generally supported Clinton's constrained internationalism. A plurality of around 45 percent in polls even backed the 1995 Bosnian troop deployments. All indications are that presidents are still able to sell the US public a version of post-Cold War internationalism, so long as it recognizes limits, keeps troop casualties low, and avoids the language of "foreign policy as social work" (Graham, 1994; Rielly, 1995).

Post-Cold War presidents retain the ability to control much of the foreign policy agenda by the traditional means of invoking national security, national interest, and patriotism. Yet this ability may be lessening. To the extent that post-Cold War policy-makers have succumbed to foreign policy "channel surfing," they have been responding to a more complex and quick-changing policy environment. It is an environment in which the news media play an enhanced role. According to James Schlesinger (1993):

> In the absence of established guideposts our policies will be determined by impulse and image . . . National policy is determined by the plight of the Kurds, or starvation in Somalia, as it appears on the screen.

Former Secretary of State George Shultz has remarked that Cable News Network "puts everybody on real time, because everyone is seeing the same thing" (quoted in Hoge, 1994). Presidents may indeed be tempted to court popularity by dancing to the tunes set by televisual discovery of new "hot spots." Television reporting, however sophisticated and technologically advanced, constantly runs the risk of conflating news and entertainment values; democratic interests are not well served by elected leaders who defer too readily. However, these dangers should be kept in proportion. A free press, in all its forms, represents an aspect of democracy, rather than a threat. Furthermore, the foreign policy media tend as much to promote inter-elite and elite-public communication, as to operate as autonomous policy entrepreneurs (Neuman, 1995; Jamieson, 1996). To the extent that new technology increases public access to information in ways which are beyond the control of (especially) presidential elites, it will be furthering the cause of democratic foreign policy.

Conclusion

It is still difficult to conceptualize the Cold War as a distinct historical epoch. The habits and inertia of the Cold War continue to affect US foreign policy: in the preoccupation with Russia; in the failure to develop defensible policies for Cuba; in continued, if waning, deference to presidential leadership; in the reluctance to rethink military and intelligence missions and commitments. However, the central foreign policy debate in the United States is structured now in a way more reminiscent of pre-Cold War than of Cold War conditions. The debate is organized between the poles of unilateralism, trade protection, and "America First" on the one hand; and multilateralism, interventionism, and resurrected Wilsonianism on the other.

The clarity of this debate is enhanced to the extent to which these two poles can be identified with the two main political parties. Of course, the Republican Party no more completely conforms to "America First" than the Democratic Party does to "assertive multilateralism." Republican internationalism has been challenged since the ending of the Cold War; it has not been extinguished. Important changes have taken place among congressional Democrats. Left liberals no longer apply the "lesson of Vietnam" to all military interventions. Activism in Somalia and Haiti was conspicuously *supported* by left-leaning legislative Democrats, including the congressional Black Caucus. Yet the Democrats in Congress include those many members who destroyed "fast track" in 1997. The experiences in Somalia still cast a long shadow over "assertive multilateralism." The dream of switching defense monies to domestic agendas has also not disappeared. It should also be remembered that post-Cold War transitional politics can produce some unlikely, trans-party alliances as between those conservative Republicans and left Democrats in opposing Most Favored Nation (MFN) trading status for China. In early 1998, independent leftist Representative Bernard Saunders of Vermont joined conservative Republican Senator Lauch Faircloth of Virginia in leading opposition to US underwriting, in the troubled Asian context, of International Monetary Fund Rescue programs.

Future years may witness a clear mobilization of the forces opposed to globalization, and its consequences both for American sovereignty and for domestic well-being. However, the contemporary debate is still essentially that inherited from the immediate post-Cold War period – a debate between (though also within) the two major parties over the proper limits of US international engagement. The debate has not been resolved, and the US still needs to make choices. In moving forward, the US must also recognise that not all positions which might conceivably be branded as "isolationist" are bad. The US *should* seriously consider issues of regional prioritization, and the matching of military missions to resources. Untrammeled free trade does endanger labor conditions and environmental protection, and governments should seek to compensate for the excesses of economic globalization. On the other hand, neo-isolationism does have real dangers; it is not a mere straw man, routinely to be invoked by internationalists. As J. G. Ruggie (1996) argues, history commands us "to be leery of the common view that isolationism requires, literally, seeking to insulate oneself from the world, or that it is necessary to harbor isolationist intentions to produce the result." Attacks on the very principle of foreign aid, and on the international budget generally, point in the direction of an untenable isolationism. As Secretary Albright argued in her 1997 confirmation hearing: "We provide a smaller percentage of our wealth to support democracy and growth in the developing world than any other industrialized nation": (*Congressional Quarterly Weekly Report*, 11 January 1997). The growth of insular trade protectionism; almost routine denigration in Congress of the purposes of the United Nations; the condemnation of ethical dimensions to foreign policy as "half-baked Wilsonianism"; the growth of populist anti-immigrant movements; legislative support for American unilateralism: all these constitute real dangers to responsible internationalism. The US should (and probably will) continue to work in a pragmatic way to establish criteria to govern a workable internationalism.

PART FOUR

CONTEMPORARY ISSUES

13

Education Policy

JONATHAN PARKER

"The answer to all our problems" President Lyndon Johnson said, "comes down to one single word, education" (Johnson, 1965). As this statement demonstrates, Americans place great value on education and subsequently expect it to solve many of the nation's most pressing problems. Johnson's words represented more than simply political rhetoric; they outlined a key governmental strategy for tackling poverty and discrimination in the 1960s and 1970s. America continues to grapple with problems of poverty and race, but now must also contend with heightened global competition in business and economic insecurity as well as high levels of crime and violence. President Clinton urged the nation to look again to education to solve the nation's most pressing and intractable problems. In his 1997 State of the Union address, he promised to make education his top priority and called for a "national crusade" for standards as well as making college learning universal to all Americans. Though the public applaud such a focus upon education, this approval does not indicate any consensus over particular solutions.

The public's exact views on education appear confused and contradictory. Though people strongly support public education, many feel the system performs poorly and is in a state of crisis. Further, though most people demand that something be done and show strong support for general reforms such as raising standards, specific policies prove highly controversial and divisive in practice. The high visibility and saliency of problems in education and simultaneous lack of agreement over solutions creates an insidious cycle of failure. High public anxiety encourages political leaders to promote education as an answer for social problems without any clear notion of how to accomplish such aims. These ambitious promises lead to conflict, unfulfilled expectations, and, ultimately, disillusionment. Though the public continues to value education, many people have lost confidence in a system that has promised so much more than it could achieve.

President Clinton has championed education reform for much of his political career, and this zeal for reform has continued in both his terms as president. Congress, whether controlled by Democrats or Republicans, has proved a willing partner in this effort. Under Democratic control, Congress passed Clinton's Goals 2000 plan, supporting the development of voluntary national standards in education. Originally dubbed America 2000, it was developed at the 1989 education "summit" between President George Bush and the National Governor's Association, led by then Governor Clinton. Congress refused to pass the plan under President Bush, but, once elected, President Clinton continued to press for its passage and ensured its eventual success.

The 1994 elections brought to power a conservative Republican Congress very hostile towards President Clinton. Nevertheless, both president and Congress cooperated in 1997 to pass sweeping reforms in higher education. Public anxiety over the high cost of attending colleges and universities forced this issue onto the national agenda. When asked in a national survey about their greatest fears over raising children, more parents listed college costs (52 percent) than any problem other than kidnapping and violent crime, and these two examples of sudden tragedy only beat out college costs by two percentage points (*Newsweek*, 1997). Higher education costs have persistently risen faster than the average incomes, and may deter even middle class students. President Clinton proposed tax breaks for college expenses, returning to the theme of middle class tax cuts which appeared in his 1992 and 1996 campaigns. The issue attracted strong bipartisan support from the now Republican Congress, resulting in a massive increase in governmental aid for students. Though President Clinton and Congress have been particularly active in education reform at all levels, the federal government can more effectively influence higher education because of its prominent leadership in that area. This power does not often extend to primary and secondary education, which the national government has historically avoided, so reforms in this area have less impact.

Though recent federal reforms have proved particularly vigorous, these efforts represent only a small part of education policy. State and local governments wield the most influence in education. The American system of government, with its separation of powers and multiple, overlapping levels (see Chapter 6) creates a situation in which no one is clearly in charge or responsible for education. Each level and branch of government plays an important role. Even the most decisive federal action cannot easily alter the education system, and such action rarely occurs. The arena of education policy is fraught with competing interests of all types and political views. This combination of diverse interests and strongly held beliefs makes consensus over any policy very difficult to achieve. Even with such an agreement at the national level, such as Goals 2000, coordinating policy across the different levels and branches of government proves highly complicated. As a result, education policy often appears hopelessly fragmented. Making coherent and effective policy, which has never been easy, now presents an increasingly complex and difficult challenge, and any attempt at comprehensive reform must negotiate these obstacles. Though a remarkable level of consensus has been achieved by the national government, its options remain limited. Despite concerted action by president and Congress, the national level of government plays a relatively restricted role in this area.

State and Local Control of Elementary and Secondary Education

Responsibility for education formally rests at the state level. Despite this formal control, however, most power remains firmly lodged at the local level. Local governments historically established and administered public education, and the compelling vision of neighborhoods and communities running their own schools remains a potent political force today. Local control of schools endures because of two factors. First, the fragmented nature of education policy discourages any real alternatives. Secondly, much of the funding for schools comes from local governments, largely from property taxes. Thus, local districts and counties oversee both the financing and administration of the schools.

Local control has weakened since the 1960s, however, as the federal government expanded its role towards protecting disadvantaged groups such as racial minorities, the poor, the disabled, non-English speakers and women. Despite these sweeping changes at the national level, the major erosion of local control has been to state governments (Elmore, 1984). The expansion of national regulations stimulated the development of larger and more professional state education departments. States organized large staffs of skilled civil servants in order to enforce the new federal rules. In turn, these modernized departments provided the means to expand state supervision of education policy. Thus, federal regulations, by forcing states to monitor their treatment of disadvantaged groups, enabled states to intensify their control over areas such as school finance, curriculum development, testing and teacher certification. Federal intervention intensified in the 1960s due to concerns over equity issues such as race and poverty, but these issues also influenced agendas at the state and local levels. One of the most perennial and controversial of these issues is school finance.

Local financing of education occurs largely through property taxes. However, this method of funding creates tremendous disparities in expenditure, both between individual states and between districts within each state. Wealthy areas have larger tax bases and can provide more lavish budgets at lower rates of taxation. By contrast, poorer districts often levy higher tax rates but raise much smaller amounts. In the 1970s, some state supreme courts began to rule that educational finance systems violated state constitutions. Since the first case in 1971, 17 state finance systems have been declared unconstitutional and 18 have been upheld (ECS, 1998). Even when states win their cases, the threat of legal action often prompts finance reforms. These reforms attempt to further centralize state funding of education, which should allow for greater distribution of resources to poorer districts. Typically, states provide a minimum level of funding per pupil and let local governments fund the rest. Therefore, the larger the state proportion of funding, the less any single district must make up from its own taxes. The proportion of centralized funding varies widely by state, from Hawaii, which provided 86.8 percent of funds in 1990, to New Hampshire, which has a strong tradition of local control and provided only 7.8 percent of education expenditures (NCES, 1993).

Although most people agree that students should receive a good education, no matter where they live, finance reforms have failed to eliminate or even reduce funding disparities between districts. In order to equalize funding, states must either shift money away from wealthier districts or limit their spending. The political clout of these districts blocks such measures in most cases. Instead, states try to "level up" the system by providing more money overall with extra resources for poor areas, which does not make any district worse off. Unfortunately, such plans require huge sums of money to have much impact, and such funding is rarely forthcoming. Despite widespread reform efforts and increased judicial intervention, centralized funding has changed little over time. Most states reformed their finance systems after 1971, 17 of them under court orders, yet the state proportion of funding has barely risen from just under 40 percent in 1970 to just over 45 percent in 1994 (NCES, 1996). Local districts continue to pay a larger proportion of school financing than states, and, therefore, the funding disparities continue. Though finance reforms remain a state and local matter, they arose due to concerns over equity, and these issues achieved more success at the federal level.

The Limited Role of the Federal Government

Direct national involvement in education did not really begin until the 1950s, when the launch of Sputnik by the Soviet Union shocked the country and brought attention to the poor condition of science and math instruction. In response, the government provided support for curriculum development and research, which cost relatively little and imposed no requirements on states. Issues such as government aid for religious education, racial segregation and fears that federal action would ultimately usurp state and local control generated intense controversy, and these issues created intractable political conflict in which any attempt to provide national assistance floundered. Eventually, issues of race, poverty and social justice produced a coalition in the 1960s that achieved landmark reforms such as the protection of civil rights and creation of the welfare state. This coalition overcame the obstacles to federal assistance and brought sweeping changes to American education.

From the mid-1960s, the national government massively expanded its involvement in education, concentrating its efforts on four major areas. First, it attacked racial discrimination by outlawing segregation and discrimination in public schools, producing dramatic improvements, although racial problems still afflict education. Secondly, the government assisted poor and deprived children by providing extra assistance through compensatory programs. Thirdly, it guaranteed disabled students an "appropriate" education, provided in regular classrooms wherever possible, forcing widespread integration of disabled students into mainstream classrooms. Finally, student grants and loans provided access to higher education, resulting in one of the highest participation rates in postsecondary education throughout the world.

Education plays a key role in American social policy, and government assistance to primary and secondary education takes up half of all federal education spending (NCES, 1997). The Elementary and Secondary Education Act (ESEA) of 1965 created the largest and most prominent federal program. The act sought to alleviate poverty by providing categorical grants to state and local governments to create compensatory education programs, designed to help deprived children overcome barriers to educational success. Bilingual education was added to ESEA in 1967, providing assistance and requiring services for non-English speaking students. ESEA also encouraged state and local governments to develop and expand their bureaucratic departments to oversee education policy. This expansion helped create the institutional capacity through which states increased control over educational policy-making.

In the 1970s, the protection of disabled children provided a new and significant addition to federal intervention. The Education for All Handicapped Children Act of 1975, renamed the Individuals with Disabilities Education Act (IDEA) in 1990, set up legal requirements for the identification and education of students with disabilities. States had neglected the treatment of this group, and many children languished in mental institutions or received no education at all. Lawsuits prompted states to enact reforms in the early 1970s, but the national law preempted these reforms. It set standards by offering financial assistance but compelling states to follow strict regulations in return. Further, this education would take place in the "least restrictive environment" possible, requiring schools to teach children in regular classrooms wherever possible.

These requirements developed into detailed legal prescriptions for schools, resulting in a separate administrative and legal system for disabled students. Each state and local district now employ a battery of specialist staff to identify disabled children, provide some education, and supervise their treatment. Such services are mandatory, even if it means hiring new staff or paying for places at private schools. In effect, special education programs get first claim to funds. When shortfalls occur, special education is protected from cuts, which can concentrate reductions on regular classroom services. Further, providing these services to disabled students costs over twice as much as for other students (Chaikind *et al.*, 1993). Disabled children now comprise around 10 percent of all students, so the additional costs to states are staggering. To offset this burden, Congress promised up to 40 percent of the funding for these programs but has neglected to provide anything near this level. Currently, the national government provides about $3.25 billion per year, while the states are estimated to pay between $25 and $30 billion in extra costs (Chaikind *et al.*, 1993), though others claim the figure may be as high as $50 billion (Finn, 1996). Thus, the federal government only provides between 7 and 13 percent of the extra cost. Though widespread support for special education continued, states grew less enthusiastic about federal regulation and legal requirements as their financial costs multiplied. Special education retains powerful political backing and public sympathy. Despite Republican calls to end unfunded mandates and devolve power to the states, Congress has made no move to change substantially its control over special education.

The case of special education demonstrates how the national government exercises influence over education beyond its modest financial contributions. Federal programs enhance services for needy or deprived groups by providing money and imposing regulations on states. Both the level of aid and number of groups covered expanded in the 1970s. Nevertheless, even at its highest point federal spending never provided more than 10 percent of education funding. The proportion dropped from over 9 percent in the 1970s to about 7 percent in 1995 (NCES, 1996). Despite this decline in the proportion of funding, federal influence expanded through the use of mandates and regulations. Though unwilling to pay for new programs, the national government demanded additional spending by state and local governments. The use of mandates and regulations has become particularly powerful because of the increasingly detailed and vigorous oversight applied by federal courts. This branch of government initiated, supported and ultimately forced the national presence in education.

The Role of the Courts

The controversial role of the federal courts in education began over the issue of racial discrimination long before any other national involvement occurred. Though many cases dealing with race led up to the decision, in 1954 the Supreme Court unanimously declared separate schools to be inherently unequal and unconstitutional in *Brown* v. *Board of Education.* However, little action occurred over the next decade. Federal judges became increasingly active as states flagrantly defied orders to desegregate schools. Finally, in *Swann* v. *Charlotte-Mecklenberg* in 1971, the Supreme Court allowed forced busing to be imposed on districts in order to achieve desegregation. Judges could devise their own desegregation plans and even take over individual school districts if governments disobeyed their rulings. The Supreme Court subsequently restricted the scope of desegregation plans to individual school districts, and "white flight" from urban areas led to a resegregation of many areas. Predominantly minority inner cities have no means to integrate within their borders, but districts must still ensure racially balanced schools. Despite this mitigated success, judicially imposed desegregation achieved sweeping changes in education whose effects continue today.

In addition to highly visible issues such as race, the federal courts much more aggressively enforce the overall national regulation of education. Schools cannot violate student rights to privacy, religious freedom or discrimination on the basis of race, sex, language, or ethnic origin. All aspects of education must take these legal requirements into account. Every district in the country maintains a legal office, and contending with lawsuits has become an everyday part of administration for most areas. The threat of legal action serves to maintain the strong national influence over education, despite its weak financial contribution.

Education Reform

Education reform movements sweep the country in fairly regular intervals (Ravitch, 1983) and such movements have had a consistent presence in the latter half of the twentieth century. A strong focus on equity issues such as race and poverty dominated the reforms of the 1960s and 1970s. Federal support rapidly expanded but, unsurprisingly, could not cope with such difficult problems. At the same time, a decline in standardized test scores occurred nationwide. The failure to overcome the legacies of racial discrimination and poverty, combined with a fall in student achievement, shattered public expectations which had been fuelled by overly ambitious claims and helped undermine confidence in public education. Further, economic distress in the 1970s and 1980s brought concern over worker productivity in the face of increasing global competition. Many business leaders worried that students did not acquire the knowledge and skills that companies required of workers in order to compete effectively. These conditions brought a change in the focus of reform, heralded by the report *A Nation at Risk* (National Commission on Excellence in Education, 1983).

The release of *A Nation at Risk* signalled a new focus upon educational quality instead of the equity concerns that dominated the previous two decades. The report warned of a "rising tide of mediocrity that threatens our very future as a Nation and a people" and stated that if a foreign power imposed the current level of educational standards on the country it would be regarded as an act of war. This concern cut across party and ideology, and virtually every state enacted some package of reforms. States increased spending, particularly on teacher's salaries, raised graduation requirements, enacted tests for teacher certification, and required student competency testing for high school diplomas. However, these reforms did little to change conditions inside the classroom (Fuhrman, 1993). Test scores failed to rise, and calls for more sweeping reforms soon followed.

The second wave of "restructuring" reforms have occurred since the late 1980s. Restructuring generally follows one of two potentially conflicting strategies. The first approach uses classical bureaucratic models, in which you improve performance by clearly defining goals and hold organizations accountable for achieving these goals. This type of reform promotes higher educational standards by creating a common curriculum with challenging goals and assessing student performance (Fuhrman, 1993). Champions of this approach note that little or no agreement exists on exactly what schools should teach or how to test what students have learned. State curricula appear vague, and classroom teachers create and administer most examinations, which does not allow comparison across states, schools, or even individual classes. Statewide or national exams, which allow more comparison, take the form of standardized multiple choice tests which are devoid of any direct connection to what students learn. The standards movement seeks to establish a curriculum reflecting a consensus over what students should learn, test students on this subject matter in a meaningful way, and hold schools accountable for teaching these skills and content to students (Fuhrman, 1993).

Though individual states have progressed unevenly and also differ across subjects, the standards movement has achieved far more success in the states than at the national level. Goals 2000, which promoted the creation of national standards, has encountered stiff political opposition. Though the public overwhelmingly approve of raising standards as a general concept for reform, specific plans attract vocal opposition from both the left and right. Conservative groups, particularly the Christian right, oppose Goals 2000 because they feel it would result in a strong national curriculum under federal control. They also remain highly suspicious of state curriculum content, particularly in the areas of health education and moral values. Ironically, the left also attack the standards movement, portraying rigorous standards and assessments as a threat to the underprivileged. Since poorer areas, particularly inner cities, face tremendous social problems and funding inadequacies, they cannot hope to compete with the test scores from districts in wealthier, less deprived areas. Thus, the environment of poorer districts would lead to lower test scores for their students. The comparatively higher scores from other districts would add yet another disadvantage for students in deprived areas, which could lead to even further deterioration of conditions. Thus, a bizarre coalition of left and right opposition to standards often derails reform efforts. Nevertheless, despite setbacks for Goals 2000, forty-five of fifty states have moved to create new curriculum frameworks and methods of assessment (Pechman and Laguarda, 1993).

The Republican takeover of Congress in 1994 created radical changes in the federal government. It also brought many opponents of federal involvement in education to power and produced great antagonism between the legislature and the president. Goals 2000 funding has been broadened so that states can now use the money for uses other than the development of new standards, such as purchasing new technology. In order to continue moving standards forward, President Clinton proposed new national tests in mathematics and English to begin two years later. These tests encountered strong opposition, particularly since Clinton sought no approval from Congress beforehand. In such a politically charged atmosphere, states have been loathe to adopt the tests and their future remains unclear. Nevertheless, standards reforms continue to spread throughout the country on a state by state basis. The enthusiasm of states for developing their own standards ensures that these reforms will endure, regardless of attitudes in the national government, though the ultimate effects will only become known over time. The second type of reform, market-based organizational approaches, have proved no less controversial than higher standards.

Decentralization represents the other type of "restructuring" reforms. By reducing centralized bureaucratic organizations and power, these reforms can provide more control and accountability to local communities and allow those closest to the classroom to influence policy decisions (Smith and O'Day, 1991). Many decentralization plans, though not all, use market-based conditions to drive innovation and improvements in schools. School choice programs represent the most common of these reforms and allow parents to choose the schools which their children attend. Choice plans incorporate many different variations, the most controversial of which involve vouchers that pay a specific sum towards the cost of attending any school, public or private. Public school choice plans prove less contentious and only allow parents to choose which public school their child will attend. Charter schools present yet another approach to this idea. Organizations, including school districts, nonprofit agencies, or other groups may set up their own schools, receive government funding based on the number of pupils, and retain most authority to run the schools. President Clinton endorsed the latter, less controversial approaches to school choice, which attract widespread support. Thus far, 30 states have passed charter school legislation and 28 states have enacted school choice of some sort (ECS, 1998). School-based management represents a less market-oriented reform but takes a broader approach to decentralization by devolving power to each school, rather than choosing a select few as charter schools. Representative bodies consisting of teachers, administrators, parents, and local community members govern each school, providing stronger ties to local communities. Many forms of decentralization reform exist, though all present clear alternatives to the increased state authority sought by the standards movement.

The standards movement and decentralization comprise two clearly distinct types of education reform that use very different approaches to improve education which appear contradictory. Higher standards provide strong state control of what is taught by designing a common curriculum and assessing how well students have learned. This process strengthens centralized state oversight and control over the classroom. By contrast, decentralization reforms seek to strip away centralized control in order to empower those in the classroom to make decisions. Despite the apparent conflicts between the approaches, many proponents of "restructuring" efforts embrace a combination of both types of reforms. The rationale behind this approach claims that standards should be set and measured at more centralized levels, but the governance of schools and classroom practices should be left to those closest to the action. Thus, states set challenging standards and provide a mechanism for determining how well a student has learned the curriculum. In turn, the schools are left to carry out the business of teaching, the area they know best. Individual schools can tailor their programs to meet the needs of the students, and accountability will be provided by the state curriculum and assessments (Smith and O'Day, 1991). These ideas appear similar to those used in industry, such as Total Quality Management systems, which set goals for which employees will be accountable but then decentralize decisions about how to meet those goals to those employees. Regardless of how effectively these two approaches to reform complement one another, both continue to expand throughout the states and represent the cutting edge of education reform in the 1990s.

Higher Education

Over 60 percent of Americans currently receive some higher education, achieving one of the highest participation rates in the world. However, the cost of attendance has reached a crisis level for many people. Tuition costs have risen far above the level of inflation and income growth for many years, making access difficult for poor and even middle-class students. In response to this problem, President Clinton and Congress approved a series of tax incentives to alleviate these costs. The long history of federal involvement in higher education makes such direct action at the national level both more possible and more effective, unlike many reforms in elementary and secondary education. The national government supported higher education in the nineteenth century by providing land grants for colleges and universities. Following World War II, more extensive support came through the GI Bill, which met most of the expenses for veterans to attend higher education. This program began a massive post-war expansion of participation in higher education that accelerated when grants and loans were extended to most students in the 1960s.

This federal leadership has been tested in recent years. Spending on higher education dropped by almost 30 percent between 1980 and 1996 (NCES, 1996) while tuition costs climbed rapidly. Further, the prominence of federal support tends to mask the critical role of states, which own and govern most colleges and universities. The proportion of students in these public institutions rose from 50 percent in 1950 to 78 percent in 1994 (NCES, 1996). States provide heavy subsidies in order to keep tuition low and encourage access for all citizens. Such appropriations make up over one-third of revenues for public colleges and universities, and have a substantial impact upon costs. The total cost of public institutions averaged $9,000 per year, as opposed to almost $20,000 per year for private institutions (NCES, 1996). The rising cost of higher education became an increasing public concern and, eventually, prompted a national response.

President Clinton made higher education reform part of his "crusade for education" and proposed making college education as universal as secondary education. The primary weapon in Clinton's arsenal was a tax credit for tuition costs, which appealed to both the public and the Republican Congress. The new plan offers students $3500 in tax credits over four years. President Clinton claimed the plan will make the "largest increase in investment in higher education since the GI Bill a half-century ago." Along with additional tax breaks, the level of aid should reach $36 billion over five years. This amount would provide an average $7.2 billion per year, which represents almost a 50 percent increase in federal funding for students (NCES, 1997). The tax credits will clearly benefit low income students, though most benefits go to middle class and wealthy students. The program attracts immense popularity as a middle-class tax break, and fulfills one of Clinton's election promises, even if the effects on enrollment prove less dramatic. Participation levels of 60 percent are already the highest in the world, and tax credits are unlikely to seriously increase student access, and the plan will likely reduce costs as opposed to boosting enrollment.

Prospects for the Future

The effects of President Clinton's various reforms are unlikely to live up to his ambitious rhetoric, but they do represent sweeping change at the federal level. The tax benefits for college tuition constitute the most dramatic federal action for over two decades and should help alleviate student costs, though they are unlikely to raise enrollment levels significantly. The movement for national curriculum standards and testing at the federal level provokes too much conflict and controversy to achieve much progress. However, lack of a federal consensus does not mean that change will not occur. States continue to adopt similar reforms on their own, and stronger curricula and assessment procedures continue to spread. Decentralization reforms have not achieved such widespread success. Further, federal regulations and strong judicial oversight hamper efforts to decentralize power and authority in education.

The fragmented system of education hinders rapid change throughout the entire nation, though it allows reform on a state by state basis. Education policy continues to experience widespread change, despite these obstacles. Some efforts, such as standards, succeed on a state by state basis despite a lack of national consensus. However, the ultimate impact of these policies on the classrooms and individual students remains to be seen. Will higher standards and decentralization actually improve the educational experience of students and help alleviate problems of economic stagnation, inequality, and poverty? The American experience with previous educational crusades provides some indication. Widespread reform will occur, and improvements may indeed result. Despite any successes, however, the results will never live up to expectations because people demand more of education than it could possibly deliver. Therefore, the future of education policy in the United States can be predicted to offer more of the same.

14

Affirmative Action and the Politics of Race

Richard L. Engstrom

In June 1997, Bill Clinton announced that he intended to use his presidential office to lead the United States in "a great and unprecedented conversation about race." Clinton recognized that it would be a conversation in which "emotions may be rubbed raw," but said that it was necessary because racial discrimination remained "the greatest challenge" his country faced.

Such a conversation will be emotive, because race is one of America's most sensitive and divisive issues. African-Americans report that racial discrimination is still widespread in the United States. In a Gallup survey taken only a few months before Clinton's speech, in January–February 1997, 45 percent of the African-American respondents reported experiencing discrimination, based on their race, within the previous thirty days. Interestingly, whites and blacks in the survey were in rough agreement about the existence of white prejudice, provided the measure of prejudice was based on what whites report about "other whites" and not themselves.

The Gallup survey asked respondents to identify how prejudiced they themselves and others were against blacks. Response options ranged from 0 through 10, with 0 indicating "not at all" and 10 "extremely prejudiced." When whites reported on their own feelings, the average placement on the scale was only 2.1, with 27 percent placing themselves at 0 and only 14 percent at 5 or higher. When whites were asked about "other whites," however, far more prejudice was reported. When the referent was no longer personal, the average response increased to 4.2. The percentage placing other whites at 0 dropped to only 7, while the percentage placing them at 5 or higher increased to 44. Blacks actually reported less prejudice among whites than did whites. While 44 percent of the blacks also placed whites at 5 or higher, 21 percent responded with 0, with the average placement being 3.9 (Gallup Organization, 1997).

While whites and blacks may be in rough agreement when it comes to acknowledging the existence of prejudice, there has been much less agreement between them on how the country should respond to it. At the center of this dispute has been a concept called "affirmative action." The idea behind affirmative action is that conscious actions that benefit African-Americans, and members of other disadvantaged minorities as well, are needed if the United States is to be a society in which "opportunity" is equal in fact, not just in theory. These actions are to help compensate for past discrimination, a way of "levelling the playing field" so that minorities can compete on an equal basis. The actions have taken a variety of forms, ranging from deliberate efforts to make members of minority groups aware of various opportunities, to giving preferences to members of minority groups when "other things are equal," to giving preferences even when other things may not be equal, such as setting aside jobs, contracts, and seats in universities for minorities.

Affirmative action has become a "wedge issue" in American politics. The racial divisions over it are large, and the emotions it stimulates often intense. According to the Gallup survey, African-Americans favor an expanded application of the concept. When asked whether the government should increase or decrease affirmative action programs, a majority of the African-American respondents (53 percent) said that they should be increased, whereas only 12 percent said they should be decreased. A plurality of the white respondents (37 percent), in contrast, favored decreasing affirmative action programs, while only 22 percent favored an increase. One recent study even reports that affirmative action is not simply opposed by many whites, but is also a source of great resentment among them. It was estimated, through an experimental survey design, that demands for affirmative action by African-Americans make virtually all (98 percent) of the whites residing in the South, and 41 percent of those outside the South, angry (Kuklinski *et al.*, 1997)

Affirmative action is an issue that will be at the center of President Clinton's national conversation on race. Whether that conversation succeeds in reducing the racial divide in America will no doubt depend heavily on the public's response to that issue. Clinton hopes to convince the country that these actions are an important medium for helping to relegate its racial problems to its past. In starting the conversation, Clinton stated:

> I know affirmative action has not been perfect in America . . . but when used in the right way, it has worked.

Divisions over issues like affirmative action, however, cause others to be more skeptical about the results of a national conversation. Such a dialogue, some fear, might "do little more than confirm how far we remain apart" (Cose, 1997).

Compensatory Action as Policy

There is no single affirmative action policy in the United States. It is not a program that is neatly bundled in a few legal pronouncements or bureaucratic regulations. At the federal level, for example, there is no Affirmative Action Act as there is a Civil Rights Act of 1964, Voting Rights Act of 1965, or Fair Housing Act of 1968. As noted above, a variety of actions can fall under the concept, and which deserve to be so labelled and which do not is sometimes a matter of debate. Provision requiring race-conscious actions that are intended to be benign are contained in numerous statutes, executive orders, bureaucratic regulations, and Court decisions at all levels of government.

The first use of the expression "affirmative action" in such a document was in Executive Order No. 10925, issued by John F. Kennedy in 1961. The order concerned equal employment opportunities and specified that contracts issued by the federal government require contractors to:

> take affirmative action to ensure that applicants are employed, and that employees are treated during employment, without regard to their race, creed, or national origin.

The responsibility for overseeing compliance with this provision was placed with the president's Committee on Equal Employment

Opportunity, which was created by the order. This language was then repeated in President Lyndon Johnson's Executive Order No. 11246 in 1965, in which the oversight responsibility was transferred to the Department of Labor.

It is usually Richard M. Nixon, however, who is credited with providing substance to the concept by attaching specific numerical goals to affirmative actions. The Nixon Administration in 1969 developed what was popularly called the "Philadelphia Plan" for implementing the federal contractual employment requirement. Under this arrangement, federal contractors are required to agree to explicit "goals and timetables" for hiring minorities on their projects. Contractors failing to attain these goals are required to show that they had in fact made a "good faith effort" to achieve them (see Hood, 1993). If such an effort cannot be demonstrated, the contract is subject to termination. The use of numerical standards to evaluate affirmative actions made the concept much more controversial, with critics equating the goals with *de facto* quotas.

Compensatory affirmative actions are now applied to many areas in which government is involved. The congressional Research Service (CRS) in 1995, for example, identified over 160 provisions in federal statutes, orders, and regulations that "prefer or consider race, gender, or ethnicity as factors in federal employment or the allocation of federal contracts or grants to individuals and institutions." The CRS reported that the areas covered by these provisions concerned employment, housing, education, and governmental contracting (CRS, 1995). There are also many affirmative action provisions administered by state and local governments in the United States, and affirmative action plans within the private sector as well.

White Reactions to Affirmative Action

A 1996 analysis of public opinion surveys concludes that the political differences between the white majority and the black minority in the United States:

> are enormous, quite unlike any other social cleavage, and cannot be explained by black–white differences in income or educational

> attainment or indeed anything else. The racial divide . . . is really racial. (Kinder and Sanders, 1996)

These differences are especially pronounced, as noted above, on affirmative action, where white hostility seems to be especially acute.

Affirmative action is justified as a remedial necessity. It is intended to compensate for the history of discrimination and its contemporary consequences. These race-conscious actions are said to be required because, as a former Supreme Court justice once expressed it, "In order to get beyond racism, we must first take race into account" (*Regents of University of California* v. *Bakke*, 1978). Supporters of affirmative action often make this point by quoting a portion of a commencement speech given by President Johnson at Howard University in 1965, in which Johnson noted:

> You do not take a person who, for years, has been hobbled by chains and liberate him, bring him up to the starting line of a race and then say, "You are free to compete with all the others," and still justly believe that you have been completely fair.

Compensatory actions, in short, are necessary if "equal opportunity" is to be more than a rhetorical expression in America.

These compensatory actions have not been popular with whites, however, who often interpret them as discriminatory toward themselves. Whites complain that affirmative action results in "reverse discrimination." They claim that they are now the victims of discrimination, losing jobs, promotions, contracts, and seats in schools simply because they are white, rather than less deserving. In making up for past discrimination, the concept of "merit" is said to have been discarded. Opponents of affirmative action also have a favorite quotation from a famous speech. They are fond of reciting the passage from Martin Luther King's "I Have a Dream" speech at the 1963 March on Washington in which he stated, "I have a dream that my four little children will one day live in a nation where they will not be judged by the color of their skin but by the content of their character." Affirmative action, they claim, is inconsistent with King's dream, emphasizing color over character.

While racial matters are an especially sensitive area for survey research, white hostility to affirmative action has been well documented through that medium. Responses to survey questions dealing with race are no doubt frequently contaminated by "social desirability" effects. Many respondents are believed to provide "an insincere, 'right' answer" to queries concerning race, especially those who are in fact the most prejudiced (Kuklinski *et al.*, 1997). Question wording is therefore considered particularly important when it comes to racial concerns. This seems to be less of a problem when the issue is affirmative action, however. Whites show little restraint in responding negatively to affirmative action, regardless of the question wording employed. A few examples from national surveys illustrate these negative feelings (Steeh and Krysan, 1996).

A question about affirmative action in employment included in a CBS/*New York Times* survey taken in 1995 provided the respondents with a positive cue, a reason for them to favor affirmative action. The question asked, "Do you believe that where there has been job discrimination against blacks in the past, preference in hiring and promotion should be given to blacks today?" Despite this limiting condition – where there has been job discrimination in the past – only 21 percent of the white respondents provided a positive response, while 68 percent responded negatively.

The National Election Study (NES) conducted by the Survey Research Center at the University of Michigan in 1994 contained a more balanced question about affirmative action and employment. It asked, "Some people say that because of past discrimination, blacks should be given preference in hiring and promotion. Others say that such a preference in hiring and promotion of blacks is wrong because it gives blacks advantages they haven't earned. What about your opinion – are you for or against preferential hiring and promotion of blacks?" Only 10 percent of the white respondents said they were in favor, while 88 percent indicated they were opposed (68 percent "strongly" so).

Another question in the 1994 NES asked respondents about providing "special favors" to African-Americans in light of the discrimination they have suffered. This item, however, contained a negative cue, a reason to reject the need for special assistance. Respondents were asked whether they agreed or disagreed with the statement, "Irish, Italians, Jewish and many other minorities overcame prejudice and worked their way up. Blacks should do the same without any special favors." Over three-quarters of the white respondents (77 percent) agreed, with 37 percent "strongly" agreeing with the statement. Only 12 percent disagreed.

Providing preferences for African-Americans to make up for past discrimination is clearly not popular among whites, many of whom, as noted above, resent it. Donald Kinder and Lynn Sanders (1996) have argued that "When it comes to . . . affirmative action, nothing explains variation in white opinion as well as racial resentment" (see also Sears *et al.*, 1997). The causal ordering within this statement has been questioned, however, as others have argued that affirmative action is itself a cause of racial divisions.

This is the conclusion reached by Paul Sniderman and Thomas Piazza (1993), based on an experiment with survey respondents. They conducted what they called the "mere mention" experiment in which they deliberately varied the order of questions within a survey. Half of the respondents were asked first about their support for affirmative action, and then about their images of black people. The other half were asked first about their images of blacks, and then their support for affirmative action. The question concerning affirmative action was as follows:

> In a nearby state, an effort is being made to increase dramatically the number of blacks working in state government. This means that a large number of jobs will be reserved for blacks, even if their scores on merit exams are lower than those of whites who are turned down for the job. Do you favor or oppose this policy?

Sniderman and Piazza report that when this question about affirmative action is asked first, white respondents are more likely to describe black people as irresponsible and lazy. Among the white respondents who were asked about black people before being asked about affirmative action, 26 percent said that blacks were irresponsible and 20 percent said that they were lazy. Among those presented with the affirmative action question first, however, the percentage identifying blacks as irresponsible increased to 43, and the percentage saying lazy increased to 31. Both differences were statistically significant. Sniderman and Piazza (1993) interpret these results as indicating that affirmative action provokes a dislike of blacks, thereby exacerbating the racial division in the country.

A survey question referring to jobs being "reserved" for blacks that are presumably less "meritorious" may hardly qualify as providing a "mere mention" of affirmative action. But this is no doubt the impression that many whites have of how affirmative action is implemented. It has been reported that up to two-thirds of whites think it is likely that a white will lose a job or promotion to a black due to affirmative action, and that half of white youth think that there are more whites adversely affected by "special preferences" than blacks adversely affected by racial prejudice (Hochschild, 1995). Despite the fact that other groups, such as women, Latinos, and the disabled, have benefitted from affirmative action programs, it is when the beneficiaries are black that the hostility is the greatest (Steeh and Krysan, 1996). One study of the history of the affirmative action issue concludes that it is essentially racial, that the opponents of affirmative action have "focused on, and the public only seemed to care about, *racial* preferences" (Skrentny, 1996).

Affirmative Action as a Political Issue

Affirmative action is both a political issue and a legal issue. On the political front, it has been described as "the ultimate political wedge issue of the mid-1990s" (Williams, 1996). On the legal front, it provides yet another confirmation of Alexis de Tocqueville's observation, made in 1835, that "Scarcely any political question arises in the United States which is not resolved, sooner or later, into a judicial question" (de Tocqueville, 1956). The US Supreme Court, at least as currently constituted, has been a particularly receptive forum for white complaints about affirmative action.

White politicians have made subtle, even less than subtle, racial campaign appeals through references to affirmative action. The most famous instance occurred in the senatorial campaign of Jesse Helms in North Carolina in 1990. Helms was a Republican US senator running for reelection against a black Democrat. During the week before the vote, his campaign ran a television commercial featuring a white man receiving a job rejection letter. This image was accompanied by a voice-over stating, "You needed that job, and you were the most qualified. But they had to give it to a minority because of a racial quota. Is that fair?" The white vote for Helms, estimated at around 65 percent in an exit poll, carried him to victory.

Bob Dole, the Republican presidential nominee in 1996, became a critic of affirmative action while positioning himself for that nomination in 1995. Dole had previously been a supporter of affirmative action programs. Indeed, William Bradford Reynolds, the chief architect of the Reagan Administration's efforts to roll back affirmative action (see Wolters, 1996), identified Dole as playing a critical role in blocking that assault (Reynolds, 1996). But in the spring of 1995, while he was his party's leader in the US Senate, Dole announced his intention to introduce a bill that would prohibit the federal government from giving preferential treatment to members of minority groups, saying that "the race-counting game" had gone too far. The bill, entitled the "Equal Opportunity Act of 1995," was introduced that summer. It would have prohibited any such preference being granted in connection with any "federally conducted program or activity."

Not surprisingly, proponents of affirmative action began to fear that the issue would become, in 1996, "a new version of Willie Horton" (Fletcher, 1996; see also Patrick, 1996). Horton was a young black male who became a subject of controversy in the 1988 presidential campaign. He was serving a life sentence for murder in a Massachusetts prison when, while on a weekend furlough from prison, he raped a white woman and stabbed her husband. The Republican candidate George Bush, then the vice president, used the Horton incident to attack his Democratic opponent, Michael Dukakis, who as governor of Massachusetts supported the furlough policy. While the Republicans claimed that they were addressing the crime issue through the Horton story, the Democrats, and many others, considered it a blatant racial appeal to white voters (see Mendelberg, 1996).

The affirmative action issue did not assume the saliency expected of it in 1996, however. Dole never used the issue in a way comparable to Bush's use of the Horton incident. The issue did not play a featured role in his campaign except in California, where an anti-affirmative action proposition was on the ballot along with the presidential contest. The California proposition, known as the California Civil Rights Initiative, stated:

> The state shall not discriminate against, or grant preferential treatment to, any individual or group on the basis of race, sex, color, ethnicity, or national origin in the operation of public employment, public education, or public contracting.

California voters made the proposition state law, with 54 percent voting for it. An exit poll placed white voter support at 63 percent, whereas Latino and African-American support was at 24 percent and 26 percent, respectively. Dole's endorsement of the proposition did little for his own vote, however. Clinton defeated Dole in California, 51 percent to 38 percent. According to one study, affirmative action was a salient issue to conservative Republicans, but not to the potential swing voters that Dole needed. Improvements in the state's economy during Clinton's first term overshadowed affirmative action for these voters (Cain and MacDonald, 1997).

One reason affirmative action was less salient than expected was no doubt Clinton's effort to defuse the issue. In the summer of 1995, Clinton was also taking a position on affirmative action. He continued to support the concept, he said, because minorities were still being systematically excluded from opportunities. But he also stated that the implementation of it was at times problematic. There were, he said, "legitimate questions about the way affirmative action works." Clinton summed up his position with the slogan "Mend It, Don't End It." He then announced that he was starting the mending process by ordering all federal agencies to make sure that their affirmative action programs complied with "four standards of fairness" which were:

> no quotas, in theory or in practice;
> no illegal discrimination of any kind,
> including reverse discrimination;
> no preference for people who are not
> qualified for jobs or other opportunities;
> and as soon as a program has succeeded,
> it must be retired.

The "Mend It, Don't End It" stand reduced the contrast between Clinton and Dole on this issue and defused much of its electoral impact. White voters across the country, like those in California, opposed affirmative action, but the issue did not cause a large swing to Dole. The balanced question about affirmative action discussed above was repeated in the 1996 NES In that survey, 12 percent of the white respondents favored affirmative action and 88 percent opposed it, with 71 percent strongly opposed. The division of the vote among whites opposed to affirmative action, however, was 44 percent for Clinton to 46 percent for Dole. This is almost identical to the division of the overall white vote recorded in the Voter News Service (VNS) exit poll, which was 43 percent for Clinton and 46 for Dole. Clinton won 84 percent of the African-American vote in the VNS poll, and 72 percent of the Latino vote, thereby defeating Dole in the total vote. (This was the eighth straight presidential election in which black voters and white voters differed in their choice for president.)

Affirmative Action as a Legal Issue

Affirmative action, as noted above, has also been a legal issue. Whites have taken their complaints about affirmative action programs to the courts, arguing that they violate the racial neutrality required of state and local governments by the Fourteenth Amendment's Equal Protection Clause and of the federal government by the Fifth Amendment's Due Process Clause (on the latter, see *Bolling* v. *Sharpe* (1954)). One month prior to Clinton's "Mend It, Don't End It" speech in 1995, the Supreme Court also made an important decision about federal affirmative action programs. The Court held, in *Adarand Constructors* v. *Pena*, that the federal programs, like those of state and local governments, must be strictly scrutinized by the courts.

American courts normally uphold government actions that treat people differently as long as the actions are rationally related to accomplishing some legitimate purpose. But if the difference in treatment is based on race, then the action is held to a higher standard known as "strict scrutiny." Under that standard, an action is permitted only if it is "narrowly tailored" to accomplish a "compelling governmental interest." These expressions, which are "exceedingly vague terms of art" even for lawyers and judges (Edley, 1996), are intended to impose a very difficult burden of proof on the government taking the action. The significance of this elevated burden is revealed in the popular summary of the strict scrutiny test, which is that it is "strict in theory but fatal in fact."

The strict scrutiny standard was adopted to prevent governments from discriminating against racial minorities. Affirmative action programs, however, raised another question – are the race-based actions of governments that are intended to benefit rather than harm racial minorities subject to the same scrutiny? The Supreme Court had been unable to resolve this issue in its first few confrontations with affirmative action programs. In *Regents of California* v. *Bakke* (1978), the Court held that the University of California at Davis could not continue to set aside a specified number of seats in its medical school for minority students. In *Fullilove* v. *Klutznick* (1980), the Court upheld a 10 percent set-aside for minority-owned businesses contained in the federal Public Works Employment Act of 1977. And in *Wygant* v. *Jackson Board of Education* (1986), the Court precluded a school board from laying off white teachers before black teachers with less seniority. But in each of these cases the outcome was arrived at without a majority of the Court agreeing on the basis for the decision.

This changed in 1989 when the Court concluded, in *Richmond* v. *Croson*, that state and local affirmative action programs must satisfy the strict scrutiny standard. At issue in *Croson* was a set-aside program adopted by the city of Richmond, Virginia. Under this program, 30 percent of the value of the city's construction contracts was to be allocated to businesses owned by members of minority groups. Strict scrutiny was again "fatal in fact," as the Court found the program violated the Equal Protection Clause. The city, the Court concluded, failed to demonstrate a compelling interest for its remedial set-aside program because it had failed to provide any evidence of "identified discrimination in the Richmond construction industry". In addition, the Court found that the city's use of "a rigid numerical quota" was not a "narrowly tailored" approach to remedying whatever past discrimination there may have been (see generally Drake and Holsworth, 1996).

One year after *Croson*, the Court confronted another affirmative action program, this one adopted by the Federal Communications Commission (FCC). The FCC had adopted two policies promoting diversity in radio and television broadcasting, in compliance with its responsibilities under the Communications Act of 1934. One policy provided a preference for minority ownership and management in the awarding of new broadcast licenses, the other a preference for the transfer of licenses to minority enterprises. In this case, *Metro Broadcasting* v. *Federal Communications Commission* (1990), the Court chose not to impose the strict scrutiny test. A five-person majority held instead that:

> benign race-conscious measures mandated by Congress . . . are constitutionally permissible to the extent that they serve important governmental objectives within the power of Congress and are substantially related to achievement of those objectives.

These policies, the Court found, satisfied this standard.

The composition of the Court changed by the time of the *Adarand* decision in 1995. In *Adarand* a different five-person majority expressly overruled *Metro Broadcasting*'s determination of the level of scrutiny appropriate for federal programs. The new majority concluded that federal programs must be strictly scrutinized, just like those of state and local governments. At issue in *Adarand* is a US Department of Transportation program that provides contractors with additional compensation if they subcontract work on their projects to minority-owned businesses. The Court remanded the case to the lower court, instructing it to evaluate the program under the strict scrutiny standard.

Affirmative action programs face an uncertain future under the strict scrutiny test. What interests qualify as "compelling," and what exactly "narrow tailoring" entails, are questions that have not been clearly answered by the Supreme Court, which has been closely divided on affirmative action questions. Whether strict scrutiny will continue to be fatal in application, and even whether strict scrutiny will continue to be required of federal programs, will no doubt depend on future changes in the Court's personnel.

The Uncertain Future of Affirmative Action

The Clinton Administration's review of affirmative action had resulted, by the summer of 1997, in the termination of only one program, a set-aside policy for the awarding of contracts by the

Department of Defense. The administration's efforts to "mend" other programs received little public attention. The Department of Justice concluded that, due to persistent discrimination in contracting markets, the government does have a compelling interest in making benign race-conscious decisions in the awarding of contracts. New procurement regulations designed to satisfy the narrow tailoring requirement were expected to be announced by the department in the Fall of 1997. Changes were also expected in the programs administered by the Small Business Administration and the Department of Transportation.

The concept and implementation of affirmative action will no doubt receive much more public attention, however, during Clinton's national "conversation" on race. At the center of the conversation will be the question of whether affirmative action is still needed. There is no question that affirmative action has increased the access that African-Americans and other minorities have had to jobs, contracts, and educational opportunities. The most systematic study of the long-term effects of affirmative action, a matched comparison of graduates of the University of California at Davis medical school, reports that those admitted as a result of affirmative action and other special considerations have been just as successful in their postgraduate training and subsequent professional activities as those that satisfied the school's regular admission criteria (Davidson and Lewis, 1997). Opponents of affirmative action argue, however, that minorities can now compete on an equal basis without the special preferences affirmative action entails. Proponents, in contrast, express concerns about the "resegregation" of many aspects of American society, business, and education if affirmative action programs are curtailed.

Evidence from California suggests that the concerns about resegregation cannot be easily dismissed. The law school of the University of California at Berkeley, for example, returned to a policy of disregarding the race and ethnicity of applicants for admission in 1997. The result was the admission of about 25 percent of the white applicants, compared to 10 percent of the Latino applicants and only 5 percent of the black applicants. (It has been reported that none of the fourteen African-Americans who were admitted chose to attend the school.) These disparities prompted the Office of Civil Rights in the US Department of Education to investigate allegations that the admission criteria employed by the law school are racially discriminatory (see Wallace, 1997).

Affirmative action is an issue that stimulates an emotive response among Americans. The debate over it has been characterized by a "high ratio of claims to evidence" (Hochschild, 1995). Hopefully Clinton's "national conversation" will stimulate more evidence. Without it, the conversation may indeed "do little more than confirm how far we remain apart."

15

Campaign-finance Reform

JASON F. KIRKSEY

The 1996 reelection of President Bill Clinton brought with it more questions than answers about the next four years. One of the most pressing questions is how the president (and Congress) intend to curb the enormous cost of running for Congress and the presidency. Campaign finance reform regulations generally focus on four basic goals: contribution restrictions, limiting campaign spending, public disclosure, and implementing a system of public financing (Alexander, 1992). Campaign finance reform is not only intended to lower the cost of running for office, but also to lessen the influence of money, especially that from special interests in the political system. The influence of political donors is a major concern of the American public (Yang, 1997). The proliferation of political action committees (PACs) and their impact on electoral outcomes, mainly as a result of campaign contributions, is the focus of public concern. Both major parties have alleged that the other has engaged in unethical and illegal campaign fund-raising activities, including accepting contributions from foreign sources. These charges, coupled with the record spending levels of candidates, political parties, PACs and individuals in the 1996 presidential and congressional elections, has left the public outraged and demanding a change.

Efforts to reform the American campaign financing system are not a recent phenomenon (Smith, 1996; Alexander, 1992; Sorauf, 1992). In 1905, President Theodore Roosevelt urged Congress to ban corporate contributions in federal elections. Between 1907 and 1966, Congress enacted legislation that attempted to regulate campaign spending in federal elections, required public disclosure of campaign financing, and sought to limit the influence of wealthy citizens and special interest groups in federal elections. In 1971, Congress enacted the Federal Election Campaign Act (FECA) which marked a major turning point in the history of campaign finance reform (Alexander, 1992). This law required full disclosure of political funding. Amendments to FECA in 1974 resulted in the most comprehensive campaign finance reform legislation ever enacted (Smith, 1996; Alexander, 1992; Sorauf, 1992). The new law established the Federal Election Commission (FEC). This independent regulatory agency enforces federal campaign law, facilitates public disclosure of campaign finances, and administers public funding for the presidential election. The 1974 amendments also established contribution limits on individuals and groups to candidates, political parties and PACS. Individuals are limited to contributions of $1,000 per candidate per election. The total annual limit on individuals for contributions to candidates, parties, or PACs is $25,000. PACs are limited to $5,000 per candidate per election. PACs, unlike individuals, do not have a cumulative annual spending limit, and the 1996 national elections illustrated the ability of political actors to sidestep the current campaign finance laws.

The 1996 Elections

The 1996 elections have been described as a "political fault line," and the elections that "overwhelmed the nation's fragile campaign finance laws" (Marcus and Babcock, 1997). It is estimated that over $2.5 billion was spent by candidates, parties, special interest groups, and individuals. These elections were clearly the most expensive in American history, exceeding the previous record-setting mark by an estimated 25 percent. An examination of the financing of the 1996 presidential and congressional elections indicates how the record-setting levels were achieved.

The presidential election

During the 1996 presidential primary election season the major and minor party candidates spent a total of $237 million of the

$245 million raised, according to the FEC. This amount nearly doubled the amount spent during the same period in 1992. The largest source of primary funding for the candidates in 1996 came from individuals. Slightly more than half of the money raised in 1996 was from individual contributions. PAC contributions accounted for only 1 percent of the 1996 primary funding.

Eligible presidential primary candidates also received public funds. To gain eligibility candidates must raise $5,000, in matchable contributions from individuals of $250 or less, in each of twenty states, for a total of $100,000. Contributions from PACs or party committees are not matchable. Candidates who accept public funds must agree to use these funds only for campaign expenses, as well as comply with the established spending limit. Approximately one-quarter of the money raised in 1996 came from public matching funds. This total was lower than previous years because two Republican primary candidates, Steve Forbes and Morry Taylor (both millionaires), did not participate in the matching-funds program.

The FEC-formulated $37 million legal spending limit for the 1996 primary election campaign appears to have been exceeded by both President Clinton and his Republican challenger, former US Senator Robert J. Dole (R-Kans.). The FEC estimates that President Clinton made approximately $41 million in primary campaign expenditures and Dole about $43 million. Both candidates received slightly more than $13 million in federal matching funds, and therefore were required to adhere to the $37 million spending limit. However, as this examination will show, this infraction pales in comparison to the campaign finance abuses that each of the major parties alleges of the other in their respective efforts to get their candidate elected to the presidency.

In the general election, President Clinton and Republican-challenger Dole received $61.8 million in public funds. During this period no private funds can be raised for campaign purposes. Perot, by virtue of receiving 19 percent of the popular vote in the 1992 presidential election, was also eligible for public funding. Although he received $29 million for the 1996 general election campaign, Perot was permitted to raise private contributions to reach the $62 million spending limit. As of April 1998, the FEC had not yet released the final spending figures for the candidates in the general election.

"Soft" money

The use of "soft" money is the activity that pushed spending in the campaign to record levels. "Soft" money consists of unlimited contributions to political parties by corporations, unions or individuals. "Soft" money is categorized differently by the FEC from "hard" money. "Hard" money consists of funds raised within the legal limits of FECA, and can therefore be used for federal campaigns. Soft-money contributions are for "party-building" activities like voter registration and generic party advertising, and are therefore legally different from direct contributions to candidates. In 1996 (as well as in recent previous elections) soft money served as a loophole that enabled candidates and contributors to evade the current rules.

Soft-money contributions proved to be a major focus of the 1996 presidential election campaign spending controversy. FEC figures indicate that during the 1995–6 election cycle there was a dramatic increase in soft-money contributions to both major parties. The Democrats spent $122 million in soft money, an increase of 271 percent from 1992. Republican soft-money contributions increased by 178 percent between 1992 and 1996. The Republicans spent $150 million in soft money in 1996, a 224 percent increase from 1992. While less than half of the soft-money contributions to the two major parties was used in the presidential campaign, the amounts that were spent led to both President Clinton and Bob Dole spending almost double the legal limit.

The most troubling aspect to the American public of the soft-money controversy in the 1996 presidential race appeared to be how the contributions were raised (Drew, 1997b). Some of the most prominent elected officials in the United States were accused of engaging in a "shakedown" of their contributors. The most prominent of the alleged abuses were attributed to President Clinton and Vice President Gore (Farris, 1997).

President Clinton was also accused of "selling" (or at least renting) rooms in the White House. During the president's first term individuals who had contributed large amounts to the Democratic Party stayed overnight at the White House, often in the Lincoln Bedroom. Funds from these soft-money contributors to the Democratic Party are estimated to be about $10 million.

Another alleged fund-raising impropriety involved the Democratic National Committee (DNC)-organized White House "coffees." Between 1995 and 1996, over 100 coffee meetings were hosted at the White House for donors and supporters. About one-third of the attendees made large contributions (approximately $27 million) to the Democratic Party near the time of their appearance at these events, although the president said that no fund-raising took place at these meetings.

The White House released videotapes from some of the "coffees." Republicans argue that the tapes provide more evidence that President Clinton engaged in illegal fund-raising activity. The Democratic response was to produce videotapes showing President Reagan meeting with Republican Party donors at the White House, alleging that the fund-raising activities of President Clinton were not any different than those of the former president.

Vice President Gore also engaged in several questionable fund-raising activities. The most serious of the alleged improprieties was the solicitation of contributions over the phone from his White House office (fund-raising on federal property is prohibited by law). While the Vice President vowed to discontinue this practice, questions concerning the legality of such activities inevitably emerged.

The most egregious of the alleged funding abuses involved millions of dollars in foreign contributions to President Clinton's reelection effort. Donations from foreign citizens or businesses are prohibited in US elections. It was alleged that one of the foreign contributors, the Chinese government, attempted to funnel several million dollars into US political campaigns, including the presidential contest. The charge of illegal activities in the presidential race centered around President Clinton's relationship with John Huang. Huang, a former US executive of the Indonesian-based Lippo conglomerate, was appointed by the President to a mid-level position at the Commerce Department after the 1992 election . He eventually took a job as a fund-raiser for the DNC, where he raised approximately $3 million in donations to the Democratic Party from the Asian-American community. Although Huang denied any wrongdoing in his fund-raising tactics, the DNC returned most of the money due to the questionable nature of its source, refunding a total of $2.8 million in suspect contributions and also releasing information indicating that $2.2 million of these funds had been raised by three fund-raisers, John Huang, Johnny Chung and Charles Yah Lin Trie (Balz, 1997).

The Republican Party seemed to emulate some of the questionable fund-raising tactics of the Democrats in 1996. The Republicans are accused of selling access to key elected officials. In their efforts to raise soft-money contributions, the Republicans allegedly promised "special treatment" to donors of $250,000 or more (Marcus and Babcock, 1997). An additional alleged fund-raising impropriety involves the creation of a questionable organization by former Republican National Committee (RNC) Chairman Haley Barbour to raise undisclosed funds, including some from abroad. Barbour's National Policy Forum has been part of an investigation into Republican campaign finance abuses, in particular contributions from foreign sources. The RNC has returned over $100,000 in contributions after determining they were from illegal foreign sources; the Democrats argue that the RNC should return more than $2 million dollars in illegally donated funds (Balz, 1997).

Questions surrounding the fund-raising tactics of the Democrats, particularly the roles of President Clinton and Vice President Gore, led to Republican calls for a Justice Department investigation. In September, Attorney General Janet Reno answered these calls by conducting a 30-day review of the fund-raising activities of the president and vice president (Clymer, 1997). It was speculated that these reviews were a precursor to the appointment of an independent counsel. In October Reno announced that she would need another 60 days to determine whether campaign contributions were illegally solicited from the White House. In the end, the Attorney General, much to the dismay of Republicans, decided against the appointment of an independent counsel. As the presidential fund-raising controversy contined to unravel, the American public became less optimistic that the whole story would ever be known.

Congressional elections

At the congressional level, spending during the 1995–96 election cycle also increased over the previous two-year election period (1993–94). In an analysis of the 2,605 congressional candidates in

1996 the FEC found increases of 7 percent in receipts and 5 percent in expenditures. A total of $790 million was raised by the candidates, with $765 million being spent. The magnitude of the increased campaign spending in 1996 can be put in perspective by comparing it to a previous election. During the 1991–92 election cycle there were 2,950 candidates whose total spending was $680 million. The results of this comparison indicate that in the 1996 congressional elections, 350 fewer candidates than in 1992 spent approximately $100 million more in their efforts to win office.

In the House, 2,289 candidates spent $478 million in 1996. This represented an 18 percent increase over the 1993–94 cycle. The 853 Republican candidates outspent the 827 Democratic candidates $252 million to $221 million. Winning candidates spent approximately $300 million. This results in the average successful House campaign costing about $700,000. These successful candidates spent $123 million of $156 million of the money contributed by PACs.

In the 1996 Senate elections, the 316 candidates raised $285 million and spent $288 million. These figures represented about a 10 percent decrease from 1993–94. Successful Senate candidates spent $128 million including $30 million of the $46 million PACs contributed. Based on these figures, the campaigns of Senate winners in 1996 averaged approximately $4 million.

The two major parties raised $881 million in federal receipts during the 1995–96 election cycle. This was an increase of 73 percent over the previous presidential election cycle (and a 97 percent increase over the previous two-year cycle) according to the FEC. The Republican Party raised $549 million compared to $332 million for the Democrats. The largest increases for both parties occurred among soft-money contributions. Republican national party committees (i.e. congressional campaign committees, senatorial campaign committees, etc.) disbursed approximately $150 million in soft money, an increase of 224 percent over 1992. In 1996, Democratic national party committees showed a 257 percent increase in soft-money spending over 1992. These committees disbursed $117 million of the $122 million raised by the party.

The financial activity among PACs also increased in 1996. According to the FEC, PAC spending during the 1995–96 election cycle totaled $430 million. Federal candidates received $218 million in PAC contributions. This amount represented a 15 percent increase over both the previous two-year election cycle (1993–94) and presidential election cycle (1991–92). The 1996 election was the first time in several election cycles that Republican candidates received more PAC money than their Democratic opponents. This is a probable result of the Republicans' recently gained majority in Congress.

Independent expenditures

Another area of campaign funding that is a target of controversy is independent expenditures. According to the FEC, an "independent expenditure" is a public communication or advertisement that expressly advocates the election or defeat of a clearly identifiable candidate made independently of any federal candidate or her/his committee. Independent expenditures are not subject to any spending limits. These expenditures must be reported to the FEC by the committee making the expenditures. Individuals must also report independent expenditures if the amount exceeds $250.

In *Buckley* v. *Valeo* (1976), the US Supreme Court held that independent expenditures made by individuals could not be constitutionally limited due to the free speech provision of the First Amendment. The Court, however, held that contributions were distinct from independent expenditures, and therefore could be limited. Twenty years later, in *Colorado Republican Federal Campaign Committee* v. *Federal Election Commission (FEC)* (1996), the Supreme Court ruled that the First Amendment also precluded limits on independent campaign expenditures by political parties. According to the FEC, in 1996, the two major parties spent $11.5 million independently of their respective candidates' campaigns, with the Republicans significantly outspending the Democrats $10 million to $1.5 million.

In the 1996 congressional elections, about $21 million was spent independently, either in support of, or against, candidates. Most of these expenditures occurred in Senate races. Approximately $16 million was spent independent of the senatorial candidates' campaigns. The expenditures were split evenly in ads for ($8 million) and against ($8 million) candidates. Nearly $10 million in these expenditures were for Republican senatorial candidates compared to almost $6 million spent on Democrats. In House races, independent expenditures totaled roughly $5 million. The majority of these expenditures went for ads in support of candidates. Almost $1 million in independent expenditures favoring or opposing Democratic candidates were made in the campaign. Over $4 million was spent independently on Republican House candidates.

Over $10 million in independent expenditures for and against candidates were made by PACs in 1996. This figure nearly doubled the amount of independent expenditures of PACs in the 1994 elections. Almost $7 million in 1996 independent expenditures were in support of candidates. PACs focused the overwhelming majority of their independent expenditures on congressional elections. In the presidential contest, PACs spent just over $1 million independently of the candidates' campaigns. This figure represented a decrease from the 1992 presidential election, in which $4 million in independent expenditures were made by PACs. One possible explanation for PAC independent expenditures in 1996 is the perception early on that Dole was unable to defeat President Clinton; however, control of Congress was "up for grabs."

Despite the warnings of elected officials, and the public's outcry for reforms that limit the influence of special interests in federal elections, the 1996 elections achieved record proportions in receipts and expenditures. The two major parties' reliance on soft-money contributions to elude existing campaign finance rules, particularly in the presidential race, demonstrates the vulnerability of the American electoral system to wealthy contributors. The Court's reluctance to allow limits on independent expenditures left the door open for campaign spending to remain an issue in future elections. With no apparent end in sight, the American public could only wonder about the impact of this trend on the future of the political system.

Prospects for Campaign-finance Reform

In his 1997 State of the Union message, President Clinton set a deadline of July 4 for the Congress to send him a new campaign finance law. Congress failed to meet this deadline. In October, both the House and the Senate agreed to debate campaign finance legislation during the fall of 1997 (Schmitt, 1997). Among the numerous campaign finance reform bills introduced in Congress, the legislation proposed by Senators John McCain (R., Ariz.), and Russell Feingold (D., Wisc.) appeared to have the most support. This bipartisan effort attempts to alter dramatically the existing campaign financing system. Under this legislation, PAC contributions would be prohibited. PACs currently are limited to $5,000 contributions per candidate per election. Soft-money contributions would also be banned (currently, these contributions are unlimited and unregulated). Contributions from individuals not qualified to vote in federal elections such as non-US citizens would also be forbidden under this proposal. The legislation also calls for those candidates who voluntarily agree to spending limits to receive some free television time, as well as discounted postal rates and advertising rates. President Clinton said he would sign the McCain–Feingold Bill. A similar bipartisan proposal has been introduced in the House by Representatives Martin T. Meehan (D-Mass.), and Christopher Shays (R-Conn.).

While Congress failed to meet the July 4 deadline, President Clinton appeared to be moving forward with his campaign finance reform efforts. On June 4, 1997, following an earlier request (May 16, 1997) by five members of Congress (Meehan and Shays along with Representatives Zach Wamp (R-Tenn.), James P. Moran (D-Va.) and Marge Roukema (R-N.J.)), the President petitioned the FEC to ban soft-money contributions. While there has been no clear determination of whether the FEC has the authority to eliminate soft money, given the agency's past record it is unlikely that any changes will occur regardless of the decision. The President's petition bypassed Congress, which up to that point had refused to enact new campaign-finance reform legislation.

Groups attempting to increase public sentiment in favor of reforming the current campaign-financing system have increased their efforts as well. Earlier in 1997, grass-roots reformers began a petition drive called "Project Independence." Chaired by former US Senator Bill Bradley (D-N.J.), this campaign had hoped to collect 1,776,000 signatures supporting the McCain–Feingold Bill by the President's July 4 deadline. By October, 1 million signatures were on the petition, well short of the July 4 goal.

The inability of the FEC to curb the abuses in 1996 served as a further disappointment to the American public. The historical ineffectiveness of the FEC to punish abusers raises questions about the enforcement of any new campaign finance reforms. The FEC, for a variety of reasons, has been described as a failure. The boastful spending in the 1996 elections evidences the virtual impotency of this regulatory agency charged with overseeing federal campaigns. FEC rulings on improper funding usually date back a campaign or longer (President Clinton's 1992 campaign was fined by the FEC), with the resulting penalties (if any) serving little or no purpose to the offenders. The consistent under-funding of the agency, coupled with its bipartisan configuration, has exacerbated its weaknesses (Alexander, 1992; Sorauf, 1992).

Campaign-finance reform opponents

Most Americans clearly believe that the current system of campaign finance needs to be reformed (Broder, 1997; Cass, 1997). Opponents of reforming the existing rules, however, are not optimistic that any reforms will be successfully implemented. The most prominent argument against reforming the law is that banning soft money or placing spending limits on independent expenditures violates the First Amendment's guarantee of free speech. This position has been consistently supported by the Supreme Court.

One of the leading, and certainly the most outspoken, opponents of legislation reforming campaign finance, including a proposed constitutional amendment, has been Senator Mitch McConnell (R-Ky.). McConnell's opposition to reform proposals was supported by eleven citizens' groups including the National Rifle Association, the Christian Coalition, the National Right to Life Committee, the American Civil Liberties Union, and the National Education Association. This unusual ideological coalition opposed reform legislation, the McCain–Feingold Bill in particular, on the basis of the First Amendment.

While the public wants to see a change in the nation's campaign finance laws, most Americans have little confidence that the president and/or the Congress will make any changes (Cass, 1997). Even if the unlikely passage of the McCain–Feingold Bill were to occur, it is doubtful that the government will ever be able to eliminate the corrosive effect of money on politics. If candidates and contributors are unwilling to abide by the current campaign finance restrictions, it is highly improbable that they will adhere to even tighter restrictions.

Congressional hearings

On March 11, 1997, the Senate voted 99–0 to authorize the Senate Governmental Affairs Committee to conduct an investigation into the "illegal or improper activities in connection with the 1996 federal election campaigns." While the focus of the investigation was to examine federal elections, the emphasis was quickly narrowed by the Republican majority to the presidential election. The Committee began holding Special Investigation hearings on July 8, 1997. The hearings were scheduled to be held throughout July and possibly into August. On October 31, 1997, after hearing testimony from almost 100 witnesses for approximately four months, Senator Fred Thompson (R-Tenn.), chairman of the Senate Governmental Affairs Committee, announced that the hearings were being suspended, and that the probe would not be extended beyond the December 31, 1997 deadline. Thompson cited declining support for the investigation among his Senate colleagues as leading to the decision (Kellman, 1997).

President Clinton declined an invitation to testify before the Senate committee. The unusual request was issued following Dole's offer to appear before the Senate panel. The hearings failed to substantiate most of the major Republican alleged improprieties against the Democrats, and specifically President Clinton. The last remaining opportunities for the 105th Congress to enact campaign reform legislation virtually ended in the House on March 30, 1998 as a result of the manipulative efforts of the Republican leadership. The Senate, in February 1998, killed the McCain–Feingold Bill. With major legislation reforms either defeated or blocked, the last shred of hope for reform legislation had rested with efforts to convince twenty-two House members to join 196 of their colleagues by signing a discharge petition circulating in the House.

Conclusion: The Future of Campaign-finance Reform

With a new campaign-finance scandal being reported on what seems to be a daily basis, the question that many Americans have asked themselves is whether Congress will ever pass, and the president sign, major campaign-finance reform legislation? The record spending levels reached in the 1996 elections produced a disgruntled American public. Intense media scrutiny exposed the "selling" of the White House, as well as questionable campaign contributions and fund-raising tactics on the part of both major parties. Such media reports, coupled with the urging of current and former legislators, catapulted the issue of campaign-finance reform to the top of the public agenda. Despite the heightened focus, the chance of any major (or even minor) campaign-finance reform legislation being enacted at the national level remains unlikely.

One option for reforming the current campaign-financing system is for candidates and parties to enact self-imposed restrictions. Amid the numerous fund-raising controversies surrounding the 1996 elections, the DNC announced voluntary restrictions. While this may be analogous to "the fox guarding the hen house," it is at least a recognition of public concern by the DNC The DNC will no longer accept contributions of more than $100,000 per year from any one donor, whether individual, corporate or union. The DNC also will no longer accept contributions from noncitizens who are permanent residents or contributions from American subsidiaries of foreign-owned companies, both of which are currently legal. This appears to be a potential route of campaign-finance reform rather than legislative action by the president and Congress.

The public's skepticism toward seeing any legislative changes in the existing campaign finance rules is warranted given the realization by members of Congress and the president, that even minor changes in the system will have a considerable impact on their respective parties, and possibly their own political careers. The future of campaign finance reform, however, may not be as bleak as the preceding analysis (and public sentiment) indicates. Campaign-finance reform proposals have been enacted (usually through the initiative process) in a number of states. This may serve as the eventual route (all of the proposals are currently under legal challenge) for altering the nation's campaign-financing system. While establishing campaign-contribution limits, and implementing public financing for state-level elections does not directly impact federal elections, it may stimulate the public no longer simply to express the desire for change, but instead to crusade actively for national politicians to reform the campaign-financing system. Only time will show the effect of state-level campaign-finance reforms on the American political system.

16

The Regional City: Governance and Competitiveness in Pittsburgh

Brian D. Jacobs

This chapter highlights recent developments in urban and regional governance in the United States. It develops a theme covered in Vice President Al Gore's 1997 seminar series, "Community 2020: A New Future for the American City." The seminars have identified the need for effective policies for sustainable development, crime reduction, educational betterment and improved race relations. However, the following concentrates on the seminar theme of cities as important regional hubs where public–private partnerships contribute to economic competitiveness. The Pittsburgh case illustrates the strengthening ties between local and regional economic development policies and the efforts of the public and private sectors to promote regional growth through complex policy networks.

Cities are Important

The discussion about the future of the cities launched during the Clinton Administration's second term is significant because it recasts the "urban question" in a broad setting. Community 2020 is about the role of metropolitan regions in the new global high-technology economy. The administration has therefore adopted a broad perspective that promises to refocus "urban policy" outwards to the wider global and regional contexts. This suggests that coordinated regional policies can effectively help to overcome local problems such as unemployment and poor housing. This view represents a significant theoretical rehabilitation of "the city" as well as a practical recognition that cities will play an important part in sustaining the nation's competitiveness in the new millennium.

Until recently, it has been fashionable to assume that big-city governments no longer play an important role because they are powerless and at the mercy of the disruptive forces of globalization. Ohamae (1990, 1995) predicted the end of the nation state and the rise of global regions in a technology-driven "borderless world." For Ohamae (1995), national interest had become "a declining industry" since corporations organized production globally. Other writers asserted that America's big cities were so vulnerable to global economic forces that city governments could not influence events in the market (Kantor, 1995; Sassen, 1995). Market trends hastened the political decline of cities and increased the difficulties of governing them (Schockman, 1996). Similarly, urban "hyper-pluralism" portrayed diverse interests contending for influence over urban policy while wealth and political power shifted to the suburbs that were the new growth poles (Thomas and Savitch, 1991). Urban political coalitions broke up as economic activity located at "edge city" (Garreau, 1991). Urban regimes, consisting of coalitions of community and business interests, found it difficult effectively to respond to changing market conditions as government fragmented between diverse networks that politicians could not control (Stone and Sanders, 1987).

Despite its superficial appeal and its germ of truth, this "weak-government" perspective does not satisfactorily account for the changed role of cities in the United States in the 1990s. Certainly, the old political machines and coalitions have gone, and cities have suffered reduced funding for many public services. Subnational government is fragmented, and many cities rely on powerful business leadership groups to promote economic development. However, in spite of the loss of influence of cities over many of their traditionally strong public provisions, urban policy-makers still enjoy substantial political influence within and without their cities. Indeed, Clarence Stone (1989), who has long argued that modern urban political elites have lost power, now calls for a reassessment of the urban political machine. He argues that "many practices" associated with the political machine "linger on" (Stone, 1996) through patronage politics and officeholders who seek electoral support by offering favors to hold on to power. Indeed, Eldersveld *et al.*, (1995) argue that modern male-dominated urban elites are so powerful that they often neglect the problems that face poor urban communities and minorities.

However, there are other factors, apart from patronage and power-seeking, that help to sustain the political influence of city politicians and public officials. As in business, where corporate executives work in networks that bring together organizations with common interests, cities have discovered the importance of collaboration. Put simply, mayors and public officials have become more extensively networked than ever before as they have sought to position their cities as important players in the economic market. Gruberg (1996), in a study of Milwaukee, shows that modern city mayors are often highly influential in national and regional political networks. Schneider *et al.* (1995) refer to the successful new "public entrepreneurs" of the 1990s who are the mayors, politicians, and public officials most keen to work in the competitive market to develop global strategies that extend their political influence. Policy networks give public officials a political salience that they would not otherwise enjoy. As Peters (1997a) argues, the globalization of the economy has enhanced the role of market-oriented governments that have extended their range of policy interests by establishing new relationships with the public and private sectors. In this setting, the new urban public entrepreneurs have taken advantage of the opportunities presented to them by regional networking and they have realized that regional action can effect change at the local level (Orfield, 1997).

The Reagan Administration stimulated this process by encouraging the states and cities to work with the private sector and to enhance competitiveness through less reliance on federal government. This led the public sector to borrow management techniques from the private sector to run community services (Bledsoe, 1993) and to work more effectively with business leadership groups. By the late 1990s, according to Vice President Al Gore, "businesslike" federal government had come to behave so much like the private sector that it was more efficient, more customer-oriented, and less encumbered by wasteful bureaucracy (Gore, 1997). It is easy to over-state the managerial similarities of governments and companies, but "reinventing government" efforts have produced interesting comparisons of state governments and multinational corporations in terms of their size and revenue-generating activities. For example, a *Congressional Quarterly* (*Congressional Quarterly*, 1997) study, using 1994 data, compared state governments to "Fortune 500" US corporations. The study found that the State of California generated $89.8 billion in revenues placing it above Wal-Mart and only below General Motors, Ford, and Exxon in the revenue league. *Congressional Quarterly* presented a "Governing 100" with California at the top of the list, New York State second and New York City third. The Commonwealth of Pennsylvania came in fifth with revenue of $30.5 billion, only after Texas. Pennsylvania had a population of over 12 million people and employed 144,945 people on a full-time basis.

Entrepreneurial Cities

The entrepreneurialism of state and local government is not new, and this underscores a degree of continuity in governance concerning the role of cities in the national economy (Holden, 1996). Recent research has dealt with the historic entrepreneurial role of cities and the enduring links between cities and profit-driven corporations. In the nineteenth century, corporations demanded a reliable transport network developed with such substantial aid from public funds (Perry, 1995) that only periodic financial crises constrained the clamor for growth and civic advancement. Doig (1995) finds that nineteenth-century cities supported developments that powered the national economy and produced wealthy corporations committed to growth. Corporate elites frequently used politically weak local governments to promote large infrastructure projects that enhanced civic pride and competitiveness. Local governments borrowed money and incurred large debts to fund projects that produced "a buccaneering sense of political enterprise" (Monkkonen, 1995). In the 1920s, property taxes declined in importance as a source of local government revenue as federal and state support increased so that federal government assumed "a local role" by supplementing local revenues (Monkkonen, 1995).

Sbragia (1996) studies entrepreneurial cities within the changing federal system. She shows that state and local governments have been at the centre of the process of inter-governmental change in the federal system. She argues that, unlike British local authorities, the viability of US local governments derived from their frequent interventions in economic development. She maintains that the "evolution of the American private sector was intertwined with public power, frequently exercised at the state and local level, much more directly than was the British private sector" (Sbragia, 1996). This view is confirmed by Pittsburgh's situation, where a powerful business elite at the turn of the century used public provisions to boost economic growth. Industrial and banking barons such as Andrew Carnegie, Henry Clay Frick and George Westinghouse worked with political leaders to realize their civic ambitions. After the Second World War, Mayor David Lawrence, a classic Democratic power broker, created a powerful political machine (Weber, 1990) that supported business in backing local universities, funding extensive reconstruction, and transforming the city's central business district.

The Competitive Challenge in "America's New Economy"

Today, US city governments facilitate property deals, bring smaller companies together in alliances and aid corporations to relocate production (Kresl and Gappert, 1995; Savitch and Vogel, 1996). The US Department of Housing and Urban Development (HUD) report, *America's New Economy* (HUD, 1996), shows that it is now the quest for regional competitiveness that is important because cities exist in a fast-changing environment where global competition is intense. According to the report, "metropolitan regions" are centrally important in the era of information technology (IT) where new and diverse industry clusters are replacing traditional single-industry dependencies. Company downsizing, corporate reengineering and the spatial dispersion of industrial production have therefore forced cities to develop coherent regional economic development strategies. These strategies position cities within the wider context of their hinterlands and identify distinctive industrial activities and economic identities between companies located in regions. Regional cities have therefore developed policy interests beyond their jurisdictions as politicians and public officials increasingly recognize that their cities depend on the economic vitality of towns and communities that orientate towards regional metropolitan commercial and financial hubs.

The HUD report advocates closer links between business and government to coordinate competitive strategies, but competition also intensifies rivalries between regional cities. Fast-growing regional centers such as Atlanta, Denver, and Phoenix continue economically to outpace former industrial leaders such as Cleveland, Detroit, and Pittsburgh. Policy-makers in New York, Chicago, and Los Angeles want to maintain truly international status for their cities, but they confront multiple problems including social conflict, crime, and urban disorder. *The State of the Cities* report (HUD, 1997) shows that the problems for older cities arise from their urban ghettos, worn-out infrastructures and congested central business districts. In contrast, new suburban employment centers and "sunbelt" cities offer greenfield sites for development with ease of transportation and access. Cervero (1989) describes the expansion of business parks, subcities and large office corridors located along freeways forming new regional economic clusters. High-growth regions have strategies to ensure that they avoid economic obsolescence by sustaining and developing their core high-tech and commercial competencies. For example, Silicon Valley near San Francisco is the world's leading concentration of high-technology industry. It has constantly to innovate to stay ahead; business and government leaders therefore work in partnership to ensure that Silicon Valley retains its world-leader role in IT The Joint Venture Silicon Valley Network (JVSVN) is a public–private partnership co-chaired by Mayor Susan Hammer of the City of San Jose and Lewis Platt, president and chief executive of Hewlett-Packard computers. The partnership covers the whole of Santa Clara County, San Mateo County from Route 92 south, Scotts Valley in Santa Cruz County and Fremont in Alameda County. As JVSVN points out, this constitutes a region with a population of 2 million that is larger than eighteen US states (JVSVN, 1997). The JVSVN promotes a strong valley economy that retains high-technology companies and strengthens the world-class business infrastructure in the area. Silicon Valley represents a regional growth economy that provides a strong contrast with the old "rustbelt" cities of the Northeast (Deitrick and Beauregard,

1995). The valley has a high-tech economy that is geographically dispersed, flexibly organized and highly innovative.

Pittsburgh: Defending the Base

This provides daunting competition for the diverse and administratively fragmented Pittsburgh region. The city is at the heart of a wider Metropolitan Statistical Area (MSA) that suffered severe industrial decline in the early 1980s. Pittsburgh lies within Allegheny County, which contains 130 municipalities within a 731-square mile area. The city cooperates with the county in economic development and planning and with other local government bodies and public agencies that run various city services. The six-county MSA includes Allegheny, Beaver, Butler, Fayette, Washington, and Westmoreland counties (see Map 16.1). The MSA therefore provides a useful definition of the metropolitan region. The MSA definition is appropriate because it covers important clusters of companies and industries located in those counties. The MSA population declined in the 1980s and the numbers continued downwards in Pittsburgh into the early 1990s. Pittsburgh's population declined from 369,879 in 1990 to 358,883 in 1994. After 1990, the population of the whole MSA remained stable at an estimated 2,424,000 for 1995. This contrasts strongly with a 7.2 percent growth in the US population since 1985 and rapid growth rates in some other MSAs. Between 1985 and 1995, the population of the largest MSAs in the United States grew by over 7 percent while the Pittsburgh MSA reduced by 2.4 percent. Between 1990 and 1995, the US Census Bureau estimated that the Denver–Boulder–Greeley MSA had expanded by 12.8 percent, Dallas–Fort Worth Consolidated MSA by 10.2 percent, and Austin-San Marcos MSA by 14.7 percent. The Pittsburgh MSA, however, had an aging population, losing 13 percent of people in the 20–34-year-old age bracket between 1985 and 1992 (The Enterprise Corporation of Pittsburgh, 1996).

It is difficult to provide an effective regional economic development strategy to overcome this loss of ground by southwestern Pennsylvania when, even within the state, there is regional competition. Deitrick and Beauregard (1995) define four regional economies in Pennsylvania that traditionally depended on distinct

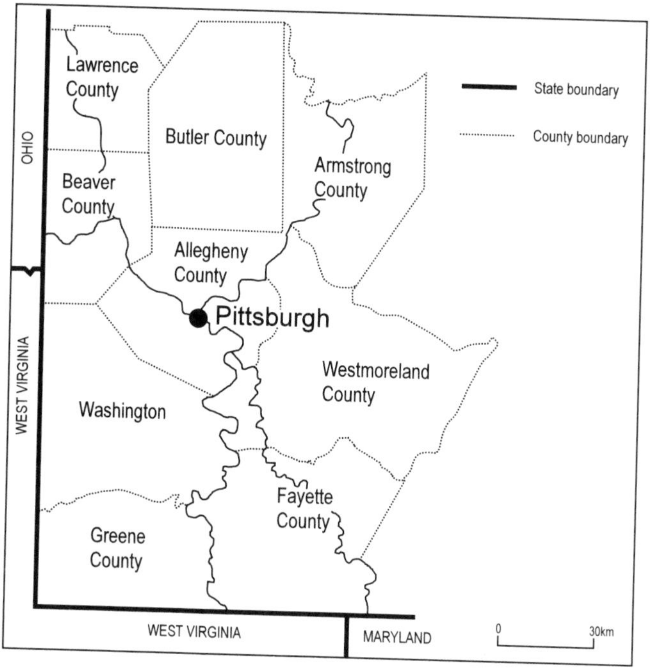

MAP 16.1 *The Pittsburgh region, including MSA counties*

core industrial and commercial activities. The center of the state specialized in agriculture. Commerce and finance clustered in the Southeast around Philadelphia while coal was located in the Northeast around Scranton. Pittsburgh was at the center of the economically diverse region in the Southwest of the state (see Map 16.1). Regional policy in southwestern Pennsylvania is also complicated by public-agency competition and the existence of jurisdictional overlaps and confusions. The Commonwealth of Pennsylvania's economic development initiatives cover the whole state, most notably through the Governor's Action Team that provides a one-stop economic development service for companies. The Southwestern Pennsylvania Planning Commission has defined the region as Allegheny County and its five adjacent counties while the Penn's Southwest Association (a public–private economic development partnership) defines nine counties making up the southwestern edge of Pennsylvania. The Pennsylvania Economy

League has defined the region as the twenty-nine counties of western Pennsylvania.

Heavy industrialization in the Pittsburgh region created a pattern of development that magnified the impact of steel plant closures and the rundown of manufacturing. The region traditionally depended upon its environmentally degrading "smoke-stack" industries, including coal, steel, glass and aluminium. Pittsburgh suffered some of the worst consequences of 1980s industrial decline and falling population. Lubove (1996) highlights the vulnerability of the Pittsburgh regional economy, listing steel closures in the valley communities where plants closed at Rankin (1982), Duquesne (1984), Homestead (1986), McKeesport (1987) and elsewhere. Corporate leaders in Pittsburgh, together with their employees, directly experienced the consequences of recession and industrial restructuring during the 1980s. Between 1982 and 1987, the Pittsburgh MSA lost 30 percent of its manufacturing sector jobs with a further 10 percent decline between 1987 and 1992. However, service industry jobs in Allegheny County increased from 23 to 39 percent of "non-farm" employment between 1969 and 1992 (University of Pittsburgh, 1994) as the region made the transition to a post-industrial economy. The University of Pittsburgh and Carnegie Mellon University reported substantial increases in spending on research and development (R & D) as the service and high-technology sectors of the economy expanded (The Enterprise Corporation of Pittsburgh, 1996).

Pittsburgh currently pursues a strongly growth-oriented local economic development strategy with high-tech robotics development as a central theme. To improve competitiveness, the city is involved in regional partnerships as well as in local economic development. The partnerships and policy strategies reflect the desire of city politicians and officials to work to defend and promote the city "base," especially the central business district. However, partnerships also serve the corporate private sector in the quest for innovation through enhanced regional competitiveness. This is important because both the city and the region contribute significantly to the industrial fortunes of the United States; a fact underlined by Pittsburgh's ranking nationally as ninth in the 1995 league of cities with "Fortune 500" corporate headquarters. Pittsburgh had eight US "Fortune 500" corporate headquarters and thirteen on the "Fortune 1,000" list. The largest corporations listed included the U.S.X. Corporation (steel), Alcoa (aluminium), Westinghouse (electricals), H.J. Heinz (food products), PNC Bank, Mellon Bank, and the Duquesne Light Company (electrical utility). However, global competition poses a challenge to Pittsburgh's "Fortune 500" corporations as well as small and medium-sized businesses (SMEs) in the region. Locally-based corporations including Pittsburgh Plate Glass and Westinghouse communicate world-wide, organize production around the world and deploy resources away from domestic production centers. In order to be competitive, the Pittsburgh region has had to adopt high-tech solutions and expand its research capabilities and has to provide commercial, financial, and legal services for corporations. The city has therefore repositioned itself in the market to be a dynamic player encouraging innovation and corporate flexibility. Public officials and "career politicians" have to be experts aware of these demanding issues (Bledsoe, 1993) in their roles as entrepreneurs in regional and local economic development. Pennsylvania Governor Tom Ridge possesses proven entrepreneurial skills and enthusiasm for a strong market economy. For example, the Governor's Action Team promotes the state and encourages inward investment. State and local public officials support regional partnerships that rely upon strong business leadership to formulate and implement a range of economic development objectives.

Networked Governance: Overcoming Fragmentation

Clarke (1993) argues that such public interventions have produced a "new localism in an era of global economic change." According to Clarke, local governments respond to global restructuring through policy activism to deal with trends that otherwise divert power away from the locality (also Clarke and Goetz, 1994). As Rhodes (1997) argues, "governance" thus refers to change in government producing new processes and networks that respond to such challenges. In corporations, there are new organizational relationships and changes to core structures achieve internal process improvements and external networking (Porter, 1985; Davidow and Malone, 1992; D'Aveni, 1994; Hamel and Prahalad, 1994; Galbraith, 1995). The pattern of the new regional governance is complicated because it involves substantial adaptation of existing organizational arrangements. Moreover, as Amin and Thrift (1995) argue, the global economy connects to the local economy through a fragmented political system consisting of private networks and public organizations. Global society and the global economy "continue to be constructed in and through territorially bound communities" (Amin and Thrift, 1995). Accordingly, big corporations articulate their interests through regional partnerships, becoming "embedded" within networks through which they lobby local governments. There is regional institutional "thickness" (Amin and Thrift, 1995) involving numerous institutions including governments, economic development agencies, chambers of commerce, and corporations. They interact, through overlapping memberships, multiple points of contact, and organizational alliances. They also defend industries that remain spatially tied to the region and that cluster there for economic reasons and access to labor and natural resources. Ahlbrandt *et al.* (1996) cite the example of the U.S.X. Clairton, Irvin, and Edgar Thompson steel plants near Pittsburgh. The plants rely upon the core labor competencies in the region and work together in the production process. Partnerships have to be adaptable enough to cater for high-tech "footloose" service companies and for companies like U.S.X. that retain a local-plant presence.

In response to corporate restructuring, city governments support networks that are often only informally arranged. Longer-established public–private partnerships usually develop a higher degree of formality because they involve partners that share commercial risks and commit resources to achieve common aims. In Pittsburgh, the most influential partnerships are generally the ones that deploy the most resources and organize regionally as well as city-wide. From the 1950s, organizational "succession" resulted from the development of specialized partnerships in the city and the region. Partnerships came into existence by succeeding older ones, and they changed their functions and developed new specialist roles to take account of economic and technological changes. Old structures that once served particular purposes at given times have given way to new arrangements suited to modern conditions. Partnerships clustered around different organizations and produced entirely new forms of public–private collaboration giving rise to hybrids that blurred distinctions between the public and private sectors. Partnerships created a variety of organizational and

TABLE 16.1 *Regional partnership development: the "layer cake"*

Era of change	Partnerships
The future era	The development of regional partnerships
Economic crisis era	Mon Valley Initiative Allegheny Policy Council Southeastern Pa. Growth Alliance Southwest Pa. Industrial Resources Center Pittsburgh High Technology Council Community development corporations Pittsburgh Partnership for Neighborhood Development Steel Valley Authority
Urban crisis era	Action Housing Model Cities–Vista Perry Hilltop Citizens' Council Homestead Economic Revitalization Corp. People's Oakland Community Technical Assistance Center
Postwar growth era	Allegheny Conference on Community Development Regional Industrial Development Corp. Urban Redevelopment Authority of Pittsburgh Smaller Manufacturers' Council Chamber of Commerce Penn's Southwest

Source: Based upon presentation in the Mehrabian White Paper (ACCD, 1993).

funding mechanisms, but frequently used the resources of public agencies to create financial mechanisms and mobilize community effort.

A team sponsored by the Allegheny Conference on Community Development (ACCD) (1993), led by Robert Mehrabian, president of Carnegie Mellon University, describes the partnership process in their "White Paper" on regional competitiveness. Table 16.1, based on the 1993 White Paper, indicates the development of partnerships in southwestern Pennsylvania after the Second World War. The Mehrabian White Paper describes the changing functional and spatial aspects of partnerships in the region. Initially partnerships concentrated upon the revitalization of Pittsburgh. Postwar growth brought corporate leaders together to tackle the legacy of haphazard industrialization and environmental pollution. The White Paper refers to the need for "planning" after the war to bring economic development efforts together at a time when the "smoky city" was synonymous with everything that was wrong and unhealthy in Pittsburgh. Corporate leaders dedicated themselves to reconstruction and the rebirth of Pittsburgh as a vibrant and pleasant place to be. The business-led ACCD provided a strategic policy that regenerated the Pittsburgh central business district in the 1950s and 1970s (known as the Renaissance 1 and Renaissance 2 periods). The emergence of a gleaming high-rise downtown became a classic in the annals of urban regeneration (Weber, 1990), but corporate leaders were keen to utilize the resources and statutory powers of public agencies. Most notably, the Urban Redevelopment Authority (URA) became a driving force behind urban regeneration. The URA, as a public authority, worked closely with the city council so that by the 1990s URA officials assumed the roles of financial and property development experts who took risks and clinched deals to benefit the city. For example Mulugetta Birru, who in 1997 was the Executive Director of the URA, headed a team that had an intimate knowledge of the real estate and property development sector. Together with officials in the Mayor's Office, the URA team now possesses expertise that has come to rival any in the private sector.

In the 1960s, the ACCD mobilized private resources for city revitalization and the improvement of urban communities. Federal, state, and local government worked together with the ACCD and the URA in urban regeneration. Local initiatives such as Action Housing and the federal Model Cities program typified the community orientation of partnerships at the time. However, the ACCD also developed a stronger regional interest as large corporations expanded their global horizons. During the era of economic crisis after the 1970s, the ACCD further developed its regional outlook as new partnerships formed to deal with the decline of heavy manufacturing industry. The partnerships that developed during this period had wider spatial coverage and attended to the development of new technologies to ensure the economic prosperity of the region. The White Paper refers to the "post-industrial layer of organizations" (ACCD, 1993) that built upon the experiences of the partnerships created in earlier eras. The "layer cake" depended upon inter-organizational learning and the transfer of competencies between organizations. It produced innovative partnerships and policy solutions that developed from the complicated policy and organizational arrangements previously established. However, as Mehrabian's White Paper concludes, the layer cake produced a "legacy of innovations" that produced benefits, but which, by the 1990s, consolidated administrative fragmentation and inter-agency duplication.

This highlights the essential problem of the modern infatuation of federal, state and local policy-makers with networking and partnership. While public–private partnerships undoubtedly do provide conditions conducive to regional innovation, they can dissipate the kinds of core organizational competencies commonly associated with government. Partnerships promote flexibility and organizational innovation, but they reduce consistency and coherence in policy (Jacobs, 1996). Chisholm (1997) argues that privatization in urban government undermines competencies, such as high public service standards, competency in institutional reform, and electoral accountability. The autonomy of the partnership weakens democratic accountability and depoliticizes important strategic policy decisions by taking them out of public view and subjecting them to "visionary" consensus (Jacobs, 1996). The "shared vision" substitutes for political debate about alternative priorities often by marginalizing community organizations and over emphasizing the interests of the corporate private sector. Partnerships tend initially to be open and accessible, but they become hierarchical and more exclusive as they expand and become more professional. Mintzberg (1996) identifies a tendency towards the top-down "machine" in large companies as decentralized networks are controlled and politically restrained by chief executives and line managers. Similarly, public–private partnerships develop hierarchical organizational structures and service delivery structures, especially when they draw substantially upon public resources or corporate donations. In their attempts to overcome the shortcomings of the market, partnerships thereby create new organizational bureaucracies and dysfunctions.

Policy-makers are often aware of these problems. The Mehrabian White Paper recommended greater coordination between economic development organizations to overcome the dysfunctional fragmentation and lack of policy coherence in economic development. Mehrabian's team produced a strategic overview of the regional economy by defining a Pittsburgh metropolitan region that had spatially grown beyond the city. The region had significant international economic influence that made it vital that business leaders should coordinate their efforts with state and local governments. Corporate frustration with fragmented government required renewed efforts to overcome the conflicts between agencies and the lack of strategy for regional economic development. The White Paper adopted a tone of immediacy because action to improve regional competitiveness was crucial. Following the White Paper, public and private sector partners formed the Working Together Consortium to promote regional economic growth and coordination within the complex state, county and local government system. The explicit emphasis upon regional competitiveness, the development of economic support mechanisms and the focus upon technology contrast with the downtown-centered economic development perspectives of the 1950s and 1970s (see Table 16.2).

Community Empowerment

The Clinton Administration also advocates a shift away from an inner-urban preoccupation. The administration supports the linking of inner-city residents to the regional economy to enable the unemployed in local communities to contribute to the wider economy. In spite of federal pleas to connect inner-city and regional policies, community organizations in socially distressed areas often remain marginalized in regional policy. Community organizations tend to work outside the sophisticated regional networks, frequently on the periphery of the policy process. As *The State of the Cities* report (HUD, 1997) indicates, there has been progress in improving minority involvement in local programs, but the urban poor still demand greater access to the policy process (see also Glazer, 1994; Hunt, 1997). Communities suffering high unemployment, social disadvantage and communal tensions have been encouraged by HUD to be more self-sufficient through neighborhood enterprise (Taub, 1994), but groups still lack influence over

TABLE 16.2 *The Working Together Consortium: aims and partners*

Aims

Build on the strengths that hold the key to future job growth
Invest in wealth and job creation assets
Revive our entrepreneurial vitality
Make Greater Pittsburgh a leading destination for world visitors
Create an economic climate for the 21st century
Establish a new spirit of teamwork in economic development
Connect workers and students to jobs of the future
Building one economy
Making it happen

Examples of Working Together partners

The following is a sample of the members of the Working Together Consortium in 1996:

City of Pittsburgh
Sony Electronics
Mellon Bank
Pittsburgh Public Schools
Southwestern Pa. Industrial Resource Center
PPG Industries
IBM
Alcoa
Duquesne Light Company
Minority Enterprise Corp. of Southwestern Pa.
Carnegie Mellon University
Westinghouse Electric Corp.
Duquesne University
University of Pittsburgh
PNC Bank Corp.
Pittsburgh High-Technology Council
Allegheny Ludlum Corporation
Price Waterhouse
The Enterprise Corporation of Pittsburgh
Allegheny Conference on Community Development
Commonwealth of Pennsylvania
The Greater Pittsburgh Chamber of Commerce

Source: The Working Together Consortium (1996).

key decisions. In Pittsburgh, Ferman (1996) points to a close relationship between the city council and community organizations where city officials regard groups as legitimate participants in the policy process. However, as Ferman argues, community groups are constrained by narrow official perceptions of what constitutes "legitimate" access to the political system (Ferman, 1996).

Nevertheless, federally supported Empowerment Zones (EZs) and Empowerment Communities (ECs) do provide opportunities for legitimate access. They provide cities with the opportunity to compete for federal funds to regenerate local communities suffering the ravages of economic decline, unemployment and criminality. Central to the EZ–EC approach is the formation of public–private partnerships involving community groups, companies and local government. A HUD evaluation of the EZ–EC programs examines the factors that make successful partnerships in urban revitalization. The HUD studies point to "comeback communities" in Detroit, Boston, Baltimore, Atlanta, and elsewhere. However, the HUD analysis of the Pittsburgh EC concentrates upon the difficulties of creating a partnership involving disparate communities and encouraging a spirit of enterprise and initiative. Regional and local policies therefore need to develop strong community initiatives if communities are not to be permanently excluded (Dodge, 1996; Imbroscio, 1997). Corporations pursue corporate social responsibility programs to involve companies in communities. A wide range of community empowerment initiatives in US cities have been successful in generating local economic activity, but the successes have tended to be patchy especially where political conflict has resulted.

Conclusion

Networking enables policy-makers to work free from jurisdictional constraints and restrictive local government institutional rules. City officials advise companies and advance corporate interests. However, networked governance represents a degree of continuity in public administration despite reorganizations and reinvention in city government. Networks have not resolved the problems of regional organization; instead, they have redefined the problems of control and effectiveness within a fragmented context. Nevertheless, networking does undermine many of the traditional core competencies of democratic local government. Networks fragment the policy process and enable remote bureaucrats to manage programs removed from effective public accountability.

17

The Media and US Politics

PHILIP JOHN DAVIES

Politicians in the US have to be constantly aware of the media. Almost every household in America tunes into radio and television, and with an average of 5.6 radios per household and 2.2 televisions per household, all the family can listen and watch. The 80 percent of households with VCRs spend \$6.6 billion on film rental, and cinemas receive a further \$6.5 billion in receipts. Total newspaper distribution is around 60 million. The media in all its facets provides the formats through which politics, policies, the polity and politicians are viewed by the American electorate. Politicians are anxious to be in the media spotlight, but are concerned that thereby they expose themselves to independent analysis by the powerful branches of the communications industry. It is not surprising, then, that a tense relationship exists between American politicians and the media.

All's Fair in Love and War

President Clinton found himself under intense media attention in early 1998, when allegations of an affair with a one-time White House intern, Monica Lewinsky, became widespread. Clinton has faced claims of sexual philandering before, but the added element of possible harassment of a young volunteer worker made this the only story in town. The national and international news media camped out on the White House lawn and chased the actors in this drama wherever they appeared. Presidential press conferences with visiting dignitaries Yassir Arafat and Tony Blair, were blown off course by insistent questioning around the one topic of the President's sexual behavior. Speculation took on a slightly hysterical note, and there was wild media talk of resignation or impeachment being imminent.

The White House reacted with a powerful effort to spin the media coverage and public perception of Clinton's leadership in a more favorable direction. The President appeared at what would otherwise have been a low profile White House public relations meeting on education in order to respond with a forcible denial to one question about the Lewinsky matter. Hillary Clinton went on CBS News' *60 Minutes*, defended her husband unblinkingly, and counter-attacked with talk of a right-wing conspiracy against the President. Former Clinton campaign executive James Carville went on NBC News' *Meet The Press* to launch a vitriolic attack on the president's opponents, and especially on Kenneth W. Starr, special prosecutor investigating the Whitewater affair, whose enquiries seemed to spread into ever broader areas of presidential activity. White House press secretary Mike McCurry took the opportunity afforded by a Harvard University seminar to attack inaccurate coverage, lousy reporting, and to claim that the media was damaging its own credibility.

The Clintons' family image was boosted by the existence of photographs of apparently private romantic moments on the beach between Bill and Hillary Clinton, and daughter Chelsea took a break from her studies in California to be by her father's side. At the same time Bill Clinton walked a firmly presidential line. He hosted a White House policy conference between his advisers and those of Prime Minister Blair as a backdrop to the claim that they were developing a trans-Atlantic moderate "third way" on which to build policy. He made a State of the Union speech claiming the policy high ground in a country where the economic and business signs were good, and presenting the possibility of the first balanced budget in a generation. His role as head of state was highlighted by the re-emergence of difficulties with Iraq, and the threat, led by the USA and the UK, to use force against Saddam Hussein.

The strategy seemed to work. A *Washington Post* poll found that more respondents believed the president's enemies were to blame for the scandal than blamed the president's own behavior, 56 percent felt the media coverage of the scandal was unfairly biased against Clinton, and 75 percent considered the coverage to be excessive. Sam Donaldson, veteran reporter and then White House correspondent for ABC News, was impressed by the Clinton spin operation, considering it superior to that of any earlier president. In this encounter said Donaldson of the Clinton media managers, "They won."

Such a victory has its limits. The ongoing legal investigations did not stop, as they have a life of their own. Nor was the public convinced that Bill Clinton the man was wholly to be trusted. While there was 66 percent approval for "the way Bill Clinton is handling his job as President," only 21 percent had a strongly positive impression of "Clinton as a person," and 43 percent had a disapproving impression of Clinton the person. While they were willing to be convinced that the president of an economically successful America should not be unduly harassed, there was a skepticism about the potential diversionary stimulus behind the administration's sabre-rattling in the Middle East. The administration was saved from having to test its ability to rally the nation behind a foreign adventure when Kofi Annan, Secretary-General of the United Nations, negotiated a compromise with Saddam Hussein. When *Wag the Dog* portrayed a president attempting to deflect attention from sexual scandal by foreign policy adventures it dovetailed neatly with contemporary public assumptions about Clinton's tactics.

The Hollywood Sign: The Fear and Fascination of Mass-Media Entertainment

Washington is fascinated by Hollywood, and vice versa, but the latter part of the twentieth century has been a time of considerable cross-over. Ronald Reagan had ceased to be a film actor for many years before he entered the White House, but he had not lost his presentation skills, and a speech-writing team led by Peggy Noonan provided him with scripts he could work eloquently. His address to the nation after the *Challenger* disaster was a masterly example. The Reagan campaign team were no less aware of the political virtue of media projection, and the 1984 "Morning Again in America" Reagan reelection campaign was a presentation of an uplifting vision of America with the Reagan product placed at the center.

The culture of celebrity in politics and in media significantly connects Washington and Hollywood. Campaign advertising has continued to look towards cinema and television for technique and inspiration. The practicalities of campaigns draw politicians to the western base of American entertainment media. California, with fifty-four Electoral College votes, is a powerful force in the presidential election. Election campaigns cost hundreds of millions of dollars – film celebrities have the resources to donate, and to raise, substantial amounts of money. Positive exposure is everything in election campaigns, and association with major film celebrities is helpful. Nonetheless, the media in all forms are autonomous and powerful, and the benefits that can be gained by politicians are accessed at considerable risk.

Drawing a Line in the Sand: Grandstanding against Cultural Threats

The main players in the US entertainment industry depend on large profit products. Movies, together with the work that is created for television and for the music industry, need to attract a mass market. The need to cater broadly tends to ensure a product moderated not to offend the political or moral mainstream. That said, the market does include areas where bad taste will sell. Cultural rebellion has long been a pastime of the young; some people love to be shocked and thrilled. As the market has become larger, the potential to make a modest profit from a narrow sector, rather than relying on mass appeal, has grown, though there seems little for the industry to gain from truly subversive material. Politicians, however, seem unable to stop themselves from commenting. The huge audiences for mass media entertainment make any controversy newsworthy. An appropriate criticism can give a politician authenticity with a mass audience. The temptation to opportunist commentary by politicians yearning for politically valuable limelight is considerable, but the politically motivated critic risks being exposed as out of touch with contemporary cultural reality.

Reagan's Secretary of the Interior, James Watt, temporarily banned the Beach Boys from playing on the Mall in Washington, D.C., for fear of the deleterious effect of their California surfing music on America's youth. Tipper Gore, when her husband Al was still on Capitol Hill, led a campaign to have warning labels stuck on records that might offend sensibilities similar to her own. Vice President Dan Quayle attacked TV character "Murphy Brown" (acted by Candice Bergen) for having a baby out of wedlock. President George Bush claimed that he wanted more American families like *The Waltons* and fewer like *The Simpsons*. In each of these cases the politician received his or her comeuppance. Watt reinstated the Beach Boys to public acceptability at a press conference where he admitted shooting himself in the foot. Gore accompanied her husband to make peace with senior figures in the entertainment industry when his presidential ambitions became serious. Quayle found that he had taken on a major battle; he undoubtedly expected the anger of feminists, but he forgot that Candice Bergen was the daughter of Edgar Bergen, a ventriloquist whose model, Charlie McCarthy, was one of the most loved family entertainers of his day, and is now a permanent exhibit in the Smithsonian. In attacking Candice's character, Quayle was casting aspersions on Charlie McCarthy's more modern, less plain, but equally charming, sister. Anyway, most people had no quibble with a well heeled and independent character bringing up her own child. Quayle made a feeble apology, sent roses to Ms Bergen, and withdrew from the fray. The creators of *The Simpsons* inserted the Bush comment into an episode, and the Simpson family, shown regularly to be full of faults, but fundamentally loyal, loving and willing to sacrifice for each other, shared with the audience their amazement at being so ill-used.

In the 1992 presidential race Bill Clinton used an attack on the entertainment media rather more skillfully, when he took to task Sister Souljah, a black rap artist, for the inflammatory lyrics in her work. Clinton used this technique to position himself with regard to racial issues within the Democratic Party, and in the public eye, without having to confront directly the ideas of the black political leaders within his own political party. Bob Dole was not so successful in 1996 when denouncing the exploitative violence and sexuality of contemporary movies. The point might be well made given the electorate of moderates to whom Dole appealed, but the admission that he had not seen any of the movies he named, and the careful exemption from criticism of Republican donors and serial "tough guy" actors Bruce Willis and Arnold Schwarzenegger inevitably undermined the power of the comments made.

The Media Market

If the entertainment mass media fascinate electorate and politicians alike, the news-carrying mass media are much more significant to politicians on a day-to-day basis. In the United States, the mass media carriers of news and entertainment are privately owned businesses. Newspapers and television channels for the most part depend on advertising revenue for their profits, and their audience determines their success. Traditionally the size of market alone determined advertising charges. For general-purpose newspapers and television channels, this is still the rule of thumb, but some media specialists recognized years ago that contemporary developments, especially in the delivery of television, would alter the definition of the audience.

Surveys of public opinion and tastes have from their beginning reported not just global figures, but have broken down results to give figures for identified groups within the total. These techniques have become increasingly sophisticated as new generations of computers have been able to amalgamate masses of survey research, census data, audience returns, and other resources to identify sectors of the population with increasing clarity. Advertisers have welcomed these breakdowns for their value in determining what groups most appreciate their products, and therefore in acting as a guide on how to pitch further advertising. The resulting advertising has been designed to appeal to potentially receptive segments of the global market, but often the vehicle for the advertising has still been the general purpose newspaper or television channel.

In some cases the segmented market could also be approached through a purpose-built media channel. Magazines are often aimed at specific groups of buyers, and the advertising inside the pages reflect this. Even on general-purpose channels, some individual television programs will be aimed at particular viewers, indeed in the early days of radio and television this kind of targeting was demanded by advertisers as a condition of their sponsorship. Political operatives also recognized the value of this ability to identify the viewing audience. For example, when the Reagan presidential reelection campaign became concerned about the "gender gap" of higher support for Democratic candidate Walter Mondale among women than men, it responded with a series of advertisements during day-time TV The spots stressed the dangers of inflation and higher prices in case of a Mondale victory, and were aimed at the large segment of US middle-aged, home-based women who watch TV soap operas and light entertainment quiz games. Reagan's pollster Richard Wirthlin claims that while these women formed only 6 percent of the electorate, the fact that they responded with a rapid shift towards Reagan limited the damage that the gender gap could inflict on the Republican incumbent.

Segmentation of Provision

The past twenty years has seen the development of electronic media that segment the market channel by channel. Satellite and cable distribution of television brought to US households the potential of many channels from a multitude of providers. Even viewers far distant from major urban media markets would now have the potential to view scores of channels, if they were willing to invest a little for equipment and services.

The customer's necessary initial investment was not negligible, and a selling point made by Ted Turner in 1978, pitching advertisers for his Atlanta-based "superstation" was that "we're not wired to the ghettos" (Turow, 1997). He managed to persuade advertisers to pay premium rates. As cable and satellite development has continued the upscale nature of the audience has remained important: in 1991–92 over 70 percent of adults with household income over $50,000 were watching cable, as opposed to fewer than 50 percent of adults with household income lower than $30,000 (Stanley and Niemi, 1994). However, as important to those wishing to communicate with an audience was the development and expansion of specialist channels and networks: the Christian Broadcasting Network, the Fox system, MTV (Music TV), the Home Shopping Channel, CNN (Cable Network News), C-SPAN (Cable-Satellite Public Affairs Network), ESPN (sports), the Weather Channel, the History Channel, the Science Fiction Channel, the Disney Channel, Nickelodeon (children and family channel), and a range of variously targeted media providers. This added to the traditional form of "broadcasting" the complementary style of "narrowcasting."

While average TV viewing has remained around seven hours per day since the early 1980s, the challenge to traditional television networks, ABC, CBS, and NBC, presented by alternative providers has been considerable. The share of the total TV audience for the big three networks declined from 90 percent to 60 percent in the decade up to 1990. Simultaneously the percentage of households with cable TV grew from less than 20 percent in 1980 to over 60 percent in 1992.

The Developing Information Environment

The variety of broadcast news sources now available to US viewers is greater than it has ever been. Twenty-four hour news, led on television by CNN, is available at the flick of a switch. C-SPAN and its sister channel C-SPAN2 carry live coverage of congressional business from the debating chambers and committee rooms of Capitol Hill. Regional public-interest cable channels around the United States cover state and local political happenings with a similarly unstinting documentary gaze. Many other channels present news as part of their programming, and news reporting and political information is moving out of the news studio and into other broadcast forms.

The US public does not have much confidence in "the national news media" (about 40 percent expressed "very little confidence" in a February 1997 public opinion poll by Hart and Teeter), but news anchors themselves are among the most trusted of public figures. The only groups more trusted than local news anchors are ministers and doctors (Roper Center poll, January 1997). News presenters have long been an important feature of television channels' appeal to their public. These presenters have achieved celebrity status, and their authority in US society is well recognized. As long ago as 1980 independent presidential candidate John Anderson reportedly invited national TV newscaster Walter Cronkite, one of the most trusted men in the United States, to be his vice-presidential running mate. Dan Rather, anchor for CBS, became the *bête noire* of some parts of the political right, convinced of the liberal bias of the national television news. In May 1997 Tom Brokaw of NBC was reportedly offered a $7 million salary to move to CNN

News programs have adopted formats designed to attract viewers and advertisers, with attractive presenters, often a male–female team, referred to by some as the "Barbie and Ken" model, and the introduction of daily "human interest" stories to lighten and personalize the news. Investigative crime programs, and crime fiction series, have come to look increasingly like each other as the hand-held camera style makes the fiction look fashionably realistic, and the access offered by publicity-hungry (and budget-hungry) emergency services makes the edited documentary look increasingly dramatic.

Ed Fouhy, formerly Washington bureau chief for ABC, latterly creator of the Pew Center for Civic Journalism, states that the producers of news shows are under intense market pressures, and that in the search for markets, "You start to censor yourself. You start to pull punches on what kind of stories you do" (Kurtz, 1997a). Sensationalism rules in the news rooms especially in the "sweeps months." These are the periods, three times a year, when the media audience is surveyed in-depth. The advertising rates for the next quarter are set on the basis of the size and quality of audience recorded in these survey periods, so there is immense temptation to go to extremes in the pursuit of audience at these times.

News, information, and social and political debate has increasingly been turning up in alternative formats such as talk shows, and phone-ins. Some of these shows, such as *Larry King Live* regularly concern themselves with political and social matters, but *Oprah*, *Rikki Lake*, and other audience-participation entertainments, attract huge audiences for their wide-ranging, and sometimes sensationalized, debates. The 1988 abolition, by the Federal Communications Commission (FCC), of the "fairness doctrine," on the grounds that it was contrary to the spirit of the First Amendment, opened the way for the development of very polemical commentary in the media. Radio talk shows saw the earliest evidence of this, with the growth of shows centered on highly opinionated hosts. "Shock jocks" were found to attract audiences; while many of these would defy political bracketing, it is certainly true that conservative political commentators have flourished in "talk radio." Conservative critic Rush Limbaugh has, for example, proved very successful in attracting loyal fans (so loyal that they claim to agree with all that Limbaugh says, calling themselves "ditto-heads"), and has shown that the format can also attract television audiences.

While the range of news and information offerings has apparently increased, substantial parts of the electronic media spectrum are now effectively "news-free zones," and channel-hoppers need never come into contact even with distorted versions of public debate. The public affairs C-SPAN channels are finding themselves squeezed from cable systems as more entertainment channels and well financed alternative providers come onstream for cable systems already at full capacity. The market strength of Rupert Murdoch's companies, especially in the satellite TV sector, has led to concern about concentration of ownership in the developing media sectors. In spite of the many outlets for news and information, international comparisons suggest that American citizens are less well informed than the citizens of many other countries, which leads to further concerns about the quality of the information being transmitted.

The Traditional News Media

Most recent development has been in the electronic media, but newspapers remain very important, and have also undergone modernization. In 1992, over 60 percent of US adults reported reading daily newspapers, and over 66 percent reported reading a Sunday newspaper. Total circulation of daily newspapers in 1991, at almost 61 million, was at about the same size it had been for twenty years. New technology has changed the way that newspapers are written, produced, and circulated.

Almost all American newspapers are essentially local, but some major papers, such as the *New York Times* and *The Wall Street Journal* have developed distribution networks across the nation. *USA Today* has emerged as a well intentioned, if relatively superficial, national newspaper. Regions of the United States often have locally available a high-quality newspaper, such as the *Boston Globe*, *Los Angeles Times*, and in some areas there will be competing newspapers, such as Chicago's *Tribune* and *Sun-Times*. There are large areas of the country, however, where there is a single provider of local print news, and where that provider is not necessarily of the highest quality.

The major newspapers retain considerable influence. Having maintained a tradition of investigative journalism, printing the Pentagon Papers, beginning the exposure of Watergate, chasing the details of the Iran–Contra connections and the Whitewater affair, these news outlets carry weight, and notoriety. A newspaper carries far more words than any television or radio news broadcast, and is capable of more in-depth coverage of a broader range of topics than a news show. The range and depth of stories and analyses carried by the major papers located in political and economic centers, together with the quality of the journalism in these papers, considerably influence the news agendas adopted by the electronic news media at local, regional, and national levels.

It is often said that politicians need the press, and the press need politicians. The politicians need the "oxygen of publicity" to gain support towards their ends; the press need the stories to maintain the interest of their audience. Each side has at times been accused of manipulation or distortion. Learning from the British control of press coverage in the Falklands War, the American government managed to limit access to cover the invasion of Grenada, and the Pentagon's presentation of the Gulf War was masterly. Only now is it being admitted that the American bombing raids were not so accurate, nor the "smart" bombs so gifted as was claimed, and accepted, at the time. Not wishing to miss a story, especially one that is highly marketable, reporters have been accused of indulging in a "feeding frenzy" when something meaty comes along. The pursuit of any touch of deviation from some assumed moral norms in the life of candidates for major political office may be seen as evidence of this aspect of contemporary journalism. The appearance in recent years of substantial information resources on the Internet has encouraged journalists to browse more widely, and to analyze deeply, contributing to the emergence of "computer aided reporting." The sparring between political actors and journalists may be healthy in principle, but audiences are won by sensation, and the translation of this tension into a culture of shocked revelation may not be so positive. It feeds into the feelings of cynicism and disaffection with politics and the political which have grown in recent years. Some trace this trend to the Vietnam War and Watergate. Wherever it began, it forms the background against which American politicians now have to present their campaigns for policies, and for their own elections.

The Political Campaign and the Media

American politicians and candidates communicate with the electorate through the media. Given that television is the major single information source for most citizens, it is inevitably the major single communication channel for those in and seeking high office.

A campaign for major state office or higher is effectively invisible if it does not feature on the television; in some communities even offices with smaller constituencies than the state are now being contested on the air. Coverage in other media is still significant, given the agenda-setting, and in-depth coverage functions of the press, and given that in a country with around half a million elected offices, many of these contests are small-scale and localized. Between elections media exposure is important to office-holders who are promoting their favored policies in the increasingly entrepreneurial US political environment.

The changes in the media market and the information environment are as significant to politicians as they have been to advertisers. Politicians are the purveyors, and to some extent the products, in a political market-place. The contemporary political office is incomplete without survey researchers, consultants, market strategists, media advisers, and image consultants to advise politicians on how to promote their ideas, preferred policies, and career with the electorate. Targeting political messages to likely receptive audiences has always been important, and the modern media allow this to an unprecedented degree.

In a country dedicated to the principle of free speech it is difficult sometimes to distinguish between messages that are in the public interest and those that are politically motivated. Increasingly local, state, and national government bodies are providing access and information through the Internet. Feedback through E-mail-based "electronic town halls" has been possible since the early 1980s in some communities. The "Thomas" web site of the Library of Congress provides a world-wide web equivalent of a public affairs–public access political information channel, and even Supreme Court decisions – not covered in depth in other media – can be accessed almost immediately through computer links. The Internet also carries a great deal of partisan information, and was used extensively in the 1996 presidential election campaigns by the candidates and political parties. While the computer-channeled message was getting through to only a modest portion of the population, it gave some of the most attentive public an opportunity to observe the campaigns closely. It also gave journalists the chance to download copy and quotations at ease. That political information, both public-interest and partisan, is increasingly available is certainly true; there are, however, concerns that the targeting of this information through new media is leading to a growing information gap between those who can afford to be plugged in to the new channels of information, and those who cannot. This division may do nothing to alter the already low, and socially skewed, electoral participation.

Recent elections show many tendencies that have been well established for some time. Candidate teams work hard to "earn" free spots on the media by constructing events that reporters will find it hard to ignore. Campaign speeches are written with an eye to the "soundbite" phrase that will show the candidate well, and that will jump out of the material made available to the news editor. Particular attention is given to those parts of the electorate defined by the survey research as important to the campaign, and therefore to those media outlets that can access the required groups. Novel information channels have been explored to get to these groups. Bill and Hillary Clinton's 1992 preemptive appearance on a talk show to challenge allegations of his sexual impropriety gave them far more control over the message than an alternative format such as a press conference. Ross Perot's announcement of his candidacy on *Larry King Live* drew further coverage because of its novelty. Bill Clinton's saxophone playing on *The Arsenio Hall Show* has become legendary for its *chutzpah* and charm.

1996

In 1996, the Dole presidential campaign found it difficult to maintain discipline over the messages that it was trying to get across. The team was changed too often, Dole and his vice-presidential nominee never appeared comfortable together, and there were reports of Kemp distancing himself from responsibility for the faltering campaign well before election day. Giving reporters good access to the candidate is one way to magnify the chances of getting into the media, but Dole's handlers knew that this entailed the risk of uncontrolled and potentially disadvantageous off-the-cuff remarks being exchanged. Dole media events had been well organized in Iowa, the early caucus covered intensively by the mass media, but his poll victory had not been decisive. While the Dole campaign achieved the nomination of its candidate, the first half of

1996 was spent in a savage, and widely reported, intra-party battle between the ideological camps of the Republican Party.

The Clinton–Gore campaign remained focused, learning well from the 1980s campaigns run by Ronald Reagan's advisers. With no Democratic opponents for the nomination, Clinton could remain above the fray, and use his media opportunities to enhance his presidential status, and to attack the Republicans. Clinton used the power of incumbency to attract media attention. Three bills were signed by President Clinton in the White House Rose Garden in the week before the Democratic National Convention, and an attack on tobacco was launched by the President, all as part of a planned, news-grabbing foundation for convention coverage. Clinton and Gore and their families took part in a whistle-stop rail trip to the convention, providing well staged photo- and video-opportunities along the way.

Both campaigns achieved considerable control of the media message at the convention stage. The Republican convention was characterized by pundits as "a four day infomercial," and Democratic leaders happily introduced the Democratic meeting as "a four day press conference." The Republicans purchased time on a minor, family-oriented TV network to ensure that the full impact of the convention was available to potential supporters. The Democrats established a comprehensive array of localized links to the hundreds of local stations around the country, fronted by relevant local Democratic officeholders and delegates. The national network TV audience was down by about 25 percent from the 1992 figures. The party managers claimed not to be worried; they opined that conventions were naturally evolving from debating conferences to ratification ceremonies – configured to be viewer-friendly showcases for the nominee. The messages had been targeted, and had been reported satisfactorily, and each party had received a public opinion poll boost in line with previous years when the TV audiences had been larger.

The presidential and vice-presidential debates used a variety of formats, none of them very confrontational. Reform Party candidate Ross Perot lost out by dint of not being allowed access to the debates. Clinton came out on top, displaying calm confidence, command of the material, and remaining at ease. Dole was well briefed, but could not overcome the knowledge that he was sniping from behind.

None of this campaign management comes cheap, but the paid advertisements are the largest single element of the campaign budget. The Democrats began, using Democratic National Committee (DNC) money, with a first advertisement running on June 27, 1995. These were classed as "party-building" messages, and therefore outside the limits imposed by campaign-finance laws (see Chapter 15). They portrayed a positive vision of the president's record on highly salient issues – crime, education, Medicare – and painted the Republicans as the enemies of the public interest. Showing a sophisticated understanding of the political economy of the media, these advertisements were shown in markets outside the major media markets. The major journalistic organs of the nation, in their big-city confines, did not notice the campaign for months. By the time they did so, at least $25 million had been spent massaging the Clinton image in 42 percent of the US media market. The major journals called this a "stealth campaign," a term that Clinton adviser Bob Squier found risible, and no doubt very satisfying. The advertising campaign shifted focus over the next year-and-a-half, as surveys and focus group research fed back into the campaign's management.

Republican advertising had also started early with a spot from presidential hopeful Lamar Alexander aired in Iowa on June 19, 1995. The self-financed campaign blitz of another Republican hopeful, Steve Forbes, increased the pressure in Iowa and other early primary and caucus states. In Iowa alone an estimated $4 million was spent by Republicans chasing the presidential nomination. The intra-party competition was aggressive. Negative ads are said to increase public skepticism of politics in general, and potentially to reduce voter turnout, but they move the relative polling figures between candidates quicker than any other form, and regardless of good intentions the managers in a close fought campaign will reach for the negatives as polling day approaches. The Republican primary battle was no exception, with attacks on Forbes' political inexperience, Dole's career as a political insider, and deal-maker among the topics covered.

The infomercial, a 30-minute advertisement style brought into prominence by Ross Perot in 1992, did not feature strongly in 1996 even in the Reform Party campaign. Spot ads, sometimes highly targeted and made at speed with ever-improving technology, dominated the paid media. This high-octane, high-cost campaigning is expensive, even given the ruling that campaign ads have to be aired at the lowest relevant advertising rate. Presidential campaigns receive considerable grants from the public purse towards their costs, in return for accepting certain spending limits, but ways do exist to spend other money ("soft" money) in parallel to the official campaign. At the congressional and other levels no federal limits on campaign spending exist, though there are strictures on how the money can be raised. According to Anthony Corrado (1997) the seventeen major candidates for the presidency raised $245 million in the prenomination period. Once nominated Clinton, Dole, and Perot received a total of around $153 million in federal grants for their campaigns. Candidates for the US House of Representatives spent over $400 million, and for the US Senate, over $200 million. National party organizations also spent well, for an overall total expenditure on the federal election campaigns exceeding $2 billion, an increase of about 50 percent over the 1992 total.

Such considerable sums of money were raised from many and various sources, including very large single and corporate contributions that avoid financial limits by being routed through party committees. The range and variety of fund-raising techniques has led to concern that the limits of the law, as well as of propriety may have been breached in some cases, including a fund-raising event involving Vice-President Al Gore, which was held at a Buddhist temple in California. But other visits to California were less controversial. Victory in this state was crucial to the Clinton–Gore campaign, and so a concentrated effort here was to be expected. In addition, the lure of Hollywood continues to be strong; the entertainment media once again provided celebrity Friends of Bill, and proved a successful engine for generating both the funds and the media exposure essential to the contemporary political campaign.

Conclusions

The media in all its forms is a permanent feature of American political life. The general context for social and political discussion and analysis is established and reinforced in the mass media. Individual political issues and actions are examined in detail. Fiction, faction, and powerful documentary are produced to equally high standards. Unable to live without the oxygen of publicity, politicians are inevitably drawn into a tense and continuous relationship with the media. Officeholders, administrations, and candidates attempt to get their voice heard, to establish some authority, to impose some order, and to control, or at least to delimit the messages carried. This may have success at some levels in some communities, but while the national multi-media environment responds to political pressures, it evades control. The media environment becomes ever more complex with new technological developments in communications, ensuring that politicians and the media will remain in the future, wary partners in a careful, watchful, and occasionally frenzied dance.

PART FIVE

AMERICAN POLITICS AT THE CENTURY'S END: AN OVERVIEW

18

The American Political System in Transition to a New Century

ALAN WARE

The ancient Chinese curse, "May you live in interesting times," appeared to have fallen on both American politicians and the American public during the early-to-mid 1990s. In a variety of ways politics had become less predictable, more conflictual, and, in some respects, simply nastier than it had been in earlier decades. This is not to say that the 1990s are comparable with the 1850s, 1890s or 1960s – decades in which massive upheavals threatened to disrupt the American polity; they are not. However, given that the 1990s might well have been expected to be an era of "quiet" politics, it is curious that this has not been so. More important, it may be asked whether the "unquiet" character of the polity in the 1990s will persist into the twenty-first century. The object of this chapter is to outline what seems to have changed in American politics, to suggest why, at first glance, the 1990s seems to be an unlikely decade for turbulent and conflictual politics, to examine the factors that have contributed to these developments, and, finally, to ask whether this turbulence is likely to continue after the year 2000.

Evidence of Turbulence and Conflict

An obvious place to begin is with American electoral behavior. Between 1990 and 1996 huge shifts in electoral fortunes occurred. 1990 had produced a fairly typical post-1945 result for a first-term president: a small number of seats were lost in the House, while the balance between the parties remained the same in the Senate. In 1992 the electorate turned on the president, though not on his party. George Bush became only the second popularly elected president since 1932 to lose his bid for reelection, and only the third since Benjamin Harrison lost in 1892. Since the advent of competitive party politics in the 1830s seventeen popularly elected presidents had sought reelection, and only two of them (Taft in 1912 and Hoover in 1932) had experienced a greater decline in their share of the vote than did Bush.

However, voter discontent with Bush was not accompanied by a strong surge of support for either Bill Clinton or, more generally, for the Democrats. Clinton secured only 43 percent of the popular vote and in Congress the Democrats were in a slightly worse position than they had been after the 1990 elections; they lost ten seats in the House, although their overall majority in the Senate remained the same as before the 1992 election. Then the national electorate moved in a direction that had not been seen in America since the major depression of the early-to-mid-1890s. A party that had captured the presidency lost its congressional majorities, and lost them decisively, in the mid-term elections two years later. Paralleling their experience in 1894, the Democrats in 1994 sustained major losses of seats in both House (fifty-two) and Senate (eight), with the House Speaker among the defeated candidates. Even Woodrow Wilson, whose election in a three-cornered contest in 1912 most superficially resembles Clinton's this century, had been able to retain control of both chambers in 1914; that comparison provides a crude measure of the extent of the Democrats' collapse in 1994. Similar losses were sustained by the party at the state level; in 1992 they held thirty of the fifty governorships, but by 1996 this was reduced to a mere eighteen. Yet, by 1996 the Republican surge had been halted and partly reversed. Bill Clinton retained the presidency relatively easily, although the Republicans still controlled Congress, acquiring a slightly larger majority in the Senate and a slightly smaller one in the House.

As had been the case 100 years earlier, rapid changes in support for the parties were paralleled by internal conflict within one of them. In the 1990s it was the Republicans who were divided, and the issues dividing them were social rather than economic ones.

This had hurt them initially in 1992 when George Bush's renomination was damaged badly by the candidacy of Pat Buchanan, whose right-wing policies on matters like abortion were anathema to some traditional Republican activists and voters. The right's drive for power within the party was bolstered by the electoral successes of 1994 when, with a much lower voter turnout, it appeared that there might be popular support for a sharp turn to the right; in particular many of the incoming Republicans in the House had been committed to a highly conservative political agenda. Unity among Republicans proved short-lived, and in 1996 Buchanan's right-wing populism once again threatened to disrupt the party. However, the support he displayed in some of the early presidential primaries and caucuses could not be sustained, and tight management of the national convention prevented another debacle, but not a general election defeat.

One interesting similarity between the period 1890–96 and 1990–96 is that in both cases the party that appeared, at last, to have made a major breakthrough found its advantage crumbling very quickly. In the early 1890s it was the Democrats who seemed to have gained the initiative:

> Had the Democrats been able to hold onto what they had gained in 1890–92, they would have been in a position to dominate national politics in a way that no one had been able to do for thirty years past. (Silbey, 1991)

But the Democrats' advantage then was quickly wiped out in the 1894 mid-term election and the 1896 presidential election. Similarly, in early–mid-1995 it appeared as if a significant shift in the balance between the parties had occurred. In this case, it was the Democrats who, like the Republicans in 1890–92, appeared to be losing the battle. They had lost control of both chambers for the first time since 1953–55, some Democratic members of both chambers (including two Senators) had switched or were switching parties, and the Democratic president was on the defensive as the House Republican leadership sought to enact its Contract With America. Yet within a year the Republicans had lost the initiative.

It was not just in the electoral arena that there was evidence of disquiet among the American public. Poll evidence from mid-1995, for example, revealed that 65 percent of respondents were not satisfied "with the way things are going in the United States," and in 1996 less than a third of respondents "believed the United States would be in better shape in the year 2000 than it is today." These attitudes went hand-in-hand with, on the one hand, a reduced confidence in the ability of government to improve the situation, and, on the other, a high level of satisfaction with their own lives (Golay and Rollyson, 1996). The pattern of public opinion, in relation to factors such as whether people trust government, belief that government benefits all the people and so on, has been consistently in the direction of a decline in confidence in government. After the rise in confidence in the early-to-mid 1980s, the trend evident in the period from the late 1960s to the mid-1970s has reappeared (Stanley and Niemi, 1994). Significantly, perhaps, for developments in the next century, the four years of prosperity under the first Clinton Administration did not seem to have produced a contented public.

At the local and state levels, people's concerns about "the way things are going" have had at least one notable consequence: laws, often proposed in initiative referendums, to limit the rights of others. Thus, Colorado passed a law prohibiting its cities from giving special protection to gay rights, California removed various rights from illegal immigrants and their children, and there have been several attempts to eliminate bilingualism from public affairs. The courts found some of these measures unconstitutional, but the interesting point about them is the light they shed on conflictual aspects of contemporary American mass politics. Moreover, at the fringes of politics, there were a number of developments that indicated a growing intolerance of normal political processes; these included the rise of militia movements, a spate of arson attacks on black churches in the South, murders by anti-abortion activists of employees at abortion clinics, and the 1995 bombing of a federal government building in Oklahoma City. Such incidents raised questions about the future of political violence in the United States.

Increasing intolerance has also been evident among political elites, especially in the House of Representatives. Comity had been declining since the 1980s (Uslaner, 1993). However, from the beginning of the 1990s civility declined even further. Both before the Democratic defeat in 1994 and afterwards the House conducted its business on far more partisan lines than had been evident earlier. The strategy of the Clinton Administration in 1993 had been to drive legislation through Congress on the back of its majorities in the two houses; the problem with this was that a sufficient number of Democrats were always willing to defect on particular measures so that margins of victory were not always secure. In 1995 Newt Gingrich was similarly to utilize a partisan approach, this time against a Democratic president and in support of the legislation to which the House Republicans were committed in the Contract With America. But the House in the 1990s was not just more divided by party than it had been earlier, there was also much greater personal antagonism dividing the partisans. This atmosphere affected the work of the committees – the heart of congressional life. Committees, such as Agriculture and Appropriations, moved from being arenas in which bipartisanship was practiced to being forums for partisan conflict.

Most commentators regarded the overall atmosphere of the House as being more unpleasant than it used to be. Rancor came to characterize much of the business of the chamber, extending into unusual places. The most unlikely arena for this perhaps, but one which illustrates just how much the House had changed, was the Science and Technology Committee. Both the policy area covered by this committee and its lack of power and prestige in the chamber meant that it had been a haven of bipartisanship. By 1996 the situation had changed so much that the Democratic ranking member could describe the Republican chair as "the most autocratic, nondemocratic chairman I have ever had the pleasure of working with," while the latter said that the Democrats' "bitterness over losing control is so deep within the committee, it is actually being destructive to the legislative process" (*Congressional Quarterly Weekly Reports*, May 11, 1996).

In the Senate there was less scope for a shift towards a more partisan and conflictual mode of operating. The smaller size of the chamber has always made for a more personal, rather than a party, style of coordination; the narrower electoral margins of incumbents pushes them towards moderate policy stances; and the party leaderships have fewer resources with which to control their members, so that the kind of leadership exercised by Newt Gingrich before 1996 would be counter-productive in the upper chamber. Nevertheless, in electing Trent Lott as Robert Dole's successor in June 1996 the Senate Republicans opted for a relatively junior member (first elected in 1988) who had made his name in the House as an ally of Newt Gingrich and who, like Gingrich, had had a reputation for being both aggressive and very conservative. Although he had modified his style when he became the Senate whip, his election as majority leader provided some evidence of pressures towards militant partisanship even in the Senate.

Finally, the balance between president and Congress that had been established since the advent of the modern presidency under Franklin Roosevelt, was challenged in 1995 by Newt Gingrich. In 1994 Gingrich was a major innovator in American politics in the way that he drew House Republican candidates together to fight the mid-term elections on the basis of a legislative program they would all support, if elected – the Contract With America. Having secured a majority in the House, Gingrich then proceeded to act as if he now had a mandate that superseded the one that the president acquired in 1992. In Garry Wills's words, "It would be hard to overstate the audacity of the Contract With America. No one had ever before tried to create a national mandate from congressional elections" (Wills, 1996a). In effect, Gingrich acted as if his new position as Speaker was rather similar to that of the French prime minister during a period of *cohabitation*; he presented himself to the American public as the driving force of domestic policy initiation in American government to whom the president would have to concede.

Of course, Gingrich had no control over the senators, who would kill or modify many of his proposals when these were unlikely to go down well with their voters. Nor would any president give in to a usurpation of power, and Clinton could choose to make his stand on the grounds most favorable to him. The dispute over the budget, and the partial shutdown of the federal government, enabled Clinton to lay the blame on the Republicans, and Gingrich in particular. Gingrich's remark to the press that he had shut down the federal government because Clinton had snubbed him by confining him to the back of the presidential plane on a diplomatic mission crystallized growing public hostility to the Speaker. By early 1996 Gingrich had the worst "negative ratings" in opinion polls of any politician since Richard Nixon at the time of his resignation and, furthermore, much of the Contract With America legislation had either not been enacted at all or not enacted in anything like the form in which it had been proposed. The Speaker's confrontation with the president was resolved largely in favor of the latter, and public dislike of Gingrich was used by the Democrats in the 1996 campaign with prominence being given to photographs of Bob Dole standing next to him. The response of some House Republicans, even those who had been enthusiastic supporters of the Contract With America, was to distance themselves from the program and from Gingrich; in seeking to portray themselves as centrists, and not extremists, association with the Speaker became dangerous. Together with Clinton's strategy of being seen to work with Congress, this seemed to produce greater cooperation between the two branches of government by mid-1997 – culminating in agreement over the budget. However, the potential for discord was still high, as partisanship within Congress remained relatively high – as the investigations into election funding and into the contested Louisiana Senate election result revealed.

Would We have Expected the 1990s to be an Era of Political Conflict?

Superficially, at least, there are a number of reasons why the conflict and turbulence evident in the 1990s is surprising. First, as noted in Chapter 10, it has been a period of relative prosperity. Despite Bill Clinton's well known memo to himself during the 1992 election campaign – "It's the economy, *stupid*" – the American economy overall was quite strong, even at the beginning of the decade. The recession of 1990 and 1991 was minor by comparison with the depressions of either the 1890s or the 1930s, both of which were severe enough to affect party politics for several decades. In fact, the decline in GNP in 1990 and 1991 was rather less than it had been in either of the two previous recessions, in 1974–75 and 1981–82.

Secondly, unlike, say either the 1850s or the 1960s, the role of Afro-Americans in American national life was not a fundamental issue around which conflict could develop. The extreme turbulence of both those decades can be traced, in part, to the issue of race, as indeed it can in the case of the 1890s. However, although issues like the beating of Rodney King by the Los Angeles police, the trial of O.J. Simpson, and the passage of an anti-affirmative action referendum in California in 1996 exposed clear and continuing racial divisions in the United States, as with the American economy in the 1990s, the overt problems were far less intense than they had been in several previous eras.

Thirdly, the United States was not engaged in unpopular foreign wars. American engagement in foreign wars can be a catalyst for electoral revolt, for demonstrations and for more extreme forms of mass political intervention. The Korean War produced a major backlash against the Democrats in 1952, while the Vietnam War destroyed the Johnson presidency. But in the 1990s few American soldiers died in action; the Gulf War was relatively popular – being both of short duration and with relatively few casualties in the field. Peacekeeping operations by America in Somalia, Haiti, and Bosnia attracted considerable criticism but were never issues of high political salience simply because American forces were not involved in bloody military actions.

Fourthly, the Cold War had ended and the military alliance that had opposed the United States for over forty years had collapsed. As a proportion of GDP, military expenditures could be reduced to nearly half the levels they had reached in the mid-1980s, being at their lowest levels since 1940. More significantly, the threat of confrontation with the Soviet Union, which had been the background to the rise of McCarthyism in the early 1950s, was eliminated.

Finally, there has been no major scandal in the first half of the decade, comparable to that of the Watergate affair (1972–74), that might have contributed to a major decline in public confidence in America's political institutions and its politicians. Whitewater, Travelgate, and other affairs which continued to dog the Clintons appeared to have little impact either on the president's popularity or in changing public perceptions of American politicians in general. Although the funding of election campaigns in 1996 did have the potential for damaging both Democratic and Republican political elites in the future (see Chapter 15), it cannot account, of course, for the turbulence in the earlier part of the 1990s.

Putting these factors together, it would look as if the decade of the 1990s should have been characterized by a high degree of stability in the political process, but it was not. So what happened?

The Sources of Political Conflict and Turbulence

The central argument developed here is that a number of different social, economic, and political factors converged in the 1990s to produce the conflict and turbulence in American politics. But it is important to begin by recognizing a continuing source of conflict from the very beginning of the Republic – namely, disagreement about the answer to the question: "who is to be included in the polity?" Many foreign observers of the United States often misunderstand this point, because they tend to assume that the kind of sentiment expressed in the famous Emma Lazarus poem on the Statue of Liberty – "Give me your tired, your poor, Your huddled masses yearning to breathe free, The wretched refuse of your teeming shore, Send these, the homeless, tempest tossed, to me" – reflects a widely held value in American society. But neither at the time that the statue was erected, nor at any point in its history, has the issue of who is, or should be, a full member of the Republic been uncontroversial.

The Republic was founded as a country for white, Protestant settlers; most assuredly, slaves and American Indians were not members of it. From the 1840s until the early 1920s mass immigration by nonProtestant Europeans provoked protests from those who believed that the basic values and life-style of the country were being undermined. The rights of black Americans in the polity were the subject of intense dispute from the 1890s to the 1960s, as were the rights of Japanese-Americans in the Second World War, and Communists in the 1950s. For much of the country's history a significant proportion of Americans have wanted either to keep various kinds of "huddled masses" from coming to the United States, to deny them full civic rights if they were inhabiting its territory, or to compel them to abandon certain aspects of their life-style. Consequently, the kind of remark made on television by Pat Buchanan in 1991 about Latin American immigration might have been made in the 1880s by a Yankee about Irish or south European immigration:

> Should we be concerned that Americans of European descent will be a minority in . . . the entire US by the middle of the next century? . . . I want to save and preserve the country I grew up in and I'll be honest. I don't want to live in the Brazil of North America (CNN's *Crossfire*, September 13, 1991).

The point is that entitlement to full political and civic rights is a matter on which Americans have rarely agreed. The kinds of liberal sentiments expressed on the Statue of Liberty have been influential in forming American public opinion, but have consistently been challenged by those who believe that one social group or another represents a threat to the American nation and should, therefore, have its rights restricted in various ways. But this raises the question of how the American economy and society may have been changing recently so as to produce new conflicts over "inclusion" of particular groups as full members in the polity.

Scholars of change in the American polity in previous eras have tended to divide between those who locate the underlying dynamic in cultural conflicts and those who see economic forces as being the primary determinant. Thus, for example, some interpretations of the 1890s posit a conflict between advocates of different kinds of Christian values and lifestyles ("pieticals" and "liturgicals") as being crucial; other interpretations have emphasized that the conflict in the late nineteenth century was one between a growing industrial sector and a relatively declining agricultural sector. In the contemporary era it is possible to point to both major long-term cultural changes and long-term economic changes that can plausibly be linked to the political turbulence, and these can now be outlined.

Antagonistic Subcultures

Turning first to culture and values. As Garry Wills (1996b) has noted: "Historic changes of great sweep were reflected on the surface of our politics by the 1970s – changed attitudes towards authority, toward sex, toward education, toward war." These changes have persisted and will continue to divide Americans in the twenty-first century. Those who have opposed many of these changes found that, even when the candidates they supported won elections, the direction of social change was not altered. Government seemed unable to stop other people following life-styles, asserting rights, and engaging in particular acts of which they disapproved, and those of whom they have disapproved include "liberated" women, gays, advocates of "secular humanism," so-called "pornographers," people who use drugs, and ethnic and racial minorities who make use of rights granted to them originally by the courts. What makes those who line up against these enemies such an important minority in the United States is the role that religion continues to play in American society. By comparison with other advanced industrial societies, the United States is unusual in the high level of religious belief and observance that is evident. Issues that would be at the fringes of politics elsewhere, simply because they are of secondary concern to most secular people, become center-stage in America. As with the clash between "pieticals" and "liturgicals" in the 1890s, this contemporary confrontation between those who would impose a return to an old moral and social order ("moralists," perhaps) and those who reject that claim (for whom the word "civicists" might be invented) has been fought out in the political arena. The "moralists" have been concentrated among Republican activists and voters while "civicists" have been found in both parties.

The Worsening Economic Position of the American Worker

At the same time, there have been changes in the economy that have, on one interpretation, exacerbated the cultural conflict, and, on another, contributed far more than a divided culture to instability in the political arena. A key development in postwar America has been the turnaround in the economic position and expectations of most American families and workers. From 1950 to 1970 Americans became much better off. Median family income (in constant 1989 dollars) nearly doubled, rising from $17,254 in 1950 to $32,540 in 1970. However, between 1973 and 1991 median family income increased only from $34,774 to $35,939 (Stanley and Niemi, 1994). These data give a strong indication of just how poorly the typical American has done since the 1973 oil crisis by comparison with the preceding twenty years or so. But there is other evidence indicating that the situation for many Americans is even worse than this. Those workers who constitute 80 percent of the workforce, and who are classified by the Bureau of Labor Statistics as being below the higher executive, managerial and technical levels, experienced a decline in their real income between 1973 and 1995 – from $315 to $278 per week. By contrast, the minority of workers with jobs above this level typically experienced large increases in pay, especially during the 1980s. Nor is the situation getting any better. American productivity did start to grow again in the 1990s; between

1990 and 1995 the productivity of nonfarm employees in the private sector increased by 10.3 percent; however, for the first time since the Second World War real wages did not increase during a period of economic recovery – real hourly wages were the same in 1994 as in 1990 (Head, 1996). Not until 1995 was there a rise (of 2.7 percent) in median household income (*New York Times*, September 27, 1996).

One consequence of this is that, for many of those who can secure employment, the only way of obtaining the level of income that their counterparts did twenty years ago is to take on additional jobs. This factor has contributed to a significant long-term growth in the number of hours people work. For those in full-time paid employment the total number of hours worked increased by about 9 percent between 1969 and 1987 (Schor, 1992). However, the lengthening of the working year in recent decades has been driven not only by the needs of workers but by pressures on employers. Fringe benefits, such as health care insurance, have become an increasingly important component of terms of employment – rising from about 17 percent of total wages and salaries in 1955 to over 36 percent in 1987. Since they are "paid on a per-person basis, rather than by the hour," they provide an incentive for firms to operate with as few employees as possible (Schor, 1992). To put the point crudely: employers want fewer workers now, and they want them to work as many hours as they can. Those in employment work longer hours, and at the same time there has been an increase in those who are either unemployed or under-employed. Schor estimates that the proportion of the workforce that is unemployed or under-employed rose from 7 percent of the total in 1969 to nearly 17 percent in 1987.

Now these developments in the American economy must be placed in context. Until the 1960s there had been a long-term decline, over many decades, in the working week. Increasingly Americans had leisure time at their disposal, and they had the income and the resources with which to enjoy it. The years after 1941 were ones of high employment levels and rising standards of living for about 80 to 85 percent of the population. A common assumption in those years was that over time the length of the working week would be reduced whilst at the same time real income would increase and opportunities for employment would remain high. These expectations have not been met for most of the population. About one-fifth of Americans have experienced rises in their standards of living, though many of the business executives, lawyers, and others in this group work longer hours than did their predecessors. Among other Americans, the situation is worse. Compared with thirty years ago a larger proportion of them are either unemployed or under-employed, and an even greater number face the threat of this. As was seen in Chapter 10, downsizing by companies has made for less secure employment, while for those in employment there is less leisure time, and, even when real income levels have been maintained, it is often because more hours have been worked.

Of course, to some extent the growth of fringe benefits helps to explain the decline in real wages and salaries; money that goes to pay for an employee's health insurance, for example, is money that could have gone into his or her pay packet. However, while health insurance is usually an important incentive for employees, it is often seen as no more than a necessity by them. The increasingly prohibitive cost of health care for "average Americans" means they cannot afford to be without coverage, but such coverage is not a mark of well-being. It is something they need, not something they would choose to spend money on if they did not have to, and one consequence of these expenditures is that they now have less real income to spend. In an obvious sense many people are better off than thirty years ago, but they are unlikely to feel better off: and most of them do not. The apparent strength of the American economy in the mid-1990s concealed how little improvement there had been in the living standards of a majority of Americans over the previous two decades. That is why an obsession with lowering taxes gripped the United States during that period, and will probably continue to do so well into the next century. If individuals' incomes were not rising, one way of increasing them was to reduce taxation; unfortunately, at the same time many Americans were also unwilling to see the government programs from which they benefitted personally reduced, and the irrationality of this made governing difficult and unpopular.

This brings us to an apparent paradox. Opinion poll evidence continues to present a picture of an American people that is seemingly content with what it is getting from the economy. A poll in April 1995 revealed that "71 percent were satisfied with their household income, 80 percent with their leisure time, 73 percent with their jobs, 75 percent with their standard of living" (Golay and

Rollyson, 1996). This might seem to suggest that most Americans either do not know what has happened over the long term or that they are content with it. The former is simply not true; there is plenty of evidence that Americans are aware that, even in the era of relative prosperity of the 1990s, the economy is not as strong as it was. So is contentment the explanation? Possibly, but there is another way of explaining the opinion poll data that helps to link it with the evidence of dissatisfaction with politicians and political institutions.

The starting point for this is the recognition, first, that government intrudes directly rather little on most people's lives, and, leaving aside obvious exceptions such as racial minorities' experience of policing in many communities, much of their immediate experience of it is not that negative; most importantly, it is not evidently worse than it was forty years ago. For most people government is not a problem – at least as it impinges on them directly. But, secondly, even if the mass media helps to illuminate feelings of discontent with politics, it cannot create that discontent. In other words, if people are worried about what is happening to the country, and how it is being governed, those concerns are not simply manufactured ones. So why is it that Americans are so worried about "the way things are going in the United States" and about their political process? A plausible answer to this is that what people want is a more prosperous and secure future, and they do not believe politicians and governments are delivering this. But how does the opinion poll evidence about standards of living cited above mesh with this claim? The answer is that except in situations of crisis people reconcile themselves to what they have personally; they can express contentment with their own lives, even at the same time as they believe that times were better in the past, and they would hope that they could be better in the future. If little can be done about the situation, and there is little that individuals can do for themselves, they accept it. Why give yourself ulcers by being embittered? But this does not mean that Americans forget the situation, or follow the biblical exhortation to turn the other cheek. Rather, they reserve their frustrations and anger for those who are presumed to be capable of making things better, and who have not done so, namely the country's political leaders. After all, they claimed, at different times and in different ways, that they could improve what was happening to the country –

but nothing very much happened, or so it has seemed to many Americans.

The fact is that, even before politicians claimed that they could macro-manage the national economy, voters reacted to adverse economic conditions by turning against incumbent politicians. For example, the Democratic electoral breakthrough of the early 1890s was destroyed by the economic depression that began in 1893. The economic circumstances of the 1990s are rather different, in that Americans have been faced by long-term, rather than short-term, decline in their economic circumstances. But the consequences are rather similar. People are inclined to vent their frustrations at the polling booth, and to blame those in public office for what has been happening. But this leads to another puzzle. Why should the long-term decline in the economic circumstances of most Americans have produced voter rebellion in the 1990s and not, say, seven or ten years earlier?

The Impact of the End of the Cold War

This brings the discussion to another factor that has contributed to the 1990s being an era of mass political frustrations – the ending of the Cold War. The Cold War helped to stabilize American domestic politics; it provided an anchor that helped to fix many aspects of domestic electoral competition. It was largely consensual, in that Democrats and Republicans agreed on the objectives and many of the means for realizing them. Usually, the Republicans benefitted from this, in that their presidential candidates could use it to their advantage in seeking election or reelection.

While we might well surmise that defeat in the Cold War, in whatever form that might have taken, would have had a cataclysmic effect on American politics, victory has also been disruptive. Obviously, we know from opinion poll evidence that, normally, foreign policy plays a relatively small role in determining voter choice, so that it would be highly implausible to assert that a major shift in voting alliances could have been expected after 1989. But the Cold War did have a solidifying effect on voter coalitions. Nowhere was this more evident than with Ronald Reagan's campaigns of 1980 and 1984. Already in 1980 the forces of the religious right (the "moralists") that were to play such a destructive role in the Republican Party in the 1990s, were displaying their strength within the party. They were important in defeating a number of Democratic senators that year, and they contributed to the Reagan coalition. But by focusing on a combination of tax cuts, on which there was some cross-party agreement anyway, and America's perceived weakness in the world, Reagan was able to sideline the religious right within the party, ensuring that they did not scare off its more centrist supporters. In office, the conservative social agenda of the religious right was given lower overt priority than either the administration's economic agenda or its challenge to the Soviet Union.

However, by the 1990s the situation had changed in two respects. First, the Republicans had lost one of their key electoral advantages in presidential contests; it was much more difficult to appeal to the need for a strong national defense in the absence of a Soviet threat. Secondly, the fissures in the Republican Party that had been evident in 1980 could no longer be concealed by an appeal to Cold War politics. Sidelining the religious right, and making its political agenda seem removed from that of the party, was far more difficult in the 1992 and 1996 presidential-nominating process than it had been earlier. That there was not a politician with the charisma of a Ronald Reagan who could attempt to paper over the great differences between the religious right and moderate Republicans on social policy exacerbated the problem.

Increasing Ideological Cohesion in the Political Parties

For much of American history the major division within American society has tended to affect both parties. This has constrained the ways in which the parties can oppose each other and it has contributed to the (false) belief among some foreign observers that there is little that actually distinguishes the two parties. One of the most important political developments of the last thirty years has been the erosion of the minority wings of the two parties. Old-style liberal Republicanism has shrunk as a political force, primarily because of the growing insurgence of conservative grass-roots activists from the early 1960s onwards. At the same time the conservative wing of the Democratic Party, which was a much greater force in their party than the liberal Republicans were in theirs, has declined dramatically as the Republicans have mobilized in the South. The impact of this was already evident in Congress by the early 1980s; the Republicans were a more uniformly conservative party on most economic issues than they had been earlier, while the Democrats were a more uniformly moderate-to-liberal party. In this world of more clear-cut partisan differences, intra-party divisions were potentially that much more threatening to a party because there were no related ructions gripping the other party at the same time. So it was to become for the Republicans over the social agenda of their right-wing religious supporters – once the intervening factor of the Cold War had been removed with the implosion of the Soviet Union at the end of the 1980s.

The electoral realignment in the South has had a further "disquieting" effect on the polity. The norms of courtesy in the Congress had been very much associated with the style of politics practiced by the southern Democrats. It was in their interest that northern liberals in their party did not come to resent the disproportionate influence the southerners exercized through their control of congressional committees. A conflictual style might have precipitated such a reaction, and most southerners had done their best to reinforce norms of courtesy.

The Consequences of Congressional Reform in the 1970s

While the growing distinctiveness of the two parties has been an important factor influencing the development of a more conflictual style of politics within Congress and between Congress and president, there was another factor at work. This was the reforms of Congress in the 1970s – reforms which removed the traditional hierarchies that had centered on the congressional committees and their chairs. For sixty or so years after the revolt against Speaker Cannon in 1910, the conduct of business in the House of Representatives centered on the committees, and the committees tended to operate in a spirit of partial bipartisanship. Cooperation between majority and minority was the norm. As is well known, the 1970s' reforms provided for greater power for individual members, who were less constrained by the need to "go along to get along," and also to the party leadership. The old norms of cooperation were not jettisoned immediately, but the new conditions provided opportunities, especially in the ranks of the minority (Republican) party, for individuals to build careers on the basis of a more pugnacious style within the House. Challenges to other politicians and to ways of conducting business of a kind that would have been political suicide earlier were now possible and careers could be built by those who took advantage of this. Newt Gingrich, first elected in 1978, was the most prominent and the most successful of the new breed of "street-fighter" politicians in Congress. His hounding of Democratic Speaker Jim Wright from 1987 to 1989 led to the latter's downfall over a financial scandal, and it helped Gingrich to a narrow but decisive victory in the election for minority whip in 1989; this was a style of politics that had been alien to older Republicans, irrespective of their political ideology.

However, political ideology was relevant to what was to happen to Congress in the 1990s in that, from the first year of the Reagan Administration (1981), a shared ideology had facilitated a much greater cohesion among congressional Republicans. They sought to vote together in support of the president's agenda, and during the next decade and a half voting scores in Congress were to reveal more partisan divisions than had been evident in earlier decades. A partisan legislature does not mean that a legislature is divided by personal enmity and bitterness; for example, for much of this century, the British Parliament has been highly partisan but also characterized by cross-party friendships in the chamber. But with the growing success of Gingrich in embarrassing the Democrats, and his consequent rise (and that of his allies) in the Republican Party, the growing partisanship in Congress was to develop in the late 1980s and 1990s along lines that connected it with a style of opposition to Democrats that produced rancor and bitterness along party lines. The Democrats' response to this, exploiting their long-term control of the House for partisan ends, encouraged even greater conflict within the chamber in the years before 1994.

The Role of Individual Politicians

An obvious question to ask is: To what extent can the conflict within Congress, and between Congress and the president, be understood as the result of the ambitions and personalities of particular individual politicians? Two arguments can be made against the importance of this factor. The first is one already mentioned; the post-reform Congress provided opportunities for politicians to develop new routes to political power, so that, even if Newt Gingrich had never existed, it is likely that other politicians would have taken the path he did. The second point is that the swelling budget deficit in the 1980s, one of the most important effects of the Reagan tax cuts, constricted the policy choices open to president and Congress alike; because it was now less possible to accommodate competing demands for federal government expenditure, politicians with different policy priorities were placed in direct conflict with each other. This was reinforced by growing public resistance to any tax increases.

Consequently, the kind of conflict evident in the 1990 budget crisis between George Bush and the Democratic Congress can be explained by the logic of the situation facing them – a situation that was very different from that ten years earlier. However, this kind of explanation cannot account, for example, for Gingrich's attempt to take over the policy agenda from the president after the 1994 election. Of course, a Democratic president would surely have been in conflict with a Republican Congress, whoever its leaders were; after all, this was the situation facing Harry Truman after the 1946 mid-term election. Gingrich's approach, though, went far beyond anything that the Republicans had attempted in 1947 and 1948. He sought to sideline the president in the belief that he had obtained an electoral mandate that overturned the one Clinton had received in 1992.

Thus, Gingrich's behavior cannot be explained away simply by the logic of the situation. Just as Richard Nixon's personality is crucial in explaining how the Executive Branch came to organize its business between 1970 and 1974, so is Gingrich's in accounting for the way in which the attempt to drive through the Contract With America was made. Hubris was an important factor here: Newt Gingrich over-estimated how much the country backed his policy agenda and he over-estimated how much the 1994 elections changed the position of the Speaker in the complex set of institutional relationships. His admission in late 1995 that he had allowed the government shutdown over the budget crisis to develop because the president had slighted him in the Air Force One incident (see Chapter 3) illustrated the significance of his personality in explaining key aspects of the assertion of congressional power that year.

More generally, the point can be made that, as minority whip and then Speaker, Newt Gingrich did make a significant difference to the worsening personal relations within Congress in the 1990s. Although he was the whip, and not the minority leader in the House, Gingrich was the real leader in the early 1990s (Sinclair, 1996). By 1990 it had already become less easy to cut deals and to prevent partisan competition from becoming heated in Congress, but Gingrich's style of leadership further encouraged this. The Democrats responded in kind. Especially in 1993, the Clinton Administration tried to get its legislative agenda through Congress on the basis of its nominal majority, and it paid relatively little attention to building cross-party links on individual bills with potentially sympathetic Republicans. The Democrats, though, found it much more difficult than the Republicans to prevent defections from their own ranks, and the result was to confirm Gingrich's belief in the value of his partisan approach.

There is no question about Gingrich's attributes as a skilled political operator, even though he allowed hubris to cloud his judgment at key points in his conflict with the president. Yet his ability to use his skills was constrained by the incoming House Republicans in 1995 who believed wholeheartedly in the Contract With America. Many were unwilling to make the compromises that Gingrich saw were necessary, and, in part, it was their intransigence that contributed to the conflict over the budget – the conflict that both enabled Bill Clinton to rebuild his own standing in the opinion polls and also saw Newt Gingrich's reputation plummet. By 1996 Gingrich had become a major electoral liability for the Republican presidential bid. In 1997 his weakened position made it much more difficult for the House to take the lead in challenging the Clinton policy agenda – that role fell more to the Senate – and in July 1997 it also helped to produce an aborted coup against Gingrich's leadership of his party in the House.

The Future of the Unquiet Polity

It is evident from this discussion then that the causes of the current turbulence and conflict within the American polity are complex, though some of the factors that have contributed to the development of the "unquiet polity" are connected to each other. The "unquiet polity" has been a long time in the making, and the next question to consider is whether it is likely to persist into the next century.

One way of approaching this matter is to think about which of the factors, if any, are already weakening, or might disappear eventually. Obviously, one possibility is that there might be different politicians in key positions: the attempt in 1997 to oust Gingrich raises the possibility of whether he might be replaced by someone whose style was very different and with whom the Democrats would respond with a return to the politics of cooperation. Moreover, there is another factor, discussed above, that is certainly changing – by 1997 the budget deficit was already declining.

However, the impact of these two factors may well prove to be limited. Even if Gingrich were to be toppled, it is far from clear that he would be replaced by a "consensus" politician. One of the causes of the attempted coup against him appeared to be dissatisfaction by some House members with the progress of the party's conservative political agenda. As for the elimination of the budget deficit, it is of itself unlikely to do much to reduce the obsession with low taxes within the American public. Even without a deficit, the zero-sum game nature of competing public policies today may remain, so that the potential for enduring conflict between the parties would persist.

Moreover, there remain a number of other factors that probably will not be very different in 2000 or 2005 than in 1997. America will still be a country in which who is to be included within the polity, and who excluded, is a possible source of mass conflict. Women are not going to return to the domestic sphere, gays will not return to the closet, and ethnic minorities will not become Uncle Toms, but neither are the "moralists" in the American public going to accept these newer life-styles, so that the conditions for cultural conflict remain. The prospects for the American worker, with respect to trends in both real income and leisure time, are not likely to be as good as they were in the years 1941–73, even if the relatively better economic conditions of the 1990s continue. The Cold War cannot be reinvented, so that there seems to be little that could modify or ameliorate the conflict over the social agenda within the Republican Party.

The fact is that the political turbulence of the 1990s does not appear to have been primarily the result of short-term factors, but rather follows from the convergence of a number of long-term factors, none of which is likely to be reversed. It would seem only a short step from this to the conclusion that instability will persist in American politics: electoral majorities will be overturned, as, successively, each of the parties fails to satisfy the coalitions that have supported them. Intolerance will be fuelled by politicians seeking short-term electoral benefits and support from mass publics that cannot understand why politicians cannot provide the conditions in which the "good life" can be led. Nevertheless, there is an obvious objection to this conclusion. If we look back to previous eras, the pattern in the United States is for turbulence to be replaced by a new political settlement – a settlement that was not foreseen by participants in the political process a few years earlier.

Consider again the first half of the 1890s – a period in which there are, at least, some superficial parallels with the 1990s. Electoral majorities were overturned and then overturned once more; Republican Party elites had been struggling to reduce the influence of moralistic insurgents (mobilized by the issue of Prohibition) who could make the party unelectable (as it did in Iowa in the late 1880s); mass discontent in the South and West had led by 1892 to the rise of a third party as a national force (the Populists); and populist appeals by political leaders found an enthusiastic response among some key groups in American society. Yet by the later 1890s a new political settlement was in place. In federal elections the years between 1894 and 1910 were dominated by the Republicans, and there was no repeat of the Populist challenge to the two-party order; the great issue (of gold as the sole unit of account), which had so divided the parties in 1896 was marginalized as prosperity returned and it became apparent that industrial, not rural, America was now the key to electoral success; in the South the introduction of the Jim Crow laws and the disenfranchisement of nearly all black people stifled any possibility of an alliance between blacks and poor whites; prohibitionists' tactics changed, and they moved away from the infiltration of party politics in the pursuit of their goals. By 1905 the conditions of political action were very different; the factors that threatened to destabilize politics had been removed; the old political order was in the process of being changed but not by the forces that seemed to be undermining it in the early 1890s, nor in the direction that would then have been predicted.

This example is a salutary reminder that political dynamics are complex and that predicting the distant future is foolish, even when the persistence of certain long-term trends is evident. But what disrupts an emerging pattern of conflict? One of the most famous explanations of this is that of Walter Dean Burnham (1970, 1982). Burnham argued that American politics had been characterized by a tension between a highly developed economy and an under-developed political system. In a sense the political system could not cope with the economy, and every so often (according to Burnham, about every thirty years) pressures would build up and the result would be a realignment of the parties. The tension would then ease – as with an earthquake in relation to the earth's tectonic plates – and a long period of stability would follow until the process was repeated three decades later. Of course, at the time the significance of what had happened might be far from clear. Often it is difficult to distinguish short-term switches of support by various social groups from longer-term changes in patterns of voter support. Hardly anyone in 1898 or 1902 understood just how much the political order had changed and was changing; the gap between the political worlds of 1892 and 1902 would be much more apparent in later decades than it was in 1902.

So we must consider the possibility that the divisions evident in the first half of the 1990s represent the building up of socio-economic tensions that will be relieved, or are in the process of being relieved, by shifts in the basis of party support and hence in the pattern of interests the two parties represent. An obvious objection to this argument is that Burnham's model seemed not to work the last time the conditions for realignment appeared to be present. On the thirty-six year cycle Burnham identified, 1968 should have been at the heart of an era of realignment, but there was no evidence of major shifts in partisanship then. Rather, some writers argued there was a long-term withering away of voter attachments to any parties; this was now the era of the individual politician who used his or her own resources to secure election. Nor is there any evidence that this shift away from parties and towards individual candidates has been reversed since the 1960s. Moreover, while the realignments Burnham identified produced a decisive advantage for one party, the present state of the parties is balanced: for example, in 1996 the share of the vote obtained by all House candidates was almost the same as for all Republican candidates. Consequently, it seems that a new long-term electoral majority can provide the basis of a political settlement that will defuse conflict among Americans. But in the 1890s were there other factors that were important in stabilizing politics that might also be relevant in the 1990s?

One possible factor is the role played by the Supreme Court in settling particular areas of social conflict. Today the 1893 case of *Plessy* v. *Ferguson* is recognized as immoral because, in legitimizing the "separate but equal" doctrine, it permitted the southern states to practice racial segregation. However, while there is no denying this, the case did help to contribute significantly to the emergence of political stability because it resolved for sixty years a major conflict, by allowing white southerners wide latitude in their treatment of black people. (This case is a powerful reminder that, while political stability is generally a desirable goal, the price that may be paid in achieving it may be far too high.) What the Supreme Court decides can shape the context in which political disputes are conducted, and, in doing so, it can help to defuse overt conflict in the polity.

In this regard, one recent case commands particular attention. This is the 1996 decision in *Romer* v. *Evans* (see Chapter 4), in which the Court struck down Colorado's anti-gay legislation, noting that "it is not within our constitutional tradition to enact laws of this sort." The language used by the Court surprised many commentators, indicating perhaps that even the conservative Court of the Rehnquist era might take clear decisions that favored the rights of those who were under attack from the "moralists" in American society. Were this to be the case, it might be imagined that the Court might play a role similar to its predecessor in the *Plessy* era, by coming down firmly on the side of the political forces that seemed capable of aligning themselves in the majority. In other words, despite its conservatism, the Court of the 1990s would construct decisions that would allow a political settlement that favored the "civicists," just as in 1893 it came up with a decision that recognized the political advantage the white, segregationist South then enjoyed – at least in relation to the South itself.

However, it is by no means clear that, the language of the *Romer* decision notwithstanding, the Supreme Court has cleared the way for victory for the "civicist" cause. The decision in this case (and also in another 1996 case requiring the admission of women to the Virginia Military Institute) is written in a way that leaves it open to doubt whether it has general applicability. The *modus operandi* of the Rehnquist Court has been the very opposite of that of the Warren Court of the 1950s and 1960s, which did take bold steps in the pursuit of general policy objectives. The Court in the 1990s has tended to move very slowly away from the status quo. If this interpretation of its behavior is correct, then *Romer* may be more of a curiosity than a case that will help define a new political settlement.

Nevertheless, there is another factor that may help to ameliorate political conflict in the short term, even if its long-term effects are weaker. This is that, having contributed to the development of political turbulence, politicians may come to believe that in the interests of the future of the polity, their own behavior should be modified. Speaking of the election of 1896, VanderMeer (1985) noted of Indiana politicians:

> Many were concerned about the bitterness, hostility, and divisiveness this election engendered. Fearing this might continue and perhaps expand beyond the bounds of electoral politics, and afraid of the apocalypse that each had predicted, members of both parties modified their rhetoric and lowered their voices . . . Even though partisanship and party conflict did continue thereafter, the day of less bitterness . . . was at hand.

Furthermore, it is not just a concern for the long-term future of the polity that can induce change in the behavior of political elites. Their beliefs about the attitudes of key groups of voters to a conflictual style of politics can also lead to a modification of behavior. Indeed, this is precisely what seems to have happened in the 1996 election campaign. Voter hostility to the approach adopted by Gingrich, particularly his willingness to "close down the federal government" during the dispute with the president over the budget, meant that the presidential campaign had to be conducted on a very different basis. Even so, although the Republicans produced a rather bland election campaign, the evidence from the party's focus groups suggested that the Dole campaign may not actually have gone far enough to adopt a campaign style that voters found acceptable (*New York Times*, October 5, 1996). Yet the campaign the Republicans did produce was still a rather bland one. Furthermore, the belief that a conflictual style did not sell well with the public guided both the president and the Republican congress leadership in 1997: their deal over the budget was possible because neither side wished to appear to be the "spoiler."

Here, at last, there appears to be a factor that might help to moderate the political turbulence of the 1990s and thereby make for a less conflictual start to politics in the twenty-first century. Yet the effects of this may not last that long. As noted earlier, many of the factors that contributed to the "unquiet polity" of the 1990s are likely to be present then, and unlike the beginning of the twentieth century, it would not appear that a new long-term political settlement is emerging. The potential for the reappearance of a highly conflictual style of politics remains, and the ancient Chinese curse – of living in interesting times – may well be experienced again in the American polity.

Guide to Further Reading

Chapter 1 Introduction

Lowi (1995) and Dionne (1996) offer stimulating interpretations of recent developments in American politics. Wilson (1998) addresses the issue of American exceptionalism. Schlesinger (1991) raises important questions about American national identity.

Chapter 2 The Presidency

Journalistic accounts of the Clinton Presidency include Drew (1994), Woodward (1994) and Walker (1996). Early scholarly appraisals can be found in Campbell and Rockman (1996). Morris (1997) and Reich (1997) provide lively insider accounts of the Clinton White House. Skowronek (1993) provides an interesting theoretical framework which seeks to explain patterns of presidential power.

Chapter 3 Congress and Partisan Change

Foley and Owens (1996) places the contemporary Congress in its historical and institutional context, as do Loomis (1996), Smith (1995), and Davidson and Oleszek (1998). The Republican takeover of Congress is considered more fully in Owens (1997), McSweeney and Owens (1998), and Dodd and Oppenheimer (1997). Good, relatively short accounts of the first 100 days of Republican rule are Wilcox (1995) and Gimple (1996). A particularly good journalistic account of the Republican "revolution" is Maraniss and Weisskopf (1996).

Chapter 4 The Supreme Court and the Constitution

O'Brien (1996) and McKeever (1993) provide good introductions to the role of the Supreme Court. A radically different view of the power of the Court is provided by Rosenberg (1991). The jurisprudence of the Rehnquist Court is examined by Gillman (1991). Those interested in constitutional law should consult Fisher (1995).

Chapter 5 The American Federal Bureaucracy

Osborne and Gaebler (1992) is the obvious place to start an investigation of the reinventing government initiative. Good appraisals of recent developments are Kettl (1994), Kettl and DiIulio (1996), and Kettl *et al.* (1996).

The annual reports of the National Performance Review also contain good information about changes in the federal bureaucracy.

Chapter 6 The Changing Federal System

Good introductions to the changing patterns of American federalism are Zimmerman (1992) and Walker (1995). Peterson (1995) offers an excellent, if controversial, theoretical model to explain national-state relations. Gray and Jacob (1996) provides a good introduction to politics at the state level.

Chapter 7 Political Parties

Epstein (1986) provides a good general overview as does McSweeney and Zvesper (1991). Rae (1989 and 1994) offers an interpretation of the parties which concentrates on factionalism. Mayhew (1986) is very useful on the distinctive state character of parties. Shafer (1983) is the authoritative work on Democratic Party reform. Bibby and Maisel (1998) is an excellent up-to-date overview.

Chapter 8 Organized Interests

Petracca (1992) and Cigler and Loomis (1995) are both excellent collections of essays on interest group politics. Heinz (1993) is an interesting discussion of the changing geometry of contemporary interest groups. Birnbaum (1993) offers a lively insight into the actual workings of interest groups.

Chapter 9 Electoral Politics

Pomper (1997) and Nelson (1997) provide excellent overviews of the 1996 elections. Polsby and Wildavsky (1996) is a good introduction to the structure and politics of presidential elections while Jacobson (1997c) offers a similar introduction to congressional elections. For a discussion of voting patterns see Miller and Shanks (1996). King (1997) offers an insightful analysis of the pervasiveness of electioneering in American politics.

Chapter 10 Economic Policy

Hall (1998) examines the role of economic ideas. Kettl (1992) and Savage (1988) examine the impact of the deficit and the demand for a balanced budget on American politics.

Chapter 11 Social Policy

The problems of welfare in the United States are examined in Janssen (1993), Bane and Ellwood (1994) and Noble (1997). The Clinton

Administration's efforts to reform health care are examined in Mann and Ornstein (1995), Skocpol (1996), and Marcus and Craven (1997). An overview of recent domestic policy is provided by Stoesz (1996). Howard (1997) looks at the "hidden welfare state" created by government tax loopholes.

Chapter 12 Foreign Policy

The various options facing the US after the end of the Cold War are discussed in Cox (1995) and Lieber (1997). Nordlinger (1995) gives a spirited and intelligent defense of neo-isolationism, which is well answered by Ruggie (1996). Hirst and Thompson (1996) provide an excellent, if controversial, interpretation of the economic context of contemporary US foreign policy. Dumbrell (1997b) discusses the making of American foreign policy in the contemporary world.

Chapter 13 Education Policy

For a comprehensive overview of the politics of education see Wirt and Kirp (1992). Ravitch (1983) provides an excellent history of reform movements in American education in the postwar years which puts current conflicts in a larger context. The increasing legalization of education policy and its effects are discussed in Kirp and Jensen (1986). Chubb and Moe (1990) strongly criticize the current education system and promote the case for market based reforms. See Smith and Meier (1995) for a strong rebuttal of the case for school choice plans. Finally, Fuhrman (1993) discusses the merits of more conventional restructuring efforts, typified by the educational standards movement.

Chapter 14 Affirmative Action and the Politics of Race

Belz (1990), Drake and Holsworth (1996), Edley (1996), and Skrentny (1996) are good introductions to the changing nature of affirmative action programs. More general discussions of civil rights legislation include Buimiller (1992) and Nieman (1991). The best discussion of the effect of the Voting Rights Act in the South is Davidson and Grofman (1994). Peacock (1997) offers a more recent examination of developments post-*Shaw*. General examinations of the role of race in American politics include Hochschild (1995) and Kinder and Sanders (1996).

Chapter 15 Campaign Finance Reform

Alexander (1992) is an authoritative account of campaign financing. Discussions of the role of PACs in funding campaigns include Clawson *et al.* (1992), Greiden (1992), and Makinson (1992). Sorauf (1992) provides a balanced view of issues in campaign finance.

Chapter 16 The Regional City: Governance and Competitiveness in Pittsburgh

Good up-to-date overviews of the general problems of American cities can be found in Monkkonen (1995) and Sbragia (1996). Ferman (1996) focuses on the issue of growth while Imbroscio (1997) looks at economic options for cities. Savitch and Vogel (1996) examines regional politics while Kresl and Gappert (1995) places American cities in the context of the global economy.

Chapter 17 The Media

A good overview of the role of the media in politics is Graber (1997, 5th edn). Kurtz (1997b) discusses the effect of the talk show culture on American political life. General discussions of the changing nature of the media include Gilder (1993) and Wriston (1993).

Chapter 18 The American Political System in transition to a new century

Nye, Zelikow and King (1997) offers an excellent overview of the political culture. Samuelson (1995) is also insightful. Shafer (1997) explores the causes of American discontent in the 1990s.

Bibliography

Aberbach, Joel D. (1996) "The Federal Executive Under Clinton," in Colin Campbell and Bert A. Rockman, eds., *The Clinton Presidency, First Appraisals*, Chatham, N.J., Chatham House.

Ackerman, Bruce (1991) *We the People*, Cambridge, Mass., Harvard University Press.

Ahlbrandt, R. S., R. J. Fruehan and F. Giarratani (1996) *The Renaissance of American Steel*, New York, Oxford University Press.

Alexander, Herbert E. (1992) *Financing Politics*, 4th edn, Washington, D.C., Congressional Quarterly Press.

Alexander, Lamar and Chester E. Finn, eds. (1995) *The New Promise of American Life,* Indianapolis, The Hudson Institute.

Allegheny Conference on Community Development (ACCD) (1993) *Toward a Shared Economic Vision for Pittsburgh and Southwestern Pennslyvania*, Pittsburgh, Carnegie Mellon University.

Amin, A. and N. Thrift, eds. (1995) *Globalisation, Institutions, and Regional Development in Europe*, Oxford, Oxford University Press.

Babson, Jennifer (1995) "Armey Stood Guard Over the Contract," *Congressional Quarterly Weekly Report*, April 8.

Bacevich, A. J. (1996) "The Impact of the New Populism," *Orbis*, 40, pp. 31–43.

Bacon, Donald C., Roger Davidson and Morton Keller, eds. (1995) *The Encyclopedia of the United States Congress*, New York and London, Simon & Schuster.

Baker, James A. (1995) *The Politics of Diplomacy*, New York, G.P. Putnam's Sons.

Balz, Dan (1997) "Democrats Return $1.4 Million in Questionable Donations," *Washington Post*, June 28.

Bancroft, Ann (1998) "California Drops Bilingual Education Requirement," *Boston Globe*, March 14.

Bane, M. J. and David T. Ellwood (1994) *Welfare Realities: From Rhetoric to Reform*, Cambridge, Mass., Harvard University Press.

Barber, James (1972) *The Presidential Character*, Englewood Cliffs, N.J., Prentice Hall.

Barnes, James A. (1995) "Haley's Comet," *National Journal*, February 25.

—— (1996) "Lott: The Senate Broker," *National Journal*, December 21.

—— (1997) "Ready on the Right," *National Journal*, January 25.

Barry, John M. (1989) *The Ambition and the Power*, New York, Viking.

Baumer, Donald C. (1992) "Senate Democratic Leadership in the 101st Congress," in Allen D. Hertzke and Ronald M. Peters, eds., *The Atomistic Congress*, Armonk, N.Y., M.E. Sharpe.

Beer, Samuel (1978) "In Search of a New Public Philosophy," in Anthony King, ed., *The New American Political System*, Washington, D.C., American Enterprise Institute.

Begley, Sharon and Pat Wingert (1997) "Teach Your Parents Well," *Newsweek,* 129, 17, p. 72.

Belz, Herman (1990) *Equality Transformed*, New Brunswick, N.J., Transaction Books.

Bennett, William (1988) *Our Children and Our Country: Improving our Schools and Affirming the Common Culture*, New York, Simon & Schuster.

Bennett, William (1992) *The Devaluing of America: the Fight for our Culture and our Children*, New York, Summit Books.

Betts, Richard K. (1995) *Military Readiness: Concepts, Choices, Consequences*, Washington, D.C., Brookings.

Bibby, John and Louis Maisel (1998) *Two Parties or More?*, Boulder, Co., Westview.

Bingham, R. D. (1997) *Industrial Policy – American Style,* Armonk, N.Y., M.E. Sharpe.

Birnbaum, Jeffrey (1993) *The Lobbyists*, New York, Random House.

Blanchflower, D. and A. Oswald (1994) *The Wage Curve*, Cambridge, Mass., M.I.T. Press.

Blasi, Vincent, ed. (1983) *The Burger Court*, New York, Alfred Knopf.

Bledsoe, T. (1993) *Careers in City Politics*, Pittsburgh, Pittsburgh University Press.

Bork, Robert (1990) *The Tempting of America*, New York, Simon & Schuster.

Bowling, Cynthia J. and Deil S. Wright (1997) "Public Administration in the Fifty States," Chapel Hill, Institute for Research in Social Science, University of North Carolina.

Bradley, Jennifer (1997) "Livingston Feuds With Leadership," *Roll Call*, June 2.

Brady, David W. and Philip Althoff (1974) "Party Voting in the US House of Representatives, 1890–1910, Elements of a Responsible Party System," *Journal of Politics*, 36.

Bright, Stephen B. (1997) "Political Attacks on the Judiciary," *Judicature*, 80, pp. 165–73.

Broder, David S. (1997) "Campaign Reform Maze," *Washington Post*, March 23.

Brown, K. B. (1996) *Taxing America*, New York, New York University Press.

Brown, W. Q. and D. H. Dunn (1996) *American Security Policy in the 1990s*, Aldershot, Dartmouth.

Browning, Graeme (1996) "Please Hold for the Election Results," *National Journal*, November 16.

Brownstein, Ronald (1992) *The Power and the Glitter: The Hollywood–Washington Connection*, New York, Vintage.

Bryce, James (1891) *The American Commonwealth,* London, Macmillan.

Buchanan, James M. (1995) "Federalism as an Ideal Political Order and an Objective for Constitutional Reform," *Publius*, 25, pp. 1–9.

Buimiller, Kristin (1992) *The Civil Rights Society*, Baltimore, The Johns Hopkins University Press.

Burnham, Walter Dean (1970) *Critical Elections and the Mainspring of American Politics*, New York, W.W.Norton.

—— (1982) *The Current Crisis in American Politics*, Oxford, Oxford University Press.

Cain, Bruce E. and Karin MacDonald (1997) "Race Was a Dull Wedge in California's 1996 Presidential Campaign," *Public Affairs Report*, 38, pp. 10–13.

Campbell, Colin and Bert A. Rockman (1996) *The Clinton Presidency: First Appraisals*, Chatham N.J., Chatham House.

Capitol Source (1997) *The Who's Who, What, Where in Washington*, Washington, D.C., National Journal.

Caplan, Lincoln (1987) *The Tenth Justice: The Solicitor General and the Rule of Law*, New York, Alfred Knopf.

Carelli, Richard (1996) "Chief Justice Says Independent Judiciary is Vital," *News and Reports* (April 11, 1996)

—— (1997) "Scalia Calls Move to Impeach Liberal Judges A Nonstarter," *News and Reports* (May 20, 1997), AP Wire Service, http://www.sddt.com/files/library/96W.

Carroll, James and Walter Broadnax (1997) "Governance, Accountability and Welfare Reform," unpublished paper.

Cass, Connie (1997) "Americans Want Campign Reform," *Washington Post*, March 23.

Center for Education Reform (1996) *The National Charter School Directory*, Washington, D.C., The Center for Education Reform.

Center for Public Integrity (1995) *Well-Healed: Inside Lobbying for Health Care Reform*, Washington, D.C., Center for Public Integrity

Cerny, Philip C. (1997) "Paradoxes of the Competition State: The Dynamics of Political Globalization," *Government and Opposition*, 32, pp. 251–74.

Cervero, R. (1989) *America's Suburban Centers*, Boston, Unwin Hyman.

Chaikind, Stephen, Louis Danielson and Marsha Brauen (1993) "What Do We Know about the Costs of Special Education?," *Journal of Special Education*, Vol 26 No 4.

Chisholm, D. (1997) "No Magic Bullets: Privatization's Threat to Urban Public Administration," *Journal of Contingencies and Crisis Management*, 5, pp. 140–50.

Chisman, Forest P. (1995) "Can the States Do Any Better?," *The Nation*, May 1.

Choate, Pat (1990) *Agents of Influence*, New York, Alfred Knopf.

Christopher, Warren (1995) "America's Leadership, America's Opportunity," *Foreign Policy*, 98, pp. 6–28.

Chubb, John and Terry Moe (1990) *Politics, Markets and America's Schools*, Washington, D.C., Brookings.

Ciambala, Stephen J., ed. (1996) *Clinton and Post-Cold War Defense*, Westport, Ct., Praeger.

Cigler, Allan J. and Burdette A. Loomis, eds. (1995) *Interest Group Politics* 4th edn, Washington, D.C., Congressional Quarterly Press.

Clarke, Jonathan (1996) "Gone to the Lake: Republicans and Foreign Policy," *The National Interest*, 42, pp. 34–45.

Clarke, Susan E. (1993) "The New Localism: Local Politics in a Global Era," in E. G. Goetz and S. E. Clarke, eds., *The New Localism*, Newbury Park, Calif., Sage.

Clarke, Susan E. and Martin R. Saiz (1996) "Economic Development and Infrastructure Policy," in Virginia Gray and Herbert Jacob, eds., *Politics in the American States*, 4th edn, Washington, D.C., Congressional Quarterly Press.

Clarke, T. N. and E. G. Goetz (1994) "The Antigrowth Machine: Can City Governments Control, Limit, or Manage Growth?," in T. N. Clarke, ed., *Urban Innovation*, Thousand Oaks, Sage.

Clausen, Aage R. (1973) *How Congressmen Decide*, New York, St. Martin's Press.

Clawson, Dan, Alan Neustadtl and Denise Scott (1992) *Money Talks: Corporate Pacs and Political Influence*, New York, Basic Books.

Clayton, Cornell (1992) *The Politics of Justice: The Attorney General and the Making of Legal Policy*, New York, M.E. Sharpe.

—— (1994) "Separate Branches – Separate Politics: Judicial Enforcement of Congressional Intent," *Political Science Quarterly*, 109, pp. 843–72.

—— and Howard Gillman (1998) *Institutional Approaches to Supreme Court Decision Making*, Chicago, University of Chicago Press.

Cloud, David S. (1995a) "Lott Has Pole Position in 'Race' for Leader," *Congressional Quarterly Weekly Report*, February 17.

—— (1995b) "GOP Moderates Refusing to Get in Line," *Congressional Quarterly Weekly Report*, September 30.

—— (1995c) "Santorum Pushing Senate To Be More Like House," *Congressional Quarterly Weekly Report*, October 28.

Clough, Michael (1994) "Grass Roots Policymaking: Say Good-Bye to the 'Wise Men'," *Foreign Affairs*, 73, pp. 2–7.

Clymer, Adam (1997) "Reno Finds There's Little Room To Move," *New York Times*, October 15.

CNN, *Crossfire*, September 13 1991.

Cohen, Richard E. (1995) "Whipping the Senate GOP Into Shape," *National Journal*, January 7.

Congressional Quarterly (1993) *CQ Guide to 1990 Congressional Redistricting*, Washington, D.C., Congressional Quarterly Press.

—— (1997) *State and Local Sourcebook '97*, Washington, D.C., Congressional Quarterly.

Congressional Quarterly Weekly Reports, May 11 1996.

Congressional Quarterly Almanac (1992) Washington, D.C., Congressional Quarterly Press.

Congressional Research Service (C.R.S.) (1995) "Compilation and Overview of Federal Laws and Regulations Establishing Affirmative Action," Washington, D.C., CRS.

Connelly, William F. and John J. Pitney (1994) *Congress' Permanent Minority?*, Lanham, MD, Littlefield Adams.

Cooper, C. J. and J. O. McGinnis (1995) "The Republican Congress and the Constitution in Foreign and Military Affairs," *Common Sense*, 2, pp. 75–88.

Corrado, A. (1997) "Financing the 1996 Elections," in G. Pomper *et al.*, *The Election of 1996: Reports, Interpretations*, Chatham, N.J., Chatham House Publishers.

Corwin, Edward S. (1950) "The Passing of Dual Federalism," *Virginia Law Review*, 36, pp. 1–24.

Cose, Ellis (1997) "Dialogue of Dishonesty," *Newsweek*, June 30.

Cox, Gary W. and Matthew D. McCubbins (1993) *Legislative Leviathan*, Berkeley, University of California Press.

Cox, Gary W. and Samuel Kernell, eds. (1991) *The Politics of Divided Government*, Boulder, Co., Westview Press.

Cox, Michael (1995) *US Foreign Policy after the Cold War*, London, Pinter, Royal Institute of International Affairs.

D'Aveni, R. A. (1994) *Hyper-Competititon*, New York, The Free Press.

Dahl, Robert (1957) "Decision-Making in a Democracy: The Supreme Court as a National Policy-Maker," *Journal of Public Law*, 6, pp. 279–95.

Davidow, W. H. and M. S. Malone (1992) *The Virtual Corporation*, New York, Harper Business.

Davidson, Chandler and Bernard Grofman, eds. (1994) *Quiet Revolution in the South*, Princeton, N.J., Princeton University Press.

Davidson, Robert C. and Ernest L. Lewis (1997) "Affirmative Action and Other Special Consideration Admissions at the University of California, Davis, School of Medicine," *Journal of the American Medical Association*, 278, pp. 1153–8.

Davidson, Roger H. (1985) "Senate Leaders, Janitors for an Untidy Chamber," in Lawrence C. Dodd and Bruce I. Oppenheimer, eds., *Congress Reconsidered*, 3rd edn, Washington, D.C., Congressional Quarterly Press.

—— (1994) "Congress in Crisis . . . Once Again," in Gillian Peele, Christopher J. Bailey, Bruce Cain and B. Guy Peters, eds., *Developments in American Politics 2*, London, Macmillan.

Davidson, Roger and Walter J. Oleszek (1998) *Congress and Its Members*, 5th edn, Washington, D.C., Congressional Quarterly Press.

Davies, Philip John and Brian Neve, eds. (1981) *Cinema, Politics and Society in America*, Manchester, Manchester University Press.

—— (1992) *Elections USA*, Manchester, Manchester University Press.

Davis, Richard (1995) "Media: Becoming an Autonomous Force," in Philip John Davies, ed., *An American Quarter Century: US Politics from Vietnam to Clinton*, Manchester, Manchester University Press.

Deitrick, S. and R. A. Beauregard (1995) "From Front-Runner to Also-Ran – The Transformation of a Once Dominant Industrial Region: Pennslyvania USA," in P. Cooke, ed., *The Rise of the Rustbelt*, London, UCL Press.

Delli Carpini, Michael X. and Scott Keeter (1996) *What Americans Know About Politics and Why It Matters*, New Haven, Ct., Yale University Press.

Department of Defense (1997) *Report of the Quadrennial Defense Review*, Washington, D.C., GPO.

Derthick, Martha (1996) "Whither Federalism?," Washington, D.C., The Urban Institute.

Dethloff, H. C. (1996) *The United States and the Global Economy Since 1945*, New York, Harcourt Brace.

de Tocqueville, Alexis (1956) *Democracy in America*, New York, Mentor, original edn published in 1837.

Dionne, E. J. (1996) *They Only Look Dead: Why Progressives Will Dominate the Next Era*, New York, Simon & Schuster.

Dodd, Lawrence C. (1986a) "The Cycles of Legislative Change," in Herbert F. Weisberg, ed., *Political Science, The Science of Politics*, New York, Agathon.

—— (1986b) "A Theory of Congressional Cycles, Solving the Puzzle of Change," in Gerald C. Wright, Leroy N. Rieselbach and Lawrence C. Dodd, eds., *Congress and Policy Change*, New York, Agathon.

—— and Bruce I. Oppenheimer (1997) "Congress and the Emerging Order: Conditional Party Government or Constructive Partnership?," in Lawrence C. Dodd and Bruce I. Oppenheimer, eds., *Congress Reconsidered*, 6th edn, Washington, D.C., Congressional Quarterly Press.

Dodge, W. R. (1996) *Regional Excellence*, Washington, D.C., National League of Cities.

Doherty, Carroll (1996) "Clinton's Big Comeback Shown in Vote Score," *Congressional Quarterly Weekly Report*, December 21.

Doig, J. W. (1995) "Politics and the Engineering Mind: O.H. Amman and the Hidden Story of the George Washington Bridge," in D. C. Perry, ed., *Building the Public City*, Thousand Oaks, Sage.

Donahue, John D. (1997) *Disunited States*, New York, Basic Books.

Dougherty, Regina, Everett C. Ladd, David Wilbur and Lynn Zayachkiwsky (1997) *America at the Polls*, Storrs, C. N., The Roper Center.

Drake, Willie Avon and Robert D. Holsworth (1996) *Affirmative Action and the Stalled Quest for Black Progress*, Urbana, Ill., University of Illinois Press.

Drew, Elizabeth (1994) *On the Edge*, New York, Simon & Schuster.

—— (1996) *Shutdown: The Struggle Between the Gingrich Congress and the Clinton White House*, New York, Simon & Schuster.

—— (1997a) *Whatever it Takes: The Real Struggle for Political Power in America*, New York, Penguin.

—— (1997b) "A Gourmet's Guide to the Campaign Finance Stew," *Washington Post*, March 23.

Dumbrell, John (1997a) *American Foreign Policy: Carter to Clinton*, London, Macmillan.
—— (1997b) *The Making of US Foreign Policy*, 2nd edn, Manchester, Manchester University Press.
Duncan, Phil and Steve Langdon (1993) "When Congress Had to Choose, It Voted to Back Clinton," *Congressional Quarterly Weekly Report*, December 18.
Edley, Christopher (1996) *Not all Black and White: Affirmative Action and American Values*, New York, Hill & Wang.
Edsall, Thomas (1984) *The New Politics of Inequality*, New York, W.W. Norton.
Education Commission of the States (1998) "Clearing House Notes", Denver, ECS.
Edwards, George C., Andrew Barrett and Jeffrey Peake (1997) "The Legislative Impact of Divided Government," *American Journal of Political Science*, 41, pp. 545–63.
Ehrenhalt, Alan (1982) "Every Man is an Island in the Senate of the 1980s, Team Spirit has Given Way to the Rule of Individuals," *Congressional Quarterly Weekly Report*, September 4, pp. 2175–202.
—— (1995) "Out in the States, It's Not the 1930s Anymore," *Governing*, 9.
Eisner, M. A. (1991) *Anti-Trust and the Triumph of Economics*, Chapel Hill, University of North Carolina.
Elazar, Daniel J. (1962) *The American Partnership*, Chicago, University of Chicago Press.
Eldersveld, S. J., L. Stromberg and W. Derksen (1995) *Local Elites in Western Democracies*, Boulder, Co., Westview.
Ellwood, David T. (1993) "The Changing Structure of American Families: The Bigger Family Planning Issue," *Journal of the American Planning Association*, 59, pp. 3–8.
Elmore, Richard (1984) "The Political Economy of State Influence," *Education and Urban Society*, 16, pp. 125–44.
The Enterprise Corporation of Pittsburgh (1996) *The 1996 Entrepeneurial Vitality Scorecard: Pittsburgh Metropolitan Region*, Pittsburgh, The Center for Economic Development, Carnegie Mellon University.
Epstein, Lee (1986) *Conservatives in Court*, Knoxville, Tenn., University of Tennessee Press.
—— and Jack Knight (1997) *The Choices Justices Make*, Washington, D.C., Congressional Quarterly Press.
Epstein, Leon (1986) *Political Parties in the American Mold*, Madison, Wisc., University of Wisconsin Press.
Evans, C. Lawrence and Walter J. Oleszek (1997) "Congressional Tsunami? The Politics of Congressional Reform," in Lawrence C. Dodd and Bruce I. Oppenheimer, eds., *Congress Reconsidered*, 6th edn, Washington, D.C., Congressional Quarterly Press.
Fallows, James (1995) "A Triumph of Misinformation," *The Atlantic Monthly*, January.
Farhi, Paul (1997) "Is Rupert Murdoch Looking to Be Master of the Universe," *Washington Post National Weekly Edition*, March 24.

Farris, Anne (1997) "Unfolding Story Swelling Like A Sponge," *Washington Post*, April 6.

Ferman, B. (1996) *Challenging the Growth Machine*, Lawrence, Ks., University Press of Kansas.

Fink, Evelyn and Brian D. Humes (1996) "Party Conflict and Institutional Change in the US House of Representatives, 1st–99th Congress," unpublished paper.

Finn, Chester E. Jr. (1996) "How Special is Special Education?," Indianapolis, The Hudson Institute.

Fiorina, Morris (1996) *Divided Government*, 2nd edn, Boston, Allyn & Bacon.

Firestone, William, Beth Bader and Diane Massel (1992) "Recent Trends in State Educational Reform: Assessments and Prospects," *Teachers College Record*, 94.

Fisher, Louis (1995) *American Constitutional Law*, 2nd edn, New York, McGraw-Hill.

Fletcher, Arthur A. (1996) "A Personal Footnote in History," in George E. Curry, ed., *The Affirmative Action Debate*, Reading, Mass., Addison-Wesley.

Foley, Michael and John E. Owens (1996) *Congress and the Presidency: Institutional Politics in a Separated System,* Manchester and New York, Manchester University Press and St Martins Press.

Fried, Charles (1988) "Jurisprudential Responses to Legal Realism," *Cornell Law Review*, 73, pp. 331–67.

—— (1995) "Forward: Revolutions?," *Harvard Law Review*, 109, pp. 13–77.

Fuhrman, Susan (1993) *Designing Coherent Education Policy: Improving the System*, San Francisco, Jossey-Bass.

Funston, Richard (1975) "The Supreme Court and Critical Elections," *American Political Science Review*, 69, pp. 795–811.

Galbraith, J. R. (1995) *Designing Organizations*, San Francisco, Jossey-Bass.

Gallup Organization (1997) "The Gallup Poll Social Audit on Black/White Relations in the United States," Executive Summary, Final Revised Version, June 10.

Gallup Poll Monthly (1996a) "The Clintons: Comparative Favorability Trend," January.

—— (1996b) "Gallup Short Subjects," April.

—— (1996c) "Clinton's Commanding Lead Returns After Conventions," September.

Gamble, Andrew and Anthony Payne, eds. (1996) *Regionalism and World Order*, London, Macmillan.

Garreau, J. (1991) *Edge City*, New York, Doubleday.

Gilder, George (1993) *Life After Television*, New York, Norton.

Gillman, Howard (1993) *The Constitution Besieged*, Durham, NC, Duke University Press.

Gilmour, John B. (1994) *Majority Rule in the Senate*, Working Paper 94–6. Berkeley, Institute of Governmental Studies, University of California.

Gimple, James G. (1996) *Fulfilling the Contract*, Boston, Allyn & Bacon.

Gingrich, Newt (1995) *To Renew America*, New York, HarperCollins.

Ginsberg, Benjamin and Martin Shefter (1990) *Politics by Other Means*, New York, The Free Press.

Ginsberg, Ruth Bader (1992) "Speaking in a Judicial Voice," *New York University Law Review*, 67, pp. 1885–904.

Gitenstein, Mark (1992) *Matters of Principle: An Insider's Account of America's Rejection of Robert Bork's Nomination to the Supreme Court*, New York, Simon & Schuster.

Glazer, Nathan (1994) "Divided Cities, Dual Cities: The Case of New York," in S. Dunn, ed., *Managing Divided Cities*, Keele, Ryburn Publishing.

Golay, Michael and Carl Rollyson (1996) *Where America Stands 1996*, New York, John Wiley.

Goldberg, Lenny (1995) "Come the Devolution," *The American Prospect*, 24, pp. 66–71.

Goldman, Sheldon and Elliot Slotnick (1997) "Clinton's First Term Judiciary: Many Bridges to Cross," *Judicature*, 80, pp. 2554–73.

Gottlieb, Sanford (1997) *Defense Addiction: Can America Kick the Habit?*, Oxford, Westview.

Governors' Bulletin (1996) "States Feel Relief from Unfunded Mandates," June 17.

Graber, Doris (1997) *Mass Media in American Politics*, 5th edn, Washington, D.C., Congressional Quarterly Press.

Graber, Mark (1996) *Rethinking Abortion*, Princeton, N.J., Princeton University Press.

Graham, T. W. (1994) "Public Opinion and US Foreign Policy Decision Making," in David A. Deese, ed., *The New Politics of American Foreign Policy*, New York, St Martins Press.

Gray, Colin S. (1996) "The Continued Primacy of Geography," *Orbis*, 40, pp. 247–59.

Gray, Virginia (1996) "The Socioeconomic and Political Context of States," in Virginia Gray and Herbert Jacob, eds., *Politics in the American States*, 4th edn, Washington, D.C., Congressional Quarterly Press.

Gray, Virginia and Herbert Jacob, eds. (1996) *Politics in the American States*, 4th edn, Washington, D.C., Congressional Quarterly Press.

Greenblatt, Alan (1997) "Both Chairmen Claim Bragging Rights," *Congressional Quarterly Weekly Report*, August 16.

Greiden, William (1992) *Who Will Tell the People? The Betrayal of American Politics*, New York, Simon & Schuster.

Grodzins, Morton (1960) "The Federal System," in *Goals for Americans: The Report of the President's Commission on National Government*, New York, Columbia University Press.

Gruberg, M. (1996) *A Case Study in US Urban Leadership: The Incumbency of Milwaukee Mayor*, Aldershot, Avebury.

Gugliotta, G. and I. Chinoy (1997) 'A System Out of Control," *Washington Post Weekly*, Vol. 14, No. 17, February 24, 1997.

Hall, P. A. (1988) *The Power of Economic Ideas*, Princeton, N.J., Princeton University Press.
Hamel, G. and C. K. Prahalad (1994) *Competing for the Future*, Cambridge, Mass., Harvard Business School Press.
Hames, Tim (1993) "Foreign Policy and the American Elections of 1992," *International Relations*, 11, pp. 315–30.
Hanson, Russel L. (1996) "Intergovernmental Relations," in Virginia Gray and Herbert Jacob, eds., *Politics in the American States*, 4th edn, Washington, D.C., Congressional Quarterly Press.
Hanuschek, E. A. (1987) "Formula Budgeting: The Economics and Analytics of Fiscal Policy Under Rules," *Journal of Public Policy Analysis and Management*, 6, pp. 3–19.
Hart, Henry (1959) "The Time Chart of Justices," *Harvard Law Review*, 73, pp. 84–129.
Hatcher, P. L. (1996) "How Local Issues Drive Foreign Policy," *Orbis*, 40, pp. 45–52.
Head, Simon (1996) "The New Ruthless Economy," *New York Review of Books*, February 29.
Healey, Jon (1996) "Clinton Success Rate Declined to A Record Low in 1995," *Congressional Quarterly Weekly Report*, January 27.
Heinz, John P. (1993) *The Hollow Core: Private Interests In National Policy-Making*, Cambridge, Mass., Harvard University Press.
Henig, Jeffrey (1985) *Public Policy and Federalism*, New York, St. Martin's Press.
Henwood, P. (1995) "The Business End," *Left Business Observer*, 70.
Herrnson, Paul S. and Kelly D. Patterson (1995) "Toward More Programmatic Democratic Party? Agenda-Setting and Coalition Building in the House of Representatives," *Polity*, 27, pp. 607–28.
Hinckley, Barbara (1994) *Less Than Meets the Eye: Foreign Policy Making, The Myth of the Assertive Congress*, Chicago, University of Chicago Press.
Hirst, Paul and Graham Thompson (1996) *Globalization in Question*, Oxford, Polity.
Hochschild, Jennifer L. (1995) *Facing Up to the American Dream*, Princeton, N.J. Princeton University Press.
Hoge, J. E. (1994) "Media Pervasiveness," *Foreign Affairs*, 73, pp. 136–44.
Hood, J. Larry (1993) "The Nixon Administration and the Revised Philadelphia Plan for Affirmative Action: A Study in Expanding Presidential Power and Divided Government," *Presidential Studies Quarterly*, 23, pp. 145–67.
Hosansky, David (1996) "GOP Confounds Expectations, Expands Federal Authority," *Congressional Quarterly Weekly Report*, 2 November.
Howard, Christopher (1997) *The Hidden Welfare State*, Princeton, N.J., Princeton University Press.
Hrebenar, Ronald J. and Clive S. Thomas (1995) "The Japanese Lobby in Washington: How Different Is It?, in Allan J. Cigler and Burdette A. Loomis, eds., *Interest Group Politics*, 4th edn, Washington, D.C., Congressional Quarterly Press.

Housing and Urban Development (HUD) (1996) *America's New Economy.*

Housing and Urban Development (HUD) (1997) *The State of the Cities.*

Hughes, J. R. T. (1991) *The Government Habit Redux: Economic Controls from Colonial Times to the Present*, 2nd edn, Princeton, N.J., Princeton University Press.

Hunt, D. M. (1997) *Screening the Los Angeles "Riots,"* Cambridge, Cambridge University Press.

Huntington, Samuel P. (1993) "The Clash of Civilizations," *Foreign Affairs*, 72, pp. 22–49.

Ikenberry, G. John (1996) "The Myth of Post-Cold War Chaos," *Foreign Affairs*, 75, pp. 79–91.

Imbroscio, D. L. (1997) *Reconstructing City Politics*, Thousand Oaks, Sage.

Ingraham, Patricia W. (1995) *The Foundation of Merit*, Baltimore, The Johns Hopkins University Press.

—— (1997) "A Laggard's Tale: Civil Service and Administrative Reform in the United States," unpublished paper.

—— James R. Thompson and Ronald S. Sanders, eds. (1997) *Lessons from the Federal Reinvention Laboratories*, San Francisco, Jossey-Bass.

Iyengar, Shanto and Richard Reeves, eds. (1997) *Do the Media Govern?*, Thousand Oaks, Sage.

Jackson, Jesse L. (1996) "Race-Baiting and the 1996 Presidential Campaign," in Geroge E. Curry, ed., *The Affirmative Action Debate*, Reading, Mass., Addison-Wesley.

Jacobs, Brian (1996) "A Bureau-Political Model of Local Networks and Public/Private Partnerships: Responses to Crisis and Change," *Journal of Contingencies and Crisis Management* 4, pp. 133–148.

Jacobson, Gary C. (1997a) "Reversal of Fortune: The Transformation of the US House Elections in the 1990s," unpublished paper.

—— (1997b) "Congress: Unprecedented and Unsurprising," in Michael Nelson, ed., *The Elections of 1996*, Washington, D.C., Congressional Quarterly Press.

—— (1997c) *The Politics of Congressional Elections*, 4th edn, New York, Longman.

Jamieson, A. M. (1996) "The Messenger as Policy Maker," *Democratization*, 3, pp. 114–32.

Janssen, B. (1993) *The Reluctant Welfare State*, 2nd edn, Pacific Grove, Calif., Brooks/Cole.

Jensen, Richard (1971) *The Winning of the Midwest, 1888–1896*, Chicago, University of Chicago Press.

Johnson, Haynes and David Broder (1996) *The System: the American Way of Politics at Breaking Point*, Boston, Little, Brown.

Johnson, Loch K. (1994) "New Directions for US Strategic Intelligence," in J. E. Winkates, J. R. Walsh and J. M. Scolnick, eds., *US Foreign Policy in Transition*, Chicago, Nelson-Hall.

Johnson, Lyndon (1965) *Public Papers of the Presidents of the United States: Lyndon Johnson 1963–64*, 482, Washington, D.C., USGPO.

Joint Venture Silicon Valley (J.V.S.V.N.) (1997) *Joint Venture Silicon Valley Information*, San Jose, Joint Venture Silicon Valley.

Jones, Charles O. (1981) "House Leadership in an Age of Reform," in Frank H. Mackaman, ed., *Understanding Congressional Leadership*, Washington, D.C., Congressional Quarterly Press.

—— (1982) "Senate Party Leadership in Public Policy," in David C. Kozak and John D. Macartney, eds., *Congress and Public Policy*, Homewood, Ill., Dorsey.

—— (1994) *The Presidency in a Separated System*, Washington, D.C., Brookings.

—— (1995) *Separate But Equal Branches*, Chatham, N.J., Chatham House.

Jones, Vernon Dale (1995) *Management Strategies for Reinvention and Downsizing in the Federal Government*, unpublished PhD., Syracuse University.

Jost, Kenneth (1996) "The States and Federalism," *CQ Researcher*, September 13.

Kagan, Robert (1995) "A Retreat from Power?," *Commentary*, 100, pp. 19–25.

Kantor, P. (1995) *The Dependent City Revisited*, Boulder, Co., Westview Press.

Kaplan, Lawrence S. (1996) "NATO after the Cold War," in Jarrod Wiener, ed., *The Transatlantic Relationship*, London, Macmillan.

Keith, Bruce *et al.* (1992) *The Myth of the Independent Voter*, Berkeley, Calif., University of California Press.

Kellman, Laurie (1997) "Fund-Raising Hearings Suspended," *Washington Post*, October 31.

Kernell, Samuel (1986) *Going Public*, Washington, D.C., *Congressional* Quarterly Press.

Kettl, Donald F. (1992) *Deficit Politics*, New York, St. Martin's Press.

—— (1994) *Reinventing Government: Appraising the National Performance Review*, Washington, D.C., Brookings.

—— and John DiIulio, eds. (1995) *Inside the Reinvention Machine*, Washington, D.C., Brookings.

——, Patricia W. Ingraham, Ronald Sanders and Constance Horner, eds. (1996) *Civil Service Reform*, Washington, D.C., Brookings.

Killian, Linda (1998) T*he Freshmen: What Happened to the Republican Revolution?*, Boulder, Colo., Westview Press.

Kinder, Donald R. and Lynn M. Sanders (1996) *Divided by Color*, Chicago, University of Chicago Press.

King, Anthony (1997) *Running Scared*, New York, The Free Press.

King, Desmond S. (1992) "The Establishment of Work-Welfare Programs in the United States and Britain: Ideas and Institutions," in S. Steinmo, K. Thelen and F. Longstreth, eds., *Structuring Politics*, New York, Cambridge University Press.

Kirp, David and Donald Jensen (1986) *School Days, Rule Days: The Legalization and Regulation of Education*, Philadelphia, Falmer.

Kirschten, Dick (1995) "Ethnics Resurging," *National Journal*, February 25.

Klare, Michael T. (1992) "US Military Policy in the Post-Cold War Era," in Ralph Milliband and Leo Panitch, eds., *The Socialist Register 1992*, London, The Merlin Press.

Kresl, P.K. and G. Gappert, eds. (1995) *North American Cities and the Global Economy*, Thousand Oaks, Sage.

Krugman, Paul (1994) "Competitiveness: A Dangerous Obsession," *Foreign Affairs*, 73, pp. 28–44.

Kuklinski, James H., Michael D. Cobb and Martn Gilens (1997) "Racial Attitudes and the 'New South'," *Journal of Politics*, 59, pp. 323–49.

——, Paul M. Sniderman, Kathleen Knight, Thomas Piazza, Philip E. Tetlock, Gordon R. Lawrence and Barbara Mellers (1997) "Racial Prejudice and Attitudes Towards Affirmative Action," *American Journal of Political Science*, 41, pp. 402–19.

Kurtz, Howard (1997a) "Journalist, Heal Thyself," *Washington Post National Weekly Edition*, June 23.

—— (1997b) *Hot Air*, New York, Basic Books.

—— (1998) *Spin Cycle: Inside the Clinton Propaganda Machine*, New York, The Free Press.

Ladd, Everett Carl, ed. (1995) *America at the Polls*, Storrs, Conn., The Roper Center.

Langdon, Steve (1994) "Clinton's High Victory Rate Conceals Disappointments," *Congressional Quarterly Weekly Report*, December 31.

Lasser, William (1985) "The Supreme Court and Periods of Critical Realignment," *Journal of Politics* 47, pp. 1124–87.

Laurent, Anne (1996) "The Cutting Edge," *Government Executive*, 29, pp. 10–19.

Lawrence, R.Z. (1997) "Is it Really the Economy, Stupid?," in J.S. Nye, P.D. Zelikow and, D.C. King, eds., *Why People Don't Trust Government*, Cambridge, Mass., Harvard University Press.

Lawson, R. and W.J. Wilson (1995) "Poverty, Social Rights, and the Quality of Citizenship," in K. McFate, R. Lawson and W.J. Wilson, eds., *Poverty, Inequality and the Future of Social Policy*, New York, Russell Sage Foundation.

Layne, Christopher (1994) "Kant or Cant: The Myth of Democratic Peace," *International Security*, 5–49.

Leadership Directories (1997) *Congressional Yellow Book: 105th Congress Roster*, Washington, D.C., Leadership Directories, Inc.

Lehmann, Nicholas (1997) *The New Republic*, July 28.

Levi, Edward (1949) *An Introduction to Legal Reasoning*, Chicago, University of Chicago Press.

Lewis, Neil A. (1997) "Clinton and Jones Lawyers To Talk About A Settlement," *New York Times*, September 15.

Lewis-Beck, Michael (1988) "Economics and the American Voter: Past, Present, Future," *Political Behavior*, 10, pp. 5–21.

—— and Tom Rice (1992) *Forecasting Elections*, Washington, D.C., Congressional Quarterly Press.

Lieber, Robert J. (1997) *Eagle Adrift*, New York, Longman.

Lindsay, James M. (1994) *Congress and the Politics of US Foreign Policy*, Baltimore, Mass., Johns Hopkins University Press.

Llewellyn, Karl N. (1931) "A Realistic Jurisprudence – The Next Step," *Columbia Law Review*, 30, pp. 431–65.

Loomis, Burdette (1996) *The Contemporary Congress*, New York, St. Martin's Press.
Lowi, Theodore (1995) *The End of the Republican Era*, Norman, Okla., University of Oklahoma Press.
Lowry, William R. (1993) *The Dimensions of Federalism*, Durham, NC, Duke University Press.
Lubove, R. (1996) *Twentieth Century Pittsburgh*, Pittsburgh, Pittsburgh University Press.
Luttwak, Edward N. (1995) "Towards Post-Heroic Warfare," *Foreign Affairs*, 74, pp. 109–22.
Makinson, Larry (1992) *Open Secrets: The Cash Constituents of Congress*, Washington, D.C., Congressional Quarterly Press.
Mandelbaum, Michael (1996) "Foreign Policy as Social Work," *Foreign Affairs*, 75, pp. 16–32.
Mann, Thomas E. and Norman J. Ornstein, eds. (1995) *Intensive Care*, Washington, D.C., Brookings AEI.
Maraniss, David and Michael Weisskopf (1996) *Tell Newt to Shut Up*, New York, Touchstone.
Marcus, Alan and Hamilton Craven (1997) *Health Care Policy in Contemporary America.*
Marcus, Ruth and Charles R. Babcock (1997) "System Cracks Under Weight of Cash," *Washington Post*, February 9.
Markus, Gregory B. (1992) "The Impact of Personal and National Economic Conditions on Presidential Voting," *American Journal of Political Science*, 36, pp. 829–35.
Marmor, T. R. (1994) *Understanding Health Care Reform*, New Haven, Conn., Yale University Press.
Mayer, William G. (1994) "The New Electoral Map," *The Public Perspective*, November–December.
Mayhew, David (1986) *Placing Parties in American Politics*, Princeton, N.J., Princeton University Press.
—— (1991) *Divided We Govern*, New Haven, Conn., Yale University Press.
—— (1996) "Innovative Midterm Elections," in Philip A. Klinkner, ed., *Midterm: The Elections of 1994 in Context*, Boulder, Colo., Westview.
Maynes, C. (1997) "A Closing Word," *Foreign Policy*, 106.
McCurdy, Dave (1995) "Glasnost for the CIA," *Foreign Affairs*, 73, pp. 125–40.
McKeever, Robert (1993) *Raw Judicial Power*, Manchester, Manchester University Press.
McKuen, Michael B. (1983) "Political Drama, Economic Conditions, and the Dynamics of Presidential Popularity," *American Journal of Political Science*, 27, pp. 165–92.
McSweeney, Dean and Zvesper, John (1991) *American Political Parties*, London, Routledge.
McSweeney, Dean and Owens, John E. (1998) *The Republican Takeover of Congress*, London, Macmillan.
Mead, L. M. (1986) *Beyond Entitlement*, New York, The Free Press.
—— (1992) *The New Politics of Poverty*, New York, Basic Books.

Mellich, Tanya (1996) *The Republican War Against Women*, New York, Bantam Books.
Mendelberg, Tali (1996) "Executing Hortons: Racial Crime in the 1988 Presidential Campaign," *Public Opinion Quarterly*, 61, pp. 134–57.
Miller, Warren E. and J. Merrill Shanks (1996) *The New American Voter*, Cambridge, Mass., Harvard University Press.
Mintzberg, H. (1996) "The Structuring of Organisations," in H. Mintzberg and J. B. Quinn, eds., *The Strategy Process*, London, Prentice-Hall.
Mitchell, Alison (1997) "Clinton Shifts Tax Cut Debate To His Liking," *New York Times*, July 27.
Monkkonen, E. H. (1995) *The Local State*, Stanford, Stanford University Press.
Moore, David W., Lydia Saad, Leslie McAneny and Frank Newport (1994) "Contract With America: A Gallup Poll Special Report," *The Gallup Poll Monthly*, November.
Morin, Richard (1996) "Tracking Down America's Party: A Little Math Indicates the Views of GOP Convention Delegates are Closer to Those of All Voters," *The Washington Post National Weekly Edition*, September 2–8.
Morris, Dick (1997) *Behind the Oval Office*, New York, Random House.
Moynihan, Daniel P. (1995a) "The Professionalization of Reform II," *Public Interest*, 121, pp. 23–41.
—— (1995b) "Rearranging Flowers on the Coffin," *Congressional Record*, December 12.
Muravchik, Joshua (1996) *The Imperative of American Leadership*, Washington, D.C., American Enterprise Institute.
Nathan, Richard P. (1996) "The Devolution Revolution: An Overview," *Rockefeller Institute Bulletin*, New York, SUNY.
National Academy of Public Administration (NAPA) (1997) "Making Devolution Work," Washington, D.C., NAPA, Panel on the Federal System.
NCES (1993) *Digest of Education Statistics*, Washington, D.C., NCES.
NCES (1996) *Digest of Education Statistics*, Washington, D.C., NCES.
NCES (1997) *Digest of Education Statistics*, Washington, D.C., NCES.
National Journal, January 24, 1998, *States of the Union. Then & Now*.
National Commission on Excellence in Education (1983) *A Nation at Risk: The Imperative for Educational Reform*, Washington, D.C. NCES.
National Performance Review (1993) *Creating a Government That Works Better and Costs Less*, Washington, D.C., GPO.
—— (1994) *Annual Report*, Washington, D.C., GPO.
—— (1995) *Annual Report*, Washington, D.C., GPO.
—— (1996) *Annual Report*, Washington, D.C., GPO.
—— (1997) *The Blair House Papers*, Washington, D.C., GPO.
Nelson, Michael, ed. (1997) *The Elections of 1997*, Washington, D.C., Congressional Quarterly Press.
Neuman, Johanna (1995) *Lights, Camera, War: Is Media Technology Driving International Politics?*, New York, St. Martin's Press.
Neustadt, Richard (1960) *Presidential Power*, New York, Wiley.

Newman, Jon O. (1997) "The Judge Baer Controversy," *Judicature*, 80, pp. 156–64.
Newsom, David D. (1996) *The Public Dimension of Foreign Policy*, Bloomington, Indiana University Press.
New York Times (1996) "Portrait of the Electorate," November 10.
Nieman, Donald G. (1991) *Promises to Keep*, New York, Oxford University Press.
Noble, Charles (1997) *Welfare as We Knew It*, Oxford, Oxford University Press.
Nordlinger, Eric A. (1995) *Isolationism Reconfigured*, Princeton, N.J., Princeton University Press.
Norquist, Grover (1996) "Spirit of '96," *Policy Review*, May/June.
Nye, Joseph (1990) *Bound to Lead*, New York, Basic Books.
Nye, Joseph, Philip Zelikov and David C. King (1997) *Why People Don't Trust Goverment*, Cambridge, Mass., Harvard University Press.
O'Brien, David (1988) "The Reagan Judges: His Most Enduring Legacy," in Charles O. Jones, ed., *The Reagan Legacy*, Chatham, N.J., Chatham House.
—— (1996) *Storm Center: The Supreme Court in Politics*, 4th edn, New York, Norton.
—— (1998) "Institutional Norms and Supreme Court Opinions," in Cornell Clayton and Howard Gillman, eds., *Institutional Approaches to Supreme Court Decision-Making*, Chicago, University of Chicago Press.
O'Connor, Karen and Lee Epstein (1989) *Public Interest Law Groups*, New York, Greenwood Press.
Ohamae, K. (1990) *The Borderless World*, New York, HarperCollins.
—— (1995) *The End of the Nation State*, London, HarperCollins.
O.M.B. (Office of Management and Budget) (1997).
Orfield, M. (1997) *Metropolitics*, Washington, D.C., Brookings.
Ornstein, Norman J., Thomas E. Mann and Michael J. Malbin, *Vital Statistics on Congress 1995–96*, Washington, D.C., Congressional Quarterly Press.
Osborne, David and Ted Gaebler (1992) *Reinventing Government*, Reading, Mass., Addison-Wesley.
Owens, John E. (1997) "The Return of Party Government in the US House of Representatives: Central Leadership–Committee Relations in the 104th Congress," *British Journal of Political Science*, 27, pp. 247–72.
—— (1998) "Taking Power? Institutional Change in the House and Senate," in Dean McSweeney and John E. Owens, eds., *The Republican Takeover of Congress*, London, Macmillan.
Pagano, Michael A. and Ann O'M. Bowman (1995) "The State of American Federalism," *Publius*, 25, pp. 1–21.
Papacosma, S. Victor and Mary Ann Heiss (1995) *NATO in the Post-Cold War Era*, Basingstoke, Macmillan.
Patrick, Deval L. (1996) "Standing in the Right Place," in George E. Curry, ed., *The Affirmative Action Debate*, Reading, Mass., Addison-Wesley.

Peacock, Anthony A. (1997) *Affirmative Action and Representation*, Durham, N.C., Carolina Academic Press.
Pechman, Ellen and Kate Laguarda (1993) *Status of New State Curriculum Frameworks, Standards, Assessments and Monitoring Systems*, Washington, D.C., Policy Studies Association.
Peele, Gillian (1984) *Revival and Reaction*, Oxford, Clarendon Press.
Perry, D. C. (1995) "Building the City Through the Back Door: The Politics of debt, Law and Public Infrastructure," in D.C. Perry, ed., *Building the Public City*, Thousand Oaks, Sage.
Perry, William J. (1996) "Defense in an Age of Hope," *Foreign Affairs*, 75, pp. 64–79.
Peskin, J. (1995) "The Changing Child Support Environment," *CBO Papers*, Washington, D.C., CBO.
Peters, B. Guy (1997a) "The Institutions of Regulation in the American Economy," in G.B. Doern and S. Wilks, eds., *The Institutions of Regulation: A Comparative Analysis*, Toronto, University of Toronto Press.
—— (1997b) "Shouldn't Row, Can't Steer: What's a Government To Do?," *Public Policy and Administration*, 12, pp. 51–61.
Peters, B. Guy and Donald Savoie (1996) "Managing Incoherence: The Coordination and Empowerment Conundrum," *Public Administration Review*, 56, pp. 281–9.
Peters, Ronald M. (1990) *The American Speakership*, Baltimore, Mass., The Johns Hopkins University Press.
Peterson, Paul E. (1992) "The Rise and Fall of Special Interest Politics," in Mark Petracca, ed., *The Politics of Interests*, Boulder, Colo., Westview Press.
—— (1995) *The Price of Federalism*, Washington, D.C., Brookings.
Petracca, Mark (1992) *The Politics of Interests*, Boulder, Colo., Westview Press.
Phillips, Kevin *(1994) Arrogant Capital: Washington, Wall Street and the Frustration of American Politics*, New York, Little Brown.
Polsby, Nelson W. (1983) *Consequences of Party Reform*, Oxford, Oxford University Press.
—— and Aaron Wildavsky (1996) *Presidential Elections*, 9th edn, Chatham, N.J., Chatham House.
Pomper, Gerald M. (1997) *The Election of 1996*, Chatham, N.J., Chatham House.
Porter, M. E. (1985) *Competitive Advantage*, New York, The Free Press.
Proceedings of the First Reinvention Conference (1996) unpublished papers.
Quirk, P.J. and J. Hinchcliffe (1996) "Domestic Policy: The Trials of a Centrist Democrat," in Colin Campbell and Bert A. Rockman, eds., *The Clinton Presidency: First Appraisals*, Chatham, N.J., Chatham House.
Rae, Nicol (1989) *The Decline and Fall of the Liberal Republicans*, Oxford, Oxford University Press.
—— (1994) *Southern Democrats*, Oxford, Oxford University Press.

Ravitch, Diane (1983) *The Troubled Crusade: American Education 1945–1980*, New York, Basic Books.
Reich, Robert (1991) *The Work of Nations*, New York, Alfred Knopf.
—— (1997) *Locked in the Cabinet*, New York, Alfred Knopf.
Reynolds, William Bradford (1996) "An Experiment Gone Awry," in George E. Curry, ed., *The Affirmative Action Debate*, Reading, Mass., Addison-Wesley.
Rhodes, R. A. W. (1997) *Understanding Governance*, Buckingham, Open University Press.
Richman, Alvin (1996) "What the Polls Say: Issues of Concern to American Voters," *US Foreign Policy Agenda*, 1, pp. 17–21.
Rielly, John E. ed. (1995) *American Public Opinion and US Foreign Policy 1995*, Chicago, Chicago Council on Foreign Relations.
Rieselbach, Leroy N. (1994) *Congressional Reform*, Washington, D.C., Congressional Quarterly Press.
Ripley, Randall B. and James M. Lindsay, eds. (1993) *Congress Resurgent: Foreign and Defense Policy on Capitol Hill*, Ann Arbor, MI, University of Michigan Press.
Rivlin, Alice M. (1992) *Reviving the American Dream*, Washington, D.C., Brookings.
Roberts, J. M. (1995) "New Keynesian Economics and the Phillips Curve," *Journal of Money, Credit and Banking*, 27, pp. 975–84.
Roberts, P. C. (1984) *The Supply-Side Revolution*, Cambridge, Mass., Harvard University Press.
Rockefeller Institute Bulletin (1996) "American Federalism Today," New York, SUNY.
Rockman, Bert A. (1984) *The Leadership Question: The Presidency and the American System*, New York, Praeger.
Rodman, Peter (1996) *America Adrift*, Washington, D.C., Nixon Center for Peace and Freedom.
Rohde, David W. (1991) *Parties and Leaders in the Post-Reform House*, Chicago, University of Chicago Press.
Rose, Richard and B. Guy Peters (1978) *Can Government Go Bankrupt?*, New York, Basic Books.
Rosenberg, Gerald (1991) *The Hollow Hope*, Chicago, University of Chicago Press.
Rosenbloom, David (1993) "Got an Administrative Fix? Don't Forget the Politics," *Public Administration Review*, 53, pp. 503–507.
Rosenstein, Thomas (1995) "Why Newt Is No Joke," *Newsweek*, April 10.
Rosner, Jeremy D. (1995) *The New Tug-of-War*, Washington, D.C., Carnegie Endowment for International Peace.
Rubinstein, Alvin Z. (1996) "The New Moralists on a Road to Hell," *Orbis*, 40, pp. 277–96.
Ruggie, John G. (1996) *Winning the Peace*, New York, Columbia University Press.
Russett, Bruce M. (1993) *Grasping the Democratic Peace*, Princeton, N.J., Princeton University Press.

Rust, Michael (1996) "The Revenge of the Grown Ups," *Washington Times*, June 24.

Salisbury, Robert A. *et al.* (1992) "Triangles, Networks and Hollow Cores: The Complex Geometry of Washington Interest Group Representation," in Mark Petracca, ed., *The Politics of Interests*, Boulder, Colo., Westview Press.

Samuelson, Robert (1995) *The Good Life and its Discontents: the American Dream in the Age of Entitlement*, New York, Times Books.

Sandel, Michael (1996) *Democracy's Discontents*, Cambridge, Mass., The Belknap Press.

Sassen, S. (1995) "On Concentration and Centrality in the Global City," in P. L. Knox and P. J. Taylor, eds., *World Cities in a World System*, Cambridge, Cambridge University Press.

Savage, J. D. (1988) *Balanced Budgets and American Politics*, Ithaca, N.Y., Cornell University Press.

Savitch, H. V. and R. K. Vogel, eds. (1996) *Regional Politics*, Thousand Oaks, Sage.

Sbragia, A. M. (1996) *Debt Wish*, Pittsburgh, Pittsburgh University Press.

Schattschneider, E. E. (1960) *The Semi-Sovereign People: A Realist's View of Democracy in America*, New York, Holt, Rinehart & Winston.

Schlesinger, James (1992) "Quest for a Post-Cold War Foreign Policy," *Foreign Affairs*, 72, pp. 14–20.

Schlesinger, Arthur M. (1974) *The Imperial Presidency*, London, André Deutsch.

—— (1992) *The Disuniting of America: Reflections on a Multicultural Society*, New York, Norton.

Schlozman, K. L. and J. T. Tierney (1986) *Organized Interests and American Democracy*, New York, Harper & Row.

Schmitt, Eric (1997) "House Plans Debate on Campaign Finance Bill," *New York Times*, September 25.

Schneider, M. and P. Teske, with M. Mintrom (1995) *Public Entrepreneurs*, Princeton, N.J., Princeton University Press.

Schockman, H. E. (1996) "Is Los Angeles Governable? Revisiting the City Charter," in M. J. Dear, H. E. Schockman and G. Hise, eds., *Rethinking Los Angeles*, Thousand Oaks, Sage.

Schor, Juliet B. (1992) *The Overworked American*, New York, Basic Books.

Schwarz, John E. (1988) *America's Hidden Success*, New York, W.W. Norton.

Sears, David O., Colette Van Laar, Mary Carrillo and Rick Kosterman (1997) "Is it Really Racism? The Origins of White Americans' Opposition to Race-Targeted Policies," *Public Opinion Quarterly*, 61, pp. 16–53.

Seay, Douglas and Wesley Smith (1996) "Federalism," Issue '96: *The Candidates' Briefing Book*, Washington, D.C., The Heritage Foundation.

Segal, Jeffrey and Howard Spaeth (1993) *The Supreme Court and the Attitudinal Model*, Cambridge, Cambridge University Press.

Seidman, Louis M. and Mark V. Tushnet (1996) *Remnants of Belief*, Oxford, Oxford University Press.

Shafer, Byron (1983) *Quiet Revolution*, New York, Russell Sage.

—— ed. (1997) *Present Discontents: American Politics in the Very Late Twentieth Century*, Chatham, N.J., Chatham House.

Shannon, John (1994) *Reflections on the Fourth Stage of Federalism*, Washington, D.C., The Urban Institute.

—— (1997) "Middle-Class Votes Bring a New Balance to US Federalism," *The Future of the Public Sector*, Washington, D.C., The Urban Institute.

Shuman, Milton H. (1992) "Dateline Main Street: Courts v. Local Foreign Policies," *Foreign Policy*, 86, pp. 158–77.

Sicherman, Harvey (1997) "The Revenge of Geopolitics," *Orbis*, 41, pp. 7–14.

Silbey, Joel H. (1991) *The American Political Nation, 1838–93*, Stanford, Calif., Stanford University Press.

Silverstein, Mark and Benjamin Ginsburg (1987) "The Supreme Court and the New Politics of Judicial Power," *Political Science Quarterly*, 102, pp. 371–88.

Sinclair, Barbara (1982) *Congressional Realignment*, Austin, Tex., University of Texas Press.

—— (1983) *Majority Leadership in the US House*, Baltimore, The Johns Hopkins University Press.

—— (1985) "Agenda, Policy, and Alignment Change," in Lawrence C. Dodd and Bruce I. Oppenheimer, eds., *Congress Reconsidered*, 3rd edn, Washington, D.C., Congressional Quarterly Press.

—— (1989a) *The Transformation of the US Senate*, Baltimore, The Johns Hopkins University Press.

—— (1989b) "House Majority Leadership in the late 1980s," in Lawrence C. Dodd and Bruce I. Oppenheimer, eds., *Congress Reconsidered*, 4th edn, Washington, D.C., Congressional Quarterly Press.

—— (1992a) "The Evolution of Party Leadership in the Modern House," in Allen Herzke and Ronald M. Peters, eds., *The Atomistic Congress*, Armonk, N.Y., M.E. Sharpe.

—— (1992b) "The Emergence of Strong Leadership in the 1980s House of Representatives," *Journal of Politics*, 54, pp. 657–684.

—— (1993) "House Majority Party Leadership in an Era of Divided Control," in Lawrence C. Dodd and Bruce I. Oppenheimer, eds., *Congress Reconsidered*, 5th edn, Washington, D.C., Congressional Quarterly Press.

—— (1995) *Legislators, Leaders, and Lawmaking*, Baltimore, The Johns Hopkins University Press.

—— (1996) "Trying to Govern Positively in a Negative Era: Clinton and the 103rd Congress," in Colin Campbell and Bert A. Rockman, eds., *The Clinton Presidency: First Appraisals*, Chatham, N.J., Chatham House.

—— (1998) "Leading the Revolution: Innovation and Continuity in Congressional Party Leadership," in Dean McSweeney and John E.

Owens, eds., *The Republican Takeover of Congress*, Basingstoke, Macmillan.
Skocpol, Theda (1996) *Boomerang: Clinton's Health Security Effort and the Turn Against Government in US Politics*, New York, W.W. Norton.
Skowronek, Stephen (1993) *The Politics That Presidents Make*, Cambridge, Mass., Harvard University Press.
Skrentny, John David (1996) *The Ironies of Affirmative Action*, Chicago, University of Chicago Press.
Smith, Bradley A. (1996) "Faulty Assumptions and Undemocratic Consequences of Campaign Finance Reform," *Yale Law Journal*, 105, pp. 1049–91.
Smith, Kevin and Kenneth Meier (1995) *The Case Against School Choice: Politics, Markets and Fools*, New York, M.E. Sharpe.
Smith, Marshall and Jennifer O'Day (1991) "Systemic School Reform," in Susan Fuhrman and Betty Malen, eds., *The Politics of Curriculum and Testing*, Philadelphia, Falmer Press.
Smith, Rogers (1988) "Political Jurisprudence, the New Institutionalism, and the Future of Public Law," *American Political Science Review*, 82, pp. 89–108.
Smith, Steven S. (1992) "The Senate in the Postreform Era," in Roger H. Davidson, ed., *The Postreform Congress*, New York, St. Martin's Press.
—— (1993) "Forces of Change in Senate Party Leadership and Organization," in Lawrence C. Dodd and Bruce I. Oppenheimer, eds., *Congress Reconsidered*, 5th edn, Washington, D.C., Congressional Quarterly Press.
—— (1995) *The American Congress*, Boston, Mass., Houghton Mifflin.
—— and Christopher J. Deering (1997) *Committees in Congress*, Washington, D.C., Congressional Quarterly Press.
—— and Eric D. Lawrence (1997) "Party Control of Committees in the Republican Congress," in Lawrence C. Dodd and Bruce I. Oppenheimer, eds., *Congress Reconsidered*, 6th edn, Washington, D.C., Congressional Quarterly Press.
Sniderman, Paul M. and Thomas Piazza (1993) *The Scar of Race*, Cambridge, Mass., Harvard University Press.
Solomon, Burt (1993) "A Modish Management Style Means Slip-Sliding Around the West Wing," *National Journal*, October 30.
—— (1995) "With a Smoothy Behind Podium, President Cuts President Slack," *National Journal*, June 3.
Sorauf, Frank J. (1992) *Inside Campaign Finance: Myths and Realities*, New Haven, Conn., Yale University Press.
Stanfield, Rochelle L. (1995) "The New Federalism," *National Review*, November 28.
Stanley, Harold W. and Richard G. Niemi (1994) *Vital Statistics on American Politics*, 4th edn, Washington, D.C., Congressional Quarterly Press.
Starr, Paul (1997) "An Emerging Democratic Majority," *The American Prospect*, No. 35 (November–December), pp. 18–27.

"Statistics on the 1995 Term" (1996) *Harvard Law Review* 110, pp. 367–76.
Steeh, Charlotte and Maria Krysan (1996) "Affirmative Action and the Public, 1970–1975," *Public Opinion Quarterly*, 60, pp. 128–58.
Stidham, Ronald, Robert Carp and Donald Songer (1996) "The Voting Behavior of President Clinton's Judicial Appointments," *Judicature* 80, pp. 16–21.
Stockton, Paul N. (1995) "Beyond Micromanagement: Congressional Budgeting for a Post-Cold War Military," *Political Science Quarterly*, 110, pp. 233–59.
Stoesz, D. (1996) *Small Change: Domestic Policy Under the Clinton Presidency*, White Plains, N.Y., Longman.
Stone, Clarence (1989) *Regime Politics: Governing Atlanta, 1946–1988*, Lawrence, KS, University Press of Kansas.
—— (1996) "Urban Political Machines: Taking Stock," *Political Science and Politics*, 3, pp. 446–50.
Stone, P. H. (1996) "Grass-Roots Goliath," *National Journal*, July 13.
Stone, C. and H. Sanders, eds. (1987) *The Politics of Urban Development*, Lawrence, Kans., University of Kansas Press.
Strange, Susan (1995) "Political Economy and International Relations," in Ken Booth and Steve Smith, eds., *International Relations Theory Today*, Oxford, Polity.
Sunstein, Cass (1996) "Forward: Leaving Things Undecided," *Harvard Law Review* 110, pp. 4–103.
Swett, C. (1995) *Strategic Assessment: The Internet Office of the Assistance Secretary of Defense*, July 17, 1995.
Talbott, Strobe (1996) "Democracy and the National Interest," *Foreign Affairs*, 75, pp. 47–63.
Taub, R. P. (1994) *Community Capitalism*, Cambridge, Mass., Harvard Business School Press.
Taylor, Andrew (1995) "House's Magnum Opus Now Subject To Senate's Tender Mercies," *Congressional Quarterly Weekly Report*, April 1.
Thomas, J. C. and H. V. Savitch (1991) 'Introduction: Big City Politics Then and Now', in H. V. Savitch and J. C. Thomas, eds., *Big City Politics in Transition*, Newbury Park, Sage.
Thompson, James R. (1996) *Public Organizational Change and the Reinvention Laboratories*, unpublished PhD, Syracuse University.
—— and Patricia W. Ingraham (1996) "The Reinvention Game," *Public Administration Review*, 56.
Thurber, James (1991) *Divided Democracy,* Washington, D.C., Congressional Quarterly Press.
Tucker, Robert W. and David C. Hendrickson (1992) *The Imperial Temptation*, New York, Council on Foreign Relations.
Tufte, Edward R. (1978) *Political Control of the Economy*, Princeton, N.J., Princeton University Press.
Tulis, Jeffrey (1987) *The Rhetorical Presidency*, Princeton, N.J., Princeton University Press.
Turow, Joseph (1997) *Breaking Up America*, Chicago, University of Chicago Press.

Tweedie, Jack (1997) "Welfare: What Now?," National Conference of State Legislatures.

University of Pittsburgh (1994) *Economic Benchmarks*, Pittsburgh, University of Pittsburgh.

Usborne, David (1997) "New York State Hands Industry Licence to Pollute," *The Independent*, May 21.

US Bureau of the Census (1996) *Statistical Abstract of the United States 1996*, Washington, D.C., GPO.

US General Accounting Office (1995) *Comments on the Report of the National Performance Review*, Washington, D.C. GPO.

US Office of Management and Budget (1996) *Budget of the US Government*, Washington, D.C., GPO.

USA Today/ PBS, Labor Day Poll (1997) September 1.

Uslaner, Eric M. (1993) *The Decline of Comity in Congress*, Ann Arbor, Mich., University of Michigan Press.

VanderMeer, Philip R. (1985) *The Hoosier Politician: Officeholding and Political Culture in Indiana, 1896–1920*, Urbana, Ill., University of Illinois Press.

Verba, Sidney *et al.* (1995) *Civic Voluntarism in American Politics*, Cambridge, Mass., Harvard University Press.

Victor, K. (1995) "Leading Labor into Hostile Territory," *National Journal*, May 6.

Vobejda, Barbara and Judith Havemann (1995) "Traditional Welfare Constituencies Put Out By Lack of Reform," *Washington Post*, May 21.

Walker, David B. (1995) *The Rebirth of Federalism*, Chatham, N.J., Chatham House.

—— (1996) "Federalism and Recent Foreign Policy," in Michael Minkenberg and Herbert Dittgen, eds., *The American Impasse*, Pittsburgh, University of Pittsburgh Press.

—— (1997) "Devolution: A Big Deal or Only One Dynamic in the System," unpublished paper.

Walker, Martin (1996a) *Clinton: The President They Deserve*, New York, Vintage.

—— (1996b) "The US Presidential Election, 1996," *International Affairs*, 72, pp. 657–74.

Wallace, Amy (1997) "UC Law Schools Face Discrimination Investigation," *Los Angeles Times*, July 15.

Wallerstein, Immanuel (1995) *After Liberalism*, New York, New Press.

Wattenberg, Martin P. (1996) *The Decline of American Political Parties, 1952–1994*, Cambridge, Mass., Harvard University Press.

Weatherford, M. S. and L. M. McDonnell (1997) "Clinton and the Economy: The Paradox of Policy Success and Political Mishap," *Political Science Quarterly*, 111, pp. 403–36.

Weber, M. P. (1990) "Rebuilding a City: The Pittsburgh Model," in R. M. Bernard, ed., *Snowbelt Cities*, Bloomington, Ind., Indiana University Press.

Wechsler, Herbert (1961) *Principles, Politics, and Fundamental Law*, Chicago, University of Chicago Press.

Weissert, Carol S. and Sanford F. Schram (1996) "The State of American Federalism," *Publius*, vol. 26, no. 3 (Summer), pp. 1–27.
Weissman, S. R. (1995) *A Culture of Deference*, New York, Basic Books.
West, Darrell M. (1991) "Television and Presidential Popularity in America," *British Journal of Political Science*, 21, pp. 199–214.
The White House (1996) *National Security Strategy of Engagement and Enlargement*, Washington, D.C., GPO.
Wilcox, Clyde (1995) *The Latest American Revolution*, New York, St. Martin's Press.
Wilcox, Clyde and Mark J. Rozell (1996) *God At The Grass Roots – The Christian Rights in the 1994 Elections*, London and Maryland, Rowman and Littlefield Publishers, Inc..
Williams, Christine B. (1996) "The Media and the Message," in Philip John Davies and Fredric Waldstein, eds., *Political Issues in America Today*, Manchester, Manchester University Press.
Williams, Linda Faye (1996) "Tracing the Politics of Affirmative Action," in George E. Curry, ed., *The Affirmative Action Debate*, Reading, Mass., Addison-Wesley.
Wills, Gary (1996a) "What Happened to the Revolution," *New York Review of Books*, June 6.
—— (1996b) "The Would-Be Progressives," *New York Review of Books*, July 11.
Wilson, Graham (1992) "American Interest Groups in Comparative Perspective," in Mark Petracca, ed., *The Politics of Interests*, Boulder, Colo., Westview Press.
—— (1998) *Only in America*, Chatham N.J., Chatham House Press.
Wilson, W. J. (1996) *When Work Disappears*, New York, Alfred Knopf.
Wilson, Woodrow (1908) *Constitutional Government in the United States*, New York, Columbia University Press.
Wirt, Frederick and Michael Kirst (1992) *Schools in Conflict: The Politics of Education*, Berkeley, Calif.,McCutchan.
Wittkopf, Eugene R., ed. (1994) *The Future of American Foreign Policy*, 2nd edn, New York, St. Martin's Press.
Wolters, Raymond (1996) *Right Turn: William Bradford Reynolds, the Reagan Administration, and Black Civil Rights*, New Brunswick, N.J., Transaction.
Woodward, Bob (1994) *The Agenda*, New York, Simon & Schuster.
Woolley, J. T. (1986) *Monetary Politics: The Federal Reserve and the Politics of Monetary Policy*, Cambridge, Cambridge University Press.
Working Together Consortium (1996) *The Greater Pittsburgh Region: Working Together to Compete Globally*, Pittsburgh, The Allegheny Conference on Community Development.
Wriston, Walter (1993) *The Twilight of Sovereignty*, New York, Scribners.
Yang, John E. (1997) "Campaign Finance Reform Not Top Priority, Poll Says," *Washington Post*, June 8.
Zakaria, Fareed (1996) "Groping for a Vision," *Newsweek*, December 16.

Zangwill, Israel (1914) *The Melting Pot*, 2nd edn, London, Heinemann.
Zimmerman, Joseph F. (1992) *Contemporary American Federalism*, Leicester, Leicester University Press.
—— (1997) "Federalism and the 104th Congress," unpublished paper.

Index

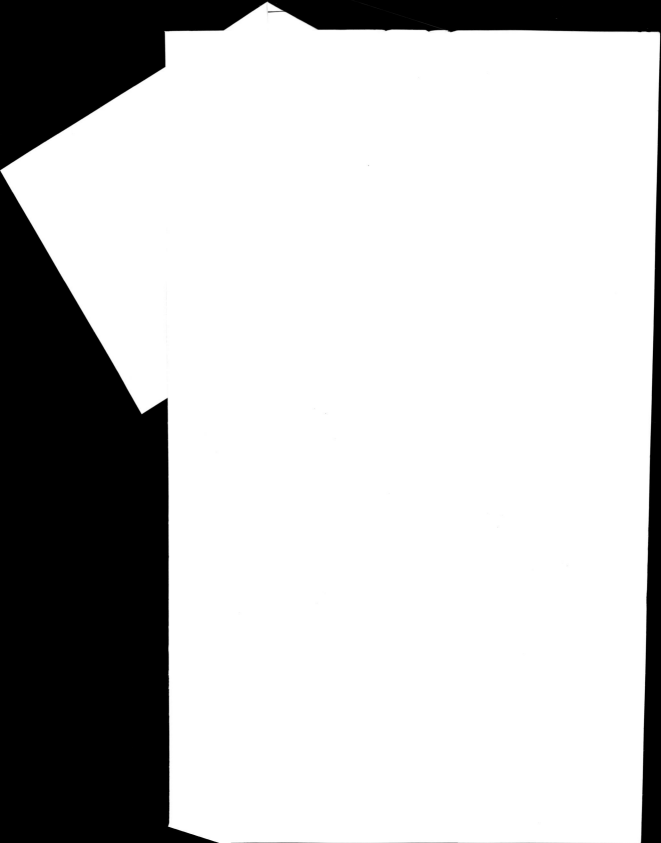

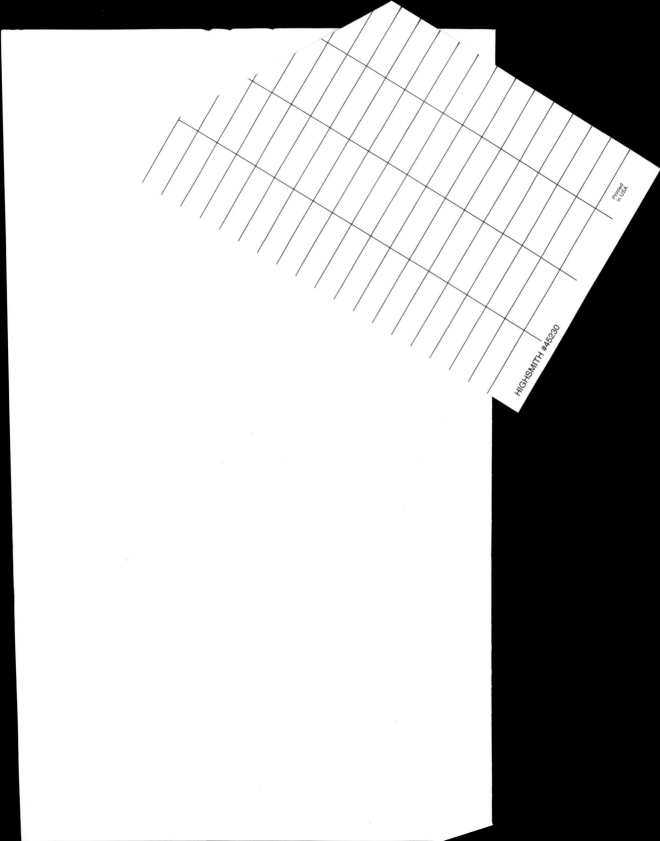